Cross-Addressing

SUNY SERIES, POSTMODERN CULTURE
Joseph Natoli, Editor

Cross-Addressing
Resistance Literature and Cultural Borders

edited by
JOHN C. HAWLEY

STATE UNIVERSITY
OF NEW YORK PRESS

Published by
State University of New York Press

Printed in the United States of America

For information, address the State University of New York Press,
State University Plaza, Albany, NY 12246

Production by Bernadine Dawes • Marketing by Theresa Abad
Swierzowski

Library of Congress Cataloging-in-Publication-Data

Cross-addressing : resistance literature and cultural borders / edited
    by John C. Hawley.
        p. cm. — (SUNY series, postmodern culture)
    Includes index.
    ISBN 0-7914-2927-X (hc : acid-free). —ISBN 0-7914-2928-8 (pbk. :
    acid-free)
        1. Literature, Comparative. 2. Literature, Modern—History and
    criticism. 3. Multiculturalism. 4. Outsiders in literature.
    I. Hawley, John C. (John Charles), 1947– . II. Series: SUNY
    series in postmodern culture.
    PN863.C76   1996
    809'.8920693—dc20   95–44770
                                                         CIP

1 2 3 4 5 6 7 8 9 10

for Noreen

CONTENTS

ACKNOWLEDGMENTS

My thanks to James Clifford and to Muhammad Siddiq for their guidance in the shaping of this book's central concerns. I would also like to thank Arturo Aldama for offering helpful suggestions with regard to my introduction, and Roger Bromley for reading the entire book manuscript before writing his concluding chapter. I am very grateful to Paul Soukup, S.J., for technical help in the preparation of the manuscript. Thanks, too, to Carola Sautter, Bernadine Dawes, Wyatt Benner, and Terry Swierzowski at SUNY Press for their patience and help in guiding the book through to completion.

Permission given by the following copyright holders and authors is gratefully acknowledged.

Ron Arias, *The Road to Tamazunchale* (1987). Copyright 1987 by Bilingual Press/Editorial Bilingüe, Hispanic Research Center, Arizona State University, Tempe, Arizona. Mayfair Yang, "Chinese-U.S. Border Crossings," from Mayfair Yang: *Gifts, Favors and Banquets*. Copyright 1994 by Cornell University. Used by permission of the publisher, Cornell University Press. Jim Wong-Chu, "old chinese cemetery kamloops july 1977," reprinted with permission from *Chinatown Ghosts* by Jim Wong-Chu (Arsenal Pulp Press, Vancouver, 1986). Brian McHale, *Postmodernist Fiction*, New York and London: Methuen & Co., 1987. From Bessie Head, *A Question of Power*, Heinemann Educational Books, African Writers Series. Copyright The Estate of Bessie Head 1974. Chris Dunton, "'Wheyting be Dat?' The Treatment of Homosexuality in African Literature" (*Research in African Literatures*, 20.3). From Nuala ni Dhomhnaill, *Selected Poems*, translated by Michael Hartnett. Copyright Edwin Higel, New Island Books; originally published by Raven Arts. From Nuala ni Dhomhnaill, *Pharoah's Daughter*, by Nuala ni Dhomhnaill et al., translated by Ciaran Carson, Medbh McGuckian, Tom MacIntyre, Michael Longley, and Paul Muldoon, by kind permission of the author, The Gallery Press (Loughcrew, Ireland) and Wake Forest University Press,

N.C. Nuala ni Dhomhnaill, *"Fáilte Béal na Sionna don Iasc,"* Mercier Books (Cork, Ireland), by permission of the author. From José Antonio Burciaga, *Restless Serpents*, Menlo Park, Calif.: Diseños, 1976, by permission of the author. From Charley Trujillo, *Soldados: Narratives of the Viet Nam War*, San Jose, Calif.: Chusma House, 1990, by permission of the author.

INTRODUCTION

The People gave her the name Euphemia or Euph-something, but when they called her that she used to toss her head like a horse and refuse to answer so they'd had to give up in the end and call her by her true-true name.
　　　　　　　　　　　　　　　—*Merle Hodge,* Crick Crack, Monkey

It is the contention of this volume that, in the words of Richard A. Schweder, "we are multiple from the start" and that our true names must reflect this fact. Whatever essentializing norms may have helped shore up our sense of identity and ways of understanding each other in past ages, our entry into the twenty-first century is marked by a heightened sense of cross-cultural and interpersonal (con)fusion.

> Our indigenous conceptions are diverse, whether they are centered in our official texts or our underground newspapers, in our public discourse or our psychoanalytic soliloquies, in our customary practices or our idiosyncratic routines, in our daytime task analyses or our nighttime fantasies. (Schweder 1991, 5–6)

As Schweder rightly notes, nowadays individuals typically share a double sense of "universal latency" and "manifest particularity" (6). The first refers to the postmodern sense of interconnection between cultures, in which an increasing percentage of the globe has immediate and overlapping access to artifacts produced by disparate and often conflictive systems of meaning. The common impression is, that it is all out there "to be had." The sense of manifest particularity, however, resists such deconstruction, implying stasis and essential difference as possibilities. Fascination, fear, and hate hold these two forces together, defining not only the movement toward hegemony by large social blocks but also the insistent doubts and individual rebellions within cultures. Following Bakhtin and Levinas, we can note that postmodern men and women typically stand in awe of the strangeness of the Other, marveling at why such a cultural "oddity" should remain so intransigently singular, and

1

are disturbed to find polyphonic others not only in "competing" cultures but in themselves, as well.

This collection of essays explores the uneasy tension implied in this interstitching of the global and the particular, the collective and the individual. What we here discuss are not simply informed and informing documents of this culture or that, but rather site-specific strategies of resistance to the imposition of identity in the terms imposed by former colonizers or implied by present totalizing norms. At the same time, the fact that many "Third World" writers are expatriates and members of intellectual elites demonstrates the "bleeding" across borders and the ambiguous forms that much "resistance" literature inevitably takes. By drawing on a widely various set of examples from around the world, we hope to consider, on a number of levels, whether or not there is a non-essentialized addressivity common to subaltern cultures—at least among those who are given voice to speak for such cultures. We propose our collection as a bridge between recent Eurocentric postmodern discourse dealing with the breakdown of the modernist stability in art, architecture, electronic media, etc. (Adam 1991), and such groundbreaking anthologies as Henry Louis Gates Jr.'s *"Race," Writing, and Difference* that problematize the issue of racial identity and literary practice (also Sollors 1986).

Richard Swiderski is among those who have conducted interesting comparative studies of people who move into a new culture and, to some extent, put it on (sometimes in both senses) like a new garment. Several of our chapters briefly discuss aspects of this "investment," but that is not really what we are about here. We are much more interested in those who have little choice in the matter, those who are inescapably of two (or more) cultures. The "cross-addressing" to which our title refers is, in fact, often as much an internal conversation as it is public. But the multiplicity that Schweder describes as a universal human characteristic is, in our essays, foregrounded less as a metaphysical or psychological donnée, and more as a compelling personal embodiment of the consequences of postmodern cultural exchange. We deal here in "other" words—in words of the other: with, for example, the words of those forced to speak a foreigner's tongue, or the words of *mestizaje* and *métissage*—with the experience of be-*longing* to (and for) more than one culture and hearing one's own cultural "homunculi" speaking in mutual interrogation and inscription. We see ourselves in conversation with the contributors to Alfred Arteaga's recent book, *An Other Tongue* (1994), who seek to interrogate "the processes of subjectification that define selves and others as the subjects of nation and ethnicity" (1).

Like Héctor Calderón and José David Saldívar, though, we feel that a "glossy version" of a postmodern world must be reinterpreted against the backdrop of the Third World and the migrant children of that world (Calderón 1991, 7). Our focus is not upon what some would describe as the *universal* deracination of our age so much as it is upon those whose "hybridized" biology or shifting locale forces their ironic confrontation not only with uprootedness but also with *rootedness*, generally in two cultures. Our collection gives voice to those who, in the words of Françoise Lionnet, "must survive (and write) in the interval between different cultures and languages" (Lionnet 1989, 1). It is *their* autography that we investigate. From Australian aboriginal and Maori to Irish, Palestinian, and South African, and on to the rich ethnic mix in North America, we hope to offer a representative and suggestive demonstration of the concerns shared by quite diverse groups—issues as fundamental as one's choice of language, one's presentation of self in society, one's "recovery" of a history.

The discussion is, of course, not only internal. The Janus-like view taken by many of our subject authors, the "unique positionings consciousness takes at these confluent streams," in Gloria Anzaldúa's words, resist accommodation to either culture:

> Living on borders and in margins, keeping intact one's shifting and multiple identity and integrity, is like trying to swim in a new element, an "alien" element. There is an exhilaration in being a participant in the further evolution of humankind, in being "worked" on. . . . And yes, the "alien" element has become familiar—never comfortable, not with society's clamor to uphold the old, to rejoin the flock, to go with the herd. (Anzaldúa 1987, iii)

This oxymoron—keeping a "shifting" identity "intact"—nicely encapsulates the postmodern condition, especially, one might argue, from the "archipelagic" ontological view of many Caribbean writers (see Benítez-Rojo and Harris), the view that Anzaldúa describes as a participation in "the further evolution of humankind." The "border" mentality, however, has little cause to celebrate this tensive coming-into-being, since it must fend off imminent annihilation. In this regard, Anzaldúa's words sound strikingly like those of bell hooks, though the experiences they reflect clearly have their particularities as well as their commonalities:

> To be in the margin is to be part of the whole but outside the main body. As black Americans living in a small Kentucky town,

the railroad tracks were a daily reminder of our marginality. . . .
Our survival depended on an ongoing public awareness of the
separation between margin and center and an ongoing private
acknowledgment that we were a necessary part of that whole.
This sense of wholeness. . . provided us an oppositional world
view. . . that strengthened our sense of self and our solidarity.
(hooks 1984, 1)

The words of writers like Anzaldúa and hooks must remain central in
anthologies such as our own, otherwise discourse among cultural elites
in these matters will be all sound and fury. If one is not a member of the
upper classes the crossing of borders, for those who actually make the
attempt, is always dangerous and frequently violent, and the danger
and violence are institutionally perpetuated. The lives we are privileged
to consider here are endangered lives.

Nor is the externalized conversation merely a soliloquy. It does elicit
a response—frequently unfriendly and simplistic, as in the ongoing
"P.C." debate. Societies, for their part, traditionally justify the marginalization they impose upon *mestizaje* by resorting to an emotional concoc-
tion of moral and biological arguments for the maintenance of the purity
of race. But this powerful totem for exclusion becomes less viable every
day. Henry Louis Gates Jr., for example, argues that "race, as a meaningful criterion within the biological sciences, has long been recognized to
be a fiction." He therefore sets out to "deconstruct. . . the ideas of difference inscribed in the trope of race, to explicate discourse itself in order
to reveal the hidden relations of power and knowledge inherent in popular and academic usages of 'race'" (Gates 1986, 4–5).[1] If race itself cannot
be isolated, it is little wonder that a meaningful characterization of *mixed*
races is even more dubious. Françoise Lionnet notes that "certain categories, such as *créole* and *métis*, are not part of any visible racial difference for the average English speaker" (1989, 14). What the words mean
is determined not by specific racial strains but by the speaker's precon-
ceptions of the individuals in question and the "racial" characteristics
they exhibit.[2] Such prejudice is nothing new. Margo Hendricks and
Patricia Parker show how the various racial terms prevalent in Europe
from the time of Columbus until 1800 were hardly in agreement: "[A]
sense of otherness led to the linking of the 'wild Irish' with the Moors,
the Scots as well as Scythians as members of a 'barbarous nation,' and
the description of Spain itself as being of 'all nations under heaven. . . .
the most mingled, most uncertayne and most bastardly'" (Hendricks
and Parker 1994, 2). If these and similar emotional descriptions are now

ridiculed, they nonetheless had a simplifying and categorizing power, and marginalized peoples today still recognize them as railroad tracks they cross at their peril. The many biracial Americans whom Lise Funderburg interviews in her recent book have little more in common than ambiguity, shifting self-definition, and a sense that the world does not welcome them.

Little wonder, then, if a debate rages over the extent to which one can and should attempt a crossing. Gates focuses several of the pertinent issues, arguing that

> we [African Americans] must determine how critical methods can effectively disclose the traces of ethnic differences in literature. But we must also understand how certain forms of difference and the *languages* we employ to define these supposed differences not only reinforce each other but tend to create and maintain each other. (Gates 1986, 15)

The strategic concerns underpinning Gates's argument reverberate throughout much of the writing under analysis in this collection. Which borders can, and must, be constantly "crisscrossed" (Martín-Rodríguez, Yaziji), and to what effect? What can be "reclaimed" (James), "transformed" (Aldama), "satirized" (Wald), "saved from extinction" (Zamora)? Which rules can be broken (O'Connor)? Which appetites dare one feed (Waxman)? As Anzaldúa notes, the place where these questions arise is never comfortable, but it is undeniably "home" (1987, iii)—a conclusion not easily come to in the essays by Yang, Quimby, and Yaziji.

As the topics of many of our chapters imply, we assert that the telling of the stories of these struggles in many cases serves as a site for their most intense realization and, sometimes, for their transformation, as well. Furthermore, while we recognize that narration is hardly the quintessence of social exchange or resistance, we believe that it historically can lead to a more conscious political struggle.[3] Furthermore, without a shared narration the political movement will almost inevitably replace one brutal injustice with another. As Wole Soyinka notes, "[T]he language of [Charles] Manson to his victims was . . . a pastiche of the very rhetoric of social revolution that is shorn of the motivating essence of communal renewal. . . . [W]hen I hear that outrageously simplistic cry of 'Culture is a gun,' I feel like reaching for my culture" (Soyinka 1994, 45). As ephemeral as any defining narrative may be in our age, such narratives *will* find a voice, and it is essential that they also find an audience.

What is under analysis here—the reaching for one's culture—is a two-tiered process. Lionnet, with Edouard Glissant, can celebrate the "recovered histories" inspiring many of these writers who are benefiting from "the egalitarian interrelations in which binary impasses are deconstructed" (Lionnet 1989, 5; Glissant 1989, 249); at the same time, with bell hooks, she will note that *métissage*, as "the site of undecidability and indeterminacy," is the place where "solidarity becomes the fundamental principle of political action against hegemonic languages" (Lionnet 1989, 6). It is much the topic of essays like McCredden's and Chao's and, in fact, all the essays in this collection were chosen with an eye for the variety of solidarities informing the strategic responses to this positioning in the larger societies.

Most of our discussion focuses on texts, and often on those that would be considered high-cultural texts. We believe it would be difficult to offer a coherent contemporary collection of essays that does justice to all significant forms of narrative, and we acknowledge that our own approach has its in-built limitations (Nelson et al. 1992, 2). At the same time, we hope to demonstrate our recognition of the larger ramifications of the terms "culture" and "narrative" in what we write, especially in light of the developments in the past decades in the field of cultural studies (Nelson et al. 1992, 1–16; During 1993, 1–25; Blundell et al. 1993, 1–102).

Like the contributors to the recent collection edited by Janice Carlisle and Daniel Schwarz, we are therefore aware that storytelling, in the traditional definition of narrative,

> is marked by its achievement of the humanistic goals of coherence, progress, and rationality. . . . [But] certain forms of recording events—in particular, annals and chronicles—fall outside such a [logocentric] notion of narrative because they do not conform to the modernist's conception of coherence, and they fail to do so precisely because they reflect earlier, culturally specific assumptions about reality. (Carlisle and Schwarz 1994, 2, 4)

Our selection of topics, various narrative formats, and sometimes obscure(d) works hopes to raise the stakes about what constitutes literary study at the end of the twentieth century. Roger Bromley's concluding essay partially addresses this concern.

The work of Clifford Geertz has been seminal in considerations such as ours. Following Max Weber's lead, Geertz defines culture semiotically, as the "webs of significance" that men and women weave, and in which humanity is suspended (Geertz 1973, 5). Following Gilbert Ryle's lead, he describes the study of these webs as an activity in "thick description" (6): a negotiation through the gestures, the "piled-up structures of inference and implication," distinguishable, within a culture, as a twitch of the eye, a conspiratorial wink, or a parody of that wink. Not only anthropologists but students of any of the liberal arts recognize that observers who do not already share the particular structure of signification that is being described will miss some of the established codes; what they consider to be data are really "constructions of other people's constructions of what they and their compatriots are up to" (9). And, thus, Geertz returns to the semiotic question: "Once human behavior is seen as . . . symbolic action . . . the thing to ask is . . . what . . . is getting said" (10). Geertz specifically denies this is the examination of "a psychological phenomenon, a characteristic of someone's mind, personality, cognitive structure"; it is instead, he asserts, an attempt to gain a greater "familiarity with the imaginative universe within which their acts are signs" (13).

Not surprisingly, Geertz finds the work of an ethnographer analogous to that of a literary critic (9), and the contributors to this volume would agree. Both sorts of writers return to the same "work" again and again, to "plunge more deeply into the same things" (25),[4] and to try in the examination of "the symbolic dimensions of social action" to "make available . . . answers that others . . . have given." In the process, both ethnographers and literary critics of a certain kind seek to "include [these others] in the consultable record" (30).

This concern for inclusion is at the heart of the present collection, and it partially explains the eclecticism of our theoretical approaches. I am not alone in this editorial preference for variety. In his latest anthology of Native American writing (1993), Arnold Krupat notes that he had, a few years ago, thought that the time for eclecticism might have passed and that it should now be replaced by collections that were rigorously feminist, or Marxist, poststructuralist, "Native Americanist," or whatever. But he subsequently concluded that such closure or regimentation was either premature or inappropriate for his subject matter—"no single thematic or perspectival orientation and no single discursive mode could be asserted" (Krupat 1993, xviii). Like Krupat, we feel that the rigorous application of a chosen theoretical approach throughout these essays would have produced an interesting book, but would have offered our collection a deceptive unity that would work against the specificity of our various subject authors. Studies in hybridity, almost by definition, demand bricolage.

Much of the literature we examine is autobiographical (Henke, especially), and in some of our analysis our own voices are also clearly audible. Using Hartwig Isernhagen's terms to characterize Western "scientific" knowledge as an insistence on "verbifying" and "meta-izing," Krupat warns that

> abstracting and distancing . . . make . . . "knowledge" suspect at best or entirely inimical to those whose lives or works it is supposed to illuminate, most particularly when, as in the case of Native Americans, it encounters constructions of the categories of "knowledge" that are hardly consonant with those of "science." (Krupat 1953, xix)

Following Krupat's lead we do not wish to adopt a magisterial tone in encounters that defamiliarize. Nor are our analyses conducted "anonymously," since many of us come to these studies from personal experiences sharing a family resemblance to topics at hand. As a gay male who, for twenty-nine years, was a Jesuit and closeted, I, for example, eventually concluded that "passing" as heterosexual was a mixed blessing, at best. The silence I had imposed upon myself increasingly manifested its complicity with larger social injustices such as those discussed by Jolly in her chapter on intersecting marginalities. In our book this compelling interest in manifestations of liminal consciousness is not surprising. In an age in which past verities offer less secure cultural borders, a growing number find themselves drawn to studies of hybridity, since so many of us now find ourselves living in various intervals *between* cultures, *amid* languages, *across* borders.

We believe our book, with its various theoretical approaches and its emphasis on the personal, also echoes the current divisions in cultural studies. In their collection analyzing the developments within that protean field, Valda Blundell, John Shepherd, and Ian Taylor note that the work of the seventies was notably political. In the eighties and nineties, however, it split, becoming interested in the cultural production of meaning, on the one hand, and, on the other, becoming involved in policy debates (Blundell et al. 1993, 8–9). Our essays share both impulses, the semiotic and the political, the postmodernist and the activist, with a decided implication that the two are intricately enmeshed and express themselves in contemporary literature in explorations of *métissage*. As Lionnet herself notes, "[W]hat is at stake in the conservative resistance to *métissage* is clearly a patriarchal desire for self-reproduction, self-duplication, within a representational space—female bodies—uncontaminated by the presence of the other" (Lionnet 1989, 12). This is hardly apolitical. In less committed language, Blundell combines the semiotic and political impulses in a succinct description of the aim of contemporary cultural studies: its practitioners seek "to learn the value of politically engaged intellectual work in understanding how forms of awareness are mediated by and contribute to the social and cultural life in which they occur" (Blundell et al. 1993, 4).

Our volume would assert that the "forms of awareness" of the man or woman standing on the border, compelling in her or his direct gaze, is especially significant in a postmodern age of imposed distraction. It is that heightened consciousness that we hope to discuss in this collection—that painful sensitivity forced upon those who stand irrevocably in two worlds:

> Across those tracks was a world we could work in as maids, as janitors, as prostitutes, as long as it was in a service capacity. We could enter that world but we could not live there. We had always to return to the margin, to cross the tracks, to shacks and abandoned houses on the edge of town. (hooks 1984, 1)

Imagining the tracks that map another's world, the transgressions that maintain another's dream, sometimes lays bare one's own true name.

Notes

1. Similar concerns fuel the defense of related canonical positions. In defense of her own poststructuralist epistemology and the postmodern condition it signals, Lionnet argues that "the criticisms leveled against poststructuralist epistemologies have very disturbing parallels in the nineteenth-century polygenists' discourse of racial purity. In both cases, indeterminacy, hybridization, and fragmentation are feared because of the risks of 'degeneration' of the human species, of the race, and of 'traditional' literary culture" (1989, 17).

2. In her book she seeks to "interrogate the sociocultural construction of race and gender and challenge the essentializing tendencies that perpetuate exploitation and subjugation on behalf of those fictive differences created by discourses of power" (Lionnet 1989, 15). Gates similarly notes that "race is the ultimate trope of difference because it is so very arbitrary in its application" (Gates 1986, 5).

3. "These linguistic and discursive relationships manifest active displacements of power, power that must be reinforced continually to maintain a particular image of the world and hierarchy of relationships" (Arteaga 1994, 1).

4. Geertz makes the distinction between "'inscription' ('thick description') and 'specification' ('diagnosis')—between setting down the meaning particular social actions have for the actors whose actions they are, and stating, as explicitly as we can manage, what the knowledge thus attained demonstrates about the society in which it is found and, beyond that, about social life as such" (1973, 27).

References

Adam, Ian, and Helen Tiffin, eds. *Past the Last Post: Theorizing Post-colonialism and Postmodernism.* New York: Harvester Wheatsheaf, 1991.

Anzaldúa, Gloria. *Borderlands/La Frontera:* The New Mestiza. San Francisco: Aunt Lute Books, 1987.

Arteaga, Alfred. *An Other Tongue.* Durham, N.C.: Duke University Press, 1994.

Benítez-Rojo, Antonio. *The Repeating Island: The Caribbean and the Postmodern Perspective.* Translated by E. Maraniss. Durham, N.C.: Duke University Press, 1992.

Bhabha, Homi K. *The Location of Culture.* London and New York: Routledge, 1994.

Blundell, Valda, John Shepherd, and Ian Taylor, eds. *Relocating Cultural Studies: Developments in Theory and Research.* London and New York: Routledge, 1993.

Calderón, Héctor, and José David Saldívar, eds. *Criticism in the Borderlands: Studies in Chicano Literature, Culture and Ideology.* Durham, N.C.: Duke University Press, 1991.

Carlisle, Janice, and Daniel Schwarz, eds. *Narrative and Culture.* Athens: University of Georgia Press, 1994.

During, Simon, ed. *The Cultural Studies Reader.* London and New York: Routledge, 1993.

Funderburg, Lise. *Black, White, Other: Biracial Americans Talk About Race and Identity.* New York: Morrow, 1994.

Gates, Henry Louis, Jr., ed. *"Race," Writing, and Difference.* Chicago: University of Chicago Press, 1986.

Geertz, Clifford. *The Interpretation of Cultures: Selected Essays.* New York: Basic Books, 1973.

Glissant, Edouard. *Caribbean Discourse: Selected Essays.* Translated with an introduction by J. Michael Dash. Charlottesville: University Press of Virginia, 1989.

Harris, Wilson. *The Womb of Space: The Cross-Cultural Imagination.* Westport, Conn.: Greenwood, 1983.

Hendricks, Margo, and Patricia Parker, eds. *Women, "Race," and Writing in the Early Modern Period.* London and New York: Routledge, 1994.

Hodge, Merle. *Crick Crack, Monkey.* London: Heinemann, 1981. Originally published by André Deutsch in 1970.

hooks, bell. *Feminist Theory: From Margin to Center.* Boston: South End Press, 1984.

Krupat, Arnold, ed. *New Voices in Native American Literary Criticism.* Washington, D.C.: Smithsonian, 1993.

Lionnet, Françoise. *Autobiographical Voices: Race, Gender, Self-Portraiture.* Ithaca: Cornell University Press, 1989.

Nelson, Cary, Paula A. Treichler, and Lawrence Grossberg, eds. *Cultural Studies.* London and New York: Routledge, 1992.

Schweder, Richard A. *Thinking Through Cultures: Expeditions in Cultural Psychology.* Cambridge: Harvard University Press, 1991.

Sollors, Werner. *Beyond Ethnicity: Consent and Descent in American Culture.* Oxford: Oxford University Press, 1986.

Soyinka, Wole. *Art, Dialogue and Outrage: Essays on Literature and Culture.* New York: Pantheon, 1994.

Swiderski, Richard M. *Lives Between Cultures: A Study of Human Nature, Identity and Culture.* Juneau, Alaska: Denali, 1991.

Toward a Critical Solidarity
(Inter)change in Australian Aboriginal Writing

LYN MCCREDDEN

Theoretical Contexts

Over the last decade, postcolonial criticism has painfully underscored the human tendency to operate through polarities—black/white, them/ us, primitive/cultured, victim/perpetrator—and it has simultaneously voiced an urgent need to reach beyond such oversimplifications. So it is that the discourses that surround and shape contemporary Australian Aboriginal writing are currently in a state of uneasy, polarizing flux. The so-called postcolonial critic,[1]—Aboriginal or white—is finding it difficult to construct registers that do not fall simplistically into mere dogmatism and/or romantically heady narratives of selfhood. Towards the monolith "Aboriginal Literature" there is also still much condescension, knowing or inept, to be found. Such cases of condescension may be deemed easier to dismiss, though they do throw back to historically responsible writers the challenge to find discourses that create real dialogue and that may become part of the crucial work of historical change. For one self-designated postcolonial (white) critic it is crucial for Aboriginal writers to "forge an authentic sense of self . . . achieve a valid self-identity . . . connect meaningfully with his past," in a process from which "redemptive wholeness can be regained by contemporary Aborigines" (Nelson 1986, 341). For another (white) critic, admiring the poetry of Aboriginal writer Colin Johnson (Mudrooroo Narogin),[2] "There is nothing 'literary' here about the language or the feeling, only an urgent drive to insist that in life as it is lived thought and feeling are one" (Brady 1987, 100). Current postcolonial debate circles around such discourses of origin—whether of identity, cultural authenticity, or ownership—and the stakes are high.[3] In the following discussion of contemporary Aboriginal and white discourses in Australia, these questions of origin and contemporary direction are investigated through the work of the Aboriginal writer Mudrooroo, which, it is argued, struggles towards a dialogic rather than a polarizing art, seeking to open itself to more problematic realities of cultural interpenetration at the same time as it seeks real political change. That is, Mudrooroo's work struggles towards a critically imagined solidarity.

The central assumption of this chapter is informed by the work of Edward Said, from *The World, the Text, and the Critic* onwards. That critical discourse does and should contribute to the nature of imaginative writing, as well as being influenced by it, and that all writing should in turn be shaped by political and social realities are central ideas of Said's work. Further, as Said expresses it:

> The history of thought, to say nothing of political movements, is extravagantly illustrative of how the dictum "solidarity before criticism" means the end of criticism. I take criticism so seriously as to believe that, even in the very midst of a battle in which one is unmistakably on one side against another, there should be criticism, because there must be critical consciousness to be fought for. (Said 1983, 28)

Said's "critical" can be a rather fluid, hybrid term, suggesting both old-fashioned literary critical analysis, broadening to include a range of theories about language and the relationship of language and politics, theory and practice. A second assumption at work in my essay, one intimately connected with this question of politically active criticism, is that it is necessary for the critic to declare to her readership the predominant boundaries within which the criticism is produced. In my case they are: white (Australian, and Scottish descent), middle-class, female, academic. Readers will necessarily find other, less-conscious assumptions at work. Postcolonial writing, particularly that of the white postcolonial critic (if this is not an oxymoron) needs to find ways of acknowledging such boundaries without resorting to silencing self-abasement (though silence has its place),[4] or waxing lyrical in romantic celebration or polemical oversimplification. If dialogue and change are desired, then the discourses struggled for must be reciprocal and change made possible for both victim and perpetrator.

So, in the following investigation of possible postcolonial discourses in Australia, a number of current literary discourses (imaginative, critical, and theoretical) and their projected audiences will be examined. A third, and connected poststructural assumption shared in, as well as mistrusted here, is that discourse, both oral and written, constructs and speaks the human subject. The variety of (mainly poststructuralist) constructivisms that at the present time hold sway in the humanities and social sciences cannot offer satisfactory theoretical, let alone practical, models for the emergent "postcolonial self." To assert this idea of the self constructed by language is only the beginning, and an unproductive cliché, unless imaginative and historical leaps can be made in the modes of representation of both colonizer and colonized.

The discourses and counterdiscourses of Australian colonization and postcolonization are legion—utopian revisions of history, by black and white writers, nativist versions of the traditions of the Dreaming, political or romantic reclamations of the sacred, social realist accounts of black deaths by white hands. The category of the sacred—imaged through narratives of the Dreaming, the clever-men, the claims to songlines and sacred sites, the often romantically depicted spirituality of the Aboriginal community—has been registered awkwardly by some critics who see the agenda as essentially political and material. Such Western polarizations as spiritual/material are being tested in the emerging discourses. For example, in much of the political negotiation for Aboriginal rights in Australia, the establishment of the status of certain discourses in their connection to an "extratextual" or "beyond" of the text has been crucial. In land rights activism and the discourses that surround and construct it, notions of the land as transcendent "text," or as political site, are under constant and changing scrutiny. Claims to land, debate over the status of pronouncements by Aboriginal elders, male and female, the evaluations of both oral and written texts of Aboriginal Dreaming all involve discourses shaped by notions of the sacred and originary now being placed under legal, economic, and literary investigation.

Other political and textual battles have sought ascendancy through simplistic polarization. The text "Australia" has of course been claimed by white colonialists as a blank page, "practically unoccupied, without settled inhabitants or settled law at the time it was peacefully annexed."[5] The terror of imprecision in that "practically" hardly needs stressing. Nineteenth- and twentieth-century texts of "the Aboriginal" in white imaginative writing are various, though they all stereotype and polarize: the Aboriginal is absence, exoticism, the erotic ("The nymph though dark is fair"), animality and the demonic, childlikeness, or the site of Christian and colonial instruction.[6]

But it is to the texts by Aboriginal writers, erupting over the past ten years, that this paper turns. In reading the critical and theoretical climate that has both produced and received this outpouring, and in an investigation of the novels of Mudrooroo, it is hoped that the theoretical assumptions outlined above will be tested. Said's disdain for a mere "flight into method and system", whose practitioners risk "wall-to-wall discourses" (Said 1983, 26) at the expense of any real social change, rings in my ears, but so too does the need to offer critical debate in the field of Aboriginal writing that does not melt into mere multicultural celebration, devoid of real intellectual—aesthetic, political, theological—inquiry; or into simple, Manichaean dogmatics, a solidarity totally devoid of criticism.

Politics, Aboriginal Writing, White Aesthetics

David Unaipon's *Native Legends* was published in 1929 and the poetry of Oodgeroo Noonuccal (earlier known as Kath Walker) has been published since the early 1960s. But with the publication of works by Bobbie Sykes, Kevin Gilbert, Jack Davis, Lionel Fogarty, Archie Weller, Maureen Watson, Ruby Langford, Sally Morgan, Mudrooroo, and many others less known nationally, Australian readers are faced with a complex voicing of Aboriginal Australia and its claims. The listing of these named writers merely has the effect of limiting the real outburst of voices emerging upon the scene in Australia. Kevin Gilbert's important anthology of poetry, *Inside Black Australia*, publishes the work of over forty Aboriginal poets. Many are preeminently oral poets, celebrated storytellers and singers within their local districts. Some are in the process of further canonization in white academia and publishing, and amongst black communities.

It is an easy move for the white postcolonial critic to select the few writers who can move, or be made to move, comfortably within sophisticated stylistics and aesthetic or theoretical self-consciousness. This helps to deal with what may be experienced by some audiences as the great threat to "Literature," all those not-necessarily-English words circling around out there in the daily lives of Aboriginal people. But a variety of questions have circulated: "Are they worth publishing?" Or the possibly less-aggressive "Should written, widely circulated inscriptions seek to stand for, replace, the oral and local words of Aboriginal poets?" Aboriginal poets themselves, through Gilbert's anthology, have answered this from their point of view by publishing. Ruby Langford, in her auto-biography *Don't Take Your Love to Town* wrestles openly and vulnerably with the reasons why she wants to write a book. Her work offended one reviewer, who openly inquired whether "so much" work needed publishing, since it met neither the artistic nor moral standards common within the white publishing industry.[7] While this may be a minority voice among professional critics in Australia, it does represent a popular opinion, met with among students in higher education and certainly among the wider reading public. And it dramatically throws up questions of "literariness" and reader/audience response so crucial to the effect of such Aboriginal writing, along with the role of the critic as possible negotiator in such a process.

This (New Critical? formalist? poststructuralist?) question of "literariness"—"aesthetics" or "stylistics," verbal complexity or self-consciousness—is dealt with uneasily by many postcolonial critics, Aboriginal and white. Underlying such uneasiness may be a sense, in many politically oriented critics, that aesthetics is a cop-out. So the critic may turn to a repudiation of formalist or close-reading techniques, in an attempt to get at the "real" issues: "You do not read poems like this for pleasure. There is little aesthetic distance. But the language has to be taken seriously because it has the weight of experience, of history at the personal as well as the public level, behind it. . . ." (Brady 1987, 99). The introduction by Kevin Gilbert to *Inside Black Australia* is vulnerable and anxious on this question of the relationship of aesthetics and politics:

> Rarely has Aboriginal poetry much to do with aesthetics or pleasure or the pastoral views . . . there is another reality, a reality that could find parallels in the experience of the indigenous peoples of South Africa or Bolivia, or of oppressed populations within the national boundaries of one culture, the Jews in Nazi Germany or the Palestinians in Israel. . . . Many critics of Aboriginal poetry, whether using polite language or digital graffiti, express some difficulty in finding comparisons and parallels. Their solemn enunciation on the aesthetics, the imagery, rhyming and metric patterns, metaphors, lucidity, fluidity, lingoism, jingoism, polemicism, chantism, phenomenalism of the Aboriginal voice, is an assurance to us that the debate will long continue. Of course, there will be many who, not wanting to reveal any overt or covert racism, paternalism, condescension, misconception, self-deception or otherwise to the value of the contribution, will dart

> like a prawn in a barramundi pond to the safety of antecedents
> ... to make comparisons with the indigenous tree and twist it to
> the semblance of the "tree back home." (Gilbert 1988, xviii)

This is apt and humorous criticism, alive to many competing voices. It manages to sum up a current white liberal paranoia about the appropriate discourses in which to venture upon discussion of Aboriginal literature (a paranoia not totally absent in this paper). Further, it gives a sharp poke at the academic publishing game, with its formalist and politically correct obsessions. But Gilbert points to another reality, or exigency, that of the interdependence of white critics and publishers and contemporary Aboriginal writers, and of the potential, along with trivializing or worse consequences, for helpful dialogue: the "assurance that the debate will long continue." He puts it up to white critics—those darting prawns in the barramundi pond—in a way that acknowledges this interdependence while maintaining his own place in the debate. Two moves for white critics are simultaneously delineated and satirized: formalist discussion running amok and liberal breast-beating that desires to praise but has only its own terms with which to lard the Aboriginal texts. But Gilbert is far from closed to dialogue, and his editorship for Penguin of *Inside Black Australia*, a book designed for a wide Australian and international audience, is proof of this. Yet it needs to be remembered that for some it is arguable, and has been strongly argued, that such a transcription of mainly oral art into a Penguin volume in English can only be a betrayal, both for black poets and white audiences.[8]

But another voice whispers seductively from beyond Gilbert's satire, in the resonances of skilled white poet and critic, unruffled by theoretical concerns about what constitutes "literariness," or perhaps too secure in his knowledge of what does constitute the aesthetic. Writing about Gilbert's anthology critic Mark O'Connor is understanding about some of the failures of the anthology:

> Gilbert's notes reveal that many of his poets have had only an
> interrupted secondary education. When they fail as poets, their
> faults are not related to Aboriginal culture, but are precisely the
> ones found in undereducated white poets: outdated poetic licences
> and archaic phrases of the "warriors of yore" variety, thumping
> rhymes and rhythms, McGonagail-style fluctuations of tone, and
> above all the reliance of abstract declamatory statements. Good
> poetry tries to convey even its more abstract ideas through con-

crete images—something the great Aboriginal song-cycles illustrate perfectly.[9]

For O'Connor, politics must submit at all times to the schooling of aesthetics: "[T]he answer to resistance is not to 'turn up the volume'"; in poetry "a platitude remains a platitude, even though there may be rednecks or self-servers who vehemently deny it" (Rutherford 1988, 251). Such white, middle-class, schooled assurance of poetic standards does not dream of different audiences possible for different poetries, even within the one reader. Nor does it ask questions about the universalism of its definitions of "the poetic," including its insistence on good form. All those unschooled Aboriginal poets out there should take note. Either get more schooling, or ask yourself whether you are a "natural poet" like one in the anthology who is praised. The critic here is, after all, interested in Aboriginal *Literature*. Here is a hierarchy of values in which politics must be served by (defined by? reliant upon?) aesthetics. No notion of white aesthetics as an impediment for a range of writers and readers, black and white. No notion of those elements of good writing that the critic prescribes—concrete images rather than avoidance of platitudes, subtle rhymes and rhythms, "their own poetic voice and range"— being possible stumbling blocks for a range of poets and readers or audiences at this particular time in Australian culture. It is a universalist, dehistoricizing white aesthetics that is being lauded, and one that seems to have little room for notions of "writing" or "textuality" unleashed for a range of audiences, purposes, effects. The critic is aware of this question of audiences, but resolves it simplistically:

> White readers may sympathise, but they will lack the Kooris' aching need for personal and racial (or national?) identity. They are more likely to ask "How *good* are these Aboriginal poets?" "Can they write about other things beside being Aboriginal? (O'Connor, in Rutherford 1988, 248)

While the position of this critic is seductive and one in which most white critics are trained and entangled, the need to break down the monoliths of "white reader" and "aching Koori" must be addressed. The image of the discerning white reader, settling back for a dose of "good" poetry, devoid of the myriad of political questions pounding in and behind every word read, is surely ludicrous.

How far can or should readers go in their separating of aesthetics and politics? O'Connor's arguments, while espousing a humanistic concern with injustice and the need for resistance, are uncomfortable with anything but aestheticized politics. But Gilbert and O'Connor, operating with distinct though connected models of human subjectivity and aesthetics, are also bound together discursively. Just as the questions raised by Aboriginal aesthetics do not have a single, static answer, but are historical and reader/audience-oriented, the question of subjectivity in their texts also needs to be examined. While O'Connor calls for "freer" Aboriginal poets, individualists who seem somehow to float just above or beyond historical, racial, and political constructions, able "to develop their own poetic voice and range," Gilbert sees "Aboriginal poets . . . identified with the freedom poets of the lately decolonized countries and as [embodying] a new perception of life around us, a new relation with the sanctity, the spiritual entity and living Presence within the earth and all life forms throughout the universe" (Gilbert 1988, xviii).

Polarities, Dialogies: The Fictions of Mudrooroo

For many white and black critics, the discourses of Aboriginal subjectivity are romantically blurred by these kinds of invocations of presence, authenticity, freedom, wholeness, and reclamation of an originary past. Whether the individual Aboriginal is imaged alone, discovering his or her "own poetic voice," or deeply entrenched within a community, a tradition or a past, what is often too easily called for in such humanist discourse is authentic Aboriginal humanity—a humanity not yet constructed by white education? desecrated by colonizing impurities? This kind of "Manichaean" approach[10]—white educator/black child, or black innocent/white polluter—is understandable, given the political reality of polemical representation and the often crude media stereotypes. But such polarization too often only leads to breast-beating guilt or a simple, powerful polemics, and is indulged in by too many. This is so, for instance, in the discourses of Christian mission and Aboriginal belief. Black American critic Emmanuel S. Nelson, writing on Mudrooroo's 1983 historical narrative *Doctor Wooreddy's Prescription for Enduring the Ending of the World*, discusses the missionary figure in the novel. The author

> invests the evangelist in his novel with a variety of colonialist motives and traits to make the missionary function as a meta-

phor for the imperialist impulse. Artistically, Johnson does not succeed as much as he does politically. His racial outrage, his secular sarcasm, and his relentless satire render Robinson a pompously self-assured buffoon, almost a caricature rather than an entirely convincing character. Politically, however, Johnson succeeds superbly in articulating the role of the missionary in the colonialist scheme: the missionary's imperial quest, like all other quests to reshape the world in European terms, inevitably fails but not before it inflicts irreparable damage. (Nelson 1989, 456–57)

In the face of the polemics of this critique, and other narratives of missionary-Aboriginal contact, the need for a reading of the text of the novel cries out. I would argue that the novel's art and its politics are much subtler and more flexible, as well as more painfully aware of verbal and human contradictions, than the critic allows. Yes, the buffoonery of the evangelist, based upon the notorious George Robinson, "Protector of Aborigines" in Tasmania, is a major feature of the representation. But such buffoonery, almost carnivalesque at points, is also a tool, I would argue, of a kind of impossible sympathy for the zealous white man full of ambiguous motives and desires, as much a physical, sexual creature as a religious one. In this way, the figures of Robinson and Wooreddy are drawn together, even as racially and historically they are perpetrator and victim. In fact, the glory of this novel, and the more recent, thematically connected narrative *The Master of the Ghost Dreaming*, is its imaginative courage to face what French critic Jean-François Lyotard in 1983 influentially described as the différend of human communications.[11] The realities of Aboriginal genocide, forced migration and Christianization are the novels' main concerns, and the instrument of government, the tool of imperialism (made up of greed, religious zealotry, class shame, sexual repression) is called George Robinson. But Mudrooroo's text is interested in the unanswerable how and why of such human actions and decisions. Robinson is the space that "functions as a metaphor for the imperialist impulse," but the novel is much more than a political diatribe. And just as the central Aboriginal character, the clever-man Dr. Wooreddy, functions as the site of black oppression and as the focus of horrific and grievous injustice, his character too is complexly represented. The novel is not chiefly realistic, but a clever working over of the genre "historical novel," employing a number of techniques and strategies one might call anti-European. The logic of realistic history writing and biography—

time as chronology, event as stable, witnessed signpost, explanation of history by personality registered as "inwardness," delineation of fact from fiction—are all questioned by the novel. The narrative at one level operates chronologically, from the childhood of Wooreddy until his death, a poor stick-figure imitation of his white friend, Robinson. But it is also a nomadic, circling narrative moving back and forward in time, in and out of the bush, characters taking on and throwing off Christianity and civilization—out of fear? greed? stoical self-survival?

Personal motives are unsure, as is the *category* of "personal motive," in the face of larger, constructing forces. Critic Kateryna Arthur is ambivalent about the representation and structural effects of these competing concepts of time in the novel. History, declares the white critic, is "a white invention":

> It depends upon a view of time as an unfolding "scroll." History proceeds sequentially, following the same kind of course as written words on a page. Because Aborigines have a different understanding of time, they do not recognize history as a distinct category. "The Dreaming" for them connects the present with the past. They have this in common with other oral communities. Lévi-Strauss writes of "the savage mind," "a characteristic feature . . . is its timelessness; its object is to grasp the world as both a synchronic and a diachronic totality." It is impossible to reproduce cyclical understanding of time in a language whose grammar operates out of a different system. And so a history like *Doctor Wooreddy* that tries to dramatize that crucial difference within the framework of a linear literary form, partially undermines its own cause while promoting it . . . although it cannot communicate the Aboriginal experience of time, the novel is a peculiarly apt form for recording a *particular* time of change and crisis. (Arthur 1985, 58–59)

Much important work has been done in the fields of ethnography and what critic Arnold Krupat calls "ethnocriticism" since Arthur's work was published. Arthur is a helpful and sensitive critic, but reassessment is needed of her monolithic categories "Aborigines," "the Aboriginal experience of time," and of course her use of Lévi-Strauss's "savage mind." While Arthur properly desires to set up difference—"them" and "us," the cyclic and the linear, white history and black experience of time—she has fallen into a Manichaean structure, which is compounded by the certainty of her delineation of "otherness." Mudrooroo's novel seeks ways of avoiding this dichotomizing effect, even as it maintains a political rage. Solidarity and critical/imaginative thought are in tension, in a way that polemics alone could not envisage. "Change and crisis" become not only the theme of his novels but characterize the nature of his discursive restlessness and experimentation.

In this way, the characterization too veers from realistic, psychological, and inward-looking to representations of subjects in a history which determines absolutely the destinies of the protagonists, white and black, leaving only parodic resistance to an already-known fate. Readers are lulled by the chronological narrative progression and character "development," but simultaneously the novel undercuts this readerly satisfaction: the ending is persistently previewed from the beginning, Wooreddy is full of wisdom and uniqueness amongst his tribe, *and* does nothing to resist the drag of history, merely "enduring." And for this passivity in the representation Mudrooroo received some strong criticism from within the Aboriginal community. The novel was seen as pessimistic, not sufficiently condemnatory of white, Christian colonization, and not revisionary enough in its depiction of Aboriginal integrity. It is not difficult to see his 1991 novel, *The Master of the Ghost Dreaming*, as an extended grappling with the textual and larger political developments started in *Doctor Wooreddy*. At the end of the earlier book's time frame, the Aboriginal tribes of Tasmania had been pathetically decimated, civilization hanging limply from them like the tattered clothes they were made to wear. The later novel tells the tale again, and therefore differently.

It could be argued of *The Master of the Ghost Dreaming* that it is written in answer to the changing political climate before and during the Australian Bicentennial "celebrations," as well as in response to more specific arguments against the European forms and the pessimistic narrative of *Doctor Wooreddy*. I do not know whether there is any direct evidence for this argument as far as the author's intentions go, but it is interesting to note that Mudrooroo has often voiced his dissatisfaction with *Doctor Wooreddy*, even in, or perhaps because of its acceptance in white academia:

> Well there is a problem, if you are an Aboriginal writer, that you never know how good you are because you are being patronized by someone or you are being put down by other ones, so you are being caught in between. . . . *Dr. Wooreddy*, my third novel, which has been praised by lots of people, I dislike, but

people tell me they like it best. (Williamson and Rudolphy 1989,
86)

It is perhaps less relevant to know how the critique of *Dr. Wooreddy* origi-
nated for Mudrooroo than to point to the differences between the two
novels. Only the bare bones of an "historical novel" remain with *Master*.
The white characters have been pared down to "Fada," "Mada," and
"Sonny," represented in the intonations of Aboriginal pronunciation. The
later novel is much more self-conscious, knows more about discourse
theory, works cleverly with parody (both thematically and generically),
and sets a determined political course, an optimistic one, for its Aboriginal characters. Fada is a loose, baggy representation of an evangelist. He
carries many of the traits of "George Robinson," though here we meet
him at the end of his mission, tired, sexually frustrated, knowing at base
the failure of his Christian/economic vision. Elements of Fada's work-
ing-class background, sexual frustration, and bodily needs are stressed.
He is an aging man, plagued by sexual desire for Ludjee, one of his
mission faithfuls. He plays at benevolent father while his "temptations"
are only too obvious to the Aboriginal woman.

The scene of chapter 4 is a condensed, individuated, and general-
ized portrait of the colonial condition. Ludjee is asked by an aroused
and self-righteous Fada to accompany him to the rocks, where he wishes
"to sketch a primitive scene for the chapter on food gathering in his
definitive work." Ludjee is at once the object of Fada's anthropological
gaze, of his sexual arousal, and she is his packhorse "carrying a heavy
armchair . . . heavy skirt dragging at her legs" (51).

The scene is charged erotically and polemically at the same time.
The polemics go completely against the old white hypocrite, and against
white sexuality generally, which covers up "under layers of thick cloth
. . . swathed in yard after yard of material" (52). The color and smell of a
white body for Ludjee is startlingly evoked:

> The colour was maggot white, the colour of fog . . . their skin in
> fact was opaque like mist and underneath veins could be seen
> pulsing with blood. This at least showed that they had blood, as
> did their cuts and wounds which ran a rich red; but it was the
> smell that alarmed her when she had to endure the actual pres-
> sure of their bodies. It was a sort of musty smell, a reeking of
> decay. And even their taste was different; rancid and bad, but
> now even her own people tasted like that. The stale ghost food

and clothing had altered their metabolism, had made them sick
and smelling of corpses. (52–53)

A great deal of the politics of the novel is concretely given here, to a
great extent through the knowing consciousness of the Aboriginal
woman. The crucial link between Aboriginal bodily and spiritual survival is negatively and powerfully imaged in the bondage of Ludjee.
The incestuous ogling of Fada at his primitive charge, who knows him
piercingly well, and the strategies for freedom, both Fada's and Ludgee's,
are tightly wound together in this chapter.

> . . . I want you to pose for me. I'll put you down on paper.
> "Capture my soul," the woman whispered.
> "But where is your net, where is your wooden chisel? It must be
> authentic. It must be as you once did.
> "Fada, we don't make them old things no more. All finished
> now same longa fish. . . . (59)

The desires of both woman and man, black and white, are given
here, in a knotted, complex relation of power. Ludjee is both superior
and submissive, knowing infinitely more of the real historical situation
than Fada but bowing out of necessity to the desires of the anthropolo-
gist/voyeur. Her "capture my soul" is a highly ambivalent, undecidable
phrase, suggesting both a desire for freedom, for her soul to be made
known and substantial, and it is an acceptance of—even a desire for?—
her bondage. The strategies of the novel, as it seeks to find a space for
survival first of all, and for new freedoms, are as complex as this phrase.
At various points in the novel we are taken with Ludjee, her "clever-
man" husband Jangamuttuk, and Wadawaka, a black African slave
washed up on the shores of Tasmania with his own stories of horror and
pitiful injustice, as they clear a way to freedom though their Dreaming
adventures/fantasies. Here in chapter 4, Ludjee literally leaps beyond
Fada's gaze:

> The female power surged within her; ancestors were connected
> in an unbroken line. The grid of the Female Dreaming flowed
> with energy. She dived into the water in a quick flowing motion
> which took her under and under. Fada frowned in annoyance,
> but she was beyond his control. She was free in her tradition. . . .
> (59)

The novel stakes much on the growing powers of the Aboriginal protagonists to take up the escape routes of their Dreaming, as they soar above the landscape with their Dreaming companions. Ludjee here is joined in a fantastic journey by Manta Ray—"free of it. Free—and the ray broke the surface of the water and flew into the air"—while Jangamuttuk watches her, excited, from the cliffs above, "with his shaman vision" (60). These lyrical and powerfully physical passages of escape and renewal through Dreaming frame the novel at its opening and closing. One level of the narrative is the progress of the central Aboriginal figures as they grow stronger in their traditional powers of Dreaming, and as they initiate two of the miserably few youths into the secrets of the old ways. A return to these ways is given as a gesture, both political and spiritual, of transcendence from the horror of the historical real. For many it will be read as merely gesture, a utopian revisioning that changes nothing of history or the present.

Another discourse, seemingly less utopian, complicates the novel to the point of straining. It is messier politically and is offered here with the knowledge that it may be accused of being a white reading irrelevant to Aboriginal concerns. But I seek here to write what has been called by a number of critics a dialogical rather than oppositional criticism. And I believe *The Master of the Ghost Dreaming* is the product of a dialogical imagination. As it seeks utopically a way beyond, of rewriting the morass of Aboriginal history and thus invigorating the present, it is at the same time dialogically alive to the ambiguities and fractures that complicate any simple oppositionality. Of such dialogism, critic Arnold Krupat writes:

[O]ne of the things that occurs on the borders is that oppositional sets like West/Rest, Us/Them, anthropological/biological, historical/mythical . . . often tend to break down. On the one hand, cultural contact can indeed produce mutual rejections, the reification of differences, and defensive retreats into celebrations of what each group regards as distinctively its own . . . on the other hand, it may also frequently be the case that interaction leads to interchange. . . . (1992, 15)

Krupat is writing particularly on white contact with native Americans. In the introduction to his volume *Ethnocriticism* he seeks to establish a methodological and ideological framework that will escape political and aesthetic polarizations. He is aware of the dangers of white diminishment of native otherness in such a stance, and is also open to the possibility that the "ethnocriticism" he seeks to write may be impossible. However, the alternatives are grim: writing "victimist history" informed by Manichaean notions of good and evil,[12] often accompanied by romantic images of perfect Indian harmony with the environment, or "nothing more than sermonizing about the Indian mind, or the evils of Western civilization." The role for critique then, is "to move away from even the majority/minority dichotomy, without, however, denying the differential relations of power it seeks to name" (25).

Multiple Strategies: Mirrors, Mimicry, Dialogue

This critical methodology may be impossible. It puts a great strain on textuality and the understandings it constructs, for the ways of registering otherness are legion and they do so often collapse simplistically into polarizations, with their attendant burden of sameness, one measure, in the end. But I would argue that *The Master of the Ghost Dreaming* can helpfully be read through this approach, because it is attempting an analogous dialogical feat. I am not sure at what level of consciousness or intention what I am about to describe exists. It exists though, perhaps in competition with the move towards reclaiming old Dreaming secrets, and often the tension between the two strategies (impulses? politics? aesthetics?) creates odd moments. What I seek to describe is partly the tension, endemic in the struggles of representation, between "the missionary function[ing] as a metaphor for the imperialist impulse" and less othering representation; between the generalizing and the textually ambiguous. Fada, Mada, and Sonny are represented in all their pathetic duplicity of motivation, though not simplistically as mere types of the hypocrite.

More controversially, I would argue that they work in the text as mirror images of Jangamuttuk, Ludjee, and their children, the boys going through initiation rites, and Wadawak, for whom "no slaves had fathers, or mothers, or sisters or brothers" (Mudrooroo 1991, 88).[13] This mirroring tells a story of sameness and difference. It scrambles fantasy and reality. It is Lacan's founding moment of identity and otherness, and the moment when desire for the other is instituted. Identity—even Aboriginal identity?—is in a compact with the other, which it sees as both murderer/castrator and as shadow of self, implicit in self. This is a potentially dangerous theory, one which could lead to a decay in any political positioning in the call for social justice. But this mirroring is there in the structures of the text and needs investigating (solidarity *with* criticism): Fada and Jangamuttuk are both clever-men, religious leaders of their people, they are aging and tired, but still full of desires—sexual, material, and spiritual. Both strive to initiate their young into the ways of their people. This white man, like all whites, is a "ghost," immensely other and yet a fantastic projection, a shadow from the imagination of the observer. What could be the relationship of this different other, this invader, to the black self? Mudrooroo's novel staggers between alternatives.

The desire to represent total otherness, Manichaean polarization of the colonizers from their victims, is certainly there in the text. One of its most puzzling and utopian strategies is the fantastic Dreaming sequences. Another is the physical revulsion expressed in the passage above. But at the very moment that otherness—revulsion, difference in color, sexuality, power, religion—is being set up, the language (or the auctorial intention) complicates the polarity with the possibility of desire *for* the other, dissemination of self in other.

In the opening chapter, a strange, parodic ceremony takes place in the bush, just as Mada and Fada are trying to sleep. Mada is furious with the loud chanting of the tribe and of Jangamuttuk "miming out perfectly words in the very voice of her husband" (10). Jangamuttuk and his people are in fact involved in a ritual of serious intent, structured through parody, mimicry, cultural cross-dressing:

> feeling out the possibilities of the play as the rhythm bounced the shaman towards possession and his people into a new kind of dance. The dancers clasped each other and began a European reel. They kept to the repetitive steps and let the strange rhythm move their feet. It became their master. Each generation including the tragically few children jigged as Jangamuttuk began to sing in perfect ghost accents. . . . (4)

Such parodic ritual reminds Protestant Fada, now watching secretly from the bushes, "of the mass of the Popish Church in Rome" (12) and he is momentarily translated into a kind of elfin anthropologist "Fascinated . . . hidden in the darkness behind the illumination of the fires . . . watching the mysterious ways of the humans" (12). No doubt readers of the text will have a number of other responses to such a scene, ranging from pity and horror at the Aboriginal submission involved to amusement at the parodic ironizing of the colonial situation by the Aboriginal players. But we are given a narrative statement of the shamanistic intention of

Jangamuttuk, a powerful (though not, of course, an exclusive) reading of the scene:

> Jangamuttuk, dreamer of the ceremony, was painted in like fashion. His work was more elaborate and detailed. A hatch design of red and white encircled his neck in a symbolic collar. Below this were painted the lapels of a frockcoat. Four buttons of a spiral design kept the coat closed. . . . His leg, and the legs of the male dancers, were painted white with a circular design at the knee.
>
> Now Jangamuttuk, creator and choreographer, checked the company for flaws before the body of the ceremony began. He was not after a realist copy, after all he had no intention of aping the European, but sought for an adaptation of these alien cultural forms appropriate to his own cultural matrix. It was an exciting concept; but it was more than this. There was a ritual need for it to be done. The need for the inclusion of these elements into a ceremony with a far different purpose than mere art. He, the shaman, and purported Master of the Ghost Dreaming, was about to undertake entry into the realm of the ghosts. Not only was he to attempt the act of possession, but he hoped to bring all his people into contact with the ghost realm so that they could capture the essence of health and well-being, and then break back safely into their own culture and society. This was the purpose of the ceremony. . . . (3–4)

So much about the scene undermines Jangamuttuk's intention here, opening out to other readings. Even as the shaman's proud desire for liberation of his people is registered, so too is the power of that other, parodied realm. But another effect of the scene is to create hybrid figures, in some ways pathetic in their submission but also figures of metaphysical and physical striving, aware of their real historical entrapment, who must make themselves powerful artistic and spiritual manipulators. We are made to read both dignity and submission in the ceremony, to register the power of both cultures through the double action of mimicry. Is it parodic power that is drawn on, the power simultaneously to acknowledge the force of the culture parodied and to limit it to its place, to make it yield up the secrets of its force? Jangamuttuk's journey into the Ghost Dreaming is represented highly ambiguously. It is a successful journey in the shaman's terms, as he returns with medicine for his people. But the final opponent, from whom he wrests "a golden flask . . . source of her good health" is represented as both violent and a victim, a fantastic mirror image of Mada:

A ghost female lay on a platform covered with the softest of skins. She was fair to behold. Stark white and luminescent was her skin beneath which, pulsing blue with health, Jangamuttuk could see the richness of her blood. Her lips were the reddest ochre and her cheeks were rosy and glowing with good health. . . . She slept the sleep of a being seemingly content in body and spirit, but Jangamuttuk with insight knew that this was an illusion. . . . Her longing extruded from her to fix his attention on a small table within reach of her groping hand. On it stood a golden flask. The source of her good health. Before the hand could clasp it, Jangamuttuk snatched it up. The eyes of the ghost female sprang open. Blue and utterly cold, they held him. Wrenched from a dream in which she was on the verge of finally and utterly achieving complete satisfaction, her hunger erupted in a scream of rage at the human. . . . (15)

We are not dealing with a single mirroring of characters or cultures here, but are positioned in a hall of mirrors, where each succeeding reflection takes on another and complicating facet. The ghost female is like Mada, perpetually unsatisfied, the keeper of the medicine upon which she relies to relieve her pain and with which the Aboriginals have been partly seduced. She is the powerful keeper of the "golden flask," a colonizer; and she is a pitiful victim, her longing taking the shape of the medical flask, just as Jangamuttuk's dream mission depends upon obtaining the flask. Mada is both powerful and empty, groping, sick. She is represented in both English and Aboriginal legendary images: rosy and clawed, a source of power and of impotence.

This scene, and following passages, are charged with a strange sexuality as the Aboriginal clever-man pits his powers against those of the ghost female (mother? lover? victim?). His song "holds" her, or is it he who is held? The song he chants envelops both protagonists:

And I groan, moan, no pain can quell,
Or hope can quench, the sorrow of my hell,
Down under, living hell down under.
                                                                        (16)

This moment of entranced battle ends with Jangamuttuk's escape back to the circle of dancers, dispensing to each of the waiting supplicants "a drop or two of seemingly precious fluid" from what looks, to the watching Fada, like "one of his wife's old medicine bottles." Fada turns from mild amusement to being "more than startled" when "the villain mimicked an awful travesty of his better half's voice."

How do readers respond to these mirroring effects? Is the mimicry politically, strategically effective, or weakly parodic, nothing more than "paralyzed gestures of aestheticized powerlessness"? [14] I would argue strongly for the impossibility of choice for the Aboriginal people represented here—or perhaps it is the contemporary novelist's impossibility of choice—and therefore for the immense courage of understanding that is realizing, through the multiple strategies necessary in the text, "identity as wound" (Spivak 1992, 770). *Master* perceives in such densely imagined passages the agonized constructions and self-construction of both victims and perpetrators. In fact it is the courage of this novel that it constructs a fictionalizing history, an interventionary history, at the same time as it struggles not to collapse back into Manichaean polarities . This struggle is of course Mudrooroo's, or the novel's, to find a discourse of empowerment, while being constantly aware of the entrapments of mere "victimist history," of mere polarizations, or of mere utopian revisionism.

The novel does not, I think, completely escape from the seductions of these smoother narrative solutions. But it is in the complex multiple mirrorings of such scenes as the one discussed above that Mudrooroo's language is seeking a discourse at once politically realistic, calling for solidarity from contemporary Aboriginals with long cultural traditions, and is also striving to write beyond us/them, colonizer/colonized, victim/perpetrator. It is not, I have argued, through any single narrative moment—utopian closure as the Aboriginal remnant head off into freedom on the stolen schooner, the fantastic possibilities of the Dreaming, the authenticity of any one character—but in the refusal of simple polemics and polarization that Mudrooroo's text brings about the grounds for dialogue about the past and the future. Such grounds are fought for in this multiplicity of discourses and are not and cannot be established with any simplistic narrative resolution. As Derrida has taught us, textuality cannot end. Such multiplicity allows the moment of victim and the moment of perpetrator, but it also enables a critical exchange where imaginative forgiveness can stimulate the dialogues of justice and (inter)change.

Notes

1. In a recent *Critical Inquiry* essay, the North American academic Sara Suleri discusses the amorphousness of the term "postcolonial": "Where the term once referred exclusively to the discursive practices produced by the historical fact of prior colonization in certain geographically specific segments of the world, it is now more of an abstraction available for figurative deployment in any strategic redefinition of marginality" (Suleri 1992, 759). My essay moves self-consciously between both of these possible definitions because, as a descendent of the white colonizing race in Australia seeking to question the rights and roles of white critics in regard to black writing, it is always questionable what place I have to play in "redefinitions of marginality."

2. "In 1988 as a Bicentennial Project Colin Johnson changed his name to Mudrooroo Narogin." Quoted from the 1989 Annual Bibliography of the journal *Australian Literary Studies*. (The Bicentennial was a series of government-induced celebration—"Celebration of a Nation"—of two hundred years of white colonization of Australia.) More recently, his novel *The Master of the Ghost Dreaming* was published under the name Mudrooroo.

3. An excellent recent article on the widely divergent positions on subjectivity and the discourses of postcolonialism is Maxwell 1991.

4. "[H]anging out in wind and water, learning not to transcode too quickly", as Gayatri Spivak describes part of this process of silent learning, of being "stripped of identity", in her provocative essay "Acting Bits/ Identity Talk" (1992, 785).

5. The view of the Judicial Committee of the Privy Council, Australia, 1889, cited in Barwick 1987.

6. A useful investigation of the figure of the Aboriginal in white fiction, from earliest contact through to the work of Keneally, Herbert and Ireland, can be found in Healy 1989. See also Terry Goldie in Rutherford 1988.

7. See for example the newspaper review by Mary Rose Liverani in *The Australian*, 28 March 1992.

8. See Arthur 1985 for two helpful essays on the relationship of Aboriginal oral and written cultures.

9. Mark O'Connor, in Rutherford 1988, 250.

10. See JanMohamed 1985 for his argument concerning "the metonymic transformation and the resulting allegory" that "come to dominate every facet of imperialist mentality." JanMohamed is writing chiefly about white imperialist fiction of the late nineteenth and early twentieth centuries. It is beyond the scope of this present essay to examine the workings of the Manichaean allegory in the writings of contemporary writers, black and white, from contemporary postcolonial communities. Other kinds of negotiating frameworks would, I think, reveal themselves.

11. Critic Simon During has written helpfully on the concept of the différend in the context of postcolonial writing and criticism in his article "Postmodernism or Postcolonialism Today," reprinted in Docherty 1993, 448–62.

12. Krupat gives a helpful summary of the "genealogy of the manichean allegory" as it applies to postcolonial work, from Frantz Fanon onwards, (1992, 14).

13. The representation of the maternal in Mudrooroo's work is complex and deserves a separate treatment. For Wadawaka, being accepted into Aboriginal Dreaming rites was being "safe at home in the womb. Feeling the warm walls constricting. . . ." (Mudrooroo 1991, 88). The push towards nativist or return-to-origin resolutions would need to be examined under this heading of the maternal, as well as through the Buddhist influences in *The Master of the Ghost Dreaming*.

14. A phrase used by Georg Lukács in *History and Class Consciousness* to describe the responses of modernism to the claims of minority voices and peoples.

References

Arthur, Kateryna. "Fiction and the Rewriting of History: A Reading of Colin Johnson." *Westerly* 30.1 (1985): 55–60.

———. "Neither Here Nor There: Towards Nomadic Reading." *New Literatures Review* 17 (1988): 31–42.

Berwick, Diana. "Making a Treaty: The North American Experience." Paper written for the Aboriginal Treaty Committee, 1987.

Brady, Veronica. Review of *The Song Cycle of Jacky* and *Selected Poems*, by Mudrooroo, *Westerly* 2 (1987): 99–100.

Docherty, Thomas, ed. *Postmodernism: A Reader*. New York: Columbia University Press, 1993.

Gilbert, Kevin, ed. *Inside Black Australia: An Anthology of Aboriginal Poetry*. Ringwood, Australia: Penguin, 1988.

Healy, J. J. *Literature and the Aborigine in Australia*. 1978. Reprint, St. Lucia, Australia: University of Queensland Press, 1989.

JanMohamed, Abdul R. "The Economy of Manichean Allegory: The Function of Racial Difference in Colonialist Literature." *Critical Inquiry* 12 (1985): 59–87.

Krupat, Arnold. *Ethno-Criticism: Ethnography, History, Literature*. Berkeley and Los Angeles: University of California Press, 1992.

Langford, Ruby. *Don't Take Your Love to Town*. Ringwood, Australia: Penguin, 1988.

Maxwell, Anne. "The Debate on Current Theories of Colonial Discourse." *Kunapipi* 13.3 (1991): 70–84.

Mudrooroo. *Dr. Wooreddy's Prescription for Enduring the Ending of the World*. Melbourne: Hyland House, 1983.

———. *The Master of the Ghost Dreaming*. Sydney: Angus and Robertson, 1991.

Nelson, Emmanuel S. "Connecting with the Dreamtime: The Novels of Colin Johnson." *Southerly* 46.3 (1986): 337–43.

———. "The Missionary in Aboriginal Fiction." *Southerly* 47.4 (1989): 451–57.

Rutherford, Anna, ed. *Aboriginal Culture Today*. Sydney: Dangeroo Press, 1988. Special double issue of the magazine *Kunapipi*.

Said, Edward. *The World, The Text, and the Critic*. Cambridge: Harvard University Press, 1983.

Spivak, Gayatri Chakravorty. "Acting Bits/Identity Talk." *Critical Inquiry* 18 (1992): 770–803.

Suleri, Sara. "Woman Skin Deep: Feminism and the Postcolonial Condition." *Critical Inquiry* 18.4 (1992): 756–69.

Williamson, John, and Ron Rudolphy. "Interview with Mudrooroo (Colin Johnson)." *Westerly* 2 (1989): 83–89.

Aboriginal Autography
The Dreaming of
Sally Morgan

SUZETTE HENKE

In *Being and Nothingness,* Jean-Paul Sartre insists that the notion of race is "purely and simply a collective fiction, that only individuals exist" (1956, 524). But what happens when that fiction is universally apprehended as a poignant reality—when collective constructions of racial difference devour our social imaginations and, like the ouroboros swallowing its own tail, roll in mesmerizing circles that hypnotize the populace into a belief in the inevitability of racial hostilities? If race be a collective fiction, it has proved one of the strongest and most invidious ideologies of social construction in postcolonial countries like Australia and the United States.

The title of Sally Morgan's Aboriginal autograph, *My Place,* might seem to an uninitiated audience deceptively simple, if not reductive—a phrase indicative of the personal quest for individuation that determines identity in the Eurocentric scheme designating one's unique place in the universe.[1] The title page, however, cunningly evinces the Aboriginal end of Morgan's quest rather than its inception: it suggests the symbolic landscape of Aboriginal Dream-time that Sally cannot fully appreciate until the book's conclusion. As James Cowan explains in *Mysteries of the Dreamtime,* "The Dreaming is . . . not so much a place as a state of being" (1949, 40). It was, furthermore, "the Aborigine's understanding of space, his ability to establish for himself a sense of 'place' while in a state of wandering, that gave him his unique human and spiritual dimension" (87).

35

Morgan implicitly infuses the title of her book with the full weight of
Aboriginal oral tradition and the Dreaming of her newfound ancestors.
Unobtrusively, she acknowledges the Aboriginal Dream-time, with its
non-European metaphysics of space and place—a belief system that
defines personal identity as a function of those godly traces and "songlines" linked to a particular geographical locale (Cowan 1989, 106–7).

Sally Morgan grew up very much on the borders of racial and cultural identity, in a household where her mulatto mother, Gladys Milroy,
and half-caste Aboriginal grandmother, Daisy Corunna, diligently
(re)constructed, against the reality of hybridized biology, a racial
counterfiction of pure Aryan ancestry. "Tell them you're Indian," Gladys
enjoined her bewildered progeny, whose schoolfellows constantly questioned the dark-skinned family's right to belong in white Australia (Morgan 1990, 38). The fantasy of Indian origins was, Gladys later explained,
a covert narrative of resistance—a fabulation meant to protect the rights
and happiness of her mixed-blood offspring from Anglo-Australian con-
tempt for miscegenation. This well-intentioned parental deception was
"only a little white lie" geared to alleviate her children's inevitable sense
of "cross-cultural and interpersonal (con)fusion" (as Hawley terms it in
the introduction to the present book) in a shockingly bigoted world. If
one associates the term Indian with the indigenous populations of North
America, mistakenly identified as Aryan by a disoriented Columbus,
then the masquerade becomes all the more convincing; it serves as a
fictive mask or convenient cloak for childhood socialization across seemingly intransigent cultural borders, while covertly asserting allegiance
to the repressed polyphonic voices of indigenous identity.

Sally, however, wears the ill-fitting cloak of racial conformity with
instinctive dis-ease from early childhood. She senses that she is inexpli-
cably liminal in white bourgeois society not only because of her
integumental hue but also by virtue of her poverty, her willfulness, her
familial solidarity, and her passionate love of nature and ecological sensitivity.[2] From the dawn of youthful consciousness, she is inadvertently
cross-(ad)dressing the split and oppositional halves of a bifurcated cultural identity. Racial *métissage* bequeaths a legacy of concealment and
incomprehension, of uncomfortable disguises and perplexing "white
lies" that repress the rich, multicultural heritage that neither Gladys
Milroy nor her offspring can fathom. Haunted by ubiquitous signs of
racial bigotry, they embrace the roles assigned by assimilationist strategies like *dramatis personae* in a grotesquely deformed (post)modern
theater of the absurd. The subaltern capitulates to white hegemony by
mimicking the values of an alien, ostensibly superior culture of aggres-

sion and conquest. Constructing a socially acceptable Aryan identity, s/he risks losing racial and historical specificity and, through patterns of amalgamation, forfeits ancestral roots that burgeon in communal meaning.

At times, Grandmother Daisy (Talahue) resembles a tribal shaman proudly presiding over the wonders of the natural world; but, at other moments, she strikes her grandchildren as a silly, superstitious old woman who fills the house with onions, garlic, and cigarette ash. Sally recalls a pivotal childhood memory of squatting in the sand and absorbing Nan's lessons in Aboriginal strategies for bush survival: "Now this is a goanna and here are emu tracks. . . . You got to know all of them if you want to catch tucker" (99).

Sally is first given auctorial permission to speak when commissioned by her uncle Arthur to record the tale of his boyhood experiences at Corunna Downs Station. "We're talkin' history," he proudly proclaims (163). With a sense of personal and racial history that ennobles the tale of his troubled coming-of-age, he offers the voice of the Aboriginal father "Jilly-yung" (176) to sanction his niece's project. Oral history proves a gift to the bewildered Sally, who proudly acts as scribe to her uncle and a vehicle of testimony for the recuperation of her newfound racial heritage.[3] Arthur's Aboriginality has, of course, been compromised by his virtual kidnapping and abduction to a white mission. He will never know the tale of his totem, the sacred and mysterious snake: "I belonged to the snake, and I was anxious to see the pretty snake's eggs, but they took me away to the mission" (176).[4] He complains wistfully, "I always wish I'd never left . . . . home" (181).[5] The rationale for his bewildering deracination was, he realized, a convenient lie: "I thought they wanted us educated. . . . I was wrong" (182). The mission, he recalls, was "just like a prison" (183), with corporal punishment a standard disciplinary practice in the training of children considered recalcitrant savages. After one particularly brutal and sadistic beating, Arthur's "thighs were running with blood" (186); he simply had no protection from being "skinned and belted around" by the irascible mission staff, even though the law that incarcerated him in this "whitefella" institution was, ironically, the Aboriginal Protection Act.[6] No wonder Sally is motivated to trace her family roots and to break the historical silence surrounding Aboriginal subaltern status: "All our history is about the white man. . . . I just want to try to tell a little bit of the other side of the story" (163–64).

In *My Place*, Sally Morgan at first appears to have embarked on a traditionally male Odyssean quest for the lost father, the paternal figure valorizing one's subject-position vis-à-vis the law and word of the father—

the social place determined by bloodline and inheritance. Sally's own biological father, Bill Milroy, is present in the mode of absence; he is an obscure figure of mental illness and inebriation whose domestic role as paterfamilias has long been de-authorized as impotent, if not invidious to domestic harmony. "Just a frame, that was Dad," Sally observes as a child (12). The father(s) of both Gladys and Daisy Corunna have been erased from personal history and must, in turn, be sought, named, "owned," and returned to the family memoir before the children of un- known progenitors can forgive paternal and colonial transgression.

Daisy's father is exposed, it would seem, as Howden Drake-Brock- man, the indomitable station owner of Corunna Downs. The mystery of Daisy's own (perhaps incestuous) mating lies at the heart of Sally's story and functions as the empty center of a complex, maternally decentered narrative. In searching for an unnamed white grandfather, Sally is left forever longing for a progenitor who refused to own or acknowledge his progeny. By the end of the story, we know and do not know the place inhabited by that central patriarchal/colonial figure deliberately exor- cised from Daisy Corunna's liberated (her)story of historical resistance.

The notion of ownership is intriguing in this text, as it is always used in two contradictory ways. On the one hand, the term signifies appropriation and slavery—an unrightful, outrageously demeaning at- tempt to keep in one's service the labor and resources of another human being. Slavery is a word rarely associated with the treatment of Aborigi- nal peoples in Western Australia. In the course of her research, Sally is startled to discover that "pastoral industry was built on the back of slave labour" (151).

Australian law and society approved of the indentured servitude of a vast multitude of people whose only recourse was flight, starvation, or slavery. "You see," says Daisy Corunna, "in those days, we was owned, like a cow or a horse" (336). The so-called Protection Act forced Austra- lian Aboriginals grudgingly to serve the needs of white settlers who colonized the territory and refused to acknowledge the rights of native people who had once made their living from the bounty of a continent that offered sanctuary to the lawless, the marginal, and the outcast from British colonial rule. Arthur Corunna poignantly recalls seeing "native people all chained up around the neck and hands" (181). He wryly notes that the colonizers preached the commandment, "Thou Shalt Not Steal," and yet "stole this country" (213).

In another context, the word "ownership" connotes the bond of blood and spirit between parent and progeny, father and child. Sally's mother and grandmother are both tormented by the ambiguity of their ancestry, the undecidability of the name and law of a father who refuses to own or acknowledge his offspring. Daisy caustically observes "[We] don't know who we belong to, no one'll own up" (325). Rape seems to have been acceptable practice for the landowners and station managers of the Australian bush, where Aboriginal women, whose dark skin made them as exotic and desirable as their status made them unknowable and unmarriageable, were coerced into servicing the sexual needs of their lascivious masters. When Daisy Corunna hints at the unspeakable history of her own sexual shame, she couches her revelations in bitter indictments: "Some men can't be trusted. They just mongrels" (337). She goes on to explain, ruefully: "I know a lot of native servants had kids to white men because they was forced" (337).

There was, of course, no attempt to know, acknowledge, or own these women in a biblical or social sense.[7] The white overlords scattered their seed with impunity and then refused to "own up" to their sexual activities or acknowledge the children they engendered. Hence the trauma that rules the life of Daisy Corunna, whose own Anglo-Australian father, Howden Drake-Brockman, apparently foisted responsibility for her paternity onto a scalawag named Maltese Sam in order to inveigle his lily-white wife Eleanor Boddington (and later, his second wife Alice) into believing the whitefella's tale of black women's sexual promiscuity.

Was it true that Howden fathered not one but two children on his own daughter Daisy—and then was responsible for the heartless abduction of her first female child on the grounds that a black woman could not be considered fit to care for her white offspring? "Howden was a lonely man," explains Arthur. "He used to go down to Daisy's room at night and talk to her" (158)—and possibly for more intimate purposes, as well. "Before I had Gladdie," confesses Daisy, "I was carryin' another child, but I wasn't allowed to keep it" (340).

Daisy's second child Gladys fared little better insofar as she was farmed out to Parkerville orphanage with a wing euphemistically called Babyland and allowed to visit her mother three times a year during holidays. Meager solace was provided by a "crying tree" in the bush and by a rag doll called Sally Jane, which she tenderly cuddled on visits to Ivanhoe. Despite her sororal affection for Alice's children, Judy, June, and Dick Drake-Brockman, Gladys could only be tolerated by this "first settler" as an occasional holiday guest. A cast-off member of the "underclass," she experienced a sense of total deprivation and injustice. While the Drake-Brockmans shared a cozy holiday feast in the dining room, Daisy Corunna ate a solitary meal of scraps in the kitchen and drank from a grimy tin mug. So much for the aristocratic family's perpetual insistence that Daisy enjoyed egalitarian status in the household as child minder and surrogate grandmother.

The warehousing of unwanted children had to be one of the greatest crimes of Australian colonialism, as half-breed mulatto offspring desperately sought a place in a world that refused them social refuge. The bond between mother and child was treated casually and broken with insouciance by the white overlords anxious to dispose of the physical evidence of their own lascivious slippage. The Other must constantly be exploited and then gotten rid of—consigned to an historical memoir, a narrative that obliterates personal responsibility and leaves the castoff remnants of desire to remain outcast by a social system that refuses to own, remember, or acknowledge its sexual/ paternal/ filial responsibilities to mixed-race offspring. From the subject position of the fatherless child, paternal absence seems a painful and perplexing mystery. Gladys tells Sally that, as a mulatto girl living in an orphanage, she used to implore God nightly for patriarchal protection; she always felt both confused and betrayed by the father/savior's failure to rescue her from bitter isolation and from the cruel taunts of her fellow inmates.

Without working through a complex theoretical structure, Sally Morgan has given the world a deconstructed postcolonial narrative. The autonomous subject, with its narcissistic ego, is deliberately decentered—erased from the center of the text and present in the mode of absence, as the perpetual quester or Odyssean adventurer in search of the history of a family whose roots have been plundered and whose historical genealogy has been virtually obliterated. Hence Morgan's unusual frame of autobiography-*cum*-oral history: she chooses to adopt the nonlinear narrative mode of Aboriginal storytelling.

Sally's own story is there, but always in shadow, giving way to the heartrending tale of a people whose heritage has been lost and memories stolen. Her marriage to Paul Morgan, for instance, is reduced to the status of a fairly casual event, reported with humor and lightheartedness, as she "nicks" into town to pick up a bridal dress on the morning of her wedding (131). The adolescent Sally matures, moves away from home, and studies psychology at the University of Western Australia, where she meets her future partner. Although Anglo-Australian, Paul offers Sally an experiential connection to the sacred, mysterious North through his upbringing in a Christian missionary family. He feels comfortable with the community of blackfellas that formed his own background and seems amazingly free of the kind of prejudice that has characterized the white males of Sally's line for several generations. Paul takes note of Nan's Aboriginal features and teases Sally for her naïveté when she suddenly becomes aware of her grandmother's dark-hued skin and distinctive physiognomy. Queried about Daisy Corunna's Aboriginality, he laughs with amusement at Sally's lifelong obfuscation of her own racial heritage. Gradually, Sally comes to realize what Paul and her sister Jill have known all along—that her origins are, indeed, Aboriginal, and that she has much to dis-cover in the bewildering search for a land and people hitherto denied her. Confronted in her early twenties with a startling realization of her ethnic identity, Sally cannot help feeling confused about the true meaning of her Aboriginal heritage: "I'd never lived off the land. . . . I'd never participated in corroborees or heard stories of the Dream-time. . . . What did it mean for someone like me?" (141).

Interestingly enough, the romance of Sally's love and courtship takes second place to the "male" romantic quest for paternity and origins that seems to characterize so much of western literature. Love there is, and mating and marrying and the getting of children. All those concerns that have traditionally centered the bourgeois novel from Jane Austen to the present simply get absorbed by the larger story of a people coming out of darkness to find themselves and their rightful heritage in a land that has been appropriated by the colonizer and stolen from beneath their feet. The colonized must rebel in a quiet way, giving voice to those polyphonic spirits long dead who rise up to comfort and solace them in times of trouble.

Spirits there are in abundance. Gladys and Nan hear the voices of Aboriginal ancestors singing in the marsh when Sally's father takes to his bed in a shell-shocked stupor or attacks the family in inebriate rage. Daisy Corunna confides to her granddaughter that she and Gladys heard ghostly "blackfellas playin' their didgeridoos and singin' and laughin' down in the swamp" (347). Since Sally's mother Gladys reiterates this (ostensibly) improbable story in her own oral narrative, it is difficult for the Eurocentric reader to doubt its psychic and cultural veracity, if not its empirical truth status.

Bill Milroy, too, hears voices, but they appear to be the hallucinatory cries of demons who goad him to kill his wife and children and amalgamate their presence with that of the German enemy lingering, still, from the prison camps of World War II. "Hide the axe," he counsels Nan; and the family takes flight to the sanctuary of a neighbor's kitchen while Dad fumes and weeps, screaming with the torments of schizophrenic hallucination.[8] Sally observes, coolly, that the voices he used to hear "kept tellin' him to kill us all, even you little ones" (347).

All those gifted with second sight in the novel hear voices of angels that comfort and counsel them. In the midst of severe domestic depression, Gladys Milroy is visited by an epiphany—the luminescent revelation of three wise men, one of whom predicts that "a great leader would be born into [her] house" (295). During life-threatening experiences of childbirth, she is buoyed up by the mystical visitation of angels of light, complete with soft, white feathers and messages of redemption. Sally, too, hears voices and experiences an epiphany—a spiritual vision that brings her into the company of those maternal ancestors she is only now discovering. "Suddenly, it was as if a window in heaven had been opened and I saw a group of Aboriginal women standing together" (227).[9]

At the end of the book, Sally's sister Jill, the most skeptical of siblings, hears the cries of an Aboriginal bird announcing her grandmother's imminent death. Daisy, fragile but at peace, acknowledges the call of this mythic creature, "the Aboriginal bird. . . . God sent him to tell me I'm going home" (357).[10] Even the dubious Anglo-Saxon reader is left with the sense that Nan's death signifies a passing rather than a termination. Because of Sally's persistent drive to recover a heritage once buried and denied, Nan will live on in memory and continue to give strength and hope to the generations that succeed her. Her descendants will proudly embrace their borderline subject positions and eagerly explore the bicultural Janus vision of hybrid cultural inheritance. Jill Milroy, once ashamed of her Aboriginal ancestry, now determines to "stand up and be counted" in honor of her spirited grandmother. Shortly before her death, Daisy Corunna poignantly confesses to her granddaughter: "I been scared all my life, too scared to speak out" (350). "I been treated rotten. . . . Just like a beast of the field. And now, here I am. . . . Just a dirty old blackfella" (352). The degradation of such racial alienation inflames her (grand)children with a passionate mission to challenge Anglo-Australian cultural hegemony.

The shape of Morgan's narrative is that of an intriguing mystery story. She circles round and round the central *aporia* of the text, burrowing deeper and deeper through the many generations who have embraced assimilationist values and have kept their family secrets hidden from a bigoted and prying specular gaze. Sally recounts her uncle Arthur's story before he dies, then the tale of her mother Gladys Corunna Milroy, and finally the story of grandmother Daisy, whose history of shame and violation always remains hidden at the unspoken kernel of the narrative. Defiantly, Nan jealously guards the "secrets" of her ineffable past. "I'll take them to the grave," she proclaims triumphantly (349). The inarticulate center of sexual and racial trauma is always hinted at, but never fully revealed.[11] It is, throughout the textual skein, the tale of a father who refuses to "own" his offspring. The incestuous patriarchal progenitor seems to have been Howden Drake-Brockman. In the end, however, the mystery of paternity is left perpetually in shadow: only the mothers are known and illuminated. Their radiant portraits give us the distinct impression of a strong, invincible matriarchal heritage gratefully retrieved by Sally's heroic quest.

When Sally, Paul, and the children visit the Pilbara for the first time, they feel overwhelmed by the gift of restored racial/historical roots, an experience of ownership that reverses the traditional discourse of gift-giving and appropriation. A full-blooded Aboriginal woman utters a prayer of gratitude sotto voce to the mixed-blood family that has so prophetically returned: "You don't know what it means that you, with light skin, want to own us" (229). Sally and her mother feel as if they have "suddenly come home" (230). "You belong to a lot of people here," insist her warmhearted Aboriginal relatives (231). "You got your place now" (232).

Seeking the nameless father, Sally has exposed, instead, the battered and brainwashed subject position of her victimized (grand)mother. Dis remains in darkness; but Demeter spurns her own fecundity, as Persephone longs for entry into those Eleusinian mysteries of parentage that must forever remain in shadow.[12] Our knowledge oscillates between certain revelation and closely guarded secrets. We suspect, but never know with certainty, that Howden Drake-Brockman spawned an illegitimate mulatto daughter, Daisy Corunna, who then served as alter ego, helpmate, and sexual mistress to a guilt-ridden father torn apart by the irreconcilable ambiguities of his position as Christian husband, landowner, station manager, autocrat, and compassionate patriarch. Gladys Corunna comments, wistfully: "When I was little, I always thought Howden was my father, isn't that silly?" (236). Her face, nonetheless, bears uncanny resemblance to an old photograph of Howden as a young man—a picture that, for Sally, seems to replicate the "spitting image" of her mother. Although Grandmother Daisy refuses to supply the missing piece of the puzzle, her hints about Gladys's paternity are deliberately tantalizing: "Everyone knew who the father was, but they all pretended they didn't know. Aah, they knew, they knew" (340). At the end of Sally Morgan's autograph, the Freudian family romance still remains shrouded in mystery, and the oedipal triangle of parent-child relationship is never finally closed.[13] "You have a sister," Nan once confided to her daughter (238). The identities (and stories) of sister, father, and grandfather are destined to remain obscure.

The best solution, however, may finally be to abandon hope of solving this inscrutable mystery, as well as all desire for traditional narrative closure. Gladys confides to her daughter after their trip to the Pilbara: "I think now I'm better off without all that business. All those wonderful people up North . . . claimed me . . . I don't want to belong to anyone else" (237). "Me either" responds Sally (237). Armed with the empowering discovery of Aboriginal ancestry, Morgan chooses a nonlinear vision of Aboriginal spirituality in lieu of the patrilineal obsessions of Eurocentric descent. The oedipal riddle has been left unanswered, the Odyssean quest unfulfilled. Having been "owned" by her Aboriginal extended family, Sally no longer needs the valorization of a patriarchal European heritage. As James Cowan explains, the Aboriginal "nomad lives in a world of openness which is only conscribed by the limitations of the imagination itself" (89). He or she harbors a "non-materialist approach to objects" and an arbitrary sense of social space (89). The European "insistence on ownership, on legal possession, is undermined by the nomad's dismissal of such values," since the Aboriginal "prefers a lack of clear definition when it comes to defining social space" (89).

In the Aboriginal scheme of things, paternity is arbitrary, since "the unborn child is an embryo of an ancestral being in the process of transformation . . . into a divine being. For the revelation or divination of an Aborigine as someone intimately identified with his Dreaming ancestor is far more important than acknowledging the accident of biological parentage. Man is not conceived as such by other individuals, but by the wilful act of the Sky Heroes" (106). It is not one's biological father, but rather one's place of conception and ancestral totem that determine Aboriginal identity. Having found her totemic place in the community of her maternal ancestors, Sally Morgan no longer desires genealogical valorization by the patriarchal world of those Anglo-Australian males who raped her foremothers and colonized the land. Turning away from the Eurocentric oedipal family romance, she celebrates her newly acquired subject position in a world of Aboriginal spirituality.[14]

"The Aborigine's insistence on the primordial sanctity of his 'country' is not an act of possession in terms of European property laws . . . but an act of being possessed by the land itself" (Cowan 1989, 44). The journey "is cyclical and involves a return to a place of origin each year" (45). "The Dream Journey on a ritual level is a way of renewing contact with themselves, since they and the land are inseparable" (48). In cyclical fashion, Sally Morgan has retraced the path from her childhood that led to the swamp, the bush, and the folk wisdom of her Aboriginal grandmother, who shared with this chosen grandchild the gifts of nature and at-onement with the earth. The white historical record, jealously guarded and interpreted by Alice Drake-Brockman and her upper-crust brood of first settler stock, has given way to the corrections of a blackened record transmitted by the oral history of an oppressed and subjugated people. The discourse of the absent father has yielded to the tribal narrative of matrilineal inheritance. Sally protests that "someone's got to tell. Otherwise, things will stay the same" (319). In a family of women gifted with mysterious healing powers, Sally herself has emerged as a mover and a shaker, a leader and a healer, bringing together those long-lost Aboriginal relatives who "own," claim, protect, and empower one another. "We had an Aboriginal consciousness now," she announces proudly (233).

Sally has come round, full circle, to a new acceptance of and respect for her grandmother's ostensibly superstitious belief in Aboriginal spirituality. "Blackfellas know all 'bout spirits," Nan insists (344). Sally Morgan tentatively offers her multicultural audience a glimpse of Aboriginal culture—a world of animism and spiritual wholeness, of family relationship, and of respect for the land. The autobiographical search for individual identity suggested by her title incorporates three oral histories that broaden the space of her narrative and yield to a more expansive consciousness alluded to in the book's epigraph, where the title "My Place" is transcended by a larger, more communal sense of "Our Place"—an awareness of recovered history poised on the verge of extinction. Sally's own cultural location and positionality are finally determined by the complex web of tribal, historical, and interpersonal relationships revealed by the deployment of new strategies for self-definition. The marginalized self, exploring frontiers and pushing back racial boundaries, must nonetheless take sustenance from a "whole people" in order to survive as an integrated, purposive, and creative subject in the complex world of twentieth-century society.

Notes

1. The Aboriginal author and critic Mudrooroo Narogin (formerly Colin Johnson) indicts *My Place* in *Writing From the Fringe* for its allegiance to what he labels the "battler genre": "The plotline goes like this. Poor underprivileged person through the force of his or her own character makes it to the top through own efforts. Sally Morgan's book is a mile post in Aboriginal literature in that it marks a stage when it is considered O.K. to be Aboriginal as long as you are young, gifted and not very black. It is an individualised story and the concerns of the Aboriginal community are of secondary importance" (1990, 149). In her

article entitled "Counter-Memories," Kathryn Trees challenges Narogin's judgment by insisting that *My Place* "moves beyond personal history to a reconstruction of the history of Aboriginal people" (Bird and Haskell 1992, 57). Morgan, she observes, "is able to make a very strong connection between the genres of [Aboriginal] oral history and European autobiography," with a resultant "displacement of the authority often appropriated by a central narrator in favour of community stories. Community is used here in the Aboriginal sense of shared labour, shared in the telling of the story" (59). Morgan's strategy of incorporating oral history into the genre of autobiography produces, furthermore, "a serial rather than a hierarchical narrative, reinforcing the displacement of the narrator's authority" (60). According to Joy Hooton, *My Place* belongs to a group of contemporary female Aboriginal life stories that manage to "expose the thoughts and emotions behind the stereotypes of the boong, the gin, the half-caste, the mission-child, and the fringe-dweller." They are "written from a position of achieved strength and pride" and tend to be "elegiac rather than declamatory, hopeful rather than vengeful; . . . they have room for wit and even light-hearted humour" (1990, 313).

2. Joy Hooton remarks that the young Sally is "a born leader. She is instinctively rebellious and non-conformist, sceptical of authority. . . . She also resembles other Aboriginal narrators in her love of the natural world, especially as it is interpreted by her grandmother, and . . . in her valuing of the imaginative and the spiritual" (1990, 334–35). Hooton explains that, in the genre of contemporary autobiography: "If white women value relatedness, it is a religion for black women; if white women privilege the personal over the public sphere, black women transform the public into the personal; if white women prefer the informal voice of conversation and the discontinuous structure, black women employ these strategies with a fresh spontaneity and conviction" (315).

3. In an interview with Delys Bird and Dennis Haskell, Sally Morgan tells us: "Arthur had a more historical perspective than I did. . . . It was only as I was researching this that I realised how many people's lives it applied to and that it was such a common story, common history" (Bird and Haskell 1992, 3). I am grateful to Delys Bird and Dennis Haskell for allowing me to be present at this interview, which took place in Fremantle, Western Australia, on 24 December 1991; and to the Fulbright Foundation for a grant that sponsored my teaching and research at the University of Western Australia and Adelaide University, respectively, during the 1991–92 academic year.

4. The cover of the original Fremantle Arts Centre Press edition of Sally Morgan's *My Place* (disappointingly, not reproduced in the American edition) offers a painting by the author that can be read as a complex visual paradigm for her narrative of family history. As Joan Newman explains, Morgan's painting "demonstrates many characteristics of traditional Aboriginal cave paintings and sand drawings—the two-dimensional plane, the stylised representation of landscape. A particularly significant image is that of the serpent, a figure in Aboriginal mythology which represents the life force, as the path of the water-

ways and as spirit of the land. In the painting the serpent's body marks major points of transition physically and emotionally for the people whose lives are narrated within the pages of the book. The mythical creature forms an over-arching frame, suggesting a governing principle that holds this group of lives together, providing "protection, meaning and harmony" (1992, 66–67). Even though Sally appears to have an aversion to reptiles in her youth and refuses to consider veterinary training for fear she might be called upon to treat a "sick snake," the adult author/artist seems to have adopted the snake as a kind of communal totem for the Milroy/Corunna family, thus resuscitating the lost totem of Uncle Arthur.

5. In discussing the enforcement of the 1905 Aborigines Act during the early part of this century, Judy Broun explains that this paternalistic legislation encouraged the "abominable policy of removing Aboriginal children from their mothers" (1992, 26). "It was reasoned that part-Aboriginal (or part-white) children could be of some value to society because of their white blood which would dilute the 'savage' tendencies and make these people 'trainable'" (27). The so-called "protectors" of the Aborigines "believed and fervently hoped that the fullblood race would die out" and that "the half-caste population could prove useful in society as a subordinate worker class" (27). Kathryn Trees finds such racist practices to be "in keeping with the coloniser's perception of indigenous people as resources, without rights" (62). Half-caste children, she observes, were "precluded from a cultural identity," as is seen when "Arthur is denied initiation rites by his tribal elders. . . . His removal to the Swan Native and Half-Caste Mission forced Arthur into no-man's land. He was ab/originated (denied any rights to his home-land)" (62). For a collection of Aboriginal oral histories describing these historical events from what Gayatri Spivak would term the "subaltern" subject position, consult Read and Read 1991.

6. Judy Broun notes, in response to Narogin, that Arthur's eventual success as a farmer, with his own land at Mukinbudin, "is not an indication that the story can be placed in the 'battler genre' but rather a testament to the will and determination of a very strong character in the face of the adversities presented by white society" (1992, 29).

7. Broun observes: "Although pastoralists often fathered 'mixed blood' children it was extremely rare that any of them claimed their children, due to the public disgrace associated with miscegenation. Although they were happy enough to indulge in sexual relations with Aboriginal women, they were reluctant to be responsible, financially or otherwise, for their half-caste offspring" (1992, 28). American readers have only to think of the still murky relationship between Thomas Jefferson and his slave mistress Sally Hemmings; or the obscure white parentage of Frederick Douglass (*My Bondage and My Freedom*); or the sexual vulnerability detailed by Harriet Jacobs/Linda Brent in *Incidents in the Life of a Slave Girl*.

8. Joy Hooton believes that Bill Milroy, despite his violent moods, self-hatred, and episodes of despair, proved to be "a powerful teacher. . . . It is one of

the paradoxes of *My Place* that this broken father should so enable his daughter, in contrast to the impairments inflicted by the absent, powerful white men or man, who had fathered her mother and grandmother" (1990, 337). In the Bird/Haskell interview, Morgan acknowledges personality traits and physical characteristics shared with her father (such as his long hands and talent for calligraphy) but adds: "Whenever I thought of Dad I thought of him in connection with the war, because he always carried it with him. He carried it in his mind and in his spirit. . . . For us it was like the war was still going on" (Bird and Haskell 1992, 7). She also confirms the destructive effects of her father's relentless devotion to drink.

9. Morgan explains in the Bird/Haskell interview that such "moments of vision" are "really common" and "not unusual in Aboriginal culture. All the people I know . . . have experiences like that, so it is just taken for granted, but people don't talk about it outside. I have probably broken the rules a bit because I have talked about it. It's only uncommon, I think, if you put it in the context of western society and rationalist thinking where those things are unacceptable. . . . So people would say that you are not having a vision, you're hallucinating" (1992, 11).

10. For a description of the Aboriginal *Chichurkna* that appears at death, see Cowan 1989, 114.

11. Fran De Groen, in an intriguing article entitled "Healing, Wholeness and Holiness in *My Place*," analyzes the "central structural contrast between speech and silence" in the text and suggests that, as the narrative unfolds, "silence and secrecy are associated with dis-ease, disharmony and oppression. Speech and openness lead to wholeness of being (physical and psychic health) and personal freedom" (1992, 35).

12. For further exploration of the mythological dimensions of mother/daughter relations, see Hirsch 1989.

13. Joy Hooton points out that Sally never manages to defeat the conspiracy of silence that has enveloped Nan, who allows her secrets to die with her. Yet much of the strength of this mystery story lies in "its Chinese-box structure, one box containing a replica of itself and so on" (1990, 340).

14. Kateryna Longley reminds us that contemporary Aboriginal autobiography tends to be "passionately polemical in its impulses" toward "two defining drives—to consolidate or reestablish links with Aboriginal communities, and to restore crucial links with traditional tribal lands" (1992, 372). She notes the anthropological importance of "women's secret ceremonies" in Aboriginal culture, as well as female responsibilities concerning "protection of the *kukurrpa* or 'dreaming'" (373). When Aboriginals speak of "my country," they are referring to "a kinship network as much as to a piece of land. Country is for them constituted inter-semiotically by storytelling and communal activity, as against geography, geology, and real estate legislation. Referring to *country*, they list the relatives through whom they claim it. . . . Ancestors, relatives, dreaming tracks and Dreaming itself are all so active in the landscape and so essential to its practical and

spiritual significance that in many cases people take the name of the land as their own name" (376). "The title of Morgan's *My Place*, in a more positive way, but still ironically, points to the centrality of place—land and cultural space—in Aboriginal cultural reempowerment" (379).

References

Bird, Delys, and Dennis Haskell, eds. "Interview with Sally Morgan." In Bird and Haskell 1992, 1–22.

———. *Whose Place? A Study of Sally Morgan's "My Place."* Pymble, NSW, Australia: Angus & Robertson, 1992.

Broun, Judy. "Unmaking White Myths: Your Laws, *My Place*." In Bird and Haskell 1992, 23–31.

Colmer, John. *Australian Autobiography: The Personal Quest.* Melbourne: Oxford University Press, 1989.

Cowan, James. *Mysteries of the Dream-Time: The Spiritual Life of Australian Aborigines.* Lindfield, NSW, Australia: Unity Press, 1989.

Davis, Jack, and Bob Hodge, eds. *Aboriginal Writing Today.* Canberra: Australian Institute of Aboriginal Studies, 1985.

De Groen, Fran. "Healing, Wholeness and Holiness in *My Place*." In Bird and Haskell 1992, 32–46.

Gare, Nene, and Patricia Crawford. "Sally Morgan's *My Place*—Two Views." *Westerly* 32, no. 3 (1987): 79–81.

Hirsch, Marianne. *The Mother/Daughter Plot: Narrative, Psychoanalysis, Feminism.* Bloomington: Indiana University Press, 1989.

Hodge, Bob, and Vijay Mishraw. *Dark Side of the Dream: Australian Literature and the Post-Colonial Mind.* Sydney: Allen & Unwin, 1990.

Hooton, Joy. *Stories of Herself When Young: Autobiographies of Childhood by Australian Women.* Melbourne: Oxford University Press, 1990.

Longley, Kateryna Olijnyk. "Autobiographical Storytelling by Australian Aboriginal Women." In Smith and Watson 1992, 370–84.

Morgan, Sally. *My Place.* New York: Little, Brown, 1990. Originally published in 1987.

Mulvaney, John. "Aboriginals in History." *Overland* 111 (1988): 92–95.

Narogin, Mudrooroo. *Writing From the Fringe: A Study of Modern Australian Literature.* Melbourne: Hyland House, 1990.

Newman, Joan. "Race, Gender, and Identity: *My Place* as Autobiography." In Bird and Haskell 1992, 66–74.

Prentice, Chris. "The interplay of place and placelessness in the subject of postcolonial fiction." *Span* 31 (1991): 63–80.

Read, Peter, and Jay Read, eds. *Long Time., Olden Time: Aboriginal Accounts of Northern Territory History.* Alice Springs, NT, Australia: Institute for Aboriginal Development, 1991.

Robertson, Jo. "Black Text, White Reader." In Bird and Haskell 1992, 47–54.

Sartre, Jean-Paul. *Being and Nothingness*. Translated by Hazel E. Barnes. New York: Philosophical Library, 1956.

Smith, Sidonie, and Julia Watson, eds. *De/Colonizing the Subject*. Minneapolis: University of Minnesota Press, 1992.

Thomas, Sue. "Aboriginal Subjection and Affirmation." *Meanjin* 47, no. 4 (1987): 755–61.

Trees, Kathryn. "Counter-Memories: History and Identity in Aboriginal Literature." In Bird and Haskell 1992, 55–65.

"Telling Our Own Stories"
Reclaiming Difference, a Maori
Resistance to Postculturalism

TREVOR JAMES

The thrust of this chapter may be simply stated. In New Zealand literature one of the ways by which Maori writers have defined an indigenous identity has been to claim a difference from a surrounding and dominant Pakeha culture. ("Pakeha" is the Maori word for New Zealanders of European descent.) This difference has been fixed in the assertion of a distinctive spirituality—a view of life that is nonmaterial, that unifies past, present and future, and that underpins Maori language, customs and the relationship with the land. However, it is at this same point, the question of spirituality, that the Pakeha critic, whether modernist or poststructuralist, has been confronted by Maori texts in which spiritual concepts are either foregrounded or at the very least an essential part of the cultural vision. In some instances the confrontation has been a hostile one and in others it has been simply one of incomprehension. Although some recent responses have been more cautious and even subtle in their positioning, it still seems (as in the case of Brown and During who are mentioned below) that there too the critic feels the necessity either to explain away the place and phenomenon of spirituality in Maori writing or at least to minimize it. When reading these critics, what seems most obvious is the clash of worldviews: on the one hand, the critic whose critical framework and discourse (setting personal beliefs to one side temporarily) seem almost invariably postreligious and secularized; on

51

the other hand, a Maori writer, whose "religious" frame of reference is hard to ignore. Between the two there seems no obvious point of meeting other than the text itself and the contention it gives rise to.

There is a further matter that needs to be considered at the outset, a matter of definition. "Spirituality" is almost inevitably a "soft" concept; it does not readily submit to specific definition. In this paper spirituality covers a wide range of possibilities. It is not limited to the European or Christian tradition. It may not be a carefully cultivated and conscious thing, such as one assumes when talking about many of the mystics, but may more commonly be an almost casual, habitual, and culturally shaped way of looking at the world. Indeed, I suspect this is precisely what is usually referred to when one talks of "Maori spirituality." Further, spirituality does not require a formally developed "theology" but it does involve—and this is probably a minimalist stance—a concern with nonmaterial aspects of being. In short, as a rough working definition, spirituality describes ways of responding to the world—including assumptions, customs and values—that are essentially nonmaterialistic and implicitly "theocentric."

I

The assertion of Maori spirituality and its presence either as an explicit or implicit center to Maori writing and culture generally has provoked in Pakeha criticism a range of responses, not all of which have been negative or dismissive. Among those critiques that have reflected a cultural or ideological "shock" a variety of positions can be discerned, and at least three are mentioned here: those views which mark cultural antipathy to expressions of Maori spirituality; those which regard Maori spirituality as a neocolonial device that continues the cultural, political, and economic subjugation of Maoris; and those which regard it as a negotiated but nonessential point of cultural distinction.

The most obvious criticism of Maori spirituality is that drawn from a viewpoint that may involve some antipathy for the subject itself. Coming under this heading are those Pakeha critics who argue that some Maori writers have presented a spirituality that has all the excesses associated with science fiction. Witi Ihimaera's stories have been particularly criticized for this—one thinks of such instances as "The Greenstone Patu" and "The Gathering of the Whakapapa." If we bear in mind that a *patu* is a Maori traditional weapon, a short-handled club often made from greenstone or hardened wood, we may read with more understanding the useful summary of "The Greenstone Patu" provided by Bill Pearson.

> A lost patu, important to the whanau, is found to be in the possession of unrelated Maoris at Porirua who will not part with it. But as the determined spokeswoman for the rightful owners insists on her claim, the sun glows on the patu in the glass cabinet and the patu is seen to swim, twisting and gliding, towards the claimants, calling its name. The glass cracks and Auntie Hiraina seizes the patu. (Pearson 1982, 174–75)

Of the critics who have found this sort of story difficult to deal with, Richard Corballis's remark that "The Greenstone Patu" is "a curious story which probably smacks rather too strongly of Star Wars for most Pakeha tastes" suggests the cultural and intellectual antipathy it has aroused (Corballis 1979, 68).

While antipathy may seem too strong a term, the "otherness" of this aspect of Maori writing was something that even Bill Pearson, the "pioneer" critic of Maori writing, seemed to feel. He found both these Ihimaera stories "less successful," tried to diminish any sense of "a supernatural intervention," and generally considered that "the outcome is perplexing" (Pearson 1982, 174–75). A footnote Pearson subsequently appended to his article marks a revision of these views with regard to "The Greenstone Patu," while clearly still registering a sense of cultural bafflement.

> Since I wrote this essay I have learned that there is a belief, widely held by older people though not freely revealed, that a greenstone weapon, once it has been prayed over with karakia and curses, can take on occult powers and might move of its own volition and swim through water to return to its owners. Clearly I have missed something in my response. . . . The question is raised, however, of the extent to which a western literary tradition, which requires of the reader no more than a willing suspension of disbelief in its tales of the supernatural, can accommodate the more deeply held occult beliefs of another culture. Witi Ihimaera's disregard for the skepticism of the unconvinced reader reflects an understandable reluctance to expose these beliefs to profane minds. For some Maori readers, I am told, he is not reticent enough. A further question is raised: whether Mr

Ihimaera, if he wishes these stories to have their full effect, is
wise to address himself only to readers who share the beliefs.
(Pearson 1982, 174-75)

Something of an aside may be appropriate here. What both Corballis
and Pearson (as two examples among many) represent is a way of thinking, and the problem their response founders upon is not simply "cultural" but religious. The way in which western thought has increasingly
marginalized religion scarcely needs comment, but even the practicing
Christian or theologian would be discomforted by a blatant irruption of
the "spiritual" into the domain of material being such as Ihimaera presents. However, it may be salutary to remember that the contemporary
western literary tradition includes writing that embraces such "irrup-
tions." For example, Charles Williams's seven "adventure" novels are
the vehicles for most uncommon insights about the nature of ultimate
reality: an obscure parish priest finds the Holy Grail in a church cup-
board; a sophisticated young woman converses face to face with a man
who had died several centuries before; a lord chief justice of England is
instantly transported across London merely by holding a certain stone
in his hand and wishing to be elsewhere. One mentions this simply as a
reminder that the way of thinking that fuses spiritual and material is
not wholly absent in the west, nor is the literature that explores it. Indeed, as the realist assumptions of modernism have been progressively
exposed, the way has become ever more open (and respectable) for
fictions that challenge realism.

The second and perhaps more serious criticism flows from poststructuralist theory, in particular an essay by Ruth Brown, who has argued that Maori spirituality is essentially a conception engineered by
western society in order to keep Maori people oppressed. Brown writes
in her *Meanjin* essay as follows:

Elision of the Maori from effective capital operation is a part of
the Westerner's version of Maoritanga, which foregrounds
spiritual inviolability while ignoring or underplaying Maori involvement in entrepreneurial enterprises, so paving the way for
continuing colonialist domination and continuing Maori resent-
ment. . . . To seize upon "Maori spirituality" as the answer to
Western society's craving for authenticity is not satisfactory
either. New Zealand is a part of Western culture, a capitalist
country . . . the Maori are the main victims of poverty, deprivation and social polarization. The valorizing of Maori spiritual-

ity may well have some connection with the failure to solve these problems. . . . Western culture's search for authenticity transforms that authenticity into a simulacrum. The world remains a monocultural nightmare, but with another marketable item added—a recording of Maori (or Aboriginal) spirituality. (Brown 1989, 257)

For later critics, especially those deeply influenced by poststructuralist thinking, the issues of representation that troubled Pearson and Corballis are insignificant. While Brown is not troubled by representation and works within a "poststructuralist" discourse, her approach to the question of spirituality is clearly grounded in a more "historicist" and "socialist" perspective, so that her critique does not address the central question of spirituality as it is assumed and presented by Maori writers. In this respect the question of representation is not raised. Another stance has been taken by Simon During who has spoken of Maori spirituality as something negotiated in a postcultural situation where there are no essential differences and identity is "open"; this During covers under the term "postculturalism."

"Postculturalism" and what During understands by it are discussed in the essay "Waiting for the Post."

It is a term which, in my usage, refers variously to an event, a programme or a mode of analysis. When one accepts that the construction of a non-modern cultural identity is the result of interaction between colonizer and colonized; when one celebrates the productive energy of mutual misrecognitions and forgettings then one enters postculturalism. It has its politics too. Somewhat in its spirit, a New Zealand identity can be constructed not simply from a Maori or a Pakeha viewpoint but by Maori-izing Pakeha formations and vice versa. This is an immensely attractive social programme: it counters the Europeanization of the Maori by constructing a non-essentialist unity across a maintained difference. . . . These reversals and displacements fill the rootlessness both of the heirs of the settlers and the urbanized Maoris. (During 1991, 34–35)

At its best it seems to me that During's "postculturalism" is a useful tool for describing the tension and the process of cultural interactions in a multiracial and bicultural society such as New Zealand. The problem is that as a way of looking at Maori culture and spirituality—and indeed of looking at Maori writing—its assumptions of loss and syncreticity, its skepticism and secularism, exclude the critic from assessing the evidence provided by Maori texts.

Before continuing with the criticisms offered by Brown and During, it is revealing to see how Maori scholars themselves have attempted to describe Maori beliefs or spirituality. In one very useful essay Rangi Walker attempts to summarize some of the key elements in Maori traditional belief. He clearly highlights the strength of Maori spirituality in its integrated vision of the things of the natural order and the spirit.

> Each of [the] divisions of nature has its own rituals and incantations to placate the presiding deity and to ensure abundance, fertility and regeneration. This commingling of religious practices with everyday pursuits indicates that Maori spiritual and philosophic beliefs unify him with nature. They teach him to live in harmony with the natural order. . . . Maori spiritual beliefs and religious practices were intertwined with temporal life in such a way that they could not be separated out in the manner of a religion or church as conceived of in western society. Spiritual and religious practices were integrated into myth, tradition and social life to produce a holistic conception of man and his place in the cosmos. It was a functional system for preEuropean Maori society, but it gave way to the new social order with its discrete division between religious and secular life. Although much has been gained from the new society in the form of material comfort, and the shedding of practices such as slavery and polygamy, the qualitative change in Maori religiosity might well prove to be a real loss in the sense that it is irreversible. (Walker 1983, 92–94)

Though Walker's essay was written in 1983 it gives little sign of the renaissance of Maori culture that was already underway. In its closing pessimistic tone he may seem initially, and on a casual reading, to justify During's concept of a postcultural society. For, if Maori spirituality has been irretrievably lost, then postculturalism may be the logical option. However, culture is not a static thing. That Maori spiritual beliefs and practices have adapted to new circumstances does not mean that they have been lost and certainly does not necessitate their relegation to a postcultural condition. In the course of the Maori renaissance how, and to what extent, has Maori spirituality been restored to Maoris who have been brought up in a wholly western tradition? Further, the role of the Maori writers themselves needs to be considered. Are Maori writers at times reinventing Maori spirituality? Since it seems that Maori tradition is not closed but open, reinvention may in fact be a natural communal process and part of the tradition. In that case it is not really cultural reinvention but cultural recovery that the Maori writer facilitates. Nonetheless, the role of the Maori writer in relation to Maoritanga seems far from straightforward. One thinks of the criticisms made of Ihimaera's presentation of some Maori material in *The Matriarch* and how many traditional Maori people felt uneasy or affronted by it.

What emerges from this reflection on critical methodology and theory is doubt whether such culturally determined critiques are capable of responding *appropriately* to Maori writers. Note that the issue is not that Maori writers be assessed differently from other writers but rather that they be read appropriately. This question arises since both During and Brown, critics who seem essentially sympathetic to Maori claims, provide perspectives that seem at odds with those views presented by Maori writers themselves and, as far as this chapter is concerned, they specifically conflict with that perception of identity which Patricia Grace unobtrusively but persistently affirms. While both Brown and During offer valuable insights, neither attends carefully enough to the evidence of the major texts themselves, and certainly neither offers a way of understanding the spirituality that underlies them.

II

Patricia Grace is probably New Zealand's foremost Maori woman writer, and she has scored some impressive firsts. Her collection of short stories *Waiariki* (1975) was the first collection of short stories by a Maori woman writer; and it is understood that her novel *Mutuwhenua: The Moon Sleeps* (1978) was the first novel by a Maori woman writer. In her fictions there is little of the ostentatious spiritual phenomena and the intensely metafictional style one finds in Ihimaera, especially his later works. Grace's preference has mainly been for a style of writing in the modernist realist tradition. Many of her stories deal with the determination of identity and the experience of cultural conflict that are part of postcolonial experience, especially in settler societies. While such stories can be read in terms of the "maintained difference" that During sees as typical of New Zealand's postcultural biculturalism, they are implicitly written against an expression of Maori spiritual consciousness that appears almost inaccessible to the Pakeha. Many of Grace's stories deal with this

question of spirituality within the terms of modernist realism, while—
especially in the novel *Potiki*—a more experimental metafictional style
indicates Grace's evolving interest in foregrounding spirituality as the
essential distinction between Pakeha and Maori.

It seems that in Grace's writing the experience of difference is neither presented as a way of finding identity, nor as a matter of choice,
negotiation, or even assertion. Instead it is represented as a given, a non-
negotiable fact that simply has to be accepted. In the first novel,
Mutuwhenua: The Moon Sleeps, Grace explores the inner dynamics faced
by a young Maori girl who falls in love with and marries a Pakeha. The
situation is one which naturally invites the writer to explore the problems of interracial conflict. However, the significant conflicts occur within
the girl herself. Since her husband is a model of sensitivity and understanding, Ripeka has to cope with her understanding of herself as a
Maori, as someone who is different. She is the inheritor of a spiritual
tradition, of a way of looking at the world that does not mesh with modern New Zealand Pakeha-driven society, and she has no choice but to
learn to accept her difficult inheritance. As Ripeka says, "I can never
move away from who I am. Not completely, even though I have wanted
to, often" (Grace 1986a, 9).

Within the first few pages of the novel Grace sets out what proves to
be the essential material for her story.

> Perhaps you and Graeme might be more different from each
> other than either of you can tell. It startled me for a moment to
> hear my own fear spill out into the room on my father's voice.
> And something made me think just then of the stone we had
> found, that was buried now at the bottom of a deep gully not
> far away. . . . I had always wanted to tell Graeme about the stone,
> which I call a stone to give less meaning, to simplify feeling. But
> I was afraid of what I might come to know about him and me,
> of what there could be between us, what differences. I have put
> many things aside over the past few years but the stone remains
> with me. The stone and the people do not let me forget who I
> am although I have wanted to many times. . . . what I'd wanted
> to tell Graeme during those days before our wedding was not
> so much the story of the stone . . . I'd wanted to tell him about
> the significance of what had happened; wanted him to know
> there was part of me that could never be given and that would
> not change . . . I can never move away from who I am. Not com-
> pletely, even though I have wanted to, often. (2–3, 8–9)

This passage reflects Ripeka's thoughts and anxieties as she prepares for her wedding. Specifically she remembers a time in her early childhood when she and some friends found a ancient stone *patu*, a Maori club, in the stream near their property. The *patu* embodies the uniqueness, specificity, and "difference" of Maoriness. The extent of that difference is further shown in the reactions of those who find it: the European man, whose son helped find it, sees it merely as an artifact and an item of economical potential, so he wishes to sell it to a museum; alternatively, the Maori protagonists are uneasy at this irruption into the present of something that has strong physical and spiritual bonds with their remote ancestors and that most particularly belongs with the dead. With the discovery of the *patu* they are aware of unspecified spiritual danger and accordingly conceal it once more in the mountains.

Though it is hidden from sight, the *patu* is present to the protagonist's memory, functioning in effect as a simulacrum of Maori spirituality. To say this is not to use the term "simulacrum" in any pejorative or minimalist sense, but to point out that the *patu* represents continuity with a whole past and a pre-European spirituality, not just in a notional way but actually makes it present. This usage therefore differs from Brown's use of "simulacrum," which is clearly pejorative, connoting a "sham"; and from During, who uses it an evasive way to denote something that is a synthetic replacement for "the sacred" (During 1991, 37). Indeed, the use of "simulacrum" in this paper has more in common with the idea of the symbol in Christian theological discourse, where it traditionally is one with its subject, participating in the reality that it signifies without in any way limiting it.

Maori spirituality is a total way of reading the world. This interpretation directly conflicts with Brown's assertion that Maori spirituality is a Pakeha construction, but then one has to say that Brown's argument simply flies in the face of the evidence provided by Maori writers themselves. Here again Grace provides the material for such an interpretation. One incident from *Mutuwhenua* will suffice to illustrate this point. Ripeka and her fiancé Graeme are taken by Ripeka's relations to a beach to gather seafood, and as the incoming tide threatens to engulf their vehicle it fails to start and one of their uncles is caught by a wave and injured on the rocks. These incidents in the natural world occur after some of the young men of the party have spoken lightly of ancient Maori ghosts in the area, and a connection between their unfortunate jokes and the near tragedy is implied. Here again the Maori way of reading the world is distinctive: the natural material world is not separated from the spiritual world; the two domains are correlated.

III

Grace's novel *Potiki* presents some particularly interesting and even compelling instances of the integration between Maori spirituality and the natural and material world of contemporary New Zealand. The material that she draws upon shows a keen political and social relevance. This is something Brown is willing to credit to the Maoris of earlier times. After commenting on the business acumen of some nineteenth-century Maoris, she remarks that "There is a model, therefore, to suggest that spirituality and entrepreneurial activity are not necessarily mutually exclusive." However, in the next paragraph she goes on to say, "The Maori way, however, did not survive" (Brown 1986, 256). Again, this is a point that Grace's writing does not accept. Instead, in *Potiki* we are shown a Maori way that has been threatened and damaged, but has endured.

Further, in *Potiki* the reader discovers a Maori imaginative consciousness that is not negotiated as During's work so far implies. Instead, it is something that exists in the face of the contradictions of Pakeha society and secular materialism, and it strenuously resists the categories that a Pakeha critic may impose upon it. Moreover, while the nature of Maori sensibility (and spirituality) is not defined and their inner processes are not fully explored, *Potiki* presents a unified sensibility that, however it evades conceptualization, is affirmed as quintessentially "Maori." Perhaps the best that can be said here is that Grace shows how the Maori can not only read the world differently, but even in a hostile and difficult situation possess the resources to discover or appropriate new materials for readings that are congruent with the hidden and undefined identity of Maori spirituality.

To place these claims in context it is necessary to have a rudimentary grasp of the story that frames *Potiki*. Even a highly oversimplified summary will give some idea of the way the story, despite its apparent simplicity, is essentially a very sophisticated work that presents not just a story but a complex synthesis of elements that, more clearly than almost any other text one can think of, demonstrates a Maori spirituality at work. The context for the novel is an isolated Maori coastal community. During a period of economic recession many of the local community return to *Potiki* from the cities where they have lost their jobs. There, in their ancestral land, they find strength and an inalienable place to stand. From the outside their security is threatened by a developer who wishes to build a leisure complex that requires access through the heart of their land. When their opposition threatens the project, mysterious happenings occur, including the flooding of their ancient *urupa* (cemetery) and the burning down of their *wharenui* (meetinghouse). Within the major narrative run a number of parallel narratives that relate to the central characters—Mary, Roimata, Toko, Hemi—though the narrative mode itself may be either in the first or third person.

All the subnarratives intertwine within the overall shape of the story, which is shaped as a communal fiction. Among the subnarratives is the story of Toko, Tokowaru-i-te-Marama, the deformed child of the simple-minded Mary and an unknown father. Toko is believed by the community to possess a special kind of knowledge, a spiritual power, which he uses to defend them against harm. Toko dies in an explosion that seems to have been an attempt to destroy the new meetinghouse, but he lives on in the carvings and the communal stories. He also marks the beginning and the end of the book: at the start we are shown a vignette from the past, a carver and a carving that is unfinished; the carving remains unfinished but is a link from the old meetinghouse to the new; at the end of the story it is Toko who is placed in the carving and he who tells the end of the tale.

The social, political, and cultural relevance of the spirituality that runs through the novel is easily illustrated. With a deft and sure feeling for her material, Grace quickly pictures the rapidly changing consciousness of Maori society in contemporary New Zealand. She outlines the mood of greater cultural confidence and the pressure to retrieve land, language, and customs from being lost. She shows how, in the midst of change and economic hardship, Maori people have increasingly returned to their ancestral communities and lands as a base for personal and communal security. In doing so she touches the essential elements of Maori spirituality.

One passage from the novel will give some idea of how she interweaves these various elements. This particular excerpt comes from a narrative belonging to Hemi, one of the key figures in rebuilding the Maori community at *Potiki*.

> These days people were looking more to their land. Not only to their land, but to their own things as well. They had to if they didn't want to be wiped off the face of the earth. There was more determination now—determination which had created hope, and hope in turn had created confidence, and energy. Things were stirring, to the extent of people fighting to hold onto a language that was in danger of being lost, and to the extent of people struggling to regain land that had gone from them years before.
> . . . And people were looking to their land again. They knew

that they belonged to the land, had known all along that there
had to be a foothold otherwise you were dust blowing here there
and anywhere you were lost, gone. . . .

. . . There were young ones here with no work to go to, who
were looking forward to doing something that was their own,
for themselves. There were those who had moved away but who
would come back as they got sent down the road from their
jobs. . . .

They'd have to make sure that they were producing enough
for their own *kai* first, and for any *manuhiri* of course. Wouldn't
be easy. Then later there'd be surplus to sell or store. They'd try
out some new crops, the markets were different now. Couldn't
wait to get into it. (Grace 1986b, 60–62)

This passage may be read in several ways. It can be taken as a primarily descriptive summary of social changes. Such a reading would
admit the emotional register that is used but take it no further. However, it seems that such a reading risks superficiality: the emotional register or weighting "is" the text. Behind this lies a view of Maori identity,
of being, which involves a strong sense of being different from Pakeha
society and in which land, language and customs are not simply extraneous materialistic adjuncts to being but manifestations of a spiritual
reality. The carefully weighted repetitions, the references to retrieval,
recovery, and return, and the metaphor in which the people without
their land are like dust—surely a metaphor signifying an essential unity
between Maori and land—become more fully comprehensible if they
are accepted as a way of viewing the world that is distinctly nonempirical,
nonmaterialist, and distinct from those secular forms of knowing that
characterize contemporary western society.

From what has been indicated above it may already be clear how in
Potiki Grace portrays a Maori imaginative consciousness that, far from
being "negotiated," stands against and distinct from Pakeha society. One
of the ways through which Grace particularly does this, and which is
central to *Potiki*, is her portrayal of a Maori mythopoeic and communal
consciousness. For instance, when she talks of the stories through which
the people of *Potiki* give shape, order, and meaning to their lives, she
displays a communal notion of textuality that is radically different from
secularized western notions of the word; it is not fixed but open to an
interfusion of stories from the past, the present, and, arguably, the future as well. This is particularly well illustrated in one of Roimata's narratives.

Then I knew that nothing need be different. "Everything we need is here. We learn what we need and want to learn, and all of it is here," I said to Hemi, but he had always known it. We needed just to live our lives, seek out our stories and share them with each other.

So I didn't become the teacher, or rather didn't become once more the teacher that I had trained to be. There was no need for a room to be changed because a boy had become five and could not find himself in schools. I became instead a teller of stories, a listener to stories, a writer and a reader of stories, an enactor, a collector and a maker of stories. But I only shared in this. What really happened was that we all became all of these things—tellers, listeners, readers, writers, teachers and learners together. . . .

I had other stories too, known stories from before life and death and remembering, from before the time of the woman lonely in the moon. Given stories. But "before life and death and remembering" is only what I had always thought. It was a new discovery to find that these stories were, after all, about our own lives, were not distant, that there was no past or future, that all time is a now-time, centred in the being. It was a new realisation that the centred being in this now-time simply reaches out in any direction towards the outer circles, these outer circles being named "past" and "future" only for our convenience. The being reaches out to grasp these adornments that become part of the self. So the "now" is a giving and a receiving between the inner and the outer reaches, but the enormous difficulty is to achieve refinement in reciprocity, because the wheel, the spiral, is balanced so exquisitely. These are the things I came to realise as we told and retold our own-center stories. (38–39)

The social and cultural vision that Grace creates here is independent of Pakeha society. Further, one can see how fully Grace's passage conforms to the spirit of contemporary postcolonial literary theory with its emphasis upon the experience of marginalization and its requirement that the postcolonial writer reappropriate the "center." The concepts of knowledge, learning, authority and meaning are redefined communally and pragmatically in accord with something that, while never clearly explicated, is essentially Maori.

However, there is also more than this. While in *Potiki* Grace offers without negotiation or apology a way of seeing the world that is imaginatively and culturally different, the vision she provides in effect "reintextualizes" Maori experience and stresses continuity and co-inherence between past, present, and future, and between the modes of material being and spiritual reality. In the last narrative Toko, now dead, speaks as the spirit of the community and the spirit of the *wharenui* itself. Though Pakeha critics are accustomed to metafiction and the devices of narrative, and though the text itself is clearly fiction and is not represented as anything else, what it portrays is clearly to be read seriously. At this point of closure the feeling that has been present throughout the text intensifies: the sense that here is a point of encounter with a way of knowing and understanding that is, on the one hand, distinct from that of the west, and, on the other hand, irreducible and not to be explained away. It is fitting that *Potiki* should have the last word.

> There is one more story to tell which I tell while the house sleeps. And yet the house does not sleep as the eyes of green and indigo brighten the edges of the world. There is one more story to tell but it is a retelling. I tell it to the people and the house. I tell it from the wall, from where yesterday and tomorrow are as now. . . . And from this place of now, behind, and in, and beyond the tree, from where I have eversight. I watch the people. . . . Because, although they listen too for the approaching shadows and the whisperings about the edges of the land, they cannot, from where they are, hear the sounds distinctly. They cannot, as I can in this time of now, distinctly hear the sounds of this now place, which is a place beyond the gentle thumbing of the eyes. (181–84)

References

Adam, Ian, and Helen Tiffin, eds. *Past the Last Post: Theorizing Post-Colonialism and Post-Modernism.* Hemel Hempstead: Harvester Wheatsheaf, 1991.

Brown, Ruth. "Maori Spirituality as Pakeha Construct." *Meanjin* 2 (1989): 252–58.

Corballis, Richard. "Witi Ihimaera: Literary Diplomacy." *Landfall* 129 33, no. 1 (1979): 64–71.

During, Simon. "Waiting for the Post: Some Relations Between Modernity, Colonization and Writing." In Adam 1991, 23–46.

Grace, Patricia. *Mutuwhenua: The Moon Sleeps.* Auckland: Penguin, 1986a.

———. *Potiki.* Auckland: Penguin, 1986b.

Hankin, Cherry, ed. *Critical Essays on the New Zealand Short Story.* Auckland: Heinemann, 1982.

James, W. T. G., ed. *The Word Within the Word*. Hamilton: University of Waikato Press, 1983.
Pearson, W. H. "Witi Ihimaera and Patricia Grace." In Hankin 1982, 166–84.
Walker, Rangi. "Maori Beliefs: An Integrated Cosmos." In James 1983, 89–94.

Breaking the Rules
Nuala Ní Dhomhnaill's
Language Strategies

MARY O'CONNOR

Nuala Ní Dhomhnaill confronts the problems associated with post-colonial identity by an exuberant refusal to be constrained within the tight boundaries of polite society—not merely that of the colonizer but also in this case, where a nativist identity is gladly taken up, polite Gaelic society. In fact, she challenges/crosses whatever borders are set up for her, invisibly deconstructing programmatic approaches from gender and cultural politics, despite her inimitable effectiveness as a raiser of women's consciousness and an examplar of anti-imperialist cultural resistance. Simultaneously more cosmopolitan and more connected to the oral tradition of Ireland than most of her contemporaries, she reincorporates the folk tradition in her poetry; but instead of using it to reconnect to some romanticized mythic past, the poet rewrites/transforms the material from the standpoint of a lived knowledge of that tradition. The effect is a pulling away from an identity shaped by the Irish literary patriarchy, which has worked out some especially constricting roles for women, including that of national icon. And by her exclusive use of Irish Gaelic in this rewriting of the folk tradition, and her use of the registers of that language that had never before been accepted as sufficiently literary for the schoolroom or the poetry text, Ní Dhomhnaill restores to Irish consciousness the sound of its authentic, aboriginal voice.

When Nuala Ní Dhomhnaill's first book of poetry was published (*An Dealg Droighin,* in 1981), she was twenty-nine years old; she had

negotiated both the rites of passage to adulthood and the almost obliga-
tory alienation and exile of the Irish artist. In Ní Dhomhnaill's case this
involved breaking from family and country and spending eight years of
exile with a Turkish husband. Returning to Ireland in 1980 with a family
of three, to be reconciled with her parents and take a job in academe, she
seemed to have steered between Scylla and Charybdis home to her self.
In her first collection, she gathered up the threads of her life again: the
early growth as the intensely focused-upon only child of professional
parents, the years with Irish-speaking grandparents during which Irish
became her first language, the academic success and rebellion, the forbidden marriage to a foreigner. Now she could settle down to the normal life of an Irish artist, which, though the artist is set apart by both the
esteem and the skepticism of the Plain People of Ireland, is far less on
the fringe than that of his or her counterparts in America.

But this woman was not about to take comfort in being in the mainstream. Her entire upbringing had educated her to the necessity, or less
positively, the unavoidableness, of a solitary stance. She tells the story
herself in a 1988 conversation with the editors of *Innti* magazine, titled
pointedly, if inaccurately,[1] "From Limbo to Grafton Street," from which
I translate the following: "I was an only child," she tells us; "it was I
who brought myself up" (41). And again: "I spoke the English of England
and the Irish of Kerry [at six, when she first came to Ireland to live with
her grandmother]. . . . Because of that [because she did not speak the
English of *Ireland*] I had no friends and I was very alone. But I was very
happy" (de Paor 1989, 42).

Ní Dhomhnaill describes herself going through this childhood in
England and Ireland as an *aonaránach*, an almost onomatopoeic word
for "solitary," if we can hear the sounds of aloneness in those long vowels. In Ireland and England she was set apart by language in her formative years. And in Turkey, "I understood that I could not go home, and I
created another person for myself. When I am in Turkey, I am as a Turk
amongst the Turks. That's three [personae] now in the same skin!" (47).

Of course, that being the nature of personas and their uses, the
aonaránach remains alone, to look out from behind the masks. Later in
the same interview she says, "I think, finally, I'm just a blow-in/trapped
bird in this life *[gur éan isteach mé ins an tsaol seo]* and that I exist for the
most part in the world of imagination I created for myself as a child, as
a protection maybe against the aloneness *[aonaránachais]*" (48). *Ean isteach*
(bird inside), a compact phrase that somehow includes the idea of the
bird's fragility, may recall the early-medieval image of a person's life as
a bird's brief passage through light and warmth between two wild dark-

nesses. But Bede's melancholy metaphor of the pre-Christian worldview in his *Ecclesiastical History of the English People* (book 2, chapter 13) privileges the hearth and promises more of the same after death for those who come to believe. Ní Dhomhnaill's point about herself is quite different. She feels out of place in this cozily lit enclosure; her true element is the dark uncertain sky outside.

Such a preparation for adult life as the one just sketched is important, because it leads to decisions which would frighten less *aonaránac* souls. Ní Dhomhnaill chose (a) to write only in Irish, in a country where an overwhelming majority of the people barely understood it; (b) to use the language in a freer way than other writers in Irish; and (c) to write from a woman's point of view about a woman's body, in a fairly prudish society, the puritanical core of which was composed of cultural nationalists (or *Gaelgóirs*, as they are known in Ireland), who were most likely to be her primary audience.

To situate our poet properly in a tradition would take another volume. Let us just for now briefly acknowledge the thin but constant stream, since the beginning of this century, of excellent writers in Irish Gaelic, poetry and prose, whose small but significant output of irreplaceable works preserves the indigenous culture and constitutes its twentieth-century glory. They range from the Blasket Island autobiographers (Peig Sayers, Muiris Ó Súilleabháin, Tomás Criomhthain) to the Galway fiction writers Pádraig Ó Conaire and Máirtín Ó Cadhain; to the poets Máirtín Ó Direáin, Seán Ó Ríordáin, and Máire Mhac an tSaoi; to the many part-time playwrights from Seán Ó Tuama to Brendan Behan—and this is not even to deal with the quite unexpected emergence of contemporary poetry in Irish in the last fifteen or twenty years, as a new generation asserted itself and its separate identity. This most recent flowering is often dated from the establishment in 1970 of *Innti*, a broadsheet representing the new movement in Irish poetry. Established magazines such as *Comhar*, *Feasta*, and *Léachtaí Choilm Cille* also continue to serve the Irish-reading community as vehicles of poetry, prose, and criticism. Since the more prosperous Fifties, all of these endeavors have been aided by grants from a state whose programs of assistance for writers in their native language led the *Times Literary Supplement* to describe the Irish Republic in 1956 as "a literary Welfare State."[2]

At the same time, and quite concurrently, the general standard of school-learned Irish, on which 95 percent of the population depend for their introduction to the language, has markedly fallen in the past forty years; the amount of broadcast media time devoted to programming in the native language is negligible compared to equivalent efforts in

Ireland's nearest Celtic neighbor, Wales; and populations of Gaeltacht, or Irish-speaking, pockets (mostly poor, rural areas) have been diminishing in a way that has been impossible to check completely, despite some flourishing new cottage industries.

Ní Dhomhnaill did not begin to write in Irish to become part of a language revival or bolster a movement. She simply discovered, while writing a poem in English at the age of sixteen, that she was unconsciously translating all the time from Irish; that writing in Irish was writing herself. It was "as if," she told a poetry workshop in St. Patrick's College, Maynooth, in 1986, "there were certain codes of sound stored in our bodies . . . for thousands of years, and when we hear certain sounds . . . those codes of memory are awakened." She experienced her first poem in Irish as a "huge leap into [her] own nature" and has not written in any other language since then (Ní Dhomhnaill 1986, 177).

The Irish language is not simply chosen as the natural voice of the poet, however: Ní Dhomhnaill believes it accommodates a range of expressiveness unavailable in English, because of its inherent concreteness, its clouds of connotation (which Ní Dhomhnaill calls reflections, shadows, extensions, echoes) and its "sensuousness of sound," in the words of the Scottish poet Somhairle Mac Gill-Eain (Ní Dhomhnaill 1986, 174–75). Whereas poetry in the English language provides images for the mind's eye, Ní Dhomhnaill maintains that Irish is written primarily for the ear. The concreteness noted by the poet is inherent in the syntax: Irish is a noun-based language. You can't, for example, say "I am hungry"; you must say "There is hunger on me." You don't welcome someone; you "put a welcome before him." This concreteness gives rise to thousands of metaphorical expressions, bringing color to a limiting speech pattern. Original similes abound in everyday speech, and "turns" (*corraí cainte*) swarm untranslatably in the most ordinary dialogue. One is, for example, "on the pig's back," when feeling lucky. Brothers of the said pig sit, "a pig on each eyebrow," when you are frowning. Luck itself is no abstraction but the capacity of a road to carry you where you want to go, incomprehensibly translated for the tourists as "May the road rise with you." Great health is "the health of the salmon," no ordinary fish in Irish mythology. Having done some feat, you pass it off modestly as being "last night's porridge." Such set expressions tell much about the culture in its appearance as mental furniture of the users of the language.

Ní Dhomhnaill's poetry, which works so well partly because it stands inside the old Gaelic tradition (rather than co-opting it nostalgically or idealistically, or treating it with an antiquarian's detached interest) is without question a force for change, in two ways. First, since Irish Gaelic is the suppressed language of a colonized people, its use becomes an act of resistance to the dominant English culture and a reenfranchisement of the people who have been dispossessed of it. Second, as a dying but "preserved" language, it has been in the hands of careful conservators and standardizers within the Irish culture; in Ní Dhomhnaill's hands, however, it is set free to follow the permutations of a living language. She revivifies rather than preserving, turning the language on its ear impudently, careless of the prohibitions of the Fathers; pointedly, she is careful of the freedom of thought and imagination thus created.

Let me show how. With reference to the first of those acts of resistance, Ní Dhomhnaill is completely persuasive (and characteristically *engagée*) when it comes to talking about her "secondary audience" and her primary reason for publishing in dual-language editions:

> My second audience is an awful lot of people in this island who've been disenfranchised: Irish is as much their right as to drink water, to breathe air, to have a job on this island, which a lot of them haven't either—and yet they have been given no choice, it has been kept from them; once they get out of school there is no functional situation where they can use it. . . . People have no choice. Even the Irish they learned in school, there's nowhere they can use it naturally, there's nowhere they can have a bit of *craic* [a really entertaining time]. . . . But there are an awful lot of people who have reasonable school Irish, and I'm very interested in this audience because I think that the reason that they haven't much better Irish isn't their fault at all. [Reading her poems in dual-language editions] they look over into the Irish and they say "Oh yeah! I can read that; I know what that word means!" (Personal interview, March 1991)

Secondly, and at greater length, let us look at what Ní Dhomhnaill does with the instrument she has chosen. To start with, she extends its range beyond the usual formal written diction permitted the writer in Irish. Despite the declared philosophy of the revivalists in the early part of the century to cleave to the language of the people rather than the language of literature (that would have meant seventeenth-century literature, since that had been the last flowering of the written language), the revival movement made every effort to standardize expressions, grammar, spelling (Bliss 1982). As we approach the end of the same century, only 5 percent of the population speaks Irish on a daily basis, and even in

Gaeltacht (Irish-speaking pockets of the country) primary schools, the emphasis falls on the rules of the standardized language (teachers will be teachers the world over) rather than on the living and vital language of everyday oral communication.

From her very first published poetry, Ní Dhomhnaill risked using demotic Kerry Irish, in defiance of the unwritten rule that the language was to be preserved in its noblest, most dignified, and correct form; she gave her audience credit for the intelligence and intuition to decode and enjoy the quirks of a spoken language. Words changed by dialect use from standard are scattered throughout her poetry: for example the use of *gártháil* for *gáirí; an burdán fearna,* where *burdán* imitates the way *bradán* is pronounced in Kerry; *it'* instead of *id',* abbreviated from *i do,* again following the pronunciation; *tá na héinne* for *tá gach éinne; tán tú* for *tá tú,* and so on. Even to a reader unfamiliar with Irish, it must be clear from these examples that something quite deliberate is being done. "This is language as it has evolved over time. It's not the clear, cleaned-up language of literature, though it is well-accepted in speech,"[3] says Dr. Tom O'Shea, a native speaker from the same area of Kerry, of Ní Dhomhnaill's poetic diction. The poet crosses the border, heavily guarded by cultural nationalists, between literary rectitude and living language, even when it involves incorporating, and therefore accepting, the mongrel language patterns of a postcolonized culture.

Besides making a place for dialectical usage in her poetry, Ní Dhomhnaill tosses in English words, such as "fags," "travelling bag," "pints," and so on, startling readers by the sudden use of words and phrases that they have not before seen in print in an Irish-language text, though they may, if they have spent any time in a Gaeltacht, have heard them in casual conversation between people who are part of the community. Referring to Ní Dhomhnaill's use of colloquialisms, neologisms, and loan words from English, O'Shea comments: "She's not *about* purity of the language, no. What's obviously more important to her is to pick up the idioms and the phrases that are circulating . . . particularly in conversational language, language that covers a whole wealth of meaning, rather than technically correct language. Technically correct language is what I was taught in school, which has usually gone into writing up to now. Her language [the use of it for poetry] would have been severely criticized . . . but she does it and she gets away with it. It should have been done before." "How would you translate something like that," I asked, "that rule-breaking thing she does with language?" "I don't know. You'd lose layers and layers of meaning by translation."

Certainly the world evoked by what Ní Dhomhnaill refers to as the clouds/swarms of associations around the places and traditions referred to in her poetry is lost to the purely English-speaking audience; but more significantly for the effect she wishes to produce, the seemingly casual, clichéd language of her speakers, shot through with the surprises of countercultural (counterpatriarchal) thought and expression—that double movement of comfort/discomfort—has been, so far, difficult to reproduce in translation.

A second, and possibly unconscious, effect of Ní Dhomhnaill's plastic use of English loan words is to debase the language of the colonizer. I was excited to find in Ketu Katrak's essay "Decolonizing Culture: Toward a Theory for Postcolonial Women's Texts" evidence of strong bonds between Nuala's work and that of the Third World women of whom Katrak writes:

> Postcolonial women writers participate actively in the ongoing process of decolonizing culture. . . . In terms of language, it is as if a version of the cultural and economic violence perpetrated by the colonizer is now appropriated by writers in order to "violate" the English language in its standard use. (1989, 169)

Is Ní Dhomhnaill debasing the master language with *phosae phinc* (pink posy), *treabhsar* (trouser), *pabhair* (power) and so on? Whatever her intention, the effect is risible. When English words are appropriated and suitably mangled by the rules of the heavily inflectional Irish language as well as by the natural erosion of rapid speech, funny things happen. To give an example from everyday speech that shows the process of the breakdown: instead of the Irish *rothar* for bicycle (from the word *roth*, meaning wheel), the word "bicycle" itself may be appropriated and inflected, and "my bicycle" becomes *"mo bhicycle"* (pronounced "mu wysicle") and even *mo bhislic* ("mu wyslic").[4] Etymologists may grind their teeth, but politically (no matter to what extent we can credit the speakers' intentions), this disrespectful transformation of English to Irish use is a neatly executed revenge for its imposition on the conquered race.

That leads us to another area in which Nuala breaks the rules: that of silence about the body. Few Irish women writers, and only a slightly larger number of men, venture to expose their passionate, joyful, or tormented imaginings, despite the early models in Joyce, though some novelists, such as McGahern and Broderick, have treated of the negative side, the abuse, inhibition, or understood prohibition. Referring to the last, Ní Dhomhnaill says that Jansenistic prudery and negativity with regard to the body and sexuality was, in Ireland,

a reaction to the trauma of the Famine. I'm convinced of that.
It's very late. My mother remembers the dancing on the crossroads. . . where the priest came out in the pony and trap and hit
and broke the melodeon. And they used to be (it was all very
harmless) courting in the bushes, and he'd come down with his
stick—my mother experienced that. I think the collective psyche
(friends of mine say I'm leaving the priests off the hook by this;
I know I am, because to act out an archetype there has to be a
level of will in it as well), the community, created the priest who
would beat you with a stick, because it's much easier to be beaten
by the priest than to have to beat yourself. Guilt is within. And
a *terror* of fertility, if your own children were to die hungry: that
was part of it. And we haven't ever worked it through emotionally yet.[5]

The poems that describe suspect activities or express open desires
are not so much about the common sinful condition of humankind as
they are a repossession of a whole area of discourse previously presided
over in Ireland by celibate males. Nor are they a reversal of values, so
much as an unraveling of the tightly woven fabric of negative judgments
on women, from Eve onwards. Ní Dhomhnaill, a woman writer celebrating the power and inherent beauty of female body, intends to be part of
an effective counterbalance to the rigidities of the neo-Puritan state,
imagined by one of its founding philosophers, Eamon de Valera, as a
sort of Gaelic-speaking Lake Wobegon:

> That Ireland that we dreamed of would be a land whose
> countryside would be bright with cosy homesteads, whose fields
> and villages would be joyous with the sounds of industry, with
> the romping of sturdy children, the contests of athletic youths,
> the laughter of comely maidens, whose firesides would be the
> forums for the wisdom of serene old age.[6]

This denial of anything but the prettiest picture of humanity (in effect, a
pathological repression of the Shadow) dominated the nation's assumed
identity through the decades, despite all evidence to the contrary, and
reemerged in a powerfully symbolic way in nationwide referendums in
the 1980s that upheld the Irish Republic's ban on divorce, and upgraded
abortion from illegal to unconstitutional. By breaking the rules, Ní
Dhomhnaill refuses to be a part of this collective fantasy and of the oppression it engenders. She owns her female body, its "grotesque" orifices, its

delights. "Thinking of you / milk fills my breasts," she says (1990b, 38–39). "We are damned, my sisters," she laughs, "we who accepted the priests' challenge / our kindred's challenge" (1988, 14–17). She is cheerfully bawdy in "Desire" about "the man / with his pouch/making me hungry" (1990, 30–31). She is open to the unromantic, but transparently human, messages of her five senses:

> It's not the crock of flowers at the head of the bed
> that makes me drunk
> but the smell of your body
>
> a mixture of blood and clay.
>
> ("I Cannot Lie Here Any More,"
> in Ní Dhomhnaill 1990, 24–25)

Both male and female bodies are presented as objects of erotic desire: from the languorous *"Leaba Shioda"*: "I'd make a bed for you / in Labysheedy / in the tall grass / under the wrestling trees"; to the more covert "Welcome of the Shannon's Mouth to the Fish," which I give below with my line-for-line translation parallel.

Fáilte Béal na Sionna don Iasc

Léim an bradáin	The salmon jumped
Sa doircheacht	In the darkness
Lann lom	A bare blade
Sciath airgid,	A silver shield
Mise atá fáiltiúil, líontach	It's I am welcoming, nets out,
Sleamhain,	Slippery/sleek
Lán d'fheamnach,	Full of seaweed
Go caise ciúin	Twisting in quiet currents
Go heireaball eascon.	Down to the swampy ends/eel-tails
Bia ar fad	This fish is
Is ea an t-iasc seo	All food/meat
Gan puinn cnámh	Without much bone
Gan puinn putóg	Without much gut
Fiche punt teann	Twenty taut pounds
De mheatáin iata	Of lowering pale fullness

Dírithe	Directed / aimed
Ar a nead sa chaonach néata.	At his nest in the neat moss.
Is seinim seothín	And I play a lullaby
Do mo leannán	To my lover
Tonn ar thonn	Wave after wave
Leathrann ar leathrann,	Verse after verse
Mo thine gealáin mar bairlín	My embers like a harbor bar
thíos faoi	under
Mo rogha a thogas féin ón	My chosen one, whom I brought
asacht.	myself from afar.

The salmon bears symbolic weight in early Irish literature, where it represents wisdom; contact with the Salmon of Wisdom is to the Irish hero what grasping the sword in the stone is for that Celt across the water, Arthur: permission to succeed, to dominate. In a satisfyingly demystifying act of revelation, Ní Dhomhnaill makes it a phallus, a wholly physical object, whose "wisdom" is founded in instinctual drives. The poem is just one of *many* Ní Dhomhnaill efforts to enact the breakdown of that artificial separation of mind and body in which the mind is the sphere of male domination and the territory of the body the domain of the feminine.

Always aware of where her stance is taking her, never narcissistic or merely prurient, the poet produces some interesting unities through her expressive and volatile art. When she's writing an intensely physical love lyric, she can break it up with a reference to the most basic, undignified bodily functions, which take it down to the human from the idealized, or perhaps even satirize or break up her earlier mood. The general effect for the reader is to suggest a Whole: body / soul, high culture / low culture, stars / mire, interconnected. We have certainly found this mixture in Joyce two generations before. But Ní Dhomhnaill's love lyrics are more serious than his. Perhaps they are patterned on Middle Eastern or earlier Irish women's poems such as the eighteenth-century *Caoineadh* of Eibhlín Dubh Ní Chonaill, so there's a greater contrast.

Translation, Translators, and Problems of Close Reading

All this talk about brave choices and artistic successes must not disguise the fact that life on the margin, on the margin of the margin, is difficult and full of ambiguity. Fellow Irish-language poet Biddy Jenkinson, in a fascinating essay for *Irish University Review* (1991, 27–34), speaks from "among the outnumbered and beleaguered but determined survivors of Gaelic Ireland" as she makes her declaration of independence from the majority, postcolonized culture: "I prefer not to be translated into English in Ireland. It is a small rude gesture to those who think that everything can be harvested and stored without loss in an English-speaking world" (ibid.). This is the voice of the hunger striker, the suffragette, the Vegan, the virgin martyr. Perhaps Ní Dhomhnaill also feels this loss sorely. Her poem *"Ceist na Teangan* / The Language Issue" describes just how frail her acts of communication seem to her at times:

> I place my hope on the water
> in this little boat
> of the language, the way a body might put
> an infant
>
> in a basket of intertwined
> iris leaves,
> its underside proofed
> with bitumen and pitch,
>
> then set the whole thing down amidst
> the sedge
> and bulrushes by the edge
> of a river
>
> only to have it borne hither and thither,
> not knowing where it might end up;
> in the lap, perhaps,
> of some Pharaoh's daughter.
> (Ní Dhomhnaill 1990b, 154–55; trans. Muldoon)

But despite the *aonoránach* feeling of not belonging to any society, and to a certain extent always isolated by language, Ní Dhomhnaill will not take a separatist stance. Not for her the austere gesture of a Biddy Jenkinson. Not for her the hard-line idealism of a Desmond Fennell, cultural nationalist and, most recently, Heaney-basher, who in a public essay asks peevishly (of the latest crop of young urban poets writing in Irish) what good it does to use the native tongue when one's very worldview is so obviously adulterated by the colonizer (Fennell 1980,

21–22). Instead she reaches out to a wide world of people and ideas. Her present project, for example, is an Irish language edition of the Turkish poet Nazim Hikmet. Though in the early years she translated a few of her own poems into English, the poet will not work in English herself any more, feeling it could infect her syntax; but nevertheless she permits and welcomes translation for the sake of her secondary audience. And recent developments show the broad recognition accruing to her despite the language barrier: she is much in demand in Ireland; she has done bilingual readings across America, from San Francisco State University to the Ivy League circuit to the Y in New York; the summer of 1992 saw her join the select band of writers honored by American Ireland Fund's Literary Award. Seamus Heaney's comment on the occasion demonstrates the rightness, from one point of view, of her outreaching stance: "She has been important in banishing the apartheid between Irish and English writings" (*Irish Independent*, 10 August 1991).

The poet is of course at the mercy of her translators. I have been critical of Hartnett's sometimes prudish, sometimes simply incorrect and misleading translations of Ní Dhomhnaill's work in *Selected Poems* (1988). *Pharaoh's Daughter*, Ní Dhomhnaill's 1990 dual-language collection, includes selected poems from her first two Irish-language collections, *An Dealg Droigin* (1981) and *Féar Suaithinseach* (1984), as well as twenty-seven of the eighty-two poems of *Feis* (1991); the translations were executed by a variety of poets working in English. The least adequate translators here let embedded forms do their thinking for them, and certain well-used and conventional solutions are enshrined as Irish-English; the best come up with little individual objects of art. Douglas Sealey's review of *Pharaoh's Daughter* (*Irish Times*, 8 December 1990) seems to assume that the real merit of the poems in this collection lies in the versions of them by the established poets in English. He contrasts "the smart raciness of Muldoon . . . ; the clotted, verbal richness of McGuckian; the conversational bite of Carson; the ornate elaboration of Longley" with the unfortunate poet's own dependence "on the nearly obliterated images of a much used coinage of idiom." Sealey's incomprehension of Ní Dhomhnaill's project—and possibly of her original language—is complicated by his expectation (he complains that "a coherent picture of the writer of the originals" is not to be had here) that the translator should deliver the author's original poem on a silver platter. But the problem with translation is that

> the semantic field of a word, the entire complex network of
> meanings it signifies, never matches exactly the semantic field

of any one word in any other language. It is primarily for this
reason that on the ideal level, all translation is distortion, and
all translators are traitors. (Holmes 1988, 9)

Prose translators get around that, but the problem is much more complex for poetry: "[T]he metapoem, if it is to achieve an effect as a poem
in English, must satisfy certain requirements that may be alien to the
original poem. . . . " (15).

Let me try to make clear the problems of discussing this poetry in
translation and show why close reading of the English produces false or
misleading results. What we want to talk about when we talk about
Nuala Ní Dhomhnaill's poetry is the poetry's total effect, which is bound
up (as is most poetry and prose in Irish) so closely with its effect on the
ear as to be impossible to demonstrate to an audience whose only route
of approach is the English translation. It is in fact an initial impoverishment not to experience the poetry in Ní Dhomhnaill's own reading! But
given the strength of her presence in the (original Gaelic) voice of the
poetry, the reading audience makes do very happily. In the following
excerpt from *Táimid Damanta, A Dheirféaracha* (We are damned, my sisters) the ear is most engaged by the long vowels: the wide and cheerful
ao and *éa* sounds (both roughly equivalent to long " a" in English, without the diphthongal ending) and the complex chiming assonances of
aoi, ío, ia, í (the mouth in position for the English long *e,* but there the
similarity ends) all of which together give a sort of smile to the five lines.
Which is in perfect apposition to the subject: loosed from their constraints
of duty and proper obedience to the male ruling class, the persona and
her sisters dance on the seashore:

> *B'fhearr linn ár mbróga a caitheamh dínn ar bharra taoide*
> *is rince aonar a dhéanamh ar an ngaineamh fliuch*
> *is port an phíobaire ag teacht aniar chughainn*
> *ar ghaotha fiala an Earraigh, ná bheith fanta*
> *istigh age baile ag déanamh tae láidir d'fhearaibh,*
> *is táimid damanta, a dheirféarcha.*

This is in the tradition of the accentual verse that first emerged—formal,
tightly structured, and elaborate—in Ireland in the seventeenth century,
replacing the older syllabic forms. Ní Dhomhnaill introduces a collo-
quial, jazz line over the ground bass of the meter and similarly frees the
verse from a strict pattern of assonances, giving an irregular but constant
repetition its own force. The lines here are almost all packed pentameters

(the first I quote showing a Hopkins-esque straining at the metrical leash); but the tension is perfectly sustained. Each verse finishes with the trimeter refrain, conclusively short, which by its repetition becomes less doomed and more defiant.

Now have a look at the Hartnett version of these lines. They are quite interesting as they stand but make little effort to reproduce the effect of the original, thereby losing something that seems to me to be the poem's most important feature.

> We preferred to be shoeless by the tide
> dancing singly on the wet sand
> the piper's tune coming to us
> on the kind Spring wind, than to be
> indoors making strong tea for the men—
> and so we're damned, my sisters!

Out of a choice of four ways in which he could have presented the poem in English: mimetic (content- and form-derivative) analogical (also content- and form-derivative, but with a certain "translation" of the form to the translator's era and culture), organic (content derivative), or extraneous (the translator uses the original as a jumping-off point for what is, essentially, a new poem of his own),[7] Hartnett has chosen to follow the content as closely as possible. His lines are shorter, more clipped, and the feeling of luxuriant freedom in the original Irish is contradicted by the (mostly) short vowel sounds massing toward the *i* and *e* end of the spectrum: on this beach one could be quite cold. The two notable long vowel sounds in "shoeless" and "tune" purse the lips into a Victorian exercise in primness that is at odds with the feeling of the original. Finally, the alliterative sounds seem almost coincidental, or, if planned, to have no purpose fitting the theme of this particular stanza. To do him justice, if I had not the original before me and could read Hartnett's version freshly, I would have different things to say: I would start with the premise of his words and his sounds and, making no invidious comparisons, be persuaded by them. In short, when one attempts a close reading of the English version of this poem, one is reading Hartnett, but not quite Ní Dhomhnaill.

To show a different choice that a translator makes, let us look briefly at a bit of Longley's translation of "Aubade." If the critic Douglas Sealey had been more sensitive to the sound effects of the original as well as to the purpose of "the ornate elaboration" of the translation, he would have seen more point to Michael Longley's beautifully analogical version, where

> the green mallard's
> Stylish glissando among reeds; on the moorhen
> Whose white petticoat flickers around the boghole;
> On the oystercatcher on tiptoe at low tide

wholeheartedly tries to match the original in its attempt at an interesting pattern of assonances. Did Sealey read either poem aloud?

It might also be instructive in this regard to compare Medbh McGuckian's magical, offbeat version of the poem *"Geasa"* (Ní Dhomhnaill 1990b, 12–13) to my line-for-line, pedestrian, and occasionally uncomprehending translation:

The Bond

> If I use my forbidden hand
> To raise a bridge across the river,
> All the work of the builders
> Has been blown up by sunrise.
>
> A boat comes up the river by night
> With a woman standing in it,
> Twin candles lit in her eyes
> And two oars in her hands.
>
> She unsheaths a pack of cards,
> "Will you play forfeits?" she says.
> We play and she beats me hands down,
> And she puts three banns upon me:
>
> Not to have two meals in one house,
> Not to pass two nights under one roof,
> Not to sleep twice with the same man
> Until I find her. When I ask her address,
>
> "If it were north I'd tell you south,
> If it were east, west." She hooks

Off in a flash of lightning, leaving me
Stranded on the bank,

My eyes full of candles,
And the two dead oars.

And now my more "accurate" version:

Banns/Taboos

If I put one hand on the blessed sanctuary
If I build a bridge over the river
Everything that is built by the craftspeople by day
Is demolished in the morning before me.

At night, a boat comes up the river
And a woman standing in it
Candles alight in her eyes and in her hands.
She has two oars.

She draws out a pack of cards.
"Will you play forfeits?" she says.
We play and she beats me all the time
And she puts the forfeit/bann/big burden on me

Not to eat a second meal in any house
Nor spend a second night under one roof
Nor snatch two winks of sleep on one bed
Till I find her. When I ask her where she lives

"If it's east, west," she says, "if it's west, east.
She goes off, flashing lightning
And I'm left there on the landing/riverbank.
The two candles are lighting still beside me.

She left me the oars.

Which of the two translations has done the Irish poet a greater service? There can be no doubt that the McGuckian version, with its complete inventions of a male presence, a "forbidden" hand, the use of all
four points of the compass, the "unsheathing" of the cards like a weapon,

even a phallic weapon, the confinement of the subject to one-night stands, "dead" oars, establishes more effectively the tension that is integral to the source poem. On the other hand, all of these inventions add a notion of greater powerlessness in the subject, making the situation more malign, we might say, than the poet intended. No, the oars are not dead: despite the eerie darkness and the difficulty of the quest, the final line of the source poem as translated literally has the revenant/female muse passing not only her light but her power to the aspiring journeywoman. But the McGuckian version pleases the ear surpassingly with its surer rhythms and striking word choices ("hooked off," "twin candles," "stranded," as well as the obvious inventions) and so is closer to the spirit of the Irish; it brings a proper shiver to the spine; it is, in fact, a freestanding poem where the other translation leans awkwardly against the original, a half-made thing.

Where does that leave us? At least when the translators are first-class poets, the dialogue between the recto and verso can provide many an absorbing inner debate. Lucky Nuala Ní Dhomhnaill, to have such excellent writers take an interest in translating her as McGuckian, Heaney, Carson, Muldoon, Ní Chuilleanáin, and Montague. If this gratifying response says anything, it is about the importance of the Irish language to the identities of Irish poets, even when they do not speak it (none of the Northerners above have Irish, for example; it's taught in few schools there). Ní Dhomhnaill's instinct about disenfranchisement is surely confirmed by their need, their bounty.

The danger of life on this very narrow border is the danger of being read without full comprehension, even by other speakers of Irish, but especially by those who read the English translations: there remains the problem of translating the rule-breaking aspect of Ní Dhomhnaill's language. The effects of her discourse depend on a vast array of associations, powerful traditional images, and *pourquoi* narratives from folklore, expressed in the formulaic, bastardized language of daily speech and the narrative patterns of the fireside storyteller, evoking a whole world—a clichéd, comfortable, conservative world—for the reader or listener. This almost smothering familiarity is simultaneously pierced with the sharp knives of discomfort caused by the iconoclastic, antiliterary usage and references to "improper" lusts and ignoble acts. How could that breaking of the rules be analogized in English by a Standard English speaker? Perhaps other oppressed groups have the best chance of representing Ní Dhomhnaill's project with full justice. In 1992 I ran across a professor from Aichi Shukutoku University, Mitsuko Ohno, who was at that time translating Ní Dhomhnaill into Japanese and struggling both with the startling effect of abjuring the traditional Japanese "women's language" in many of the poems, which seemed to call for a more active/dominant syntax, and struggling with the possible repercussions for doing so as she tried to publish. A dangerous border crossing! Ní Dhomhnaill would be pleased.

Notes

1. The inaccuracy lies in the implication that somehow the "Grafton Street" is a reality in her life, a sign of her establishment among the upper middle class, whereas, in the interview, we find it has simply been a place visited in a dream. When she finds herself there, she asks, *"Cén bhaint atá ag Laura fuckin' Ashley liomsa?"* (What does ——— have to do with me?). As she then goes on to explicate the dream, we find Grafton Street has symbolic meaning, but not exactly the one the editors permit to be implied.

2. Ó hAnluain 1986, 11. See also Dhiarmada 1987.

3. Personal interview, March 1991.

4. This example was supplied by Professor Angela Bourke, Department of Modern Irish, University College, Dublin.

5. Personal interview, June 1990.

6. From a speech delivered on 18 March 1943. Quoted in Beale 1986, 20. The author points out and illustrates that this ideal picture "bore little resemblance to the harsh reality of most country people's lives."

7. The categories are from Holmes 1988, 26–27.

References

Beale, Jenny. *Women in Ireland: Voices of Change.* Hampshire and London: Macmillan Education, 1986.

Bliss, Alan. "The Standardization of Irish." In *The Crane Bag Book of Irish Studies,* 1:908–14. Dublin: Blackwater Press, 1982.

de Paor, Louis. "From Limbo to Grafton Street." *Innti* 12 (1989): 41–54.

Dhiarmada, Bríona Nic. "Bláthú an Tradisiúin." *Comhar,* May 1987, 23–29.

Fennell, Deasún. "Cén Mhaith Scríobh I nGaeilge?" *Feasta* 33 (January 1980): 21–22.

Holmes, James. *Translated! Papers on Literary Translation and Translation Studies.* Edited with an introduction by Raymond van den Broek. Amsterdam: Rodopi, 1988.

Jenkinson, Biddy. "A Letter to an Editor." *Irish University Review,* Spring/Summer 1991, 27-34.

Katrak, Ketu. "Decolonizing Culture: Toward a Theory for Postcolonial Women's Texts." *Modern Fiction Studies* 35.1 (Spring 1989): 157–79.

Kristeva, Julia. *Desire in Language.* New York: Columbia University Press, 1980.

Mullin, Molly. "Representations of History, Irish Feminism, and the Politics of Difference." *Feminist Studies* 17.1 (Spring 1991): 29–50.

Ní Dhomhnaill, Nuala. *An Dealg Droighin.* Dublin and Cork: Cló Mercier, 1981.

——. "An Filíocht á Cumadh." *Léachtai Cholm Cille* 17 (1986): 147–79.

——. *The Astrakhan Coat.* Translated by Paul Muldoon. Loughcrew: The Gallery Press, 1990a.

——. *Féar Suaithinseach.* Maynooth: An Sagart, 1984.

——. *Feis.* Maynooth: An Sagart, 1991.

——. *Pharaoh's Daughter.* Translated by Ciaran Carson et al. Loughcrew: The Gallery Press, 1990b.

——. *Selected Poems/Rogha Dánta.* Translated by Michael Hartnett. Dublin: Raven Arts Press, 1988.

Ó hAnluain, Eoghan. "Nuafhilíocht na Gaeilge 1966–1986: úire a gus Buaine." *Léachtai Cholm Cille* 17 (1986): 7-23.

Exile and Politics of (Self-)Representation

The Narrative of Bounded Space and Action in Sahar Khalifeh's Wild Thorns

NEJD YAZIJI

Borders—which in the analysis that follows are more than just geographic lines separating Palestinians from Israelis—have to a great extent shaped Palestinian sensibilities in recent history. For the Palestinians, borders have represented an obsessive encounter with crucial limits imposed from the outside on their movements and unity as a people. Unable to find cohesiveness in space, the Palestinians have struggled since their dislocation in 1948 for a sense of unity and common destiny, realizing it largely through the national narrative. Like all other nationalist narratives, the Palestinian one has provided its community with a sense of destiny and continuity projected from a remembered past in Palestine to a desired future of return and statehood.

Yet in its linear trajectory from past to future, the Palestinian national narrative has had to displace internal divisions in the Palestinian people's present along geographic and economic borders, rifts of Palestinian existence and experience considered marginal to the struggle for nationhood or not in line with its forward movement. In a different context, Walter Benjamin has described the sense of time always projected forward as "homogeneous [and] empty"—empty, in Benjamin's view, because it does not account for the properly historical, the "time filled by the presence of the now" (Benjamin 261). What happens, then, when the temporal cohesion of the Palestinian national narrative realized by casting the conflict in terms of national identity (Palestinian vs. Israeli) is interpolated by a powerful insight into *the everyday*[1] needs and necessities of Palestinian life under occupation?

This question is powerfully engaged in Sahar Khalifeh's 1976 novel, *Wild Thorns*. Set inside the occupied territories and made to register in nearly ethnographic detail the quotidian aspects of Palestinian struggles, *Wild Thorns* reflects the interconnections between borders and economic access; borders and identities, and spatial location and the very possibility of action of Palestinian individuals. This geo-economic "determination" of the narrative of *Wild Thorns* allows the novel to articulate an "inside" view on Palestinian lives quite different from the "outside" or "exilic" one, and to configure differently the relation between "national struggle" and the claims over the occupied land. Working against a reified sense of belonging to the land sustained by means of an idyllic memory, Khalifeh describes everyday spatial practices on the land. Such everyday practices, as Michel de Certeau has argued, entail labor and work relations, consumption, organization of daily movements, border crossings, and procedures of transportation—in short, the placement of the physical body of the individual or community as a whole within the discourse of everyday life (Certeau 1984, 116). Yet this placement, as Henri Lefebvre has noted, is not equally distributed upon *all* people constituting the national body: "It weighs more heavily on women, who are sentenced to everyday life, on the working class, on employees who are not technocrats, on youth—in short on the majority of people—yet never in the same way, at the same time, never all at once" (Lefebvre 1987, 10).

The purpose of this chapter is to question the master narrative of abstract historical continuity and to establish a critique of the "natural" sense of belonging to, and recovery of, the land. In almost all anticolonial struggles the nationalist ideology is tied in to the discourse of either return to, or sovereignty over, the land, depending on the type of struggle being waged.[2] The Palestinian struggle is no exception. But recovery for whom? In this discourse, sovereignty over the land is directly and uncritically made to correspond to a "nation" and a "people" (Wallerstein 1991, 81). Yet, in this facile correspondence, the problem of cohesion within the national space—i.e., of different degrees of belonging to, and alienation from, the land—is eschewed (ibid.). In the Palestinian context, for instance, the discourse of the land will turn out to be alienating to two groups that have played a fundamental role in maintaining Palestinian struggle and peoplehood: the peasant-worker class and women (the two disempowered groups of Palestinian society par excellence). As Khalifeh's novel adumbrates, the myth of "natural" belonging to the land functions as a naturalized ideology reproducing the Palestinian privileged class's patriarchal control over the land and peasants' labor.[3] Khalifeh's *spatial* narrative brings up the tension between a "natural" (and therefore eternal and somewhat instinctive) belonging to the land, on the one hand, and everyday practices on that land in the present, on the other.

The latter dynamic, a material relationship of everyday production and consumption, labor and wages, survival and accommodation *in connection* to an economic and political space, suggests an inevitable clash with the notion of struggle inscribed in terms of eternal belonging to the land. In this sense, Khalifeh's insistence on narratives of everyday Palestinian life under occupation will redirect priorities of Palestinian struggle in terms that account for its socioeconomic and gender specificity in opposition to a fetishized grand narrative of liberation. So, while no absolute distinction can be maintained between national struggle and having a right to the land (as property), a critical distinction should be maintained as to the form of political ideologies that inform the nationalist claim.

Wild Thorns engages the issue of Palestinian employment in Israel and the new economic and political realities that Palestinians from the West Bank and Gaza came to face after the Israeli occupation of these territories in June 1967. Written just less than a decade after the occupation, the novel exposes the dramatic effects that post-1967 Palestinian "access" to the capitalist job market in Israel has had on Palestinian internal social relations and the Palestinian community's vision of its national struggle. The plot revolves around a young Palestinian from Nablus, Usama al-Karmi, who, after several years of trying his luck in inimical Arab countries, comes back to the West Bank convinced that Palestinians have no rightful place to live in the many Arab countries with which they have had to contend since the occupation. So, he believes that the "real" Palestinian struggle has to come from the "inside" and has to be fought "inside" the territories, not in the periphery.

With this ideology in mind, Usama seeks to find on the "ground" in the territories the same image his political imagination has constructed— namely, an uncorrupted and unyielding Palestinian resistance movement— a construction that soon proves incompatible with the actualities of people's daily politics there. Already embittered and alienated, Usama unequivocally rejects the notion of Palestinian work in Israel. He considers it a form of "disintegration" and, unable to understand or deal with the social and economic dynamics that make such work both desirable and feasible to the Palestinians of the territories, resolves to preempt it in a single act of self-destructive violence. He thus sets out on a mission to bomb the Israeli buses carrying Palestinian workers to Israel, including his friend Zuhdi and his cousin Adil.

Inside versus Outside

Despite the prominence of the Palestinian-Israeli national conflict whose ideologies mobilize actions, polarize points of view, and provide the context for Usama's "terrorist" event in the space of the novel, *Wild Thorns* is not about the national conflict per se (Harlow 1987, 133). While the novel is no doubt embedded in the reality of the conflict and its narrative as a whole is affected by its consequences, the author's insight turns instead on how the national crisis has forced new spatial and economic divisions on an already ambivalent and complex national space.

In *After the Last Sky* Edward Said tackles the inside-outside dichotomy that the 1967 war forced on Palestinian society. In a section with the heading "Interiors" Said writes:

> The phrase *min al-dakhil*, "from the interior," has a special resonance to the Palestinian ear. It refers, first of all, to regions of the interior of Israel, to territories and people still Palestinian despite the interdictions of the Israeli presence.... Until 1967, therefore, it meant the Palestinians who lived within Israel; after 1967 the phrase expanded to include the inhabitants of the West Bank, Gaza, and the Golan Heights, and since 1982 it has also meant the Palestinians (and Lebanese) of South Lebanon. (Said 1986, 51)

The "interior" is the "inside," or, as Said calls it, the "home"—the land from which the Palestinians departed after the early 1930s (when Jewish immigration to Palestine intensified) and especially after 1948. They were forced to leave or were exiled and, especially after the war of 1967, were turned into refugees in one Arab country or another. The "interior" also marks a difference, geographically and politically, from the "outside" or "exterior" *(al-kharij)*; it is the place where Palestinians stayed, despite their political and material dispossession, symbolizing and actualizing Palestinian resistance.

But this construction is, as Said admits, an "outside" or "exilic" construction of the "inside," one prompted by physical distance, material disassociation, and perhaps nostalgia, to idealize and privilege an uncorrupted "inside" of Palestinian internal fortitude (84). From the "inside" point of view, the picture is endlessly complicated by factors that to Palestinians from the "outside" seem altogether distant or incomprehensible.

These spatially reckoned points of view open Khalifeh's *Wild Thorns* and sustain a heightened level of tension in its narrative construction of events. When Usama, for instance, returns in the opening scene of the novel to his mother's house in Nablus, committed to staying and taking up struggle "inside" the territories, it is the distance of his perspective from that of everybody else there that strikes the reader. Only a few hours after he crosses the borders separating Jordan from the West Bank, Usama readily denounces people's acquiescence and submissiveness to the Israelis. He is struck by fellow Palestinians in the car bringing him back to his mother's house smoking Israeli cigarettes and speaking matter-of-factly of the rising cost of Israeli-produced rice and sugar; he is again outraged by a Palestinian woman in the car calling an Israeli soldier "Effendi" while imploring him to forgo the ten dinars customs' fee he insists she has to pay, but which she does not have, on items she brought home with her from Jordan:

> "Effendi! Effendi!" she calls him!" Our friend's hand almost reached out to slap the woman's black-covered head. "How can you use that word? And why the tears, woman? Ten dinars aren't worth a single tear at their customs counter. Save your tears for what will happen after the disaster and the setback. Save them for the disintegration awaiting us as long as there are people like you around."[4]

In this, as in many of the other incidents through which Usama's character is laid out to the reader, Usama's reaction is caught up in a fundamentally monologic form of consciousness: that of anti-Israeli violent struggle. His resolve, based on his own frustrated exile and now disappointed return, is that violence alone can properly redress the oppression of occupation and the complicity of the Palestinians "inside."

This unmediated idea of national struggle necessitates not only that he reject offhand what he recognizes as the people's weaknesses and passive acceptance of the status quo of the occupation, but that he denounce, equally vehemently, the signs of his own weakness and vulnerability. In an internal monologue a few moments after his reunion with "his" land, Usama reflects:

Yes, when will those tender feelings living forever inside me cease to be? This constant longing for the unknown, the feeling of melancholy that overwhelms me whenever I hear a song or smell a flower, the lift in my spirit during sun set with no limit! The yearning and nostalgia for this ever green land, its very soil, so rich and so blessed! A romantic, right? No way! Not since the training, the shooting, the crawling on all fours; such things make a man unromantic in thought and deed. (Khalifeh 1985, 9/10–11)

Here, Usama resembles what Bakhtin, speaking of Dostoevsky's heroes, has termed (after Engelhardt) "a person of an idea." This individual, Bakhtin writes, is "possessed by an idea. An idea becomes for him an idea-force, omnipotently defining and distorting his consciousness and his life" (Bakhtin 1989, 22). All other forms of feelings and emotions, including his terribly indulgent appreciation for the land to which he so strongly proclaims his belonging, have to be relinquished for his singular quest of struggle to be pursued. Later on in the narrative we will see that Usama's wistful and genuine attachment to the land is precisely what will inform his act of violence—that the structure of his undifferentiated romantic feeling towards the land he now rejects in favor of violence is what conditions the idea and commitment to violent struggle.

Meanwhile, Usama is able to live the force of his "idea" of violence only to the extent that he, as an individual, lives and instantiates a "systematically monologic context." A monologic way of cognition, Bakhtin writes, "arises only where consciousness is placed above existence, and where the unity of existence is transformed into the unity of consciousness." In other words, the force of Usama's singular "idea" is possible precisely because he does not live and share what Bakhtin has called "empirical human consciousnesses"—the struggles and oppressions of people in the "inside" (Bakhtin 1989, 81). He gains the singularity of his response by ignoring the realities of his people, like the woman confronted with the Israeli soldier at the customs checkpoint.

After this monologue, and in the process of narrating the characters' *everyday* life histories, *Wild Thorns* allows the realities of Palestinian life "inside" to speak for themselves. Once starting to unfold, these realities quickly reflect the contradictions between Usama's idea of national struggle, a monolithic political will imposed from the "outside" and representative at that historical juncture of the position of the Palestinian leadership "outside,"[5] and the multiple forms of struggle of the Palestinians "inside" that have been rendered, due to both the oppression of occupation and the persistently oppressive ideologies within Palestinian life, simply incommensurable with the singular vision of the nationalist ideology. What the reader encounters therefore are two intertwined levels of narration that synthesize the novel's radical impetus. At one level, the narrative inscribes the novel in the "real-life content" of its determining chronotopes, namely the spatial and economic realities of the decades following Israel's occupation of the territories. Yet, simultaneously, the narrative rearranges the conventional meaning of these spatial and economic realities so as to effect political implications subversive of Usama's master narrative of violent struggle. Through this twofold method of narration Khalifeh places the nationalist ideology in a dialogic relation with the "facts" on the ground—the result of this irreconcilable dialogue between the inside and the outside of Palestinian reality is reflected in the irresolution of the narrative itself, especially as seen by Usama.

The following passage, which registers Usama's first impressions of the changes overcoming his friends and relatives after his return to his mother's house, serves as an example of this narrating process and portends the author's own unconventional vision of Palestinian national struggle:

> The hardship of life doesn't show on people. They dress smartly. Walk faster. And buy without haggling. Money is aplenty and so is work. Wages are higher and people can now afford to buy meat, vegetables and fruits. . . . They eat vigorously and stuff their children. He who owned no shirt before now flaunts leather jackets. And he who could not afford to buy a scarf now warms his ears with fur collars. . . . The hips of maids have grown fat after they've become workers and clerks. Something has changed here! The occupation is still there, and so is people's crushed dignity, but something *has* changed. Maids ceased to be maids and the class ladder is less vertical. People are stuffed, *every one.* (Khalifeh 1985, 26–27/30; emphasis mine)

What has "changed" (for all but Usama) is the spatial and economic status of both the West Bank and Gaza since the occupation of June 1967—an issue that *Wild Thorns* raises as the anchor of its narrative representation of the transformation in Palestinian everyday life. Spatially, the two territories since then have become part of an expanding and militarized Israel.[6] Economically, this occupation has brought the territories from complete "economic isolation from Israel" to a state in which connection with the Israeli state has become the "predominant external economic contact" (Arkadie 1977, 105).

One of the most salient effects of this spatial-economic transformation, many analysts have argued, has been the isolation of the territories from their earlier ties with Egypt and Jordan and the creation of their dependency on Israeli economy. This happened, Salim Tamari argues in a recent essay, during the first two decades of the occupation:

> During the initial period of Israeli rule (up to 1988) the demand for unskilled wage labour in Israeli industries . . . transformed the whole relationship between family expectations, children's education and the demand of the labour market. Whole village communities, as well as refugee camps, became completely dependent for their survival on employment in Israel. . . . (Tamari, forthcoming, 5–7)

"The shift lies," Tamari adds, "in the conscious and systematic method the Israelis undertook to subordinate the economy of the two regions to the needs of the Israeli state, and—more significantly—in the appropriation of public land (and substantial private property) to serve the needs of the Jewish Settlement Councils in the occupied territories" (7).

But Khalifeh's narrative does not simply recount the socioeconomic "facts" that Salim Tamari describes above in sociological terms. Rather, her narrative elevates these "facts" to the level of an ideological force and imposes, as all narratives do, a specific morality on them (see White 1981). What Tamari describes as "dependence" and "subordination" of the economies of the West Bank and Gaza to the needs of the Israeli economy becomes in Khalifeh's narrative manipulation *a form of relative independence for traditionally underprivileged groups of Palestinians*, as reflected in the material well-being of people that shocks Usama. The tone of the preceding passage from the novel implies that the transformations in the economies of the territories in terms of their dependence on the Israeli capitalist job market have not been that detrimental for *all* Palestinians living there, since they have enabled, Khalifeh clearly suggests, some social mobility previously not available to the Palestinian masses.

At this level, then, what Ricoeur has called the "interweaving reference between history and fiction" in Khalifeh's narrative representation of the facts on the ground leads to a refiguration of the experience of national struggle itself (see Ricoeur 1988, 99). For here, the issue that Khalifeh raises goes beyond the problem of how Israel, the national enemy, has rendered the economies of the West Bank and Gaza—so far agrarian and labor-surplused—dependent on its technologically advanced and capital-intensive economy. Khalifeh is quite aware elsewhere in the novel that powerful forces and interests have operated in favor of Israel through the job market because of the sheer size of wage differentials and that the subjection of Palestinian workers to the law of the capitalist job market is not an act of Israeli benevolence. Indeed, in a scene that describes the Israeli factories, for instance, Khalifeh is blunt about the exploitative dynamics of Israeli capitalist economy that operates, albeit in varying degrees, on both Palestinian and Israeli workers. Both Zuhdi and Adil—who work in the factories and who are made to be the only pragmatic and "reliable" characters of the novel—realize that their labor in Israel will not lead to greater integration between the Israelis and the Palestinians; that the economic benefits reaped by their labors and that of their fellow Israeli workers, like Shlomo, are not mutually beneficial as long as they are controlled by the Israeli capitalist bourgeoisie and its military apparatus.[7]

Yet, while Khalifeh's critique of capitalist exploitation across national borders is integral to the social message in *Wild Thorns*, a more important Marxist critique emerges at another level in the narrative. The main issue for Khalifeh is that, through the process of what might be called forced modernization to which the territories have been subjected since their occupation in 1967, new social and economic identities have been forged on the scene of political struggle, challenging the cohesiveness of the anti-Israeli narrative of struggle. As a result of this process, the impoverished peasants who used to work on the land have become relatively prosperous as wage laborers in Israel. The hitherto weak and dispossessed workers whom Palestinian business owners hired for menial tasks now have more stable jobs and a new consciousness of themselves, while the traditionally privileged land and business owners have gradually receded in importance, their authority superseded. What Khalifeh's narrative seems to stress (and this is where her view of the Palestinian situation poses radical challenges to the nation-as-solution narrative) is that if the identities of these emerging social groups are no longer compatible with the nationalist ideology imposed from the "outside," this is precisely because the ideology has not articulated the needs and interests of these impoverished groups into its narrative vision. This is where Usama's idea of struggle is rendered futile. This critique—which chooses to unravel internal Palestinian inequities instead of simply identifying an external national enemy for the Palestinians' misfortunes, thus earning Khalifeh considerable rebuke even from leftist Palestinian critics[8]—is specifically manifested in her treatment of the kind of labor relations and property possession in the territories themselves.

Many examples could be cited to illustrate this point in the novel. For example, Zuhdi tries his hands on anything he can get in the territories, working as a mechanic, a taxi driver, and a construction worker; then he becomes an exile in Kuwait, Saudi Arabia, and Germany, and eventually comes back to become a *lishka*[9] worker in Israel. He points out to Usama that Palestinian business owners were not more "merciful" to him than his present Israeli bosses. Zuhdi's sentiment against members of the Palestinian bourgeoisie is not a unique instance in the novel. Indeed, both Zuhdi and Abu Sabir, who belong to different generations, make statements to the effect that their work in Israel has vindicated the humiliation to which their Palestinian ex-bosses had subjected them.

This is not to say that Khalifeh wants to exonerate Israel's exploitation of the Palestinians. Her narrative, rather, suggests that class inequities among the Palestinians cannot be reduced to a colonizer-colonized dichotomy; that Palestinian oppressions and failures cannot be vindicated by a monolithic national struggle; and that people's real, material choices defy nationalist identifications, even when their individual choices are referred at one point or another to the nationalist ideology. In another passage characteristic of this aporia, Zuhdi reveals stories of his oppression by fellow Palestinians while ironically narrating to Usama the story of Abu Sabir, who had been denied medical treatment in Israel after a factory incident because he was not a *lishka* worker. "Had he been a *lishka* worker," Zuhdi explains to Usama, "he would have gotten his compensation. . . . They denied him treatment, believe it or not. . . . He wanted to avoid taxes: social security we [Palestinians] don't really get, union fees and national security" (Khalifeh 1985, 77–79/87–88). Here, Abu Sabir's predicament is not that "he was illegally hired by an Israeli firm that does not provide its workers with accident insurance," as Suha Sabbagh has read it in her analysis of the novel.[10] Rather, as a Palestinian sucked into the capitalist job market of the enemy state, which gives him relatively good wages and autonomy but forces him to "contribute" to its army revenues, Abu Sabir declines paying social and national security taxes and ends up losing his health insurance in the process. The irony is precisely that Israel's health policy *does* protect Palestinian workers even when their "national security" revenues go to annex more Palestinian land. As Zuhdi puts it: "[T]he situation sucks but your wage is paid. They pull the land from under your feet and then call you brother" (Khalifeh 1985, 79/88). So, even when Palestinian oppressions, like Abu Sabir's, are "determined from without" (to use Fanon's terms) by the colonizer-colonized binary identities, their articulations in specific locales of everyday life defy a facile reduction to nationalist lines.[11]

Usama's encounter with Abu Shehadeh, an aged Palestinian peasant who worked in Abu Adil's farm along with his son Shehadeh, further demonstrates why employment in Israel has so quickly and so successfully superseded working on Palestinian land "inside." In Khalifeh's rendition, this success has more to do with the relationship of the Palestinian peasants to the Palestinian land in which they labored than with the Israeli job market per se, as Tamari's analysis suggests. Khalifeh foreshadows this link—between the relationship of the Palestinian peasant to the land, on the one hand, and his employment in Israel, on the other—in a passage where Usama goes to visit his uncle's farm:

> His uncle's [Abu Adil] farm was on the other side of the stream, hidden behind the white poplar and oleander. Usama was walking as he looked for the greens which used to cover the place, but the farms were deserted and the arboretum covered but occasional spots of the neglected land.[12]

The impact of this employment on the Palestinian community is inscribed, literally, on the land itself, which appears barren and empty. Usama, to whom the neglected condition of the land seems incomprehensible and unjustifiable, demands an explanation from Abu Shehadeh, who takes care of it: "Why doesn't Shehadeh work on this farm?" Usama asks Abu Shehadeh. "Over there is better," the old man answers. "Over there is a lot of money and fun. And none of this 'come here s.o.b., go there pimp.' . . . No one is over his head, breaking his back, making him work morning and night, like a dog" (Khalifeh 1985, 41/49).

For Abu Shehadeh and his son, then, both of whom were hired hands in the Palestinian land, work in Israel is simply changing old masters for new ones. Yet, as wage laborers in the Israeli economy, Palestinian workers are nonetheless eligible for more rights than before. But Usama, whose utter lack of touch with people's life in the "inside" is not only predicated upon his exilic perspective but also negatively determined by his privileged class position within Palestinian society, is genuinely dismayed by Abu Shehadeh's matter-of-fact answers:

> "And this farm, old man. You're leaving it for whom?" / The old man shook his head brushing a mosquito off his face as he resorted to well known idioms "How would I know!" / "Who

else would know, then? *You* don't know, the man who nourished every tree in this farm like you nourished your own son! ..." / "As if the land were really ours?" / "Whose is it then? ..." / "Would I know?" / ... "This land, whose is it sir, *Haj*, old man? Who does it belong to?" / "To its owners, Effendi, who do you think? And why are you angry at me? I am a hired hand here sir, and have always been. I have no land, nothing; my son is a hired hand too and will always be. And if the land is not mine or my son's, why should we die for it? When we were starving, you cared little for us. *Now* you care for what we do. Why?" (Khalifeh 1985, 41–42/50)

The land, then, is not an undifferentiated, abstract space that belongs to whoever lives on it. It is a piece of property belonging to the privileged Palestinian class, which has historically maintained possession and authority over it. In this instance, Usama's guileless questions to Abu Shehadeh are testimony to his political immaturity. His inability to differentiate the condition of his belonging to the land—as an al-Karmi member and heir to his family's property—from that of Abu Shehadeh and his son also conditions his discourse of struggle as a political monologue of an unmediated, binary opposition of colonizer-colonized. There is little wonder, then, why he cannot understand how a Palestinian of Shehadeh's class could accept work in Israel over staying and working in the farm, now that the Israeli occupation has provided another economic resource for those who worked on the land and did not own it.

To Usama, belonging to the land is a matter of timeless political commitment (hence, his nostalgia?), separable from what Marx has called "a definite *mode of life*"—the material relation that connects people to the social space in which they live and produce their means of subsistence (Marx 1978, 150). Connection to the land is, as he reflects after a confrontation with Adil about Shehadeh's work in Israel, a matter of "loyalty, principle, and an ethical obligation," not an economic or material relation (Khalifeh 1985, 87/95). Shehadeh is the ultimate betrayer in Usama's eyes: he bought his success and prosperity in Israel at the expense of loyalty to the Palestinian land.

Usama's class-based identification with the land, masquerading as "integrity" and an "ethical obligation," explains why the discourse of retrieving the land has been so essential to the ideology of nationalist struggle and why this discourse has not been critically tied into the issue of social class and familial legacy in the Palestinian national imagination. When Usama appeals to "integrity" and "ideals" in defending the Palestinians' obligation to the land, he is not being disingenuous, nor is his commitment to violent struggle and self-sacrifice for the sake of the Palestinian "cause" simply false. Loyalty and patriarchy are here intertwined. Usama's ideals stem from and express an old and well-sustained relation in Palestinian society between dignity, integrity, and honor, on the one hand, and property and authority over the land, on the other.

This specifically patriarchal relation is, surprisingly, what even the most progressive Palestinian thinkers still stress in their discourse on Palestinian nationalism. When discussing the effect of land confiscation in the territories on the Palestinian community's national identity, Salim Tamari writes that

> In a predominantly agrarian society (or even in an urban society with persisting agrarian values) such as the one under examination, property in terms of land and housing underlies the community's national identity. The continued confiscation of Palestinian land by the military authorities is seen not as a loss of real estate, but as the alienation of national patrimony. (Tamari, forthcoming, 10–11)

Tamari's argument confirms the relation I described earlier but fails to comment critically on it. It is precisely because the form of national identity that calls for national struggle rests on "land property" and "patrimony" that so many of the lower-class Palestinians in *Wild Thorns* fail to identify with it. Ultimately, then, what is severed through work in Israel and Israel's policy of land expropriation and control is the Palestinian upper class and landed aristocracy property rights. Hence, Usama's quest for an ethical obligation to the land is predicated upon his image of the land as a guarantor of his own identity, whose meaning and continuity stem from his legacy over, and continued entitlement to, the land. This is where Tamari's statement about "the alienation of national patrimony" uncritically collapses nationalism and patrimony into a natural or assumed correspondence where it should be thought through and articulated on a class basis. For, as Khalifeh shows in *Wild Thorns*, legacy over the land, or having a birthright to the land, is preemptive *of other Palestinians' rights to it: those who cannot claim a natural authority or continued legacy over the land.*

Yet, having leveled her critique against Palestinian patriarchy and the notion of national struggle and national sovereignty that inheres in an uncritical connection to the land, Khalifeh keenly and ruthlessly investigates the ways in which the nationalist discourse is inevitable as a dynamic for Palestinian anticolonial struggle. What Khalifeh does *not* want to relinquish is the multiplicity of voices and wills that do not combine or synthesize in a unitary voice of the author. She does not present a viable alternative to the nationalist vision, even when the discourse of the land seems alienating to the Palestinian peasants and workers and in fact secondary in terms of their material oppressions. Partly, this is because *Wild Thorns* is a *realist* novel. In terms of artistic or formal aspects, this means that the novel does not merely explore contradictory dynamics in the colonial situation; rather, its narrative as a whole is affected by their consequences.

Hence, every movement in the narrative relies on a politically constructed metaphor: characters, dialogues, monologues, even the description of nature, are all embedded in a politically symbolic sphere of language. In other words, the novel manifests a number of ideological positions that do not themselves represent "individually accented wills" or temperaments, to use Bakhtin again, but are rather made to fulfill an ideological commitment based on its chronotopic elements. The rifts that Khalifeh presents between the "inside" and the "outside," the narrative of violent struggle and that of accommodation, the discourse of loyalty to the land and that of everyday strategies of survival, all seem to be inscribed on the subjectivity of the characters themselves as Khalifeh draws them. These characters are caught up in the national narrative even when their everyday choices assert an individual strategy of survival and a will to self-interest. Every character in the novel, especially those who work in Israel, also recognizes himself or herself as part of a collective narrative of anti-Israeli, anticolonial struggle. Even when Abu-Sabir's fingers get mangled by an Israeli machine and he is denied medical treatment by the Israelis, his suffering is immediately transferred onto a collective plane of struggle of his "people." His appeal for a heroic narrative from the Arab past to redeem his not-so-heroic present reveals, momentarily at least, his need to see his humiliation as part of a larger Arab history of struggle and suffering and not as an individual or isolated event. The continuity in Abu Sabir's private and public forms of suffering, the fact that his personal injury is made to complement and radically echo that of his history at large, is testimony to the novel's allegorical level of representation (see Jameson 1986).

Similarly, Adil's character instantiates a possible alternative to the opposition between Usama's grand narrative of struggle and the status quo of total deliverance. Adil's struggles are *real* and meaningful within the realm of available choices, in contrast to his cousin's ideational *affirmation* of struggle. He supports his father's kidney machine and his brother and sister's education by (secretly) working in an Israeli factory; becomes involved with the problems of Zuhdi and other Palestinian workers despite his privileged class background; fights Abu-Sabir's legal battle for compensation in the Israeli courts; identifies with an Israeli woman whose husband Usama stabs to death; feels solidarity with Shehadeh, who rebels against his Palestinian boss (Adil's own father); and, finally, survives Usama's bombs, which kill Zuhdi and the Palestinians in the buses going to Israel when he misses work on the day of the attack to help Abu Sabir appeal an Israeli court decision denying him compensation. But Adil, too, is characterized in such a way so as to ultimately embody the Palestinian individual's incapacity to transgress the objective structures that constitute a binarism of the national conflict. As he tells Zuhdi in their last conversation:

> "I fight despair with desperate strategies. Do you understand? I cannot understand this strange blend of feelings nor can I explain what I think. Odd and indeterminate thoughts go through my head, so I can't define my stance on things with any clarity. Peace! Brotherhood! . . . I'm still dreaming of the impossible. But can I make roses from thorns?" / "Thorns don't grow roses, [Zuhdi answers] but they protect them." / "So, I go on dreaming." (Khalifeh 1985, 177/190–91)

Soon after this conversation, when Usama's explosives go off and the Israeli military vehicles arrive at the scene, the massacre of Palestinians breaks along Palestinian and Israeli national lines. Zuhdi, already injured by Usama's bomb and now caught in the line of fire, decides to protect his fellow Palestinian from the impending Israeli attack by stabbing the Israeli soldier with the screw driver he has in his hand. The contrast between this action and his earlier sentiment in the novel (when he vowed to Usama that his Palestinian ex-bosses were as exploitative of him as his Israeli bosses) rests on nothing more than a nationalist impulse. Khalifeh thus realizes that intra-Palestinian class cleavages defy a nationalist solution to the conflict but that ultimately it is the nationalist discourse that circumscribes the Palestinians' larger choices. Zuhdi is now a "thorn," another instance of the conflict's inevitable dichotomy:

> Zuhdi crawled over the dead body, the screw driver plunged in, and shivered. . . . "You killed a man, Zuhdi, what else do you expect? When Israeli men jump over you shooting at Usama?

You are a thorn, Zuhdi . . . despite yourself, despite everybody
else. . . . Carry the gun, strike! Strike. By God, I am no Christ.
And poor Shlomo with his head opened. He wasn't that bad
either. A decent man, like you and me, Usama, you pimp! But
he was a donkey like me. Two donkeys fighting for a bunch of
green clover divided up for them by the factory. Strike! Strike!"
(Khalifeh 1985, 169/196)

After this scene Usama falls dead. His final words to Zuhdi are testimony to the link between social space and consciousness:

The organizations are plagued with short-sightedness. Incorrect idiot. You just don't know what it feels like to be kicked off
a plane from an Arab airport to Lisbon. Pajamas underneath the
coat. The world's airports spit you out and your land receives
you. You cross the bridge to hear a woman screaming "swine."
You bleed and to your last breaths you still remember people
eating *kinafa* and laughing; their ears have closed off and the
pimp Shehadeh . . . smoking pipe. . . . The pimp forgets his land,
his country, and remembers his hatred. (Khalifeh 1985, 183–84/
197)

Usama's final words are haunted with the world of international airports, borders, and countries of exile and negation, where the individual's
identity and status quickly and unequivocally correspond to one's passport and nationhood. This is the social realm in which the individual's
subjectivity is constructed *for him* in relation to the institution of the nation and national identification. It is also the realm in which, as Homi
Bhabha has written, "an incommunicability . . . shapes the public moment; a psychic obscurity . . . is formative for public memory" (Bhabha
1992, 143). For, where does the act of violence itself become an assertion
of Usama's denied subjectivity as a Palestinian and where does it move
on to incorporate the space of his people at large?

Notes

1. The notion of the everyday does not emerge out of the concern with the
domestic or subjective realms only, but designates a social space in which objective forces and political conditions intersect with personal and individual choices
of a specific community. See Lefebvre 1991.

2. In the case of Palestine, the notion of return *(al-awdah)* is an important dynamic in the ideology of national struggle. Recovery of the land is inscribed in the national dream itself and this idealization of the notion of recovery is intertwined with a false sense of security stemming from the image of the land itself as an eternal and stable presence.

3. The word "land" here is used in a conceptual sense designating a geopolitical entity in association with a historical presence of a people, and in an economic one, as a "piece of property," referring specifically to the feudal system that until very recently prevailed in Palestinian society. The two senses of the word converge in this case insofar as the Palestinian national claim to *the* land seems complicit with a traditional and often patriarchal ideology of control over land. The point of this critique is not to, say, relinquish the quest for the land or declare it gratuitous in the Palestinian struggle, but rather to offer a secular vision in which such a claim revalues the class and gender dynamics of the history to which it is referenced.

4. Khalifeh 1985, 18/21. All translations from this text have been modified to ensure better correspondence to the original in Arabic. Consequently, I will give page numbers of English and Arabic texts respectively for each citation. The words "disaster" *(nakba)* and "setback" *(naksa)* have a specific resonance in Palestinian history (which is why I altered the English translation rendered as "catastrophe and defeat"): they refer to the wars of 1948 and 1967 respectively and establish a sort of hierarchy of defeats, with the loss of Palestine in 1948 as the worst and the occupation of the West Bank and Gaza as the second worst of the two events.

5. Sometime later in the narrative the reader learns that Usama's mission of blowing up the buses has been dictated by orders from the "outside." Consequently, Usama's adherence to violent struggle is not merely an individual impulse but an organized political commitment, which might explain why he as a character-individual does not develop beyond his political mission and why his idea of violent struggle does not enter into a dialogic context with other characters like Adil or Zuhdi.

6. This is true, even though the "status" and ultimate significance of these territories to the state of Israel have been adjudicated differently by different Israeli governments.

7. Muhammad Siddiq powerfully articulates this point in Siddiq 1987, 148.

8. Emil Habibi, a member of the Israeli Communist Party, took Khalifeh to task for having elevated the issue of Palestinian workers' rights and relative autonomy in Israel over the "primary issue" of the occupation of Palestinian land. See ibid., 147.

9. *Lishka* is a Hebrew word for "official." In this context *lishka* jobs refer to officially recognized jobs in Israel (similar to "legal" employment in the United States), which secure social security, medical insurance, and so forth.

10. Sabbagh 1989, 71. Sabbagh's argument about Palestinians not being eligible for Israeli benefits may be true, but the text makes it clear through Zuhdi

that Abu Sabir's case was the result of his evading Israeli taxes or having accepted an illegal employment.

11. Khalifeh goes one step further in identifying the link between Abu Sabir's predicament and the Arab tradition that skews for him a naïve authentic/ nationalist escape. Lying injured in the car carrying him to the West Bank, he asks Adil to tell him a story about Abu-Zaid al-Hilali, an Arab folk figure of heroic deeds, in a desperate attempt to salvage his disintegrating morale. Adil refuses, and Abu Sabir is denied his fictional escape. Adil later ends up fighting his legal battle for him to retrieve whatever compensation he can from the Israeli company. He wins the legal case, but the company files for bankruptcy and Abu-Sabir goes uncompensated.

12. Khalifeh 1985, 39/46. This passage, which goes on for a whole page in the Arabic original, is reduced in the English version to a four-line paragraph, so readers of English will not find an equivalent translation to this passage in the English.

References

Arkadie, Brian Van. "The Impact of the Israeli Occupation on the Economies of the West Bank and Gaza." *Journal of Palestine Studies* 6, no. 2 (1977): 103–29.

Balibar, Etienne, and Immanuel Wallerstein. *Race, Nation, Class: Ambiguous Identities*. London: Verso, 1991.

Bakhtin, Mikhail. *Problems of Dostoevsky's Poetics*. Translated and edited by Caryl Emerson. Minneapolis: University of Minnesota Press, 1989.

Benjamin, Walter. *Illuminations: Essays and Reflections*. Translated by Harry Zohn. New York: Schocken, 1968.

Bhabha, Homi. "The World and the Home." *Social Text* 31/32 (1992): 141–53.

Certeau, Michel de. *The Practice of Everyday Life*. Translated by Steven Randall. Berkeley: University of California Press, 1984.

Harlow, Barbara. "Narratives of Resistance." *New Formations* 1 (Spring 1987): 131–35.

Jameson, Fredric. "Third-World Literature in the Era of Multinational Capitalism." *Social Text* 15 (1986): 65–88.

Khalifeh, Sahar. *Al-Subbar* [Wild thorns]. Jerusalem: Galileo, 1976.

———. *Wild Thorns*. Translated b y Trevor LeGassick and Elizabeth Fernea. London: Al Saqi, 1985.

Lefebvre, Henri. "The Everyday and Everydayness." In *Yale French Studies: Everyday Life*, edited by Alice Kaplan and Kristin Ross. New Haven: Yale University Press, 1987.

———. *The Critique of Everyday Life*. Translated by John Moore. Vol. 1. London: Verso, 1991.

Marx, Karl. "The German Ideology." In *The Marx-Engels Reader*. Edited by Robert Tucker. 2d ed. New York: W. W. Norton, 1978.

Ricoeur, Paul. *Time and Narrative*. Translated by Kathleen Blamey and David Pellauer. Vol. 3. Chicago: University of Chicago Press, 1988. Reprinted in 1990.

Sabbagh, Suha. "Palestinian Women Writers and the *Intifada*." *Social Text* 22 (1989): 62-78.

Said, Edward W. *After the Last Sky: Palestinian Lives*. New York: Pantheon, 1986.

Shehadeh, Raja. *Occupier's Law: Israel and the West Bank*. Washington, D.C.: Institute of Palestine Studies, 1988.

Siddiq, Muhammed. "The Fiction of Sahar Kalifeh: Between Defiance and Deliverance." *Arab Studies Quarterly* 8, no. 2 (1987): 143–60.

Tamari, Salim. "The Transformation of Palestinian Society: Fragmentation and Occupation." Forthcoming.

Wallerstein, Emmanuel. "The Construction of Peoplehood." In Balibar and Wallenstein 1991.

White, Hayden. "The Value of Narrativity in the Representation of Reality." In *On Narrative*, edited by W. J. T. Mitchell, 1–23. Chicago: University of Chicago Press, 1981.

"Intersecting Marginalities"
The Problem of Homophobia in
South African Women's Writing

ROSEMARY JOLLY

In one of the very, very few studies of homosexuality and African literature, entitled, after Yulissa Maddy's play "'Wheyting be dat?': The Treatment of Homosexuality in African Literature," Chris Dunton examines a large variety of African texts, concluding that homosexuality in the African novel is usually "treated as an aspect of the degenerate transformation wrought on Africa through its contact with the West" (1989, 428). In this context, in which homosexuality is relegated to the status of a symptom of the effects of colonization, Dunton's choice of the word "treatment" appears particularly apt. He is extraordinarily careful, however, to avoid any consideration of the homophobia the texts exhibit as constituting a problem; nor does he question what it means to use homosexuality as a trope to illustrate the degradation suffered by Africans as a consequence of colonization. He explains:

> I am not concerned with the pejorative judgement that African writers apply to homosexuality as being a problem in itself. Rather, I am interested in showing how the treatment of homosexuality provides a convenient reference point—a closely defined narrative element—which helps reveal the general thematic concerns and the larger narrative strategy of the text. (422)

Dunton's article is revealing in its determination of its own limits: awareness of cultural relativity, and respect for African narratives of resistance to colonization, generate a silence on the part of Western critics to the problematic construction of the homosexual and lesbian in African literature.[1] That there is no shortage of examples to render this a significant field of investigation is not in question; possibly two of the best-known examples are those of Wole Soyinka's Joe Golder in *The Interpreters* and Ama Ata Aidoo's Marija in *Our Sister Killjoy*, but there are plenty of others. It is also significant to note that the awareness of cultural specificity that results in silence with respect to representations of homosexuality in African literatures has nevertheless resulted in numerous complex international debates about what might constitute an African woman's movement, and even about the desirability of such a movement.[2] That discussions of constructs of womanhood in African literatures abound, while those of the homosexual and lesbian remain unexamined, is a phenomenon that alone should render the silence that surrounds the topic suspect. We need to recognize that to refuse to discuss the issue of homosexuality or to limit ourselves to thematic discussions of the function of gender in contemporary African contexts—albeit on the grounds of limited cultural knowledge—carries its own risks.

One of these risks is evident in Dunton's piece. Dunton does, at the end of his article, comment on the silence that surrounds the topic of the African homosexual:

> the practice of homosexuality within African society remains an area of experience that has not been granted a history by African writers, but has been greeted, rather, with a sustained outburst of silence. Whether this has been carried out within or beyond the limits of the stereotype, the identification of homosexuality with the West has helped defend that silence. An "official" history has concealed the reluctance of African writers to admit homosexuality into the bounds of a different kind of discussion. (445)

Here, at last, Dunton appears to be commenting on the most striking characteristic of his topic, even if it is in the final paragraph, and even if he does attribute this silence, in a misleading gesture, only to African writers and not to Western critics. However, the brief comments he does make at the conclusion of his article on the limitations of the stereotype are severely compromised by his definition of "homosexual practice," which, because he takes it without question from the stereotypes of the texts he reads, is a thoroughly offensive one. This is his definition and its justification, which are relegated to a footnote:

> The term "homosexual practice" is used in this article to cover a range of sexual practices: male homosexuality, featured in the majority of texts under discussion, masturbation (*Blanket Boy's Moon*), pedophilia ("For Love of Therese," *Two Thousand Seasons*) and lesbianism (*Our Sister Killjoy*). *The distinctions between these practices would appear not to be relevant to the writers, and so to have little significance in discussing the ideology of these texts.* (445; emphasis added)

The non sequitur of the final sentence of the argument quoted here is a revealing one. What, one may ask, are the consequences of neglecting to examine the ideology behind describing pedophilia as a homosexual practice? How can such a move have "little significance in discussing the ideology of these texts"?

To put the question in the broader context of this discussion, how do we go about investigating the problematic intersections in postcolonial texts between narratives of liberation from racism and the constraints placed on those narratives by patriarchal constructions of gender? In the first place, we need to establish the groundwork for a discourse that is capable of articulating and evaluating the difficulties of working from a Western academic context on the construction of gender in cultures that have already been colonized. How can such a discourse avoid imposing on the texts it scrutinizes yet another paternalistic eye, this time with a view to pinpointing gender trouble as another point of colonial inferiority? Is the alternative tack to this one—that is, to accept Western responsibility for postcolonial gender trouble as another part of the legacy of colonization—any less paternalistic, or any more useful?

We can only begin to define a discourse that can deconstruct the rather futile parameters suggested by the extremes of either condemning Africa as atavistically homophobic or viewing homosexuality as the creation of the West—both equally colonialist attitudes in their own right[3]—by working on the relationship between colonial and gender oppression within very specific contexts, so that intersection between the two, in both critical and creative texts, is not divorced, arbitrarily, from its sites of cultural production.[4]

It is for this reason that I have chosen to formulate the problem I have outlined in the specific context of South African apartheid, and with particular reference to two South African women writers of different races, Nadine Gordimer and Bessie Head. For it seems to me that to overlook the problematic use of gender stereotyping in both texts is to deny a facet of both of those women writers: oppression. Such an approach results in a bifurcated reading of their works that, on the one hand, does recognize their narratives as triumphs against apartheid but, on the other, fails—or *refuses*—to acknowledge that the decolonization of the mind that is the goal of these texts does not extend to the realm of gender.[5] For both *Burger's Daughter* and *A Question of Power* exhibit strategies that, in the colonialist text, are used to "other" the racially different, but that Gordimer and Head use here to stigmatize the presence of alternative genders.

There is an incident described toward the close of the second part of Nadine Gordimer's *Burger's Daughter* that exemplifies what France represents for its heroine, Rosa Burger and, in doing so, also points unambiguously to the moral imperative of Gordimer's narrative—that is, Rosa Burger's return to South Africa and the priorities of "Peace. Land. Bread" (the ANC motto that prefaces the last part) and the 1976 schoolchildren's riots. The second part of the novel, Rosa's overseas odyssey, carries as weighty an epigram: Wang Yang-ming's "To know and not to act is not to know." What Rosa comes to know in this section of the novel, what Gordimer illustrates her heroine coming to terms with, is the decadence of the French community or, more specifically, its sanctioning of a life in which knowledge and action exist in a relationship of comfortable apartheid to one another.

The incident to which I refer is the one in which Rosa comes across a woman who suffers temporary dementia of some sort, and Rosa escorts her back to her house. Rosa describes the woman as "One of the old girls, the Lesbians or beauties from the nineteen thirties" (Gordimer 1980, 300). Rosa takes her back to her house, "away from the street that exposed through folds of blue nylon the dangle of dark nipples at the end of two flaps of skin" (301). Once inside, the woman recovers, recognizes Rosa as Arnys's friend, and carries on a conversation with her in a room filled with the mementos of a "free-range life; some of the things looked Peruvian, Mexican—American Indian." Rosa imagines herself relating the incident to Katya, her host in France, who is paradoxically both her surrogate mother and stepmother, as well as her emotional daughter:

> I wanted to go and she wanted to keep me with her in case the woman I had met in the street took possession of her again. I came flying up the hill to look for you singing while you upholster an old chair or paint a brave coat of red on your toenails. I wanted to ask you who she was and tell you what happened. But when I saw you Katya, I said nothing. It might happen to

you. When I am gone. Someday. When I am in Paris, or in Cameroun picking up things that take my fancy, the mementoes I shall acquire. (301)

The scene ends with Rosa reflecting upon Katya's—and her own—potential to inhabit, finally, the same body of the old beauty, the lesbian: a body she perceives to be incontinent, incapable of determining its own action. That the impotence of the woman's body is an infection to be resisted is clear: Rosa envisions Katya "catching the disease" and she herself, as yet another collector of mementos like the old woman, may yet fall prone to it. Of course, Rosa gives up the life of perpetual tourism that, it is implied, the French live even in their own country—for in Gordimer's France, the spectacular is an end in itself; desire for action does not exist.

Gordimer illustrates the desire for action and its fulfillment through Rosa's decision to return to South Africa to continue the work of dismantling apartheid. Yet in her portrayal of France as the decadent foil to Rosa's natural "home territory," Gordimer does employ that hallmark of *colonialist* thought—the construction of an action as a moral imperative through its opposition to a con-fusion of a number of distinct cultural practices that are viewed negatively by the auctorial voice. Thus age, lesbianism, and homosexuality are linked together in *Burger's Daughter* by adjectives that suggest incompetence, incontinence, and impotence—a satellite of cultural phenomena that render France decadent and its inhabitants politically impotent in Nadine Gordimer's terms. Rosa arrives in France to see Katya "among the elegant homosexuals with bodies of twenty-year-olds and faces like statues of which only the head remains of the ancient original" (214); the "young homosexuals" who inhabit Arnys's bar are described as desexualized, as being her family— "affectionate, bored and dependent" (248). Georges, Manolis' partner, has "a presence sure of its androgynous vitality" (256); and we leave France with Rosa, the fear of becoming that old beauty, that discarded Lesbian, burned into our memories as a caveat against obsolescence.

That a South African writer would produce homosexuality and lesbianism as con-fused—and thus misidentified—figures of androgyny, desexualization, disengenderment,[6] infantilization, and senility, and, in doing so, reproduce them as figures of political impotence is not surprising: South Africa's peculiar social history is one characterized in the case of all its population groups by entrenched homophobia and a pervasive sexism and heterosexism that ensures that intersections between political, public space and private, domestic space are determined by a patriarchy that en-genders the activity in each of those spheres according to its own notion of propriety. It makes sense that, in this restrictive context, the differences between any body perceived as "deviant"—as androgynous, homosexual, senile, and so on—is, as a matter of course, collapsed. What is more disturbing, but not surprising, is the extensive silence critics have maintained on what can be described as the predominance of antiliberationist constructions of gender in narratives of racial liberation from South Africa.

One of the ways of reading the displacement of racial trouble into gender trouble in Gordimer and Head is as a testimony to the pervasiveness of binary oppositions in the construction of South African identity—black/while, heterosexual/deviant, and so on. In this case, the novels can be read as symptoms of the very type of systemic oppression that they have partially succeeded in exposing. Such a reading has the advantage of refusing to deny the effects of patriarchal oppression on its subjects—in this case, on Gordimer and Head themselves. The international context of postcolonial criticism, however, renders heavily suspect any analogous "excuse" on its part to account for its willingness to identify the bigotry of racial essentialism while *at the same time* systematically ignoring that of patriarchy. If patriarchal postcolonialism should be a theoretical impossibility, it is, nevertheless, pragmatically speaking, a reality.

While critics and reviewers have questioned Gordimer's careful refusal to discuss *Burger's Daughter* in feminist terms, they have ignored the link between homosexuality and moral apathy prevalent throughout its French interlude.[7] In the case of *A Question of Power*, the novel to which I want to turn my attention now, Nancy Topping Bazin has been acute in pointing out the failure of earlier critics even to mention the connection Head draws between racist and sexist elements of oppression (Bazin 1985, 187). Bazin's own work, however, fails to address the obvious homophobia in the nightmare sequences of the novel, seeming to accept, once again, that the use of negative images of homosexuality to illustrate the consequences of racist and sexist oppression is unproblematic. The limit of such criticism is its inability to admit the complexity and multivalency of oppressions suffered under apartheid.

The theoretical project of identifying and thereby revealing the binary oppositions of imperialist ideology without revealing their impact on other kinds of oppression has its creative counterpart: writers who deploy the negative attributes of the Manichaean opposition by projecting them onto an-Other body whose demarcating characteristic is its engenderment as an alternative other to the other who has always been—

but should no longer be—defined in terms of heterosexual black and white.[8] Thus the gendered body, perceived from the patriarchal perspective as female due to its impotence, homosexuality, lesbianism, cross-dressing, senility, or indeed—and this is Bessie Head's most pertinent observation—its very inability to be black or white, replaces the black body as the sign of the other.

In this configuration the goal of the narrative is to identify the black body as the site of moral, psychological and social integrity in opposition to the imperialist conceptions of it fostered under apartheid. However, this replacement takes place within a cultural context that is profoundly sexist and homophobic on both sides of the color bar, so that the project of liberating the body from racist essentialism is undertaken in language that is not itself yet liberated from domination by the concept that any gender other than that dictated by the patriarchal norm of masculinity is at best an impudent mimic of that norm, and at worst, an impotent one. The black body to be liberated by writers of whatever color in the anti-apartheid project is thus constructed in a language that employs the patriarchal ideal of the male, heterosexual body as its ideal.

How then does one approach a text such as Bessie Head's *A Question of Power* in a way that takes advantage of her remarkable achievement in portraying the devastating effects of the relationship between racism and sexism, without patronizing it by ignoring the genealogy of homosexuality that forms such a prominent characteristic of Elizabeth's, her protagonist's, nightmare world? The critique I want to begin here is one that hopes to do justice to the extraordinary vision of Bessie Head without condemning her work as useless due to the homophobia it represents; that is, I want to take advantage of the opportunity the novel presents to explore the power that the habit of exclusionary thought commands even in the narrative of a writer who is desperately anxious to recognize that power and its destructive effects.

Bessie Head's narrator, Elizabeth, confounds and is confounded by apartheid categories of racial distinction. Her color, the one that falls in between those of apartheid's binaries, leads her to express the anguish of her alienation in metaphors that stigmatize figures that defy patriarchal sexual classifications, figures that she views simultaneously as both the product of and as evil as racial oppression itself. Thus Elizabeth's view of homosexuality conforms to that described by Dunton as the norm in African literature: it is a symptom of colonization and is to be rejected absolutely, along with colonialist practice itself. In this scheme, apartheid is portrayed as responsible for the emasculation of African men, and homosexuality—itself identified simplistically with transvestism,

cross-dressing, and so on—is con-fused with dirt, child molestation, incest, and bestiality to form a new other onto which Head's narrator
projects the evils of apartheid. Note also that while the "African man"
experiences his infantilization as indignity, he visits that same indignity
upon his female companion:

> In South Africa she had been rigidly classified Coloured. . . .
> They were races, not people. . . . She had lived for a time in a
> part of South Africa where nearly all the Coloured men were
> homosexuals and openly paraded down the street dressed in
> women's clothes. They tied turbans round their heads, wore lip-
> stick, fluttered their eyes and hands and talked in high, falsetto
> voices. It was so widespread, so common to so many men in
> this town that they felt no shame at all. They and people in gen-
> eral accepted it as a disease one had to live with. . . .
> An African man gave her the most reasonable explanation:
> "How can a man be a man when he is called a boy? I can barely
> retain my own manhood. I was walking down the road the other
> day with *my girl*, and the Boer policeman said to me: 'Hey, boy,
> where's your pass?' Am I a man to my girl or a boy? Another
> man addresses me as boy. How do you think I feel?["] (Head
> 1974, 45; emphasis added)

There is a telling difference, however, between Bessie Head's representation of homosexuality and that of Nadine Gordimer, in that
Elizabeth's identification with the homosexuals she describes prevents
the absolute and suspect division between the self and other that characterizes *Burger's Daughter.* The narrator makes use of this absolute division to define Rosa as politically virile in opposition to the homosexual
or impotent other. Rather, Elizabeth feels contaminated by her recognition of her affinity with the disempowered homosexuals of her nightmares, an affinity that she sees as a direct consequence of her double
oppression as black but also as not black "enough," as it were. As a
"coloured" who falls between the commanding binaries of South Africa's
racial classification system, she empathizes, reluctantly, with those whom
she perceives to have fallen between heterosexist classifications—the
homosexuals:

> As she closed her eyes all these Coloured men lay down on
> their backs, their penes in the air, and began to die slowly. . . .
> It seemed impossible then, the recurring, monotonous song

in her head: "Dog, filth, the Africans will eat you to death. . . ."
It broke her instantly. She could not help but identify with the
weak, homosexual Coloured men who were dying before her
eyes.

The narrator's obsession with clearly homophobic commentary may
at first appear to have little to offer the reader by way of explaining that
obsession. However, further examination of the image of the colored
homosexual as an other in which Elizabeth recognizes, extremely un-
willingly, herself, can shed light on the multiple facets of Elizabeth's
oppression and, consequently, the complexity of the liberation required
to dispel that oppression. The image of the colored homosexual confounds simultaneously apartheid's racial and sexual classification systems and, in so doing, reflects not only Elizabeth's "in-between" color
but also her experience of sexual impotency in the face of the grotesque
figures of sexual incontinence, both heterosexual and homosexual, that
inhabit her nightmares. These figures are torturous to her because they
continually confront her with both the necessity and the impossibility
of attaining an integrated identity under apartheid: she can only envision herself within its language, but its language cannot envision her as
colored and as woman—as human. In its language she can only be an
imperfect white and/or an imperfect black with respect to her color and
an imperfect man with respect to her gender.

Critics have been quick to point out the prevalence in Elizabeth's
nightmares of figures of racial and sexual domination. Roger Berger, for
example, explains Elizabeth's tormentors as the projections of a Fanonian
psychopathology; Elizabeth is wrestling with the fantasy of white superiority impressed upon her by her socialization under apartheid, including the myths of the demonism and sexual excesses of the black body
that fantasy exhibits (Berger 1990, 38). Joyce Johnson, on the other hand,
concentrates on the male character of the colonial fantasy, in which the
womb comes to symbolize, as Erich Neumann describes it, the "opening of the vessel of doom" whose "sucking power is mythologically symbolized by its lure and attraction for man . . . and [for] the individual
male who can evade it only if he is a hero, and even then not always"
(Johnson 1985, 171). Yet these critiques are typical in that they explain
the function of the figure of the homosexual within a discourse in which
either racial oppression, as in the case of Berger, or sexual oppression, as
in the case of Johnson, is presented as the master discourse in a hierarchy of violation. It is no wonder that this inability to perceive a number
of oppressions at work simultaneously, and not always in sympathy with

one another, results in failure to recognize the problem of putting the stigmatized figure of the homosexual to work in the service of narratives of racial or sexual liberation.

Bessie Head's stigmatization of the homosexual is clearly one which depends upon the false identification of the evils of *apartheid* with homosexuality itself. Supporting this rhetoric is the notion that homosexuality entered Africa only with the arrival of its colonizers. Such rhetoric—which mirrors that of colonialist discourse in its anxiety about contamination—and the image that it presents of homosexuals as symptoms of colonization to be targeted for extermination as part and parcel of apartheid life itself, manifests the very legacy of colonialist thought that the rhetoric itself attempts to eliminate, namely, the projection onto yet another body—the homosexual body—of the evils white fantasy projects onto the black body.

I want to make two suggestions at the close of this piece, both of which I hope will steer me away from the practice of con-fusing a series of practices into a new and disguised, yet equally pernicious other to take the place of the stigmatized body of the text—be it black, female, and/or homosexual. Firstly, I want to point out that, although Head's stated target is the evils of South African race classification rather than South African sexism—this to the extent that Lewis Nkosi has accused her of having the "profoundest conviction" of the "insignificance of sex" (1981, 102)—her choice of the figure of the colored or black homosexual does perform a covert critique of sexist classifications, and thus of the kind of thought that produces those classifications. Thus while Head's portrayal of the homosexual represents an example of the prevalence and offensiveness of the false identifications of bigoted habits of thought, it also at the same time comprises a critique, albeit a subconscious one, of the divorce between issues of racial and gender oppression that constitutes the fault line of contemporary discourses of Southern African liberation.

Finally, I suggest that in the two examples Gordimer and Head provide, and especially in the more complex work of the latter author, lies a warning to critics and teachers working on problems of racism, sexism, and homophobia in the context of postcoloniality. The fictions of Gordimer and Head constitute examples of the danger of collapsing a number of discrete practices into a single, new other to replace a now discredited construct of the other. If criticism is to avoid the reflexive property of a schizophrenic imagination that is addicted to the random embodiment of otherness—if we are to avoid constructing a new other to replace the discarded ones of the black, female, and homosexual bodies—

we need to resist collapsing those bodies into the body of criticism under the single metaphor of the colonized or the marginalized. Colonization, patriarchy, and homophobia cannot be properly comprehended by a language in which colonization is resurrected as the master narrative through its functioning as a metaphor for a number of other oppressions. Likewise, we should not be presenting postcolonialism to our students as the solution to a number of complex and conflicting marginalities. Rather, both as scholars and as teachers, we need to consider a variety of oppressions as discrete practices that intersect with one another in ways as complex and as compromised as they do in *Burgher's Daughter* and *A Question of* Power. We need to work against the ideal of mastery that has for so long been held up as the model of the critic-pedagogue; because for the postcolonial critic to claim mastery is for her or him to relinquish the most basic teaching her/his subject has to offer.

Let me rephrase my concern from the perspective of the institutionalization of post-colonial studies. The temptation is for postcolonialism, fresh from its first successes in the academy, to develop the hubris of a discourse that believes in its own ability to comprehend all the modalities of what it perceives to be parallel rather than intersecting marginalities,[9] without realizing the limitations of its own master discourse—the colonizer/colonized dichotomy. Our critical language needs to be able to accommodate the complexity of its subjects and needs to be prepared to be compromised by them, in order to conceive and reconceive of their diversity.

Notes

1. I use the term "homosexual" to refer to both men and women in this chapter. The question of terminology itself reflects the cultural construction of gender that is the subject of my inquiry: I avoid the term "gay" precisely because its meaning is determined by a Western, if not North American, cultural context. Both Margaret Cruikshank and Michael Bronski reflect this in their common reference to the Stonewall riots in Greenwich Village, New York, which began on 27 June 1969, as the point that marks the transition from "homosexual" to "gay" (Cruikshank 1992, 3; Bronski 1984, 2).

2. For an overview of the complexities involved in conceiving of feminism as a liberation movement capable of pursuing its goals internationally, without ignoring questions of cultural difference, see Mohanty 1991.

3. These claims would in any case be difficult to make in view of recent research on homosexuality in a variety of specific African contexts. For example, Gill Shepherd's work on homosexuality in Mombasa suggests that homosexuality

existed as a practice in precolonial times and that the society is certainly not homophobic in the Western sense of the word: "There are well-established rules for fitting [homosexuals] into everyday life and nobody would dream of suggesting that their sexual choices had any effect on their work capabilities, reliability, or religious piety" (1987, 241).

4.   For an astute explication of the dangers of privileging the category of race over that of gender in critiques of African women's writing, see Andrade 1990. The tendency to see the struggles of "Third World" women as either an issue of gender oppression or one dictated by racism—but not both—can itself be identified as a symptom of a contemporary, albeit subtle, orientalism.

5.   I take this phrase from Ngugi wa Thiong'o's work on decolonization and extend it to include the project of liberation from gender oppression. I do so not to suggest that the issues of gender and colonial oppression be confused, but to indicate instead that the liberation of individual subjects is a complex process involving many aspects of subjectivity—race, class, gender—whose dictates, more often than not, come into conflict with one another, rather than form themselves into easy parallels.

6.   Indeed, Gordimer's novel provides an example of a discourse in which the distinction between sexuality (in the physiological sense) and gender (the cultural construct) is collapsed in order to support a heterosexist reading of what is required from the woman who intends to live a life in the service of the public, not the family. Rosa Burger, or rather, "Burger's daughter," is represented as male-engendered: the narrative has her relinquish her relationships with her surrogate mother and sexual partners (all male) in order for her to return to South Africa as politically "virile"—a condition that is the true inheritance of her (necessarily dead) father's role.

7.   See Roberts 1990 and Driver 1990. The latter critic is particularly acute in her reading of Gordimer's unwillingness to be perceived as a feminist writer.

8.   Postcolonial criticism, following in the footsteps of Fanon and Mannoni and producing, more recently, the work of Said on orientalism and Abdul JanMohamed on Manichaean allegory, traces as a colonialist phenomenon the projection onto the black, as the object of colonialism, of attributes perceived to be negative by the ruling white subject.

9.   This phrase is taken from the title of W. D. Ashcroft's essay on the ground shared by postcolonialism and feminism. I am using the term in the context of my exploration of the fault lines that run between postcolonialism, feminism, and alternative, antipatriarchal conceptions of gender.

References

Abrahams, Cecil, ed. *The Tragic Life of Bessie Head and Literature in Southern Africa*. Trenton, N.J.: Africa World Press, 1990.
Aidoo, Ama Ata. *Our Sister Killjoy*. London: Longman, 1977.

Andrade, Susan Z. "Rewriting History, Motherhood, and Rebellion: Naming an African Women's Literary Tradition." *Research in African Literatures* 21, no. 1 (1990): 91–110.

Ashcroft, W. D. "Intersecting Marginalities: Post-colonialism and Feminism." *Kunapipi* 11, no. 2 (1989): 32–35.

Bazin, Nancy Topping. "Weight of Custom, Signs of Change: Feminism in the Literature of African Women." *World Literature Written in English* 25, no. 2 (1985): 183–97.

Berger, Roger A. "The Politics of Madness in Bessie Head." In Abrahams 1990, 31–43.

Bronski, Michael. *Culture Clash: The Making of a Gay Sensibility*. Boston: South End Press, 1984.

Cruikshank, Margaret. *The Gay and Lesbian Liberation Movement*. New York: Routledge, 1992.

Driver, Dorothy. "Nadine Gordimer: The Politicisation of Women." In Smith 1990, 180–204.

Dunton, Chris. "'Wheyting be Dat?' The Treatment of Homosexuality in African Literature." *Research in African Literatures* 20, no. 3 (1989): 422–48.

Fanon, Frantz. *The Wretched of the Earth*. Translated by Constance Farrington. Preface by Jean-Paul Sartre. Harmondsworth: Penguin, 1967.

———. *Black Skin, White Masks*. Translated by Charles Lam Markmann. Foreword by Homi Bhabha. London and Sydney: Pluto, 1986.

Gordimer, Nadine. *Burger's Daughter*. Harmondsworth: Penguin, 1980.

Head, Bessie. *A Question of Power*. London: Heinemann, 1974.

JanMohamed, Abdul R. *Manichean Aesthetics: The Politics of Literature in Colonial Africa*. Amherst: University of Massachusetts Press, 1983.

———. "The Economy of Manichean Allegory: The Function of Racial Difference in Colonialist Literature." *Critical Inquiry* 12, no. 1 (1985): 59–87.

Johnson, Joyce. "Metaphor, Myth and Meaning in Bessie Head's *A Question of Power*." *World Literature Written in English* 25, no. 2 (1985): 198–211.

Mannoni, O. *Prospero and Caliban: The Psychology of Colonization*. Translated by Pamela Powesland. New York: Frederick A. Praeger, 1964.

Mohanty, Chandra. "Cartographies of Struggle: Third World Women and the Politics of Feminism." In *Third World Women and the Politics of Feminism*, edited by Mohanty, Russo and Torres. Bloomington and Indianapolis: Indiana University Press, 1991.

Neumann, Erich. *The Great Mother*. Translated by R. Manheim. Princeton: Princeton University Press, 1974.

Ngugi wa Thiong'o. *Decolonising the Mind: The Politics of Language in African Literature*. London: James Currey, 1986.

Nkosi, Lewis. *Tasks and Masks: Themes and Styles of African Literature*. Harlow: Longman, 1981.

Roberts, Sheila. "Nadine Gordimer's 'Family of Women.'" In Smith 1990, 167–79.

Said, Edward. *Orientalism*. Harmondsworth: Penguin, 1978.
Shepherd, Gill. "Rank, Gender, and Homosexuality: Mombasa as a Key to Understanding Sexual Options." In *The Cultural Construction of Sexuality*, edited by Pat Caplan, 240–70. London and New York: Tavistock, 1987.
Smith, Rowland, ed. *Critical Essays on Nadine Gordimer*. Boston: G. K. Hall, 1990.
Soyinka, Wole. *The Interpreters*. London: Fontana/Collins, 1972.

Against Extinction
The Native American and
Indo-Hispanic Literary Discourse

BERNICE ZAMORA

I

> The earth and planets
> spinning mindlessly
> the universe
> smug in its entirety
> and you there—alone—

> . . . your existence
> primed to life
> a century ago
> and now
> exhausted in despair

> a wooden statue
> creaking
> ready to join the elements
> in silent prayer
> —Maria Herrera-Sobek, "The Last Affront"

> Nature is a haunted house.
> —Emily Dickinson

The arrangement of owning property as a means of security reflects insecurity of a criminal kind. The parallel of owning property and criminality is entirely symbolic to Native American and Indo-Hispanic authors I will consider here and is as powerful a notion as that of owning women as property. The poetic symbol for the world as ever-creative, powerful, and productive is the solid and certain Mother Earth; and Mother Earth to these writers is the activating symbol for a sleeping spirit, a living being. The physical representatives of Mother Earth, mothers, determine not only one's identity but one's place in the universe. The spirit of one's mother, like Mother Earth, is no longer sleeping. Today, such symbolic usages are analogous to matters of fact consecrated by allegiance to spaces central to life. Trenchant Native American and Indo-Hispanic writers search their dispirited communities and render unfiltered accounts of a despoiled America where inhabitants and life are thwarted. Beneath the intensity of the writers' accounts are a silent lamentation for women and for the grotesque transformations nature takes, caused, these communities believe, by the deformation of women's role as directive rulers of things earthbound. As life bearers, women require nontoxic environs for bringing forth structured life. Such areas are dimly remembered by the urban writers of these communities. Native American and Indo-Hispanic urban and reservation writers, in aggregate, give a full literary groan at the unaffected blindness that fails to see that native women rulers would never poison the people or the people's land. Nor would they have the arrogance to claim ownership to the land, although stewardship of the land is considered essential to secure life.[1]

Indo-Hispanic symbolic usage intersects with Native American usage and differs only slightly in meaning. I will discuss the point at which they intersect in order to connect disparate views and relationships to an Earth symbolized, since ancient times in the Western Hemisphere, as a feminine symbol. Cultural affinities between Native Americans and Indo-Hispanics are activated by two major factors. First, they share a common emotional sociology driven by historical displacement and by seizings of land, language, and spirit. Second, they find staggering the apathy toward Woman—forced literally by powerful, mostly violent opposition to Woman as center of the Earth. These two factors establish my point of departure and contrast with research heretofore undertaken in these, the parent and the offspring cultural literatures.

Intimidations, actual imprisonment, slavery, murder, and death by disease head an extravagant list of the types of chaos caused by the really first revolution on the American continent. Merciless fifteenth-century Europeans assured the vanishing of a relatively happy way of life for tribal people and for their careful preservation of the Earth and for Womanhood, or Unci, "The Grandmother's Way"—a way of life in which inhabitants are free and acknowledge that daughter and mother form the future. In the subsequent five hundred years, as history relates, a violent state of cruelty prevailed and the European separation of woman from the established social and Christian institutions ensued. European greed and unscrupulous social ambitions forced tribes to the misery of anarchy with its subhuman states unmatched in the Western Hemisphere's written and oral histories. The mid-nineteenth-century stuffing and mounting of Julia Pastrana, a Mexican tribal woman, for American and European circus exhibits[2] is one example; the sterilization of whole tribes of women and the disposal of tribal children are others.[3]

Each tribe faced their respective difficulties and, as is also well known, related these experiences in oral written testimonies. The science of tribal symbolic arts, practical and spiritual, coordinated with tribal instruction for control of personal survival strategies are reflected in the Native American and extended to the Indo-Hispanic written literatures today. There are traceable literary strategies, for example, that transform oral performance to transcribed written expression in the works of both cultures. It is not surprising considering the moral standard of paternalism, that in the literature, patriarchy is notably ineffective as the embodiment of intelligence and, in fact, is a polar opposite of natural harmony. Themes of external experiences include thievery, murder, homelessness—the standard designs of conquest. Themes of the internal experiences include the missing feminine principle—mother—as the hidden inspiration uniting tribal lore with spiritual wisdom.

Traditional lore foretells that the separation from female intelligence, its censure, and its opposition inhibit evolution. Tribal ancestors warned that intolerance of female authority disinherits man from his role in human exchange even with his own kind and of course from his own intellect. Traditional implications in contemporary tribal poetry, for instance, point toward a threefold loss of autonomy: material, mental, and spiritual. If maternal expression is removed as a voice of authority, reason, intuition, and memory are removed. Artistic illusions, too, flank the denouncers of women and endanger the sons of denouncers for numbered generations. The soul and spirit of such sons endanger each other. Anarchists, to be sure, fall into this threefold ruin. Certainly, similar traditions with additional meanings overlap from tribe to tribe in North and South America. The focus of the literary messages is on disastrous physical loss, intellectual dishonor, or the spiritual stalemate caused by slander of women. Understandably, tribal symbols, stylized to parallel, to redefine, or to renovate Christian symbols, limit the full interpretation of tribal symbols as they relate to feminine principles. Such use suggests a mentality successful in surmounting the violent obstacles to the practice of personal religions and, by historical extension, in the spiritual interpretations of Native American and Indo-Hispanic literatures. Impassioned lyrics, for example, echo the satisfaction of having one's own maternal representation such as Buffalo Calf Woman, Spider Grandmother, or Omecihuatl, whereas Europeans depict women as timid, unimportant, or trivial. The poetic language men use to conceal woman's representation as Earth conceals the message of men's responsibility to the land and its waters and to the skill in directing their authorities. Such a man desires to conceal his crime. Native American men and male Indo-Hispanic tribal members understand that the spirit of an abandoned woman frightens the waters and causes them to withdraw their curative and growing powers; and the earth's fruit becomes as bitter as the soul soured by the absence of Mother.

The warm Mother Earth, as we all know, is capable of awesome violence. Her tribal protectors, the rhythmic presence of spirits challengingly breathing directive songs in the cadences of nature's movements, are patient servants even in this era of anarchy. The obscured rule of conduct for living *with* women on this Earth is overwhelmingly the same as living *on* Earth. If women are absent or separated from the administration of things earthbound, then, in concentrated occurrences natural disasters are the most practical reminders of this disastrous lapse. In the minds of tribal men and women, these events are interpreted as a cleansing of the waters. They are a reminder that excessive imbalancing of the earth's resources requires severity of terrestrial adjustment. Inherent in North and South American tribal prophecies are the warnings of impending loss of water and water life, violent weather shifts, insect swarms, and other such events. A visible presence of mothers, ranked anew and honored for their work and intelligence, is necessary, or more serious revolutions can occur.[4] Tribal people note that marked ownership of property (land) or person (woman or slave) create natural disturbances that reflect in essence the violence and destruction. Property ownership distracts human attention from woman's role in the natural balancing of forces. In tribal reasoning, a world equilibrium is reflected in the personified "pairing" of feminine forces with masculine forces and is considered the natural image of stability. This is a rational view of events with feminine authority intact. Opposition to feminine connections of authority is understood by Native Americans and Indo-Hispanics as opposition to such social concepts as democratic systems of justice, education, and so on. Ample evidence points to today's excesses. Exploitation of natural resources and female labor and other injustices are mirrored in natural catastrophes: curious volcanic eruptions in areas thought dormant, earthquakes, tornados, etc. One piece of evidence is worthy of special claim: insensitivity to fellow beings, vices, and social corruptions are recognized by tribal people as the creations of ruling religious and secular organizations. Tribes rejected such excesses, described in the main as material success, and regarded lust for power and property as evil.

In the tribal world, total perfection of the spiritual individual is embodied in the female. Human females represent a powerful and dramatic poetic symbol. Opulently displayed in the material world, she represents stinginess and dullness—qualities essential to complete descriptions of an all-encompassing, potential perfection. She is undependable and, of course, extravagant, the symbol of fear and the irrational, a person not yet at home in the world of human exchange. Understandably, tribal people—men and women—hesitated to embrace the irrational, new female model.

In direct contradiction, tribal women identify with the world's women with great hesitation. Subsequent to the slaughters of tribal women, men, children, and animals, and the poisoning of waters, wells, fields and relationships, nontribal women today elect to describe tribal women with a measure of frivolity. In describing Mountain Wolf Woman, a Winnebago Native American, Nancy Oestreich Lurie writes,

> Mountain Wolf Woman likes to refer to herself as an "old Winnebago lady." This is an accurate self-assessment because among the Winnebago age carries the connotations of wisdom and dignity. It also carries the privilege of speaking frankly on the basis of knowledge and understanding derived from observing the world for a long time. (Lurie 1966, xvi)

Mountain Wolf Woman's "self-assessment" actually represents much more. An "old Winnebago lady," indicates an elder, a woman of powerful authority, a woman free to take part in the ruling of her tribe. Lurie's shallower observation becomes an erroneous one in attributing wisdom and dignity to age and then degenerates, however well-meaning, to the condescending dominant bias of the "superior" feminine system:

> Considered very pretty in her youth, Mountain Wolf Woman's face still reflects the basic beauty and the deeper beauty of serene old age. Her dark, expressive face is attractively contrasted with her perfectly white hair, which is always combed straight back into a neat bun. Although she often dresses "like a white lady," she usually wears a style of clothing typical of Winnebago women of her age. (xvi–xvii)

This depiction is a very good example of how remote the editor is from the knowledge of her subject. She describes Mountain Wolf Woman as if the choice of dress was just a matter of changing one's mind, as if the change of dress were a love of the frivolous, or game playing for coquettish purposes. In fact, at one point, the editor says Mountain Wolf Woman "frequently engaged in outrageous coquetry appropriate to their relationship," referring to Mountain Wolf Woman's relationship to the editor's husband. The tyranny from which Mountain Wolf Woman emerged and the horror of the extreme reversal of her role are completely overlooked. Instead, we are given a description of a woman competing for the affections of the editor's (presumably young) husband. Delusion follows delusion, which is graphic, to be sure, and fundamentally false in this work about a tribal elder. Arguably, the editor is a sensitive woman. But in an atmosphere of coerced compromise, Mountain Wolf Woman appears to tribal people as a tribal elder.[5] There are maddening silences in her narrative, silences that are familiar and that often accompany compromise. The narrative is absorbed in physical matters. The spiritual teachings of the Winnebago are noticeably missing in Mountain Wolf Woman's narrative, which speaks well of a tribal elder who guards even allusions to the spiritual. Certainly, one might suggest that Mountain Wolf Woman was herself a strict materialist. While the editor went to great lengths to prove their distinct realities and class identities—transcribing verbatim phonetic spellings of English words, for example—the narrative reflects a sharp conflict, the kind of mental discipline most tribal members sustain when in conversation primarily with a male or governmental authority. Since the editor interviewed Mountain Wolf Woman with a tape recorder, often in the presence of her husband, one surmises that Mountain Wolf Woman viewed Lurie as an authority figure. Evidence of narrative restraint is contained in a footnote in which are notes of discrepancies in Mountain Wolf Woman's brother's separate version of a naming ceremony.[6] While Big Winnebago's account reveals much of the naming ritual, Mountain Wolf Woman merely calls it a "feast." Mountain Wolf Woman's version is accounted for by the fact that she "was no more than eight years old and probably younger when the incident occurred. . . ." (Lurie 1966, 119). To tribal people, her version clearly shows a good deal of tact and prudence. Mountain Wolf Woman would rather appear childlike than to surrender her knowledge to misinterpretation. The responses of Mountain Wolf Woman to academic scrutiny demonstrate an intelligence faithful to the sacred traditions by flattering the academic observer, a guarded collector of academic women's own self-expression.

II

> One day a story will arrive in your town. There will always be disagreement over direc-
> tion—whether the story came from the southwest or the southeast. The story may arrive
> with a stranger, a traveler thrown out of his home country months ago. Or the story
> may be brought by an old friend, perhaps the parrot trader. But after you hear the story,
> you and the others prepare by the new moon to rise up against the slave masters.
> —Leslie Marmon Silko, Almanac of the Dead

Solamente ochente días
gobernó: terminó el mes
de Quecholli en el cual
murió. Murió de calentura. . . .
    —Salvador Toscano,
    Cuauhtemoc

El viejo barbudo
Blanco y yaciente
Ahora descansa en la mente
De la vieja viuda gorda.
    —José Antonio Burciaga
    Restless Serpents

Lack of interest in the spiritual balance of life compromises life. Indo-
Hispanics resisted for a long time changing patterns of spiritual thinking and behavior. Working in harmony with Nature requires patience,
and cyclic life becomes an awkward lifestyle, largely subscribing to a
certain insensitivity to women's attainments and authority. Such a
lifestyle has a special horror for those in the Chicano community, too.
Indo-Hispanics with courage enough to become satiated with things of
the world of excesses, yet work to uphold the have/have not axis of
social regulation, move deliberately like Mountain Wolf Woman. Mea-
sured poetically, they pay tribute to the feminine principle in tribal ways.
Chicanos who condescend to write about the experience of what it is to
destroy and disgrace human life in war, for instance, distance themselves
from the abstract, unbrotherly pleasure derived from such contempt-
ible acts. Charley Trujillo's account of Vietnam War experiences ends
his narrative chapter called "Mutiny" with this scenario:

> We were told that we were going in again in the morning. [W]e
> told them that we refused to go in again. There wasn't any sense
> in it. It was clear by that evening that the majority of the soldiers
> did not want to go back in. A new company commander was
> brought in. He seemed like a sincere man and gave us a real
> good pep talk, just like those charismatic football coaches do.
> However, that didn't convince me or many of the other soldiers.[7]
> We argued among ourselves through the night, the majority
> being against going in. . . . In the morning a few individuals
> moved out, the rest of us were more or less morally obligated to

move with them. . . . One of the first ones to get shot was the
new CO (Company Officer). He died in the Medivac (Medical
Evacuation) helicopter. There were some other deaths and one
guy was even left behind. . . . And I kept walking . . . until I was
also wounded and medivaced. (Trujillo 1990, 157–58)

Trujillo's childhood companions from a small town in California where
he grew up were his companions in the guerilla unit in Vietnam, which,
in part, accounts for his difficulty in adapting to civilian life back home
after an immoral human and ecological slaughter. The confusion of wartime—and this is especially well known of the Vietnam War—is followed
or accompanied by the use of drink and drugs by soldiers. Killing people
with familiar, family-like faces polarized the Chicano spirit. Polarity of
the human spirit in the Indo-Hispanic warrior resulted, according to
these narratives, in a departure from the Church.

My mom and grandmother made a promise to the Virgin of
Guadalupe that they would make a trip to Mexico City if I came
back alive. I didn't even know about it and I wasn't ready to go.
I didn't even enjoy myself. My grandmother went from the front
of the cathedral to the altar on her knees. I myself couldn't see
it, I guess, because I don't believe in things like that. At that
time, I wasn't old enough to vote yet, but I was old enough to
die for my country. So up to this day, I don't vote. I can't see it.
(165)

Emotional debilitation and other insanities compete with wealth and
success as the polarity of powerlessness in Native American and Indo-
Hispanic cultures' belief systems. Trujillo's war narratives of cruelty and
mindless malice demonstrate one way that powerful spiritual tradition
is reversed: "I ran up and began shooting at the dead Vietnamese in the
holes just as I had seen in the Hollywood movies" (156).

III

The contemporary literary methods used by female academics present
a substantial obstacle to those seeking access to Native American and
Indo-Hispanic literary discourse. In using contemporary literary meth-
odologies, analysts betray the cultural intuition that created the literary
works in the first place. Literary assessments to date are frustrating works

from which to extract information, because one is referring to a false document or else one is reduced to describing the void of separatist academic patterns of past and current scholarship. In either case, a hostile malleability is the order for the study of these and other literary ethnic works. The fundamental strength of this new literary tradition smacks of quarrelsome possibilities sustaining separatist practices of literary analyses. The additional implications of feminine poetic imagination and intelligence virtually guarantee devaluation of Native American and Indo-Hispanic literatures.

Native American and Indo-Hispanic literary undertakings—creative and critical—synthesize the masculine and feminine intellectual elements disguised as cognate subordination with standard interpretation. The past and current practices of established scholarship on feminine creativity justify this literary deceit. Message-bearing poetry, unfortunately, estranges the masculine from the feminine and from the synthesis of the two. The least complex divide the literary world into poles of knowing a fact, ambiguous or mysterious—exerted propositions not always befitting literary circumstance of these communities. Symbols, understandably, are the literary devices for deceit. Future research on these literary offerings promises surprising intelligent administration consistent with Native American and Indo-Hispanic forebears' intent. Freed from the inflexible, traditional literary techniques and ontological (racial) annihilation, the synthesis of Native American symbols of masculine representation (material passion) creates a wariness of things coercive (Earling 1990, 56–57). Such a synthesis renders violence an inadequate attribute for real and intellectual expression. Without the synthesis, the legacy for Indo-Hispanics' literary interpretation suffers subsequently from the mother figure representation separated from the father figure, and a discordant artistic effort results. The idea behind literary form and critical format in the struggle for Native American and Indo-Hispanic literary discourse is the conceptual need for a literary temperament that mixes opposite and unknown elements more readily without resorting to terms such as "magical realism." This serviceable reference succeeds intellectually, perhaps, but it dilutes the polarity to the restriction of baffled judgment or full error, distracting from the artistic point. The attempt to effect tribal representation to the physical world of magical realism does more to ruin Native American and Indo-Hispanic narrative interpretations. The reference "magical realism" is merely clever incoherence. Literary deceit, in the meantime, is the practical defense against ingenuousness. Trujillo's war narratives, traditional though they appear on the surface, characterize men of volatile anger, suicidal or neutralized (Dare

one say neutered?), but wholly unprepared to avenge the nation's en-
terprising tyranny in Vietnam or back home in the barrios and reservations. Literary interpretations of these war narratives, occasioned by a
heritage that recognized all life—plant, animal, and human—as sacred,
bedraggle the conscious Chicana and Chicano critic. Death's effect on
both the narrator's and critic's spirit is disquieting and difficult to reconcile once the boundaries of sacredness are ruptured. Victory itself becomes an enemy.

IV

> *She was the myth slipped down through dreamtime. The promise*
> *of feast we*
> *All knew was coming. The deer who crossed through knots of a*
> *curse to find*
> *us. She was no slouch, and neither were we, watching. . . .*
> *—Joy Harjo, "Deer Dancer"*

> *Sometime in the past the tree talked.*
> *All the elders do not know of it,*
> *But, yes, some wise ones spoke of it.*
> *When the world was becoming new here,*
> *There was one who could hear the sounds of the tree.*
> *The one who could hear it,*
> *That one told about it.*
> *They were old things from long ago,*
> *But only one could hear it.*
> *That talking stick was a long time ago.*
> *—From "U Kuta Nokame: The Talking Stick,"*
> *A Yaqui Story*

> *. . . he met her over there in the mountains*
> *and she was given to him.*
> *He was given ammunition over there.*
> *She was the one bullet he was given.*
> *Then somewhere in the wilderness he would*
> *meet up with fifty Mexican soldiers*
> *or more.*
> *He could fell them with that woman, with his*
> *single bullet.*
> *—Refugio Savala,* Autobiography of a Yaqui Poet

A creative perspective corroborates literary analysis in Native American and Indo-Hispanic literatures. Essentially traditional and double-edged in cultural aesthetics, Native American and Indo-Hispanic women authors are almost equally adept in creative literary works and in literary analysis. Their poetics, however, remains largely unknown to the world in concordance with tribal or cultural poetics. There are many reasons for this that ought to be adequately considered at some point in the future. For now, it is sufficient to note that while feminists are writing stories about the modern victorious woman, tribal and Indo-Hispanic women have ushered their works into the modern literary world with a certain reluctance. They tend to console the soul that has lived under siege and undergone horrors more atrocious than the Holocaust. Debra Earling's "Summer Humming 1946" is one tribal example:

> Loretta Two Teeth was found without blood
> Shot once in the chest close range
> In the hills above Polson.
> Summer was a hot voice that year
> A voice that lifted dry weeds to tumble
> To fences humming wire.
> And grass was humming too
> Humming over her as morning
> Pulled a dawn white sky to dust.
>
> Nattie Trout said that day
> You could hear something moving through grass
> The sound rocks make rubbing
> Red cheat to fire.
> Loretta Two Teeth quiet to sky.
> Death rattled weeds on its way to the river.
>
> Josephine Weaselhead was in Browning playing
> Stickgames. She said she saw Loretta
> Plain as day
> Three days after Loretta had died.
> . . . .
> Blood slept dry in the heat of women dying.
> A voice moved through dry weeds
> Humming the sound of women splitting wood.
>   Women spitting blood

Humming summer wind through grass.
Grandmothers you thought were dead
Hide behind trees
Knowing death
Sleeps close to rivers
The wet lips of lovers.
Fists cleanse the bones of women's ribs.
Loretta Two Teeth left the sound of breath
To Magpies.
Death is the hum of summer wind.
Death is the rattle in the weeds.
It is summer humming.

(Earling 1990, 56–57)

Such poetry of the homeland carries the suggestion that something else is to follow, for there is some reluctance to make use of Death as a symbol of conclusion. The finely modulated humming of summer is here a declaration of one tribal principle of life (and art): One violated woman violates the earth; tribes of violated women desolate the landscape, presaged in tribal prophecies in North, Central, and South America. A combination of destructive acts against tribal people is a "tragedy so tender it sticks in the throat under an indifferent enfoldment."[8] Tribal prophecies converge on one solution to the destruction: That the feminine and the female's child—male and female—be restored to the circle of sacredness for future life in the new millennium (the Sixth Sun).

The literary discourse of Native Americans and Indo-Hispanics in the Americas is not the leisurely inventing of moods, structure, or oracular exercises. Poetry serves as natural revelation to people who reside intimately in their own natural setting, as opposed to settlers, homesteaders, tourists, or linguistic anthropologists shaping human meaning in literature by distant observation. The best that can be obtained in contemporary literary discourse from tribal and Indo-Hispanic poets, for example, is a literary temperance where consolation is a matter of self-adjustment to repeated attempts at their cultural and physical extinction. Synthesizing individually and collectively the violent attempts against one's own life and one's community's with the struggle to survive is, until the attempts subside, the basis of tribal and Indo-Hispanic literary discourse. Here is one contemporary example:

FOR ANNA MAE PICTOU AQUASH,
WHOSE SPIRIT IS PRESENT HERE AND IN THE DAPPLED STARS

(FOR WE REMEMBER THE STORY
AND MUST TELL IT AGAIN SO WE MAY ALL LIVE)

Beneath a sky blurred with mist and wind,
                  I am amazed as I watch the violet
heads of crocuses erupt from the stiff earth
            after dying for a season, as I have
watched my own dark head
                appear each morning after entering
the next world
          to come back to this one,
              amazed.
It is the way in the natural world to understand the place
            the ghost dancers named
after the heart/breaking destruction.
          Anna Mae,
             everything and nothing changes.
You are the shimmering young woman
          who found her voice,
when you were warned to be silent, or have your body cut away
from you like an elegant weed.
       You are the one whose spirit is present
         in the dappled stars.
(They prance and lope like colored horses who stay with us
       through the streets of these steely cities. And
       I have seen them
        nuzzling the frozen bodies of tattered drunks
         on the corner.)
This morning when the last star is dimming
         and buses grind toward
the middle of the city, I know it is ten years since they
      buried you
    the second time in Lakota, a language that could
         free you.
I heard about it in Oklahoma, or New Mexico,
      how the wind howled and pulled everything down
in a righteous anger.
      (It was the women who told me) and we understood
      wordlessly
the ripe meaning of your murder.
    As I understand ten years later after the slow changing

                              of the seasons
        that we have just begun to touch
            the dazzling whirlwind of our anger,
        we have just begun to perceive the amazed world the ghost
            dancers
            entered
                      crazily, beautifully.

        In February 1976, an unidentified body of a young woman was
        found on the Pine Ridge Reservation in South Dakota. The offi-
        cial autopsy attributed death to exposure. The FBI agent present
        at the autopsy ordered her hands severed and sent to Washing-
        ton for fingerprinting. John Trudell rightly called this mutila-
        tion an act of war. Her unnamed body was buried. When Anna
        Mae Aquash, a young Micmac woman who was an active Ameri-
        can Indian Movement member, was discovered missing by her
        friends and relatives, a second autopsy was demanded. It was
        then discovered she had been killed by a bullet fired at close
        range to the back of her head. Her killer or killers have yet to be
        identified. (Harjo 1990, 6)

    For tribal and Indo-Hispanic people, the masculine symbol as the
    uniting principle between micro and macro worlds is the symbol of
    Death. When Death is the symbol of victory over one's enemy, Indo-
    Hispanic wisdom fancies a dance with the symbol of victory, thus secur-
    ing fancy and dance as symbolic ploy to the fulfillment of tribal prophecy:
    ruin to the "victor." The dance is necessary to disentangle the native
    good from the invaders' evils. The lavish and extravagant tradition of
    food and drink that surrounds the celebratory dance of the Mexican and
    Chicano holiday, The Day of the Dead, represents the trappings of ma-
    terial well-being. It could be said that the traditional ceremonies of
    The Day of the Dead are a check to masculine ambitions. Symbolic cel-
    ebration today includes song, dance, and social arts—a full symbolic
    encompassing of a workable alternative to the life the heirs of Adam in
    paradise proclaim for this world. Male rule governs death and is repre-
    sented by that symbol in Native American and Indo-Hispanic literary
    discourse. Symbolic death is recognized and respected as Divine Anar-
    chy, violent death, Man on the Cross, hanged, betrayed, sacrificed:

        If our art is not beautiful to your eyes, it was never meant to be.
        It is practical, it is educational. After all, what is art? What is

beauty? Is a painting of the Crucifixion by Rembrandt, El Greco or Grünewald such a beautiful sight? A man nailed, bleeding and hanging from a Cross? . . . Thing is . . . that this is my country. My forefathers were not the pilgrims as I was taught in school but the Zapotecas and the Españoles, the Mestizos. Who are these poets? They are the Browns and Blacks that never melted in your pot. . . . Who are these poets? (Burciaga 1976, 63–64)

Scholarly application of these two bodies of literature—past, present, and, one presumes, in the future as well—includes the historical categories of degradation of women and the destruction of the earth synthesized. Hence, the reluctance to use Death as a symbol of closure to poetry is a reluctance to follow the design of licentious acts of war against the texture of women's lives and against the balance of terrestrial kinship with other life. Viewing life through a glass darkly, through punch bowls, or through a gun's sight scope is depression revisited. Native American and Indo-Hispanic poets would likely agree with the poet Les Murray: "Let depression / find itself a new game" (Murray 1994).

Notes

1. Vine Deloria, commenting on Article III of the Pickering Treaty, which claims the right to purchase Seneca lands, says "Hucksterism and land theft have gone hand in hand in American history" (198830). The term *stewardship*, according to him, is not the stewardship of an individual; it refers to the tribal community sharing the responsibility and benefits of the land.

2. Wendy Rose's poem "Julia" recounts the grim circumstances of the lives and deaths of Julia Pastrana and her son. Her circus husband/manager had them both stuffed and mounted. In another of Rose's poems, "Truganinny," an Australian aborigine shared this same fate, as did her husband. Even though Truganinny, the last of the Tasmanians, requested to be buried in order to avoid the indignity placed upon her husband, she was embalmed after her death and put on display for over eighty years (Rose 1985, 69–71, 56).

3. Sterilization was only one of many methods advanced by government agencies following the 1954 Congressional "policy of termination." Deloria said of this policy that it was "a continuation of the old systematic hunt and deprivation of services. Yet this policy was not conceived of as a policy of murder. Rather it was thought that it would provide that elusive 'answer' to the Indian problem" (Deloria 1988, 54–55).

4. See Paula Gunn Allen's *Spider Woman's Granddaughters*, Olivia Castellano's *Blue Horse of Madness*, Rosario Castellanos's *Another Way to Be*, Anita Endrezze's

at the helm of twilight, John G. Neihardt's *Black Elk Speaks*, Leslie M. Silko's *Almanac of the Dead*, Stan Steiner's *Vanishing White Man*, Brian Swann's and Arnold Krupat's *I Tell You Now*, Dennis Tedlock's translation of *Popol Vuh*, William Willoya's and Vinson Brown's *Warriors of the Rainbow*, and Dhyani Ywahoo's *Voices of Our Ancestors*.

    5. Ruth Underhill, in her foreword to Lurie's work, notes, "The story was recorded on tape, exactly as it flowed from the informant's lips. Mountain Wolf Woman does not describe scenes nor explain relationships and customs. She expects these to be understood as they would be by an Indian audience" (Lurie 1966, ix).

    6. Underhill strongly suggests that Big Thunder's reminiscences were vocalized under the influence of peyote.

    7. Trujillo's company of infantry men was comprised mostly of Chicanos and African Americans.

    8. My translated excerpt is from "Sol Invernal," by César A. Gonzales. It is an elegiac poem that refers to the death of a little girl. See Armas et al. 1977, 71.

References

Allen, Paula Gunn. *Spider Woman's Granddaughters*. New York: Random House, 1989.

Armas, José, et al., eds. *Flor y Canto IV and V*. Albuquerque, N.M.: Pajarito, 1977.

Burciaga, José Antonio. *Restless Serpents*. Menlo Park, Calif.: Diseños, 1976.

Castellano, Olivia. *Blue Horse of Madness*. Sacramento, Calif.: Crystal Clear Printers, 1987.

Castellanos, Rosario. *Another Way to Be*. Translated by Myralyn F. Allgood. Athens, Georgia: University of Georgia Press, 1990.

Deloria, Vine. *Custer Died For Your Sins*. Norman: University of Oklahoma Press, 1988.

Earling, Debra Cecille. "Summer Humming, 1946." In Lerner 1990, 56–57.

Endrezze, Anita. *at the helm of twilight*. Seattle Wash.: Broken Moon Press, 1992.

Harjo, Joy. *Mad Love and War*. Middletown, Conn.: Wesleyan University Press, 1990.

Lerner, Andrea. *Dancing on the Rim of the World*. Tucson: University of Arizona Press, 1990.

Lurie, Nancy Oestreich. *Mountain Wolf Woman, Sister of Crashing Thunder: The Autobiography of a Winnebago Thunder*. Ann Arbor: University of Michigan Press, 1966).

Murray, Les. "The Bohemian Occupation." *Times Literary Supplement*, 8 July 1994.

Neihardt, John G. *Black Elk Speaks*. Lincoln: University of Nebraska Press, 1979.

Rose, Wendy. *The Halfbreed Chronicles and Other Poems*. Los Angeles: West End Press, 1985.

Silko, Leslie M. *Almanac of the Dead*. New York: Simon and Schuster, 1991.

Steiner, Stan. *The Vanishing White Man*. New York: Harper and Row, 1976.

Swann, Brian and Arnold Krupat. *I Tell You Now*. Lincoln: University of Nebraska Press, 1987.

Tedlock, Dennis, trans. *Popol Vuh*. New York: Simon and Schuster, 1985.

Trujillo, Charley. *Soldados: Narratives of the Viet Nam War*. San Jose, Calif.: Chusma House, 1990.

Willoya, William, and Vinson Brown. *Warriors of the Rainbow*. Happy Camp, Calif.: Naturegraph, 1990.

Ywahoo, Dhyani. *Voices of Our Ancestors*. Boston: Shambhala, 1987.

The Satire of Race in
James Weldon Johnson's
Autobiography of an Ex-Colored Man

GAYLE WALD

One of the effects of racial ideology in the United States has been to limit the ability of "minority" subjects to cross socially mandated and enforced lines of race. American literature and culture, especially in the twentieth century, is rife with examples of legally white subjects who have taken advantage of their privileged racial mobility to experiment with modes of racial signification as a means of political expression, personal exploration, cultural theft, or self-critique.[1] Yet such ludic or strategic border-crossing is far less available to subjects whose identities, conceived as inferior, deviant, or threatening to the norm, have historically been more stringently policed. As fetishizing legal constructs such as the "one-drop" rule attest in the case of African Americans, authority in racial naming has historically been conferred not only to visible, biological traces, but to invisible, genealogical traces of "black" blood. Such an "American grammar" of race (to borrow Hortense Spillers' useful term), while arbitrarily categorizing, nevertheless has profound, and sometimes lethal, implications.

Critical analyses of this dominant racial grammar have long demonstrated how it conceals the contradictory identities, historical impurities, and multiple instabilities that produce all subjectivities, not merely those that are typically designated as hybrid. These critiques range from Frantz Fanon's notion that formerly colonized subjects don compulsory disguises as a protective response to the distortions produced by racist representations and stereotypes, to Ralph Ellison's idea that cultural production, as well as everyday social relations between blacks and whites, is mediated through masks of authenticity and wholeness, to James Baldwin's description of his alienation, as a descendent of African slaves and therefore the bastard son of America, before the spectacle of European cultural monuments. Among feminist writers such investigations might include Spillers's analysis of the violence of racist representations of black women as Mammies, Sapphires, or the castrating heads of black households, Donna Haraway's blasphemous dream of a cyborg future, and Audre Lorde's portrait of herself as a black lesbian "Sister Outsider" who embodies shifting, and sometimes clashing, identities.[2]

Such works are justifiably celebrated as groundbreaking contributions to ongoing intellectual debates around the significance of race in African American experience and culture. Yet while contemporary scholars typically focus on nonfictional texts as the source of their critical vocabularies and theoretical paradigms, African American imaginative literature has often been engaged in a parallel exploration, albeit one that does not usually announce itself as "theory." In this essay, I focus on the literature of racial passing—narratives that represent a character's transgression of social, cultural, and legal constructs that mediate racial identities and assign relative value to these identities—as the particular site of one such inquiry in African American fiction. In particular, I seek to demonstrate, through the example of James Weldon Johnson's richly satirical *The Autobiography of an Ex-Colored Man* (1912), how the literature of racial passing engages black writers in a confrontation with the implications of racial hybridity for African Americans.

My interest in African American passing narratives in general and Johnson's text in particular lies in their ability to render narratable the salience of race in individual and collective identity-formation. Passing narratives such as the *Autobiography* not only dramatize race as a fundamental construct of all human identity in the United States; they also depict the processes by which the subject-who-passes comes to "reconcile" (to use W. E. B. Du Bois's term from *The Souls of Black Folk*) the contradictions inherent within the dominant system of racial naming. Usually centered on the experience of "mulatto" characters—subjects whose identities have historically been defined as innately, or biologically, hybridized—they illustrate how these subjects use racial passing as a strategy of bringing quintessentially "split" subjectivities to bear on dominant cultural narratives.[3] In imaginative response to the hegemonic process of racial naming, which imposes identity regardless of the mulatto subject's volition, self-interest or personal history, black-authored passing stories envision a crucial agency, a means (however conservative the ends to which it is sometimes put) by which the subject can name and rename the self. Through passing, the protagonists of these narratives claim a crucial right to cross lines of race, sex, and class in defiance of the laws, both implicit and explicit, that conspire to curb African American mobility. In the *Autobiography*, for example, Johnson imagines a process by which the Ex-Colored Man is first named, both by a paternal absence and in a traumatic scene of racial instruction, then subsequently turns the effects of this naming into a mode of cultural power.

Such an optimistic reading of passing in African American fiction is tempered, however, by two crucial observations. First, although texts such as *The Autobiography of an Ex-Colored Man* represent racial passing as transgressive in the etymological sense of crossing a line, they do not necessarily conclude that such mobility is therefore subversive of race in and of itself. In fact, the *Autobiography*'s episodic narration of the Ex-Colored Man's life—from the narrator's birth in Atlanta and childhood in Connecticut through to his decision, after witnessing a brutal lynching, to "change [his] name, raise a mustache, and let the world take [him] for what it would" (Johnson 1990, 139)—ultimately discredits the idea of a "free market" of racial identities as hopelessly (and dangerously) utopian. Although the *Autobiography* details the Ex-Colored Man's picaresque migrations through Atlanta, Jacksonville, Manhattan, Paris, London, Berlin and Washington, as well as his jaunts through various careers and social milieux, these outward signs of transportability nevertheless do not correspond to an analogous "free play" of identity. Because the very possibility and efficacy of passing depend upon the concept of stable and diametrically opposed racial identities of black and white, the Ex-Colored Man is continually fated to redraw the color line in the very process of crossing over it. When the narrator decides to pass indefinitely at the end of the text, he is not therefore transcending the cultural imperative of race; rather, in choosing a white identity (and hence constructing access to the social and economic privileges conferred by whiteness) he validates the salience of racial categories in mediating all social experience. The Ex-Colored Man's very use of passing to construct a transgressive form of self-naming attests, in other words, to the ways in which, as a legally black subject, he is ultimately still governed by dominant racial narratives.

The second reason for caution in my reading of Johnson's novel concerns the notion that the work of self-definition, like the work of autobiography, is always unresolved and always in process. While the phrase "crossing the line" implies a certain finality—as when it is used to express an irrevocable, hopeless, or irreparable situation, like the phrase "to burn a bridge"—in fact, identities are never so cut and dry, so easily discarded, or for that matter so subject to conscious control. The *Autobiography* exemplifies the intransigence of these aspects of identity in its portrayal of the narrator's predicament of attempting to construct himself as an "Ex"-Colored Man, to write a narrative of the self outside of personal history. A signifier of his self-alienation, like the "X" of Malcolm X, which it anticipates, the narrator's "Ex" exceeds the scope of his own narration, in the sense that he can never quite constitute himself from a position of total outsiderness. The paradox of the "Ex," like the paradox of autobiography as personal exorcism, thus lies in the fact that while the Ex-Colored Man seeks to abdicate or renounce a past (or "colored") self, he also recreates this self in the very process of telling his life's story. In so doing, the Ex-Colored Man stumbles upon the tension between a desire for newness and the unfeasibility of absolute novelty, a tension that links the *Autobiography* to the modernist cultural imperative to "make it new," the American Dream of immigrants who seek to reinvent themselves in the New World, and the driving force of market capitalism, which needs to perpetuate ever "new and improved" products.

Given its implicit critique of newness, it is perhaps ironic that the *Autobiography* has repeatedly been characterized as innovative or unique in African American literature. Johnson's only novel, the *Autobiography* is not only the first work of African American fiction to represent first-person interiority (Gates 1990, xvi), but it is additionally the first passing novel to confer narrative authority upon the subject who passes.[4] Johnson's conceit of the fake autobiography—a device which apparently fooled some of the *Autobiography*'s first readers and which spurred a search for the text's "real" author[5]—was also original to African American fiction. An artistic response to the dilemmas posed by centuries of black cultural dispossession, stereotypes of black artistic naïveté, and the exigencies of a patronizing, if not overtly racist, publishing establishment, the *Autobiography*'s pretense of verisimilitude allowed Johnson to draw upon the history of African American literary realism while simultaneously parodying the rhetoricity of well-known nineteenth-century black writers from Harriet Jacobs to Booker T. Washington (Stepto 1979, 96). The book's deceptively authentic "I" opened up a crucial fictional space in which Johnson could both satirize literary tropes and incorporate a critique of readerly assumptions of a literal correspondence between black authors and the narrators of their fictional creation.

As if to complement this host of "firsts," scholars have repeatedly associated the *Autobiography* with the projects, variously and sometimes idiosyncratically conceived, of literary modernism or modernity generally. Linking modernism to the market values of an emergent industrial capitalism that he envisions as at odds with authentic artistic production, Henry Louis Gates Jr., for example, writes that "more than anything else," Johnson's protagonist "embodies the alienation characteristic of modernity, as the solace of 'getting and spending' displaces all ambitions of artistic creation" (1990, xviii). William L. Andrews, author of the introduction to the 1990 Penguin edition of the novel, claims that Johnson's narrative "invokes, via an African-American's various crises of identity, the human drama of modernity in late nineteenth- and early twentieth-century America," the modern condition associated in Andrews's account with rootlessness and "ceaseless, often inexplicable, change" (Andrews 1990, xix). Defining African American literary modernism as a "contour" in which texts "respond to the post-textual call of antedating narratives," Robert Stepto asserts that Johnson's novel may be considered "modern" (1979, 96). And in her study of African American first-person narratives, Valerie Smith calls Johnson's book "our first modern case" of attempting to create a black self in language (1987, 64).

As even these brief sound bites from some of the most recognized critical accounts of the *Autobiography* suggest, scholars have often treated the novel's dramatization of passing (its thematic attention to race) and Johnson's formal innovations (the novel's place in literary history) as though these were unrelated, or largely separate, concerns. By contrast, the convergence of these two literary milestones is central to my argument that the *Autobiography* narrates race as a fundamental experience of the "modern" African American subject. I use the term "modern" here according to the definition that the *Autobiography* itself proposes in a passage in which the Ex-Colored Man describes his ideas of "modern" literature, ideas he derives from his reading of the Bible, the oldest and most authoritative text of the Western tradition. Upon discovering a copy of his mother's gilt-bound edition, the Ex-Colored Man reads the Old and New Testaments but finds himself "impatient and disappointed" with the life of Christ. "And so my first general impression of the Bible was what my later impression has been of a number of modern books," he concludes, "that the authors put their best work in the first part, and grew either exhausted or careless toward the end" (Johnson 1990, 16–17). By associating the "modern" with texts that defer narrative closure or suffer the symptoms of narrative exhaustion, the *Autobiography* links modernity to the narrator's own quixotic (and exhausting) quest for a stable and fixed identity, one that is itself always in the process of being deferred.

The price of modern black subjectivity, as the *Autobiography* demonstrates, is a kind of alienation, but one that differs quite significantly from modernist alienation as it is typically defined—that is, as a characteristic nostalgia for authenticity in the form of a "prelapsarian moment of unified, or undissociated, subjectivity" (Ross 1989, 117). Johnson's novel likewise represents passing as a "crisis" of unified identity; the Ex-Colored Man is a subject who seeks authenticity, but unlike most of the texts associated with modernism in the Anglo-American tradition, the *Autobiography* explicitly conceptualizes this "crisis" in racial terms. By portraying a character who crosses the color line to construct an alternative to the fundamentally alienating conditions of the dominant culture, which values whiteness as the sole term of prestige and power, the *Autobiography* envisions a certain kind of racial and cultural negotiation as the particularly "modern" problem of black male identity. I append the qualifier "male" to this last phrase to emphasize that while Johnson's depiction of an African American "I" may be original, his gender politics—as articulated through this "I"—may also be problematic, or at least, given the gendering of modernism among black and white literary artists, problematically representative.

Johnson initially figures the narrator's experience of alienation from the dominant culture as a paternal "gap" or absence in the narrator's personal history. From the start, the Ex-Colored Man must mediate legally incompatible maternal and paternal racial inheritances—the former permitted and recognized, the latter prohibited and denied, albeit present in the "zero degree" of the narrator's own flesh (Spillers 1987, 67). Like Frederick Douglass and the other slave autobiographers whom he tacitly cites, the Ex-Colored Man opens his narrative without being able to name his white father; he has "a distinct mental image" only of "a tall man with a small, dark moustache" (3), whom he recalls as a series of synecdochical fragments: a pair of shiny shoes, a gold chain, and a "great gold watch" (Johnson 1990, 3). Yet the Ex-Colored Man vividly recalls receiving a gift from his father before the narrator and his mother move north to Connecticut from Georgia. On the evening before their departure, the Ex-Colored Man writes,

> [My father] took me up in his arms and squeezed me very tightly; my mother stood behind his chair wiping tears from her eyes. I remember how I sat upon his knee and watched him labori-

ously drill a hole through a ten-dollar gold piece, and then tie the coin around my neck with a string. I have worn that gold piece around my neck the greater part of my life, and still possess it, but more than once I have wished that some other way had been found of attaching it to me besides putting a hole through it. (3)

As Johnson depicts it, the coin with the hole in it aptly symbolizes the hole in the narrator's history, as well as the deficit or "lack" that defines the narrator's relation to whiteness. Insofar as it is a keepsake from the narrator's father, the coin-as-trophy confers identity, but it also signifies the Ex-Colored Man's indebtedness to, or possession by, a more powerful other. A parody of the family heirloom and a metaphorical reminder of the neck-chains worn by slaves, the coin both figures the Ex-Colored Man's lack of a culturally sanctioned prerogative to his white paternal birthright—a birthright that, although it alienates him, he nevertheless has no choice but to claim. The image of the gold piece additionally emphasizes the economic terms of such a cultural (dis)inheritance, the fact that the Ex-Colored Man, once grown, will not be entitled to the wealth that typically descends from father to son. Ironically, by putting a hole in the ten-dollar piece, the Ex-Colored Man's father takes it out of the realm of commerce and turns it into a keepsake, a "sacred" object whose value, paradoxically, resides in its having been removed from commodity circulation (Kopytoff 1986, 74).

If the coin is symbolic of the economic and social value of the patronym in patriarchal culture, then a later scene demonstrates the specific effects of such a disinheritance in the process of subject formation. In *The Souls of Black Folk*, Du Bois's inauguration into a black subjectivity occurs when he discovers, through the cruelty of white schoolmates, that racial "difference"—here, difference from a European norm—carries crucial and, for him, determining social meaning. It dawns upon the young Du Bois quite suddenly "that I was different from the others; or like, mayhap, in heart and life and longing, but shut out from their world from a vast veil" (4). Likewise, in what is almost a direct (and perhaps a somewhat parodic) citation of Du Bois, the Ex-Colored Man describes his abrupt movement, as a child, across a metaphorical threshold of race. As is the case in *Souls*, in the *Autobiography* this transition is staged as a scene of instantaneous, irreversible and complete transformation, one that the narrator is doomed to repeat not only in subsequent incidents of racial exclusion or cruelty but in recollections that have the tangible quality of traumatic memories. "I have often lived through that hour, that day, that week, in which was wrought the miracle of my transition from one world into another," the Ex-Colored Man writes, "for I did pass into another world" (14).

The scene of the narrator's initiation into a "colored" subjectivity occurs, quite significantly, at school (again recalling Du Bois), in the public arena in which lessons about nationality, citizenship, and dominant cultural values are typically inculcated in children. The narrator recalls,

> One day near the end of my second term at school the principal came into our room and, after talking to the teacher, for some reason said: "I wish all of the white scholars to stand for a moment." I rose with the others. The teacher looked at me and, calling my name, said: "You sit down for the present, and rise with the others." I did not quite understand her, and questioned: "Ma'm?" She repeated, with a softer tone in her voice: "You sit down now, and rise with the others." (10–11)

If the episode with the coin symbolically represented a cultural and familial disinheritance that was nevertheless still remote from the narrator's lived social reality, then this scene powerfully attests to the consummate authority of racial naming in his experience. It is crucial, moreover, that the episode achieves its traumatic import without the teacher's ever having to name the Ex-Colored Man per se; it is enough that she designates him by means of exclusion, defining his subjectivity (as in the earlier scene with the coin) in terms of a lack—here, the lack of a social prerogative to be "counted" with the white children. The scene additionally demonstrates the process by which social constructions such as the authenticity of racial identity and the mutually exclusive nature of the terms "white" and "black" (here "white" and "other") become internalized in subjects as common sense. That the teacher is forced to reiterate the phrase "You sit down now, and rise with the others" suggests that ideological constructs such as the narrator's essential difference from the rest of the children are not self-evident but rather require repetition before subjects can incorporate them as essential truths.

It is likewise significant that the agencies of the transmission of the dominant ideology here are not necessarily those subjects who possess the most power in a general sense but rather those who have a more localized authority over him and who paradoxically are those most likely to be concerned with the Ex-Colored Man's well-being. After the episode in the classroom, and still doubtful of his teacher's instruction despite her insistence on its accuracy, the narrator runs home to his mother and appeals to her as an ultimate arbiter of racial naming. Here, crucially, it is the mother who replaces the teacher as the agent through whom dominant social values are transmitted and preserved, just as, through legal customs derived in slavery, she reproduces her own inferior social status in her son. Indeed, the Ex-Colored Man's mother is portrayed in this scene not only as the conduit of inferiority but as unknowingly complicit with the very dominating structures which later conspire to impose limitations upon the narrator's freedom and social mobility. While she thus holds tremendous social power in being able to name him, the Ex-Colored Man's mother also suffers the consequences of her own social disempowerment; in the very process of naming her son, in other words, she ironically implicates herself as an object of dominant racial narratives, not their subject. In response to the Ex-Colored Man's question, "Tell me, mother, am I a nigger?" she responds with an elliptical answer that begins with reference to herself and ends by confirming, albeit by indirection, the narrator's lack of an authenticating paternal narrative. "No, I am not white," she tells him, "but you—your father is one of the greatest men in the country—the best blood of the South is in you" (12).

This scene, in which the Ex-Colored Man demands to be informed of a stable identity and his mother defers authority for racial naming onto the Ex-Colored Man's father, encapsulates with remarkable accuracy the narrator's own problematic quest to "pin down" an identity that is itself constantly immobile, constantly in the process of being deferred. As Kimberly Benston argues in a deft reading of Johnson's novel, the narrator of the *Autobiography* is continually fated to rehearse "the spectacle of negative self-facing" (1990, 103), or the perpetual quest for self-definition in the presence of constantly shifting difference. The scene additionally introduces the idea of women (first the schoolteacher, then the Ex-Colored Man's mother) as the unsuspecting proxies of, or physical stand-ins for, the disfiguring consequences of racial naming. "Perhaps it had to be done," the narrator writes with telling ambiguity in his use of pronouns, "but I have never forgiven the woman who did it so cruelly. It may be that she never knew that she gave me a sword-thrust that day in school which was years in healing" (Johnson 1990, 12). Not only are women castrating in the Ex-Colored Man's experience but their roles are rendered all the more ambiguous by the fact that they kill with kindness, perpetrating their violent acts under the guise of compassion, as evidenced by the teacher's "soft" tone and the mother's tearful suffering on behalf of her son's pain.

Such moments in the Ex-Colored Man's narrative are instructive not only for the reasons I have already enumerated but because they under-line his vulnerability, as a child, to dominant systems of racial naming. Together, the schoolroom scene and the scene with the mother render narratable the process through which the narrator is introduced to a notion of his self as "colored." From that time forward, he writes, "I looked out through other eyes, my thoughts were colored, my words dictated, my actions limited by one dominating, all-pervading idea which constantly increased in force and weight until I finally realized it in a great, tangible fact" (14). Indeed, the rest of the Ex-Colored Man's narra-tive could be read as his ongoing attempt to recover a previously expe-rienced wholeness or stability, a striving to counteract and correct the trauma of having been robbed of the privilege (reserved for white chil-dren) of being able to conceive of his self in such terms. If previously the Ex-Colored Man had experienced himself as universal—in psychoana-lytic terms, as a pre-oedipal, or oceanic, subject—then the scene of nam-ing imposes particularity and represents a post-oedipal fall from grace and self-completion. Moreover, as in the Lacanian paradigm of subject formation, which privileges language as the medium of the child's ini-tiation into the symbolic, Johnson's novel demonstrates the central role of language as a mechanism through which the Ex-Colored Man comes to be "spoken for" by culture.

The Ex-Colored Man proposes, again following Du Bois, that the process by which he becomes "colored" constitutes a generalizable para-digm of African American subject-formation under conditions of white supremacy:

> And this is the dwarfing, warping, distorting influence which operates upon each and every colored man in the United States. . . . [This] gives every colored man, in proportion to his intellec-tuality, a sort of dual personality; there is one phase of him which is disclosed only in the freemasonry of his own race. I have of-ten watched with interest and sometimes with amazement even ignorant colored men under cover of broad grins and minstrel antics maintain this dualism in the presence of white men. (14)

As the Ex-Colored Man explains, such a necessity of filtering expe-rience and beliefs through the narrow "funnel" of race has profound psychic cost. Yet the distortions of the minstrel's mask are also a source of cultural knowledge and even, therefore, cultural power. Like the Ellisonian "Negro" trickster, who sees beyond and through the joke of the mask worn by whites, and the archetypical Du Boisian African American, who possesses a special "gift" of "second-sight" (5), the Ex-Colored Man acquires an insightfulness through naming that renders the motives and ambitions of white men transparent in his eyes. "I believe it to be a fact," he concludes, "that the colored people of this country know and understand the white people better than the white people know and understand them" (Johnson 1990, 14–15). If the hegemonic process of racial naming has a mirroring effect, insofar as it forces the named subject to apprehend his or her self through an image projected by a more powerful other, then the minstrel mask the Ex-Colored Man describes has its own reflective power as a one-way mirror which allows the black subject a privileged perspective on the white world.

In the remainder of the *Autobiography*, the narrator's pointed and purposeful donning of a minstrel mask becomes a central means by which he capitalizes upon the implications of his difference from a hegemonic white norm. Following the lead of Johnson himself, who had a rather illustrious career as part of a vaudeville songwriting team before he embarked upon his literary career, the Ex-Colored Man exploits musical performance as the medium of his self-commodification and hence the source of his ability to influence and command others. As a pianist, he writes, "I always played with feeling" (18)—the pun in "play" indicating the potential links between satire (the donning of a mask) and pleasure. The idea of the narrator's ability to "play with feeling" operates at a number of levels: literally, as a designation of his musical virtuosity, and figuratively, as the signifier of his capacity to produce effects in his audience. "Play" additionally functions as a metaphor for Johnson's own fictional enterprise, which entails the manipulation of conventions of literary realism to fool readers, to assure them of the essential trustworthiness of autobiography even as the text itself undermines such notions of trustworthiness.

In portraying the narrator's ability to manipulate the emotional response of others through a canny wearing of masks, and to revel in his ability to do so, the *Autobiography* anticipates Houston Baker's analysis of the two discursive modalities central to the production of African American literary modernism: the "mastery of form" and the "deformation of mastery." Under the former, as Baker describes it, black literary artists cannily reappropriate the minstrel's mask through rhetorical strategies of camouflage, concealment, and disguise. By thus mastering the "form" of racist representations, by assuming a black mask ironically, they transform stereotypical deformations of African American humanity (such as black dialect) into "negotiable discursive currency" (Baker 1987, 24). For writers such as Washington and Paul Lawrence

Dunbar, who for Baker exemplify this tendency in African American writing, such a strategy was inevitable precisely because of the ubiquity and universality of the minstrel image; the "mastery of form" enabled these writers to negotiate dominant cultural narratives in order to "speak back and black" (24). If the mastery of form is the adept wearing of a mask, the "deformation of mastery" is contrastingly a type of guerilla ("gorilla") action, a display of African American vernacular prowess or "badness" (50) which reinvents the forms of mastery. Exemplified for Baker in the musical bars that preface each chapter of Du Bois' *Souls*, the deformation of mastery entails the wearing of a mask that calls attention to the specificity of black cultural production (57).

Yet if Baker's analysis tends to keep these two discursive modalities distinct in order to construct a narrative of progress, in which black writers evolve from an early stage of mastering form to a more mature stage of deforming mastery, then the *Autobiography* deconstructs Baker's logic by demonstrating, through the Ex-Colored Man's performances, the inevitable interconnectedness of Baker's two terms. Not only does Johnson's literary performance master the form of autobiography in order to deform its conventions but the Ex-Colored Man's musical virtuosity enables him simultaneously to master the forms that alienate him and to deform the masters who dominate him. The musical analogues for the Ex-Colored Man's talents in this regard are his ability to master Western classical music and to "rag" the classics. The narrator's impassioned performance of a Chopin waltz for his father (come North to visit) is so effective, for example, that it brings his father to tears and wins back, albeit momentarily, the paternal recognition the Ex-Colored Man has otherwise been denied. Through musical performance, the narrator is literally able to play with some of his father's feelings, to exert a powerful agency over his emotional response. "I am certain," the Ex-Colored Man writes, that in the moments following the performance, "he was proud to be my father" (Johnson 1990, 24).

Given my earlier characterization of the pivotal role of the Ex-Colored Man's mother in inculcating dominant ideologies in her son, it is significant here that she is represented as the source of the narrator's talent and interest in music. It is through her nightly playing of the piano and singing of old Southern songs, he explains, that his own love for music flourished. That the mother conveys to her son her own capacity for musical artistry indicates that while she is an agent of ideological reproduction, her function is less limiting than the previous scene might lead one to believe. When read against one another, in other words, these two moments in the text would seem to indicate that the mother is both the conduit of cultural exigencies and the instrument by which crucial cultural knowledge is disseminated and passed on.

The Ex-Colored Man's agility as a musical performer raises the possibility that he is enacting an analogous performance for his other audience—namely, the readership of his autobiography. If the narrator can play with the feelings of his musical audiences, then what is there to keep him, by analogy, from playing with the feelings of his readers? In fact, while the *Autobiography* struggles with the dilemma of accounting for race, much of the critical writing on the novel in the last quarter-century has engaged in a parallel struggle—that of attempting to come to terms with the implications of the narrator's mixed-race identity. While virtually all of the critical commentary on the *Autobiography* has found the Ex-Colored Man in some way reprehensible as a character—most often because he sacrifices a promising musical career in exchange for upward social and economic mobility—some readers have found him additionally objectionable for seeming to reject "blackness" as a political, if not a cultural, affiliation.

The latter of these accounts—wanting, perhaps, to recuperate the *Autobiography*'s otherwise resistant narrator as a serviceable African American role model, who instructs by his own negative example—take on a morally condemnatory or remonstrative tone in relation to the Ex-Colored Man's ambiguous or unresolved racial identifications. For example, in an influential essay published in 1971, Melvin P. Garrett underscores the narrator's "reluctance to undergo the pain of honest self-analysis" (9), claiming that he wears a tragic "mask" as a form of self-protection. Michael Cooke takes this point a step further, arguing that the Ex-Colored Man is "essentially an escapist" whose narrative is characterized by persistent attempts at "self-cancellation" (1984, 48, 51). Cooke positions Johnson's text at the center of what he calls a "self-veiling" stage in the development of African American fiction, the primary motivation of whose fictional personae is survival and social accommodation in a dangerous and hostile environment (35–37). Although American law and custom historically have dictated the genetic authority of black maternal inheritance (Spillers 1987, 79–80), such critiques run the risk of assuming that, prior to any social experience, the mulatto subject is black. Ironically, they reassert a basic paradox of narratives of racial passing insofar as they insist, for the subject who passes, upon the fundamental impossibility of passing.

What I want to suggest instead is that while it confers a crucial agency, the Ex-Colored Man's ironic mastery of form—his play on white cultural traditions through music and his satire of the dominant racial discourse through passing—also has the potential to outmaster him. As I earlier suggested, neither the Ex-Colored Man's subjection to dominant cultural narratives, nor his ability to rise above these narratives, is all-determining; instead, a dialectical negotiation of the tension between these two terms is more typical of the narrator's experience. The boundaries between passing as an act of deliberate self-definition and passing as an internalization of the mask imposed by white culture rely upon the passer's ironic lack of identification with the object of his mimesis. If this is the case, however, then what happens when identification replaces lack of identification, when "straight" masquerade, to use Luce Irigaray's terms, veers into ironic mimicry?[6]

A tentative answer may be provided by the climactic lynching scene of the novel—the episode that spurs the Ex-Colored Man to relinquish a black identity and the scene in which his satire "crosses over" most explicitly into the realm of self-parody. In the lynching episode, which takes place while the narrator is visiting the South without disclosing his legal identity to those who assume that he is white, the various linguistic slippages in the narrator's account of a black man being burned alive suggest an identification—no longer ironic—with the perpetrators of racial violence:

> Have you ever witnessed the transformation of human beings into savage beasts? Nothing can be more terrible. A railroad tie was sunk into the ground, the rope was removed, and a chain brought and securely coiled around the victim and the stake. There he stood, a man only in form and stature, every sign of degeneracy stamped upon his countenance. His eyes were dull and vacant, indicating not a single ray of thought. Evidently the realization of his fearful fate had robbed him of whatever reasoning power he had ever possessed. . . . Some of the crowd yelled and cheered [as he burned at the stake], others seemed appalled at what they had done, and there were those who turned away sickened at the sight. I was fixed to the spot where I stood, powerless to take my eyes from what I did not want to see. (Johnson 1990, 136)

In this passage, the Ex-Colored Man ironically completes the process of dehumanization initiated by the lynchers through his own brutalizing description of their victim. Such metaphorical violence is epitomized in his characterization of the lynching as less dehumanizing to the villains than to the innocent man who is murdered. Such is the irony of the Ex-Colored Man's question about the "transformation of human beings into savage beasts" (137)—that the words "savage beasts" seem to apply as much to the white men as to the black man. That the Ex-Colored Man is rendered "powerless" by the spectacle completes the process by which mastery is newly replaced by submission, defiance of white supremacy replaced by obedience to its norms. Indeed, because he associates the lynching with "shame. unbearable shame"—not at the fact of being associated, by a shared humanity, with the perpetrators of the lynching but at being identified "with a people that could with impunity be treated worse than animals" (139), the lynching scene offers the Ex-Colored Man no feasible means of self-definition except in terms of self-hatred. The very fact that he is "fixed to the spot," forced to be an unwilling witness to, and therefore also a passive participant in, the lynching testifies to the degree of mastery it exerts over him.

Ultimately, this image of stasis is the one that dominates the Ex-Colored Man's narrative. Unlike its slave narrative predecessors, in other words, Johnson's *Autobiography* ends in the "loophole" of self-doubt and regret—not in freedom but in the Ex-Colored Man's rhetorical and psychological captivity (Benston 1990, 101). There is, however, some suggestion that the Ex-Colored Man—and by extension Johnson—may have the last laugh. Next to "colored men who are publicly fighting the cause of their race," the narrator writes, "I feel small and selfish. I am an ordinarily successful white man who has made a little money. They are men who are making history and a race. I, too, might have taken part in a work so glorious" (Johnson 1990, 154). The irony of these (mock) sentiments is that in creating the Ex-Colored Man's narrative Johnson has indeed made literary history, and in satirizing white supremacy indeed commented upon the very making of "race."

Notes

Thanks to Kimberly Bentson, Gwen Bergner, Joanne Gottlieb, and Wahneema Lubiano for their help in writing this essay.

1. Examples include Milton "Mezz" Messrow, a white Jewish jazz musician of the 1920s and 1930s who was one of the inspirations for Norman Mailer's infamous essay on the "White Negro"; musician, singer, and antiracist activist Johnny Otis, a Greek American who calls himself "black by persuasion"; and John Howard Griffin, whose 1961 *Black Like Me*, based on his ethno-journalistic

experiment of passing for black through the Deep South in the late 1950s, interrogates the contours of the author's own white identity. See Griffin 1972, Mezzrow 1990, and Otis 1993).

2. See, respectively, Fanon 1967, Ellison 1972, Baldwin 1964, Spillers's 1987, Haraway 1991, and Lorde 1982.

3. For a general discussion of legal and social determinants of "mulatto" identity in the United States, see Davis 1991. On mulatto subjectivity, see Spillers 1985).

4. With the single exception of Harriet Wilson, who used the first person in the opening chapters of *Our Nig* (1859), black novelists prior to Johnson generally eschewed the representation of first-person interiority.

5. In a humorous anecdote from *Along This Way*, the real autobiography he claimed to have written partly in response to the reception of the *Autobiography*, Johnson explains that "the authorship of the book excited the curiosity of literate colored people, and there was speculation among them as to who the writer might be—to every such group some colored man who had married white, and so coincided with the main point on which the story turned, is known. I had the experience of listening to some of these discussions. I had a rarer experience, that of being introduced to and talking with one man who tacitly admitted to those present that he was the author of the book." See Johnson 1990a, 238–39.

6. See Irigaray 1981 for the distinction between "mimicry" and "masquerade." Likewise, Baker's two African American literary modalities hinge upon an assumption of the subject's conscious intention. What Baker's analysis lacks, it seems to me, is a way of understanding the role of unconscious motivations and drives that might propel the subject toward a reproduction of the dominant racial discourse. Such a reading could also shed light on the novel's reproduction of dominant stereotypes of black women. Can the narrator's sexism be subsumed under the name of satire? In asking such a question, I do not mean to imply that black male writers are typically exempt from the reproduction of white patriarchal norms or that there may not be specifically black male forms of misogyny. I am instead concerned with explaining the presence of misogynist images in a text that self-consciously announces its satirical intentions.

References

Andrews, William L. Introduction to *Autobiography of an Ex-Colored Man*, by James Weldon Johnson. New York: Penguin, 1990.

Baker, Houston. *Modernism and the Harlem Renaissance*. Chicago: University of Chicago Press, 1987.

Benston, Kimberly. "Facing Tradition: Revisionary Scenes in African American Literature." *PMLA* 105.1 (1990): 98–108.

Cooke, Michael. *Afro-American Literature in the Twentieth Century*. New Haven: Yale University Press, 1984.

Davis, F. James. *Who is Black?: One Nation's Definition* (University Park: Pennsylvania State University Press, 1991).

Du Bois, W. E. B. *The Souls of Black Folk.* 1903. Reprint, New York: Penguin, 1989.

Ellison, Ralph. "Change the Joke and Slip the Yoke." In *Shadow and Act.* New York: Random House, 1972.

Fanon, Frantz. *Black Skin, White Masks.* New York: Grove Press, 1967.

Garrett, Melvin P. "Early Recollections and Structural Irony in *The Autobiography of an Ex-Colored Man.*" *Critique* 13.2 (1971): 5–14.

Gates, Henry Louis, Jr. Introduction to *The Autobiography of an Ex-Colored Man,* by James Weldon Johnson. New York: Vintage, 1990.

Griffin, John Howard. *Black Like Me.* 2d ed. Boston: Houghton Mifflin, 1972.

Haraway, Donna H. "A Manifesto for Cyborgs." In *Simians, Cyborgs, and Women.* New York: Routledge, 1991.

Irigaray, Luce. *This Sex Which Is Not One.* Ithaca: Cornell University Press, 1981.

Johnson, James Weldon. *Along This Way.* 1933. Reprint, New York: Penguin, 1990a.

———. *The Autobiography of an Ex-Colored Man.* 1912. Reprint, New York: Penguin, 1990b.

Kopytoff, Igor. *The Social Life of Things.* Cambridge: Cambridge University Press, 1986.

Lorde, Audre. *Sister Outsider.* Trumansburg, N.Y.: Crossing Press, 1982.

Mezzrow, Milton. *Really the Blues.* New York: Citadel Underground, 1990.

Otis, Johnny. *Upside Your Head: Rhythm and Blues on Central Avenue.* Hanover, N.H.: University Press of New England, 1993.

Ross, Andrew. *No Respect: Intellectuals and Popular Culture.* New York: Routledge, 1989.

Smith, Valerie. *Self-Discovery and Authority in Afro-American Narrative.* Cambridge: Harvard University Press, 1987.

Spillers, Hortense. "Notes on an Alternative Model: Neither/Nor." In *Conjuring: Black Women, Fiction, and the Literary Tradition,* edited by Marjorie Pryse and Hortense J. Spillers. Bloomington: Indiana University Press, 1985.

———. "Mama's Baby, Papa's Maybe: An American Grammar Book." *diacritics* 17.2 (1987): 65–81.

Stepto, Robert. "Lost in a Quest: James Weldon Johnson's *The Autobiography of an Ex-Coloured Man.*" In *From Behind the Veil.* Urbana: University of Illinois Press, 1979.

Tayo's Journey Home
Crossblood Agency, Resistance, and Transformation in Ceremony by Leslie Marmon Silko

ARTURO J. ALDAMA

In this chapter, I will begin with a brief examination of what many have seen to be a false dichotomy between writing and speech. Intersections between this larger question and the narrower focus of the principal argument of my chapter will soon become evident. Next, I will consider how contemporary Native American novelists in general, and Leslie Marmon Silko in particular, reclaim the novel tradition—a genre that, arising concomitant with the imperial project of Europe, has arguably perpetuated the colonialists' objectification of the Other. I will seek to show how narrative forces emerging in tribal stories and language play are "hybridizing" this narrative tradition.[1] Once I begin to analyze *Ceremony* as a narrative zone that disrupts and reclaims the processes of identity formation, I would like to consider how Tayo, a key protagonist, emerges from a site of multiple marginalization (due to his positioning as a crossblood) and moves to a decolonized state of self-acceptance.

The central question that drives my reading of this text is the way that Silko constructs the relationship of "full-blood" and "crossblood" characters to the forces of assimilation: in the process she questions fundamental relationships between race, ethnicity, and identity. At the same time, she celebrates an epistemological force moving the crucial issues of identity for contemporary tribal peoples of the Americas out of terrains defined by the dominant culture, which essentializes the relationship between race, blood quantum, and ethnicity. Specifically, Silko lifts

the complicated issues of contemporary tribal identity out of the colonially imposed "sludge" of ethnic authenticity justified by physiognomic
and blood-quantum inventions of "real Indians."[2] In doing so, Silko
critiques rigid and causal relationships between race, ethnicity, and identity, challenging racial essentialism. Instead, Silko affirms the generative power of stories and invokes Thought Women—a feminine creator
in Laguna understandings of the universe and her creation—whose
names, thoughts, and stories literary generate the universe and all its
worlds:

> Thought-Woman, the spider,
>   named things and
>   as she named them
>   they appeared.

(1)

Instead of relying on Platonic notions of pure origins and essences
of an absolute past that is lost—notions that, when applied to understanding tribal cultures, freeze and sterilize the play and the heterogeneous
vitality of ethnicity and culture—Silko offers a way of understanding
the history of the Laguna Pueblo in ways that imaginatively consider
the importance of cultural interchange and heterogeneity as points in
cycles of tribal narratives.[3] Silko, along with other indigenous writers,
empowers the struggle for identity in the wisdom of ancestors and the
changing nature of stories that literally generate meaning and create
universes. Silko deconstructs and reclaim the politics and poetics of identity in a "writing" practice that emerges from the ethnic terrains of the
Southwest—Puebloan tribal, Mexican, Anglo—and travels in and across
the borders of time, space, and cultural differences.

Writing and Ethnocentrism

Writing is considered to be one of the central indicators of Europe's sup-
posedly evolved status as holder of the "culture" and the "civilization"
during all phases of imperial expansion, up until and including the
postmodern and neocolonial social realities of the late twentieth century. On the other side of this dialectic in colonial discourse is the donnée
that so-called savage cultures remained in a primitive state of the oral
tradition—closer to the imposed Edenic understandings of "Nature."[4]
As an extension of dominating cultures, Western literary practice, which

includes the "writing of culture", whether production, criticism, or peda-gogy, has played a central role in the construction, distribution, and con-sumption of the "other," or the "savage," thus shaping still-prevailing attitudes towards race, ethnicity, culture and sexuality.[5]

Until recently, Western literary practice—in conjunction with the imposition and violent maintenance of colonies from initial contact to the present-day crisis of post- and neocolonial and postmodern real-ties—multiplied colonial discourse in two ways: (1) by constructing the other—whether it be in the Americas, Africa, or Asia in terms defined by colonial discourse—as the fierce or noble savage;[6] and (2) by deni-grating the indigenous literary practices as simplistic prewriting, as ar-tifacts of precivilization, and thereby disenfranchising the extremely complex literary practice that emerges in differing cultural matrices.[7] However, if we understand all expression—the production of meaning through social agreement—as "writing" in the Derridean sense, then we, as critics, can begin to open up the ways we understand literary production across the borders of cultural difference. We may disrupt foundations of hierarchies from which false and violent racial judgments are made.[8]

Jacques Derrida has been widely celebrated as the "father of post-structuralism" and has been credited for initializing a series of literary movements that disrupt the "fixed origin" and "immutable center" on which traditionalist literary and philosophical authority (New Criticism, neo-Kantianism, and structuralism) bases itself (Lentricchia 1980, 158–62). Even though it is not my intent to demonstrate in any rigorous way the relationship between poststructuralist thought and postcolonial cul-tural studies, I would argue that much of Derrida's work lends itself to a critique of the basis of colonial discourse, with specific regard to the relationships between language, culture, and power. My interest in Derrida is limited to how several essays in *Of Grammatology* (1976) can help us to repatriate the concept of "writing" in cultures considered too "primitive"; his ideas can add to the growing body of postcolonial cul-tural studies that (re)empower subaltern cultural production.[9]

In general, Derrida's *Of Grammatology* wrestles free from the strangle-hold of structuralist methods of practicing the human sciences (lin-guistics, philosophy, and anthropology, for example) by critiquing the relationship between transcendentality, logocentrism, and ethnocentrism. In simple terms, the dual thrust of Derrida's argument is as follows: (1) all categories of thought, meaning and language, including a priori assumptions and epistemologies guiding metaphysical authority, can-not escape from the play of signs; and (2) narcissism and ethnocentrism

guide Western man's obsession with his own transcendentality. This obsession monumentalizes categories of being and authority and attempts to
close, to contain, the "game" or "play of signifying references" (1976, 7).

Derrida considers the difference between writing and speech in a
foundational critique of the imbrication of colonial discourse in structuralist anthropology. In "The Violence of the Letter: From Lévi-Strauss
to Rousseau," he rightly criticizes the ethnocentrism of the West implicit
in its understanding of writing as existing in the "narrow sense of linear
and phonetic notation" (109). Derrida argues that "all societies capable
of producing, that is to say of obliterating their proper names, and of
bringing classificatory difference into play, practice writing in general"
(109). Derrida continues his attack on structuralist anthropology, and
specifically Claude Lévi-Strauss's dependence on Rousseau's opposition between Nature and culture. He understands writing in the limited
sense of "phonetic notation," as the activity that drives the transformation of society from primitive to "cultured": "No reality or concept would
therefore correspond to the expression 'society without writing.' This
expression is dependent on ethnocentric oneirism, upon the vulgar, that
is to say ethnocentric, misconception of writing" (109). In general, Derrida
considers writing as an activity of the play of significations across a field
of meaning, and he rightly bases his argument on the arbitrariness of
the sign as the basis of all linguistic activity. Derrida comments further
on the violence of this institutional designation of writing as the sign of
culture, noting, "Actually the peoples said to be without writing lack
only a certain type of writing. To refuse the name of writing to this or
that technique of consignment is the ethnocentrism that best defines the
pre-scientific vision of man. . . ." (83).

In another important essay, "*Of Grammatology* as a Positive Science,"
Derrida continues his critique of an ethnocentrism that sees phonetic
writing as the only writing by considering the "writing" that emerges
from differing cultural systems: Aztecan, Mayan, and Chinese (88–93).
With regards to the Aztecan codices and the Mayan glyphs—codices
and glyphs already imposed categories of understanding—Derrida argues that the picture-puzzle, a representation of the thing, signifies itself "to a thing and to a sound" (90) . The thing exists in "a chain of
differences" in space, and the sound is "also inscribed within a chain"
(90). Derrida argues for the synthetic relationship between the sound
and the thing, and summarizes by saying that, "We are dealing then
with a script apparently, pictographic and in fact phonetico-analytical
in the same way as the alphabet" (90). Regarding the ideogrammatic

and algebraic scripts of the Japanese and the Chinese, Derrida regards them not as an "unfulfilled alphabet," a precursor to the phonetic writing valued by the West as the "normal outcome, as an historical telos" (91). Instead, he argues that by understanding nonphonetic writing as different without hierarchy, "we thus have testimony of a powerful movement of civilization developing outside of all logocentrism" (90).

Such argumentation provides an important foundation to understand culturally different writing or literary practices on their own terms, disrupting colonially driven teleologies that belittle or exoticize their practice. In the case of contemporary multiethnic novelists, then, we see writers using a genre born out of a specific set of social conditions—the rise of the bourgeois family, growth of industrialism, and imperialism, and the maintenance of colonies, to name a few—and hybridizing that genre with writing practices that emerge from other cultural systems of writing: Ibo, Maori, Laguna, or Chippewa, for example.[10] What all multiethnic writers are able to do is enter the "open-ended discourse" as discussed by Bakhtin (1981) and hybridize these cultural forces of writing.[11] Specifically, writers create a zone in narrative, a time and space, or chronotope that is driven by various agencies, reflecting heterogenous identities both in form and content. And that allows writers the possibility of inscribing subjectivity in terms that can disrupt the colonially inflected logocentrism that "speaks subjects." The unfamiliar words of these recent multiethnic hybridizers liberate subjects to speak "themselves" into narrative in their own terms. Writers, then, provide counternarratives to the master narratives of the neocolonial hegemonic culture and to its imagination; they can disrupt imposed categories of understanding ethnic peoples as savage, other, primitive, or animalistic.[12]

Writing as "Other": Hybridity and Identity in Native American Novelists

In the case of contemporary Native American novelists, we can understand the novel as a hybridization of literary or writing practices, communal storytelling, and the realistic novel tradition of Europe used to create new imaginations and to reclaim those denigrated by colonial practice. Cross-cultural literary genres are created that can articulate hybrid or bordered subjectivities through epistemologies that emerge from differing cultural sites.[13] This clash or confluence of cultural trajectories can create the zones of the hybrid that liberate the spoken subject to speak in terms liberating to the self as a counterhegemonic and reclamatory force.

Contemporary Native American novelists create overlaps of differing literary practice, zones of the hybrid—writing—and we need to be wary of such easy and usually hierarchical classifications as David Murray's "myth and realism" or "oral tradition versus the modern literary tradition."[14] Leslie Marmon Silko hybridizes writing systems in her novel, *Ceremony*, to create an open-ended and polyvocal narrative zone that disrupts colonially driven expectations of identity.[15] Identity is inscribed through a simultaneous process of deconstruction and remembering, giving ultimate agency to the generative power of tribal stories and storytelling.

Bonnie TuSmith links the multiethnic writers in the United States through a shared sense of community, which she characterizes as the "dynamic interdependence of all life forms rather than the stagnant, conformist vision" (1993, vii).[16] TuSmith argues that multiethnic writers share the need to inscribe the "individual" in terms of the communal, thus breaking with the "ideology of the individualism" that views itself as "existing in a vacuum" and sees "self interest as the ultimate value" (vii). With this as the premise, TuSmith argues that the communal and relational are the ways that subjects are formed in differing narrative sites, whether authored by Maxine Hong Kingston, John Edgar Wideman, or Sandra Cisneros, for example.

With reference to *Ceremony* by Silko, TuSmith observes in the section "Storytelling as Communal Survival" that Leslie Silko's first novel, much like M. Scott Momaday's *House Made of Dawn*, "had not been 'midwifed' or mediated by a white editor/co-author" (119). This observation is important, since that gives Silko more agency as a writing subject to inscribe a consciousness in narrative that is both unmediated and liberatory—writing that disrupts, heals and transforms, a narrative of decolonization and reappropriation.[17] TuSmith points out the effects that layering or splicing tribal stories with the story of Tayo's return to Laguna has on the reader:

This splicing technique simulates the atmosphere of storytelling—as if reader were actually listening to and watching an oral performance. It effectively disabuses us of arbitrary separations such as the past versus the present, dream versus reality, and the animate versus the inanimate. In other words, with un-novel like stroke the author places us in a different reality, a

view of the world that is cosmic and holistic rather than com-
partmentalized. (122)

Similar to *Ceremony*, Louis Owens's *Other Destinies* (1992) challenges
the "westernizing" impulse of individualism as it applies to Native
American novelists. Owens enters full force into the contemporary cultural studies debates surrounding ethnicity, identity, and representation.[18]
This provocative and thorough study lifts the issues of "Indian" identity out of the federally imposed blood quantum percentages and "authenticity" invented, imposed, and circulated by Euro-American colonial
discourse. Owens states, "For American Indians, the problem of identity comprehends centuries of colonial and post-colonial displacement,
often brutally enforced peripherality, cultural denigration—including especially a harsh privileging of English over tribal languages—and systematic oppression by the monocentric 'westerning' impulse of America" (4).

Owens argues further that American Indian fiction is an attempt at
"rediscovering and rearticulating" of an identity that has been a "trea-
sured invention" in "world consciousness" (5). Owens says that contemporary writers combat the tendency to see "real Indians" living in
the absolute—and therefore vanished—past and empower the survival
and sophistication of tribal peoples (5). Owens argues that, in fact, "The
Indian in today's world consciousness is a product of literature, history
and art, and a product that, as an invention, often bears little resemblance to actual, living Native American people" (4).

The crux of Owens's argument is that Native American writers engage in either deconstructing the "verbal artifacts of Indian or mixed-
blood identity," as in the case of Gerald Vizenor, or, as in the case of
Paula Gunn Allen, "a re-membering or putting together of identity" (5).
However, I would like to argue that re-membering and deconstruction
are aspects of the same process in articulating identity; one process does
not necessarily precede another. This postcolonial challenge to
desubjectify or decolonize one's own subjectivity through the active use
of memory—remembering a way of doing things that has been forgotten in neocolonial culture—is at the center of Silko's work.

The Politics of Tayo's Journey: Blood, Identity and Entitlement

At this point, I would like to consider how Silko as a postcolonial writing subject animates Tayo as a literary force that counterwrites the way

"Indians" and crossbloods have been invented and marginalized in the colonial and neocolonial consciousness. In many ways, Silko pioneered the discussions of multiple subjectivities[19] that disrupt the colonially transmitted binarizing forces that attempt to determine mixed bloods or crossbloods as "half-savage, . . . impure. . . invisible . . . static . . . tragic" (Root 1992).

On one level, *Ceremony* is about Tayo, a person of mixed racial descent—Laguna Pueblo, Euro-American, and Mexican, a crossblood—who returns to the community as World-War II veteran,[20] charting a progression from dislocation to integration within community and universe via storytelling and ceremony. On another level, this return echoes through the generative play of natural and spiritual forces; Thought Women and these forces play through him as stories and narratives, versions of which were practiced communally before the imposition of a phonetic alphabet.

By undergoing profound transformations within Silko's narrative space, Tayo journeys "home" to a feminine heterogeneous universe. I say "home" conscious of the need to avoid the tendencies or traditions in social sciences that idealize an Edenic or prelapsarian past within tribal cultures. Such traditions deny the survival, complexity, and vitality of contemporary tribal peoples and their literary and cultural production. In addition, I want to control the interpretation of "journey" so that it is not understood as the Western telos of self-fulfillment, as seen in such classic journeys as the *Iliad*. In addition, I want to move away from the archetypal models of stasis, crisis, and resolution, such as the "Freytag's Triangle" model, that chart the development of a protagonist in terms that are linear and causal. Patricia Riley In the Woods makes an important distinction between Western expectations and the way this journey is understood in *Ceremony*:

Euroamerican culture demands for individuality in the extreme dictates that the protagonist must leave home in order to experience full self-realization. Tayo, Silko's tribal protagonist, must do the opposite. Haunted by his experiences and alienated by his "half-breed" status in tribal society that places a great deal on the value on "pure" blood lines, the road to healing lies in Tayo's ability to find his way back to his community and his traditions. (1992, 9)

This seemingly individual journey "home," Tayo's decolonial (re)-awakening, is imaginatively constructed as a continuation of stories and journeys that have been followed by the Western Pueblos, specifically the Lagunas, for thousands of years. In a broad sense, the Mother Iyatkiu—a feminine tribal state of balance of self with the human, animal, and spirit community, as well as with the land as a sacred and nurturing source of healing and regeneration—"reclaims" Tayo's personal narrative as part of a larger web of tribal stories.

By choosing Tayo rather than a full-blood to articulate the "road to healing," Silko comments on the problems of using blood quantum as the sole measurement of identity. The issue of verifying identity is of crucial importance for tribal peoples today: it could mean access to land, health care, counseling, and scholarships for higher education. Terry Wilson, a historian and scholar of people of mixed racial descent, points to the federally imposed divisions between mixed- and full-bloods:

> Indian identity with its mixed-blood, full-blood connotations stems from attitudes and ideas fostered by the majority White culture and government. Before the white man's coming there was intermarriage and interbreeding across group lines and no one marked the offspring as mixed-blood nor kept an accounting of blood quantums to determine tribal membership or degree of culture or acculturation. (1992, 116)

I would argue that through her narrative choices, Silko, a crossblood herself,[21] is in direct agreement with this critique of internalized, government-defined identity-and-membership practices.

A point of textual interrelatedness with the politics of identity in the "real world" suggests itself: the novel was published around the time of the landmark case of Santa Clara Pueblo et al. v. Julia Martinez et al. The hearings began in 1975, two years before the publication of *Ceremony*. This legal precedent dealt specifically with issues of tribal membership and entitlement to tribal privileges, cultural and economic. Julia Martinez, a Pueblo, married a Navajo man and was denied benefits for her children. The legal decision reads as follows:

> Action was brought by a female member of Indian tribe for declaratory and injunctive relief against enforcement of tribal ordinance denying membership in tribe to children of female members who married outside of the tribe while extending membership to children of male members who married outside the tribe. (436 U.S. 49, 98 S. CT. 1670)

Julia Martinez's appeal was granted and then reversed. This case decision seems to be justified by the need to uphold the matrilineality of most Western Pueblos and indicative of strict membership, even in pan-tribal unions. Used as a contextual referent, this case can help explain why Tayo was marginalized as a result of his mother's sexual union with a non-Laguna man and frames the importance of identity in the politics of the "real world."

By choosing Tayo as the narrative figure who returns to a consciousness of interconnectedness within the universe and overcomes the alienation imposed by colonialism, capitalism, and his status as a crossblood, Silko celebrates the power of tribal literary consciousness. By doing this, Silko is able to articulate a subject that is positioned in a site of multiple marginalization, what I term as an "Other's other" status common to crossbloods. Terry Wilson describes this marginalization as dark-skinned tribal peoples positioning light-skinned Indians as "second class" or of "other Indian status" (121, echoing the ambivalence that postcolonial peoples occupy, what Homi Bhabha calls "the ambivalent world of the "not quite/not white" (1984). However, in this case, the ambivalence would be "not quite/not Indian enough." Silko's narrative choice questions the tropes of racial purity and fullness of blood quanta as sole determinants in identity formation and entitlement, and provides a way for tribes to break free from federal dependency by remembering the stories of creation, change and struggle, relocating the processes of identity and place in the inclusiveness of tribal literary practice.

Trickster Tensions: Blood, Ethnicity,
and Multiple Marginalizations

The tension that is at the center of this reading of Silko is the one between full-blood and crossblood characters. The questions that drive my reading as a Chicano crossblood are how Silko plays with the colonially inflected expectations of behavior in her characters by constructing some full-bloods as assimilationist and some crossbloods as more "Indian," thus shifting the issues of Indian/non-Indian identity out of the "sludge" of racial essentialism. Specifically, Silko made me ask the following questions: Why did Silko create Tayo, a crossblood, as the protagonist? Why did the narrator construct the rich array of transformational mixed-blood characters—the Navaho and Mexican shaman Betonie, the Mexican flamenco dancer Night Swan, and the Mount Taylor spirit woman T'seh—who aid in Tayo's journey? Why did the narrator construct some of the Laguna "full-bloods" as resisting the Mother Iytakiu and actively trying to assimilate into the dominant "cultural world"?

This desire for assimilation (internalized colonialism or cultural schizophrenia in the Fanonian sense),[22] which Silko calls witchery, is seen clearly with the "full bloods" Rocky, Tayo's cousin Emo, and Tayo's auntie, his principal caregiver. Rocky deliberately avoids "the old time ways" (Silko 1977, 51), has faith in the omniscience of "books and scientific knowledge" (76), and enlists to fight in World War II to prove his patriotism. Undoubtedly, his mother, constructed as a "devout Christian, and not immoral or Pagan like the rest of her family" (77), encouraged Rocky. Emo becomes so mesmerized by the violence, both cannibalistic and erotic, produced through the United States war machine, that he becomes the key agent in "the witchery of the destroyers": "Tayo could hear it in his voice—how Emo fed off of each man he killed—how Emo grew from each killing. Emo fed off each man he killed, and the higher rank of the dead, the higher it made Emo" (61). Clearly, Emo acts out his victimization by what Jack Forbes terms the "Wetiko [a Cree word] Psychosis" in his lucid text, *Columbus and Other Cannibals* (1992). Forbes defines this colonially imported psychosis as cannibalism based on the "consuming of another's life for one's own private purpose or profit" (34).

However, Old Grandma, Josiah, and other village traditionalists are constructed in direct resistance to this cannibalizing witchery. This makes the full-blood and crossblood problematic much more complicated than simple binary reversals. This narrative tension catalyzes the need to explore issues of representation and what literary critic Tey Diana Rebolledo calls the "politics of poetics," producing commentary surrounding the narrative agency of tribal crossblood subjectivities. As a narrative force, it seems that tribal mixed-bloods disrupt imported constructs of essential, pure, and homogeneous racial subjects of the form "s/he is Indian therefore. . . , s/he is white therefore" (1990). These racial constructs have their authority colonially institutionalized by scientific traditions of biologic and genetic determinism.[23]

Tayo finds himself situated or, to use Lata Mani's term, "located" in an intense place of racial-cultural marginalization (1990, 38). He is alienated by both the Laguna and the dominant Euro-American culture. Tayo negotiates a liminal bordered space between worlds. Painfully, he lives in the interstices between contradictory discursive and material forces. To use Gloria Anzaldúa's commentary, Tayo is in a constant state of mental *nepantilism,* an Aztec word meaning torn between ways (1987,

78). This state of "mental nepantilism" positions Tayo in a cultural-psychic zone characterized by "The coming together of two self-consistent but habitually incompatible frames of reference, [which] causes *un choque* or cultural collision"(78).

The "full-blood" aunt is a Christian assimilationist. According to what Terry Wilson describes as the identity formation process by which "Blood Quanta are putatively tied to questions of culture and degrees of acculturation and assimilation," Auntie would be a contradiction in terms (1992, 109). Yet, the aunt continually marginalizes Tayo: "[S]he wanted him close enough to feel excluded, to be aware of the distance between them" (67). Auntie treats Rocky, her full-blooded son, differently: "[S]he gave Rocky little pieces of dough to play with: while she darned socks, she gave him scraps" (67). In addition, since this novel is set in the 1950s, there are such implied racist attitudes of the dominant culture surrounding the narrative world in which Tayo lives: attitudes which construct the products of any race crossing with non-European racial groups as "mongrels, diluted, invisible" (Nakashima 1992, 171).

Once his mother disappeared, the aunt took over the responsibility of raising Tayo. Through the boarding school commentary in the text, one could trace the roots of Tayo's mother running away. As a young teenager, Tayo's mother struggled to maintain her cultural identity and step into her identity as a woman. "[She was] Shamed by what they taught her in school about the deplorable ways of the Indian people" and "excited to see that despite the fact she was an Indian, the white men smiled at her from the cars as she walked from the bus stop" (Silko 1977, 68). For a young teenage girl, this is a violent message of racial inferiority, coupled with an "exoticization" of her sexuality. In certain respects, this is a continuation of early colonialist attitudes towards Native American or tribal women and their "sensual, enticing and indulgent" nature that piqued the "carnal interest" of English men (Smits 1987, 161).

As narrative commentary this already implicates the federal boarding schools in priming and perpetuating colonially "signed" sexual relationships between white men and tribal women. Through lowering cultural self-esteem to such a degree, girls seek out affirmations through relationships with the men who are supposed to be "civilized" and "superior." As evidenced by Tayo's mother own experience, this "conditioning" is false: "But after she had been with them, she could feel the truth in their fists and their greedy feeble love-making" (69). Perhaps akin to the Metis women of Canada, the price the mother pays is a simultaneous ostracism and colonial exoticism, made intense by the implied and real racial and sexual violence of the dominant culture.[24] When she leaves the Pueblo, the mother is literally and metaphorically "naked except for her high heel shoes / under that big cottonwood tree." Auntie was the last to see her go.

This "mental nepantilism" is the clash that gives birth to Tayo. As Gretchen Ronnow so acutely states, Tayo inherits "a triple dose of shame . . . the 'texts' and memories of his mother's shame" (1989, 74). This inheritance is reinforced by Auntie's acts of alienation and marginalization. She holds Tayo accountable for things he had no control over, which, in the implied and real context of discursive and material colonial violence, were understandable acts. As a narrative figure, Tayo is situated in multiple sites of disenfranchisement, victimized through replicating marginalizations enforced through Auntie. Her actions and attitudes are a terse statement of internalized colonialism.

Attempts at a Context: Origins, and Cultural Heterogeneity

To understand the politics of cultural identity further, I would like to intertextualize the novel with social, linguistic, and historical forces at play in the Southwest. Because I was raised neither by or around the Laguna Pueblo, I gathered commentary from principal anthropological and ethno-historical studies of traditional Laguna culture, so as to negotiate or reconstruct the novel's implied knowledge (or lack of it) surrounding Tayo's upbringing and to understand processes of multiple marginalization further. I did this conscious of how anthropological practice serves as an extension of colonial practice through the production and maintenance of the Other as a primitive and subhuman subject; I am also conscious of the recent interventions into the politics of writing culture by the anthropologists James Clifford and Renato Rosaldo, to name a few. I try to intertextualize the novel in a way that will contribute to a mosaic of understanding the historical importance of *Ceremony*, as a tribally centered counternarrative to the closed, sterilizing, and homogenizing impulse in ethno-historical and anthropological writing.

From the available information on the traditional Laguna child-rearing patterns and the importance of the mother, both physical and the all encompassing *Ts'its'tsi'Nako,* (Thought women), young children were born into a clan and initiated into a religious society that taught the child about its relationship to its family, culture and universe. The child was then given the teachings of the proper attitudes, ceremonies, and rituals to ensure the continuation of this harmonious relationship and the perpetuation of the Pueblo on the earth mother (Ellis 1950; Eggan 1950; Swann 1988b; Allen 1987; Parsons 1920).

Most commentaries point to the importance of clear boundaries, what is accepted and tolerated, in the Western Pueblo world (Ortiz 1972a; Eggan 1950, Ellis 1950). However, there is also significant commentary made on how the Pueblo region has served as a zone of interaction and trade between the Pueblos and the valley of Mexico. The trade continued with the Spaniards and the Europeans (Eggan 1972; Parmentier 1979; Spicer 1962). In fact, according to most historical sources, the settlement of Laguna occurred as an aftermath of the Pueblo Revolt of 1678, in which eastern and western peoples united to evict and hold the Spanish accountable for their barbarous acts of violence on the Puebloan peoples. Bands of Keresan peoples seeking refuge in Acoma migrated to what is now called "Old Laguna" (Eggan 1950; Ellis 1950, 1979).

This seems to be the "official" representation of history. With regards to what actually happened, I would feel more comfortable talking to a tribal elder at his/her choosing about the origins of the Laguna Pueblo. The Laguna Pueblo does not have the claim to "being in the same Mesa for thousands of years," as is seen with the Hopi and the Acoma. Rather, Laguna is of a mixed background sharing many principles and ceremonies with other Pueblos while retaining its own unique identity and language system. If one's origins extend geographically than just one mesa, and there was intermarriage among different tribal cultures before the onslaught of European colonialism, the concept of a "pure" origin is very problematic. The narrative tension of the full and crossbloods becomes more understandable.

Perhaps Silko wants to point out this issue of multiple origins out through her imaginative references to "the Mexican cattle who are released to go back towards Mexico," and through the importance she gives to her Mexican characters Betonie, Night Swan, and T'seh Montano. In my view, these references to Mexico evoke chronotopes of ancient times that speak of significant interconnection between the valley of Mexico and the multiple cultures of the Southwest. They also reflect the ethnic tensions between Mexicans, and Puebloans that are depicted in *Albuquerque* (1992), an important literary work by the Chicano writer Rudolfo Anaya.[25] As a narrative act, these chronotopes resist linearity and deny power to borders imposed through nation-state formations in the land of the Americas. This theme is further developed in Silko's latest work, *Almanac of the Dead* (1992), which spans the entire continent of the Americas and offers ways of understanding the conquest, colonialism, and neocolonial multinationalism as points in the cycles of tribal stories.

The Mexican people, mestizos with their "hazel green eyes," serve as role models, and healing catalysts for Tayo.[26] Their self-acceptance provides and reflects a psychic space/place that allows the polyphony of cultural confluence, and this is part of what heals and regenerates Tayo, who struggles to reconcile the multiplicity by remembering the ways of the ancestors: "'This is the only way,' [the Mexican woman] told him. 'It cannot be done alone. We must have power from everywhere. Even the power we can get from the whites" (Silko 1977, 150).

In *Cycle of Conquests*, Edward Spicer comments on how the languages of the Pueblos changed over time as they were impacted by the presence of other languages, Spanish and then English: "All observers agree that some 350 years later not more than 5% of Spanish words were included in the vocabulary of the three languages mentioned" (1972, 450). This is an incredible testament to the agency of the Pueblo peoples and their ability to resist the violent forces of imperialism (material and linguistic). With specific reference to Laguna, Spicer comments that the Keres "did not make new words after the manner of Tewa speakers, but rather extended new meanings to old words" (451). This contrasted with Eastern Pueblos, the Tewa and Tiwa, who, rather than borrowing words for new items brought by the Spanish (bread, coffin, hammer), "made their own words" (451). Perhaps this linguistic strategy could be a way to understand how Silko elides the multiple narratives in the text. Maybe Silko extends new "meanings to old words" and creates "new words." Continuing his analysis of linguistic resistance, Spicer states that: "Words for doing and acting—verbal expressions—were not borrowed, nor were other kinds of words, so that the main fabric was not at all affected by contact with Spain and Spanish speakers" (451). With regard to the impact of English on the Pueblos in the 1950s, Spicer states: "In this situation, individuals lived double lives to some extent as they became proficient in English and were attracted to the cultural world which it designated and expressed" (458). In addition, Ellis comments that "Laguna in the 1970's stands as the wealthiest and probably the most acculturated of all the New Mexico Pueblo tribes" (1979, 448). Ellis attributes this rapidity of acculturation to the proximity that Laguna had to "the rail ways and the major freeways and its proximity to the large city of Albuquerque" (447).

Representation, Authenticity, and Narrative Play

If these commentaries bear on the novel's implied knowledge, then this brings us back to questions of representation and authenticity. As mentioned before, these questions are crucial for tribal literatures and histories. The consequences of viewing both the production and criticism of Native American literature as a creative and intellectual act of imaginative pursuit without direct ethnic entitlement can be evidenced by the type of literary atrocities committed by "white" writers trying to write "Indian poem cycles." In the name of literary freedom of the writer, fame was achieved on a self-pronounced ability to enunciate, articulate, and present in a more "accurate" fashion the supposed "shamanistic" rhythm principles of the Native American ethno-oral tradition. As evidenced by their sales, popularity, and inscription into the canon of contemporary American poetry, these poets, who include Gary Snyder, Jerome Rothenburg and Jamake Highwater, were well received by the general American audience, especially in the 1970s. In the essay titled, "The Rise of the White Shaman As a New Version of Cultural Imperialism," Geary Hobson comments:

> Writing from what they generally assume to be an Indian point of view, calling their poems "shamans' songs," posturing as "shamans" and pontificating about their roles as remakers of the world through the power of the words, they seem to have no particular qualms about appropriating the transliterated forms of American Indian songs and then passing off their own poems based on those transliterations. (1980, 102)

Paula Gunn Allen, a widely published Laguna crossblood critic, poet, and novelist, illuminates another position concerning the issues of agency and representation in *Ceremony*. Allen claims that Silko is so close to the cultural truth of "it" that she accuses her of revealing a clan story: "[T]he story she lays alongside it is a clan story and is not to be told outside of the clan " (1990, 383).

For criticism and pedagogy there are many questions raised by Allen's comment. If this text is representative of traditional tribal culture, then how do we as critics celebrate its narrative richness? Are we to try to verify its cultural authenticity by examining anthropological transliterations of traditional oral narratives? Are we not to teach the text for fear of violating the sacred? Leslie Silko herself comments on her goals in *Ceremony* to June Katz: "To go beyond any specific kind of

Laguna witchery or Navajo witchery, and to begin to see witchery as a metaphor for the destroyers, or the counterforce, that force which counters vitality and birth" (Katz 1980, 193). In my view, simultaneity is central to the literary discourse surrounding Tayo and his journey. The use of "metaphor" maps local and regional knowledge-tensions surrounding crossblood agency onto concerns that are globally dispersed: (1) the destructive and life-giving aspects within all peoples; and (2) the entire global crisis of mass starvation, ecological resource depletion, biosphere destruction, and the threat of nuclear annihilation.

Clearly, this text is a literary product. Reading this literary text as culturally representative problematizes the claim made by Allen. Arnold Krupat comments on the tension surrounding narrative authority in the work of Silko: "For all the polyvocal openness of Silko's work, there is always the unabashed commitment to Pueblo ways as a reference point. This may be modified, updated, playfully construed; but its authority is always to be reckoned with" (1989, 65). In addition, Mikhail Bakhtin in *The Dialogic Imagination* (1981) explores the relationship between literary production and cultural representation in the novel. He celebrates the novel as the genre that engenders richness of language plays (time and space), heteroglossia, irony, and parody, to name a few. To deny this liberatory agency to Silko and the production of novels implies that tribal narratives should be monolithic in form and content—dead, two-dimensional narratives of little objective value. Clearly, the production of Native American novels highlights the internal "dialogic" of literary and oral narratives: "The language of the novel is a system of languages that mutually and ideologically interanimate each other. It is impossible to describe and analyze it as a single unitary language" (Bakhtin 1981, 130).

Furthermore, I argue that oral performance narratives are speech acts that are not only dialogic with their audiences but are reflective of originary speech acts and utterances that are intrinsically dialogic, heteroglossic, and heterogenous. Through language, these tribal stories speak in multiple voices of multiple worlds that overlap and reflect each other. Finally, much like Silko, Bakhtin sees the need for renewal and ceremony; for Bakhtin this happens through language:

> The literary-artistic consciousness of the modern novel, sensing itself on the border between two languages, one literary, the other extraliterary, each of which now knows heteroglossia, also senses itself on the border of time: it is extraordinarily sensitive to time in language, it senses time's shifts, the aging and renewing of language, the past and the future—and all in language. (130)

These comments clearly celebrate the "literary-artistic" power of Silko, as well as other contemporary Native American writers.

Conclusions: Dancing Away the Disease of White,
and Respect to the Mother Creator

Tayo is on the "border of time." As a narrative figure, Tayo resists the witchery brought through the white people: a witchery produced by imbalances in tribal narratives, a witchery that Betonie states taught "people to despise themselves"(Silko 1977, 132). Before Betonie draws the Sand Painting that accelerates Tayo's, he counsels Tayo: "But white people are only tools that the witchery manipulates; and I tell you we can deal with white people, with their machines and their beliefs. We can because we invented white people; it was Indian witchery that made white people in the first place" (132). This comment testifies to the power of "Indian" narrative practice, repatriating "writing" as a generative force and shattering all the dichotomies produced by colonial discourse: savage/civilized, literary/oral, Christian/pagan.

My parting response to the question surrounding the choice that Silko made with regards to Tayo is that, as a speaking subject in narrative, Tayo has the necessary "shamanic" potential to transform this sickness. What I mean is that, since Tayo is part white, he can fool the sickness to center on him—the sickness is in him; he can transform it through a type of shamanistic deception, and then purge it.

To use a term that came up in my interviews with a Northwest Coast master shaman, Tayo is a "wounded healer." Tayo's wounds, the sickness of the white culture—colonialism, alienation, and internal colonialism—and the scars he develops, best prepare him. He understands the sickness. His enunciative power is stronger than the "story of the witch's magic". When Tayo chooses not to drive the screwdriver into the skull of Emo, he enters the language play of stories and as an active subject temporarily shifts the direction, making the consequences of the stories change momentarily: "Its own witchery has returned all around it / It is dead for now." It is almost as if Tayo's "hazel green" eyes are a mask to tease the sickness out of the wounded. His dance with the disease of colonialism (external and internal) and the cultural schizophrenia it produces will transform it.

Finally, the choice to focus on the role of crossbloods in *Ceremony* is one of respect to the Mother Creator. Silko does not depend on blood quanta to determine the validity of a story; he does not say, "Oh the

Mother Creator's power stops at the full-bloods." The generative power of Thought Woman is invoked—a power both omniscient and infinite:

> Ts'its'tsi nako, Thought Woman
> is sitting in her room
> and whatever she thinks about
> appears
>
> She thought of her sisters
> Nau'ts'ty'i and I'tcts'ity'i
> and together they created the Universe
> this world
> and the four worlds below
>
> Thought-Woman, the spider
> named things and
> as she named them
> they appeared
>
> She is sitting in her room
> thinking of the story now
>
> I'm telling you the story
> she is thinking.

(*Ceremony*, 1)

Notes

1. For a discussion of the rise of the novel, growth of colonialism, formation of colonial subjects, see Azim 1993

2. See Berkhoffer 1979; Pearce 1988; Owens 1992; and Vizenor 1990

3. For a full "anthropological" discussion of the specific phases of this journey home, see Swan 1988a, 1988b. However, these readings are problematic in that they assume that Silko's text is a cultural artifact and representative of Laguna symbology, ceremony, and ritual; they deny the imaginative play of the text.

4. For an excellent summary of Rousseau and Lévi-Strauss, and of Derrida's (1976) attack on their ethnocentrism please refer to Siebers 1988, 69–97. And for discussions of "savage" in European thought, see Gerbi 1973 ; Hanke 1959 ; and Dickason 1984. In the case of the "savage" in Euro-American colonial thought and literary practice, see Pearce 1988; and Berkhoffer 1978.

5. See Gates 1985, 9–11 and D. Lloyd's introduction to JanMohamed and Lloyd 1990, as well as Clifford and Marcus 1986, and Rosaldo 1989, to understand the imbrication of Western narrative—literary/anthropological—practice in colonial discourse. To see how Native Americans are constructed by Euro-American literary practice, read the final chapters of Pearce 1988.

6. For discussions of fierce or noble savages—the extremes for understanding native peoples—in the New World and in other non-European continents, see Hanke 1959, and Gerbi 1973,

7. See Derrida 1976, 81–118; Gates 1985; and Said 1978.

8. See Derrida 1976.

9. In addition to the works by Clifford, Rosaldo, Owens, Vizenor, and Said mentioned above. With specific reference to "subaltern" I am also thinking about Spivak, Niranjana, Homi Bhabha, Trinh-Minh-Ha, Alarcón, José Saldívar, Lata Mani, and Paul Gilroy.

10. For example, see Keri Hulme's *Bone People*, Chinua Achebe's *Things Fall Apart*, Ishmael Reed's *Mumbo Jumbo*, and Gerald Vizenor's *Bearheart*, as syncretic narrative sites.

11. See the discussion of the polyphonic syncretic, or postcolonial hybrid in Ashcroft, Griffiths, and Tiffin 1989, and the emergent significatory practices in African American literary production in Gates 1988, and the final chapter of Saldívar 1991

12. See JanMohamed and Lloyd 1990.

13. See Anzaldúa 1987 and the definition of crossbloods in Vizenor 1990, vii.

14. Even though such studies as Murray's actively try to write about Native American literatures in terms that empower their cultural production and critique imperial assumptions in critical practice towards these literatures, they can still fall into simple binaries embedded within a matrix of hegemonic ideologies.

15. See Bakhtin's 1981 discussion of novelistic discourse and the tensions of the centripetal and the centrifugal.

16. For a further discussion of the relational subjectivity, see David L. Moore's incisive analysis in Krupat 1993

17. For a discussion of the power relations between "white editor/co-author" as applied to the ethnographic encounter, refer to Krupat 1985.

18. See Saldívar 1990.

19. See Anzaldúa 1987; Vizenor 1990; Saldívar 1991; and Holland 1994.

20. For a full discussion of the effects of World War II on different Native Americans, see Bernstein 1991. And in specific reference to the purification ceremonies on Navaho and Zuni soldiers before and after World War II, please refer to Adair and Vogt 1949.

21. For an interesting historical overview of the Mormons and "how they all married Laguna women and formed a small colony," please refer to Ellis 1959. To examine Leslie's relationship to her grandmother and her stories, see Silko's *Storyteller*.

22. See Fanon 1967, and Ngugi 1988
23. For a concise survey of attitudes towards race crossing, see Provine 1988. For colonial attitudes towards "Indian/White" crossing, see Smits 1987.
24. See Campbell 1973
25. See the discussion of the importance of the Montezuma myths in the Southwest—specifically, how he was said to be a sorcerer who left the Pueblos to go to the valley of Mexico and how the story speaks of the return—in the final chapter of Parmentier 1979.
26. See Jana Sequoya's discussion of "Indian" mixed-bloods, and the "stability" of the mestizo societies of Mexico and Latin America in Krupat 1993.

References

Adair, John, and Vogt, Evon. "Navaho and Zuni Veterans: A Study of Contrasting Modes of Culture Change." *American Anthropologist* 51.4 (October–December 1949): 547–61

Alarcón, Norma. "Chicana Feminism: in the Tracks of 'The' Native Woman." *Cultural Studies,* 1990, 248–56.

Aldama, Arturo. "Sacred Breath, Sacred Life Dialogues." Archives. Native American Studies Library. Evergreen State College, Olympia, 1988.

Allen, Paula Gunn. "The Psychological Landscape of *Ceremony. American Indian Quarterly* 8 (1984): 81–93.

———. *The Sacred Hoop: Recovering the Feminine in American Indian Tradition.* Boston: Beacon Press. 1986.

———. "Special Problems in the Teaching of Leslie Marmon Silko's *Ceremony.*" *The American Indian Quarterly* 14.4 (Fall 1990): 379–86.

Anaya, Rudolfo. *Albuquerque,* Albuquerque: University of New Mexico Press, 1992.

Anzaldúa, Gloria. *Borderlands/La Frontera: The New Mestiza.* San Francisco: Spinster/Aunt Lute Press. 1987.

———. *Haciendo Caras: Making Face, Making Soul.* San Francisco: Spinster/Aunt Lute Press. 1990

Ashcroft, Bill, G. Griffiths, and H. Tiffin. *The Empire Writes Back: Theory and Practice in Post-colonial Literatures.* London: Routledge, 1989.

Azim, Firdous. *The Colonial Rise of the Novel.* London: Routledge, 1994.

Bakhtin. M. M. *The Dialogic Imagination: Four Essays.* Translated by M. Holquist. Austin: University of Texas Press, 1981.

Bernstein, Allison. *American Indians and World War II* . Norman: University of Oklahoma Press, 1991

Berkhoffer, Robert. *The White Man's Indian.* New York: Vintage Books. 1979.

Campbell, Maria. *Halfbreed.* Omaha: University of Nebraska Press 1973.

Clifford, James. *The Predicament of Culture: Ethnography, Literature and Art.* Cambridge: Harvard University Press, 1988.

Clifford, James, and G. Marcus, eds. *Writing Culture: the Poetics and Politics of Ethnography*. Cambridge: Harvard University Press, 1986.

Derrida, Jacques. *Of Grammatology*. Translated by Gayatri Spivak. Baltimore: Johns Hopkins University Press, 1976.

———. *Writing and Difference*. Translated by Allan Bass. University of Chicago Press, 1978.

Dickason, Patricia. *The Myth of the Savage*. Calgary: University of Alberta Press, 1984.

Eggan, Fred. *Social Organization of the Western Pueblos*. Chicago: University of Chicago Press, 1950.

Ellis, Florence Hawley. "Keresan Patterns of Kinship and Social Organization." *American Anthropologist* 152 (1950): 499–513.

———. "The Laguna Pueblo." In Ortiz 1979, 9:432–52.

Fanon, Frantz. *Black Skins, White Masks*. New York: Grove Press, 1967.

Foucault, Michel. *The Archeology of Knowledge*. New York: Pantheon Books, 1972.

Gates, Henry Louis, Jr. *Race, Writing and Difference*. Chicago: University of Chicago Press, 1985.

———. *The Signifying Monkey*, Oxford: Oxford University Press, 1988.

Gerbi, Antonello. *The Dispute of the New World: The History of a Polemic, 1750–1900*. Translated by Jeremy Moyle. Pittsburgh, Pa.: University of Pittsburgh Press. 1973.

Hanke, Lewis. *Aristotle and the American Indians: A Study in Race Prejudice in the Modern World*. Chicago: Henry Regnery, 1959.

Hobson, Geary, ed. *The Remembered Earth*. Albuquerque: University of New Mexico Press, 1980.

Holland, Sharon P. "If You Know I Have a History, You Will Respect Me—A Perspective on Afro-Native American Literature." *Callaloo* 17.1 (1994).

In the Woods, Patricia Riley. "Standin' in the Middle of the Road: A Look at the Mixed Blood Writer as Interpreter and Mythmaker in Leslie Marmon Silko's *Ceremony*." In *Cultural and Cross-Cultural Studies and the Teaching of Literature*. N.C.T.E 1992.

Katz, June, ed. *This Song Remembers: Self-Portraits of Native Americans in the Arts*. Boston: Houghton Mifflin, 1980.

Kristeva, Julia. *The Kristeva Reader*. New York: Columbia University Press. 1986

Krupat, Arnold. *For Those Who Come After: A Study of Native American Autobiography*. Berkeley: University of California Press, 1985.

———. "The Dialogic of Storyteller. " In *Narrative Chance: Post Modern Discourse and Native American Literatures*, edited by Gerald Vizenor. Albuquerque: University of New Mexico Press, 1989.

———. *New Voices in Native American Literary Criticism*. Washington, D.C.: Smithsonian Institute Series, 1993.

JanMohamed, Abdul R., and D. Lloyd. *The Nature and Context of Minority Discourse*. Oxford: Oxford University Press, 1990.

Lentricchia, Frank. *After the New Criticism.* Chicago: University of Chicago Press, 1980.

Lodge, David. *Modern Criticism and Theory.* London: Longman, 1988.

Lukács, Gyorgy. *The Historical Novel.* New York: Humanities, 1965.

Moore, David L. "Myth History and Identity in Silko and Young Bear: Postcolonial Praxis." In *New Voices in Native American Literary Criticism,* edited by Arnold Krupat, 1993.

Nakashima, Cindy. L "An Invisible Monster: The Creation and Denial of Mixed-Blood People in America." In Root 1992, 162–81.

Ngugi Wa Thiong'o. *Decolonizing the Mind: The Politics of Language in African Literature.* London: Heinemann, 1988.

Niranjana, Tejaswini. *Siting Translation: History, Post-structuralism, and the Colonial Context.* Berkeley: University of California Press, 1992.

Ortiz, Alfonso. ed. *New Perspectives on the Pueblos.* Albuquerque: University of New Mexico Press, 1972.

———. *Handbook of North American Indians.* Vol 9. Washington, D.C.: Smithsonian Institution, 1979.

Owens, Louis. *Other Destinies: Understanding the American Indian Novel.* Norman: University of Oklahoma Press, 1992

Parmentier, Richard J. "The Mythological Triangle: Poseyemu, Montezuma, and Jesus in the Pueblos." In Ortiz 1979, 9:617–42.

Parsons, Elsie Clew. "Notes on Ceremonialism at Laguna." In *Anthropological Papers, American Museum of Natural History.* Vol. 19, pt 4. New York: Trustees of the Museum, 1920.

———. "Laguna Genealogies.". In *Anthropological Papers, American Museum of Natural History.* Vol. 19, pt 5. New York: Trustees of the Museum, 1923

———. "Early Relations Between Hopi and Keres." *American Anthropologist*: 38 (1936).

———. *Pueblo Indian Religion.* Chicago: University of Chicago Press, 1939.

Pearce, Roy, H. *Savagism and Civilization,* Berkeley: University of California Press, 1988.

Provine, William. "Geneticists and the Biology of Race Crossing." *Science* 182.4114 (1973).

Rebolledo, Tey Diana. "The Politics of Poetics: Or, What am I as a Critic, Doing in this Text Anyhow ?" In *Haciendo Caras,* edited by Gloria Anzaldúa, 346–56. San Francisco: Aunt Lute Press, 1990.

Ronnow, Gretchen. "Tayo, Death and Desire: A Lacanian Reading of Ceremony." In Vizenor 1989.

Root, Maria P. *Racially Mixed People in America.* Newbury Park, Calif.: Sage Publications, 1992.

Rosaldo, Renato. *Culture and Truth.* Boston: Beacon Press, 1989.

Ruoff, Lavonne Brown. *American Indian Literature: Redefining American Literary Arts.* New York: MLA, 1990.

Said, Edward. *Orientalism*. London: Routledge Press, 1978.

Saldívar, José. "Limits of Cultural Studies." *American Literary History* 2.2 (1990).

———. *Dialectics of Our America*. Durham, N.C.: Duke University Press, 1991.

Sequoya, Jana. "How (!) is an Indian: A Contest of Stories." In Krupat 1993.

Siebers, Tobin. *The Ethics of Criticism*. Ithaca, N.Y.: Cornell University Press, 1988.

Silko, Leslie. *Ceremony*. New York: Viking, 1977.

———. *Almanac of the Dead*. New York: Simon and Schuster, 1991.

Smits, David. "Abominable Mixture." *The Virginia Magazine of History and Biography* 95.2 (1987): 227–61.

Spicer, Edward. *Cycles of Conquest*. Tucson: University of Arizona Press, 1962.

Swann Edith. "Laguna Symbolic Geography and Silko's *Ceremony*." *American Indian Quarterly*, 12.3 (1988a): 229–49.

———. "Healing Via the Sunwise Cycle in Silko's *Ceremony*." *American Indian Quarterly* 12.4. (1988b): 313–28.

TuSmith, Bonnie. *All My Relatives: Community in Contemporary Ethnic American Literatures*. Ann Arbor: University of Michigan Press, 1993.

Vizenor, Gerald, ed. *Narrative Chance: Postmodern Discourse and Native American Literatures*. Albuquerque: University of New Mexico Press, 1989.

———. *Crossbloods: Bone Courts, Bingo and Other Reports*. Minneapolis: University of Minnesota Press, 1990.

Wilson, Terry "Blood Quantum: Native American Mixed Bloods." In Root. 1992.

Border Crisscrossing
The (Long and Winding) Road
to Tamazunchale

MANUEL M. MARTÍN-RODRÍGUEZ

I

Border crossing is the heart of Ron Arias's 1975 successful novel *The Road to Tamazunchale*.[1] Crossings, in fact, occur at every step of the narrative, from the thematic to the symbolic to the metaliterary levels. As such, the road of the title becomes a sort of literary Pan American Highway winding its way across the U.S.A., Mexico, and Peru, as well as other—literary—spaces. In this its "Pan Americanness," *Tamazunchale* is perhaps one of the most significant texts of American (in a continental sense) postmodernism, bridging together the Latin American *nueva novela* and North American contemporary fiction, as several readers have noticed.[2]

The novel deals with the last days of Fausto Tejada, a retired bookseller who lives with his niece Carmela and a mute parakeet named Tico-Tico. Although the story is not told in chronological order, the reader is able to reconstruct a certain sequence of events, if he or she so desires, that might be useful for us to recall at this point. Fausto, a Mexican immigrant, first crossed the U.S.–Mexican border on his way north, presumably in hopes of improving his lot in life. Once in the U.S., he married Evangelina, who had also crossed the border northbound as a refugee from the Mexican Revolution. In Mexico, Fausto was a street sweeper, while Evangelina came from a rich family; once in the United States, and once Evangelina has lost everything, their class differences are limited to some uppishness in Evangelina, who tends to think herself

181

better than the rest of the Mexicans on either side of the Border. We learn of her attitude upon reading about the Tejadas crossing the border southbound (as tourists) occasionally. A more or less extensive textual space is devoted to one of those trips, narrating how Fausto informally enters the Pan American Road Race accompanied by Evangelina (who constantly complains about dirty rest rooms and the like) and Carmela, for whom the trip is a cultural (and sexual) awakening. Later on, as Fausto struggles against death, he embarks upon a crusade to bring Mexican workers to the U.S., which he successfully accomplishes by disguising them in U.S. Navy uniforms he manages to get for the occasion and passing them off as drunken sailors. All the workers manage to cross unquestioned except for Fausto, who is stopped and interrogated until he recites the Gettysburg Address and other texts he had learned in the encyclopedias that he used to sell.

But, as previously hinted, the U.S.-Mexican border is not the only boundary that the characters learn to cross freely. For instance, Arias's Chicano/a characters do not seem to be confined to the space of the barrio or a rural village, as had been the case for most of the characters in previous Chicano/a novels. They roam about Los Angeles and beyond freely, and even if they are distrusted and rejected in some places (the golf course in La Jolla, for instance, where Fausto and the Mexican workers get lost), they still continue to cross those unofficial borders that would have them confined to a separate part of the city.[3]

More radical crossings occur when geographical space (as we know it) is textually rearranged to provide for unheard-of contiguity.[4] Thus, for instance, Marcelino, a Peruvian shepherd who has taken his alpacas to graze, gets lost somehow and appears in the middle of a Los Angeles freeway, where he is spotted by Fausto and Mario, a youngster who accompanies Fausto in some of the Los Angeles episodes. Or in an earlier episode (in the textual sequence), Fausto sets off for colonial Peru, where upon his arrival—by bus, reproaching himself for not having taken the plane—he places himself in command of an army of foot soldiers, harquebusiers, and lancers, writes a report to the viceroy, and embarks on a ritual journey led by a prostitute whom he first confuses with Carmela. Fausto's journey to Peru, like that of Marcelino in the opposite direction, takes a direct route that does not cross any other countries.

At another point, back in Los Angeles, Fausto and Marcelino accidentally enter the set where a movie is being filmed; thereby they transpose the border between their own novelistic reality and that of the movie (whose subject is revolution in a Caribbean republic). Later on, a nameless character (a corpse given the name David by Fausto and his neighbors) appears drowned in a dry riverbed nearby, thus transposing the boundaries between the ocean and Fausto's neighborhood. David is, in fact, a double- or triple-crosser, since he is not only crossing the aforementioned geophysical boundaries but also literary boundaries as well, as he is strongly reminiscent of Esteban, a character in Gabriel García Márquez's story "El ahogado más hermoso del mundo." Like Esteban, David crosses from the world of the dead to that of the living when he is made a part of the community and goes to "live" with the old spinster Ms. Rentería.[5] As for his coming back to life, David is not the only character who crosses the threshold of death and then comes back. Aside from Fausto, who seemingly dies a few times during the book and then comes back, Evangelina sporadically reappears during Fausto's last days to iron his pants, remind him to take his pills, reprimand him for this and that, and so forth.

Then there is another type of border crossing that has to do with transgressions from one diegetic level to another.[6] An interesting case occurs in chapter 6, when Jess (Carmela's boyfriend) is attacked by a wrestler who jumps out of the TV set while Jess is watching a wrestling match. A reversal of this episode occurs in chapter 13, when Jess has transformed himself into a TV (in the middle of a frenzy of metamorphoses that affect most characters) and Carmela and Mario go into it/him. It could also be argued that Fausto and Marcelino's crossing into the movie set transports them (albeit temporarily) to a different diegetic level, where they cease to be "characters in the book" and become "characters in the movie of the book." But this type of embedded border crossing becomes really notorious in chapter 11, where most of the main characters—with the notable exceptions of Fausto and Carmela—participate in a play entitled "The Road to Tamazunchale," in which they play the roles of themselves for an audience composed of the Mexican workers smuggled into the U.S. by Fausto (as well as several people from Fausto's neighborhood, himself included).[7]

What then, we might ask, are the reasons for this continual crisscrossing of all kinds of borders (geographical, psychological, narrative, metaphysical, and so on)? Why does Ron Arias refuse to articulate the issue of border crossing in a mostly political or historicizing way, as most other Chicano/a authors were doing in the early 1970s? How does this marked difference in the treatment of "reality" set *Tamazunchale* aside from Chicano/a literature in that decade, and what consequences does its separation have for the readers' responses and reception? These are some of the main questions I would like to address in the rest of this chapter. But in order to avoid losing sight of the radical novelty that

Tamazunchale represented when it was first published, I think it will be necessary to situate Arias's novel in its contemporary context first.

II

When in 1979 Joseph Sommers and Tomás Ybarra-Frausto edited one of the first and most influential volumes of criticism on Chicano/a literature, they opted for the title *Modern Chicano Writers*. Still very useful today, *Modern Chicano Writers* became an immediate classic in Chicano/a scholarship. Its title, however, carried something of an ambiguity (in the meaning of the word "modern"), that prompted a reviewer (Teresinka Pereira) to wonder about the intention of its editors in using the word. After pondering the issue, Pereira (who wrote her review in Spanish) chose to translate the word "modern" as *actual* (present-day, current), and she pointed out how the scholars who contributed to *Modern Chicano Writers* tried to interpret what was new in Chicano/a literature without losing sight of tradition (Pereira 1979, 58).

My own intention, in starting to contextualize Arias's novel with a reference to *Modern Chicano Writers* (a volume in which *Tamazunchale* is not critically analyzed), is to frame both books in the current debate on modernism and postmodernism. *Modern Chicano Writers* deals with books whose impulse is predominantly associated with those themes that are frequently now called modern(ist), such as an emphasis on identity (and essences), the quest for knowledge and truth, alienation, narrative fragmentation, and so forth. But there were in 1979 other books that accentuated parody and pastiche, the doubtful, the fantastic and the uncanny, the palimpsest, the mestizo, the shifting, the playful. *Tamazunchale* was, without any doubt, among the latter and, as such, it was a pioneer of a change in attitude that would come about for Chicano/a literature mostly in the 1980s with works such as Arturo Islas's *Rain God* (1984), Ana Castillo's *Mixquiahuala Letters* (1986) and *Sapogonia* (1990), Miguel Méndez's *El sueño de Santa María de las Piedras* (1989), and Alejandro Morales's *Brick People* (1988) and *Rag Doll Plagues* (1992).

As such, the fact that *Tamazunchale* was not discussed in *Modern Chicano Writers* is not as surprising as it is revealing. Arias's novel is one of the first *post*modern Chicano/a texts and was, as of 1979, too far removed from other novels to be fully accepted into the Chicano canon then in formation.[8] To be sure, there were other novels with some postmodernist impulses at the time, among them Tomás Rivera's *. . . y no se lo tragó la tierra"*(1971) and Rolando Hinojosa's *Estampas del Valle*

(1973), but in these and other novels the predominant drive was still a quest for truth and the rewriting of history, a quest that was virtually absent from *Tamazunchale,* as it was from other postmodernist texts. In order to clarify the differences between modernist and postmodernist fiction as I see them (although I do not want to engage in the polemics this debate has generated), I will resort to the hypothesis of Brian McHale, for whom a change of dominant from epistemology to ontology separates the modern from the postmodern. According to McHale, "In postmodernist texts, . . . epistemology is *backgrounded,* as the price for foregrounding ontology" (1987, 11; emphasis in the original).[9] A last warning about my use of the term postmodernist is this chapter: I am referring to a movement in the arts (and in particular in literature) that has an international dimension and that manifests itself most visibly during the second half of this century. As part of this movement (which is not bound together by any manifestos, schools, or the like), I will consider: (1) what is usually referred to as Latin American "magical realism," and (2) what has been designated U.S. postmodernism or "literature of replenishment" (Barth 1984, 193–206), as well as (3) the works of several non-American authors such as Italo Calvino and others. As John Hawley reminds us in the introduction to this volume, postmodernism implies "an interconnection between cultures," an interconnection that, as we shall see, *Tamazunchale* foregrounds.

What will differentiate my analysis from previous ones that have dealt with Arias's novel, then, is my intention to read *Tamazunchale* as part of that international postmodernity, crisscrossing from the U.S. to Latin America and vice versa (as many Anglo-American postmodernists have done).[10] While others have mentioned this possibility, their readings, as we shall immediately see, have been overwhelmingly marked by their desire (or need) to ascribe Arias's novel to Latin American magical realism, whereas my own intention will be to supplement that information with further similarities between Arias's text and others by non-Latin American authors. I will, therefore, start by reconstructing *Tamazunchale*'s critical response, in order to show other critics' accomplishments as well as what I perceive as their shortcomings.

As mentioned, *Tamazunchale* has been almost unanimously read as a magical realist novel. An early review, by Francisco A. Lomelí and Donaldo Urioste in their *Chicano Perspectives in Literature,* already stated it in its first line: "The Chicano novel here gains yet another dimension: first to be created entirely within the bounds of magical realism"(1976, 41). Virtually all Chicano/a critics and reviewers writing afterwards have confirmed that assertion and its undoubted (partial) truth.[11] Thus, without denying Arias's novel's obvious ties with contemporary Latin American fiction, it is my contention (which I will elucidate in my conclusions) that seeing the novel as just a continuation of magical realism is a problematic step taken by critics, since I believe that such an affiliation removes Arias's novel from its immediate context in the U.S. and prevents us from appreciating its constant border crossings. It is true that several critics have suggested the possibility of reading Arias's work as part of a larger context, but their efforts have been almost always limited to naming some U.S. writers without elaborating.

Thus, for instance, Carlota Cárdenas de Dwyer proposes that we ought to consider Arias's novel "wedged between the parallel traditions of modern United States writers and the so-called magic-realists of contemporary Latin American fiction" (1977, 360), and she goes on to mention a list of authors from both cultural areas (Kurt Vonnegut, William Burroughs, John Barth, Thomas Pynchon, Alejo Carpentier, Jorge Luis Borges, Juan Rulfo, Carlos Fuentes, Mario Vargas Llosa, and Gabriel García Márquez). Her essay, however, does little to clarify what the precise relations between Arias and those other writers are. In fact, the only explicit comparison drawn in her article is between Arias and Borges.

A rather similar approach is that of Ramón Saldívar in his more recent *Chicano Narrative*. Saldívar also insists on placing *Tamazunchale* in "the privileged position at the juncture of the North and South American novel" (1990, 126), as he believes that "[i]n this novel the realism of American literature is mixed with the 'magical realism' of Latin American literature to create a supernatural Chicano realism" (127). While I agree with Saldívar in placing the novel as a crossroad between Latin America and the United States, his latter quote seems to me to be far more questionable, as it oversimplifies the issue. In the first place, it is not possible to reduce Latin American literature to magical realism nor, by the same token, to reduce [Anglo-]American literature to "realism" (as a reading of many of the postmodernist texts I will refer to in my notes would demonstrate). Then, it is unclear what he means by "supernatural Chicano realism" and how it would differ from the other trends he names. Finally, as was the case with Cardenas de Dwyer's essay, Saldívar's study does not provide us with specific intertextual analysis that would support his claim, at least not in the realm of U.S. literature.[12]

Eliúd Martínez, in turn, proposes to read *Tamazunchale* as part of an international movement he calls (after the term made popular by Alain Robbe-Grillet and Carlos Fuentes) *Novela de la nueva realidad* or "New Reality Novel." This movement would be, according to Martínez, something like a bridge between modernity and postmodernity (1977, 227).

In thus contextualizing the novel, Martínez gives us a most useful start-ing point for deepening the analysis of Arias's novel as part of interna-tional postmodernism (a crosser between Latin America, U.S. America, and Europe, and the Third World). But, for some reason, he seems to prefer not to touch upon Arias's contemporaries, since most of Martínez's references in his article are to authors who wrote long before Arias did (Ionesco, Pirandello, Genet, Kafka, and Hesse, not to mention Cervantes and Goethe), with (once again) the sole exception of Latin American authors such as García Márquez and Borges. In other words, Martínez gives us the richest historical panorama of the diachronic sequence in which *Tamazunchale* inserts itself, but he does little to discuss it in terms of its synchronic literary series.[13]

Willard Gingerich, on the other hand, comes even closer to engag-ing in the exploration of *Tamazunchale*'s relation with other U.S. postmodernist texts, or so it seems at the beginning of his article, when he declares that Arias's novel "may well prove a minor masterpiece not only of 'ethnic writing,' but also of the new American fiction at large" (1977, 62). Surprisingly, after this very promising statement, Gingerich lets us down and limits himself to quoting a theoretical essay by John Barth while reverting, as all other critics, to Latin American writers, the European classics, and pre-Hispanic authors as his main points of refer-ences (this latest to his credit, since only Judy Salinas had hinted at it in her review).

A logical question poses itself immediately after reviewing criticism on *Tamazunchale*: considering that Arias has published his novel in the U.S., and in English, why is it that nobody wants to read it against the background of its immediate context—other U.S. novels written in English? Why does *Tamazunchale*'s reception look like a case of the pur-loined literary context? Or, put in another form: why is Arias's novel systematically forced across the border to become a follower of Latin American magical realism? I will come back to this question and other related issues in my conclusions, and I will then comment on the aes-thetic, historical, and ideological consequences of such a literary "de-portation." But first, let us go back to the novel for a closer look.

III

The first postmodernist trait that we may detect in *Tamazunchale* has to do with the change of dominant to which McHale refers in his *Postmodern-ist Fiction*; that is to say, what Arias's novel foregrounds is ontological praxis, not epistemological quest.[14] Fausto and the other characters are not as interested in acquiring a deeper knowledge of reality as they are in creating new realities. This was a real shock for contemporary readers already familiar with other Chicano/a novels. Clearly, *Tamazunchale* set itself apart from the then most influential genres, such as the bildungsroman, social realism, expressionism, autobiography, and the *costumbrismo*.[15] Most earlier novels presented an insider's view of Chicano/a society so as to dispel stereotypes or else they denounced social abuses against Chicanos/as; and some went deep into the mythical substrate to attempt to understand history as well as to promote ethnic pride.

But *Tamazunchale*'s narrative agenda has seemingly little to do with reality and more with creating new worlds, inventing images, and playing with conventions. In this sense, the novel's play on the ultimate ontological boundary (life/death) is significant. Life and death are not dealt with in this novel as opposites that define someone's belonging to a certain reality or not. In part this is so because Fausto and the other characters (like many others in postmodernist fiction) are clearly aware of their existence as fictional characters. As a self-conscious novelistic character, Fausto knows that as long as he is able to continue the story one more chapter, his life will automatically be extended. He is no longer the Goethian character in search of knowledge (it is symbolically relevant, I think, that he is a *retired* encyclopedia salesman), but rather a postmodern Scheherazade who manages to preserve his life by stretching out his story.[16]

In its radical departure from the narrative models prevalent at the time in Chicano/a literature, *Tamazunchale* chooses to associate with two newer ones: the deathbed monologue and the literature of travel to heterotopic worlds. Not surprisingly, these are two of the genres privileged by other postmodernist fictions.[17] The former, of course, presents a character about to cross the threshold from life to death, thus suggesting an abrupt transposition of ontological status. The latter, according to McHale (1987, 34–40), is based on the possibility of describing a universe (instead of *the* universe), that is, a world or worlds removed from our habitual experience. In the case of *Tamazunchale*, several worlds are described that overlap with one another. Those include worlds that are more or less known to us (such as colonial Peru or twentieth-century Mexico and California), as well as others that have a more virtual existence (such as Tamazunchale, which, in spite of the novel's epilogue, has little to do with the Mexican city of that name, as we shall see). After all, when fiction becomes self-conscious and abandons referentiality anything can—and does—happen. As McHale reminds us, "The space of a fictional world is a construct, just as the characters and objects that occupy it are, or the actions that unfold within it" (45).

Arias employs several strategies to create a heterocosmos in *Tamazunchale*. Among them, we could mention the textual juxtaposition of geographically separated areas (which allows Marcelino to cross the heterotopic border between Peru and Los Angeles),[18] the overlapping of worlds (the Caribbean republic inside Los Angeles),[19] anachronism (planes and viceroys coexist in colonial Peru),[20] and misattribution, where automatic associations are ruptured in postmodernist texts "parodying the encyclopedia and substituting for 'encyclopedic' knowledge their own ad hoc, arbitrary, unsanctioned associations" (McHale 1987, 48, emphasis in the original). This is what happens in *Tamazunchale* when we read in its "Postscript" (taken from Francis Toor's *New Guide to Mexico*):

> TAMAZUNCHALE . . . , former Huastec capital, is a tropical village in Moctezuma River Valley on C.N. 85; its sixteenth-century church has been disfigured by recent renovation. A naturalists' and sportsmen's Eden—river fishing from dugouts, mountain game. Moderate hotels are Texas, San Antonio, Quinta Chilla, Mirador. (Arias 1975, 108)[21]

The amazing geographical precision—which could be typical of traditional realism—becomes postmodern misattribution when we realize that the border we are crossing to get to this space is ontological rather than physical. The attribution becomes suspicious when conflicting locations or descriptions of a particular world (Tamazunchale in this case) place its reality "under erasure" (to use Derrida's familiar term). This results in Arias's novel when Tamazunchale is also revealed to be a euphemism (as Tiburcio puts it: "Whenever we don't like someone, . . . we simply send them to Tamazunchale. . . . it sounds better than saying the other, if you know what I mean" [82]), a utopian world where "we can be everything and everyone" (88), as well as the bilingual phonetic pun that sounds like "Thomas and Charley" (104).

In another episode, minute geographical detail becomes equally suspicious when the anachronic intersects spatial misattribution. Thus, when Fausto is about to enter colonial Cuzco triumphally (after a bus ride that absolutely respects the geography of Peru—the one in our maps) he realizes he is on the wrong side of the city: "But as the commander approached the new airport on the south side of the city, he winced. He should be on the *north* side. What did the map say . . . ? He had left it on the bus" (15; emphasis in the original). In heterotopic worlds maps tend to be inverted or else they are left behind, forgotten.

An important group of strategies involves the transgression of traditional boundaries, whether they are ontological or narrative, which helps to construct a space both familiar and unfamiliar at the same time. This occurs, for instance, when Evangelina comes back from the dead to iron Fausto's pants or,[22] at a different level, when Jess wrestles with the TV wrestler.[23] From an intertextual point of view, a partially similar effect takes place when characters from other books are borrowed by Arias. This phenomenon, which Umberto Eco has called transworld identity (1979, 230), has become so common in postmodernist fiction that one of the critics who has analyzed it has even affirmed that "[w]e live in an age of artistic recycling" in which authors are freely borrowing from each other (Rabinowitz 1980, 241).[24] In the case of David, whom as we saw Arias borrows from a short story by García Márquez, it is obvious that he is different from his precursor Esteban; but, at the same time, it is equally evident that he cannot be an absolutely new character in the informed reader's mind, as Eva Margarita Nieto has hinted.[25] The same could be said about Marcelino and his possible predecessor in Italo Calvino's *Le città invisibili* (1974, 152ff.), a shepherd who also wanders off his land and gets lost in a foreign city.

A consequence of these crossings is that geographical, literary, and ontological boundaries are blurred. Arias's text systematically explores the twilight zones of dreams, death, and fantasy. As a consequence, the reader cannot decide whether an episode is fantastic, strange but explainable, impossible in our world but possible in the heterotopic world of *Tamazunchale*, or simply dreamed. Occasionally, the text seems to suggest that it is all a matter of perspective. Thus, when Fausto sheds his skin in the opening scene and hands it to Carmela, all she can reply is "You want some more kleenex?" (Arias 1975, 11), suggesting that all she sees in Fausto's hand is a used tissue and not the skin that Fausto certainly sees. This type of relativism reminds us, of course, of Cervantes' *Don Quixote*, where a barber's bowl *(bacía)* is seen as such by some characters, while Don Quixote believes it to be a helmet *(yelmo),* and other characters just want to compromise in referring to it as a *baciyelmo* (barber's bowlmet?).[26]

A comparable uncertainty arises in other episodes, such as Marcelino's first appearance in the middle of the freeway (chapter 3), the snow cloud that capriciously crisscrosses Los Angeles (chapter 5), the finding of the drowned David (chapter 7), and the metamorphosis of characters into books, TV sets, flowers, and so on. (chapter 13). To further accentuate the dubious status of these episodes, most characters seem to be almost unconcerned by them. They certainly accept them without the slightest surprise, as happens in magical realist novels and in much of the rest of postmodernist fiction.[27] Even if one could interpret all such episodes as the dreams or daydreaming of the moribund Fausto (as both Cárdenas de Dwyer and Nieto have done), there would always be hints for the reader to pursue a different type of reading, more open to the ambiguous and the playful. This has prompted Gingerich to speak of a certain hesitation on Arias's part that he believes to be a fault in the novel:

> If *Tamazunchale* can be faulted in any major way, it is perhaps in Arias's hesitation to trust the fictive imagination to the fullest. He vaccillates [*sic*] between a rationalist reduction of all things fantastic to a function of Fausto's feverish brain chemistry, and a commitment to the resonant mistery [*sic*] of Fausto as image of the imagination itself. (61)

That is, for Gingerich there seem to be two possible narrative modes only, and consequently two possible readings: one would be the rationalist reduction of all episodes (close to Cárdenas de Dwyer's reading), and the other the truly fantastic option that Gingerich would like to be able to embark upon in his reading. These are two modernist types of narration that had already had their day and whose continuation in Arias's text would make for just that: a latter-day modernist novel. What I am suggesting here, however, is that Arias's hesitation is not a literary fault but the key element in his postmodernist novel. Hesitation, indecision, and doubt are ontological postmodernist states of affairs that implicitly reject both the purely fantastic and the purely rational. Needless to say, by stressing undecidability, *Tamazunchale* is asking for a postmodernist reading in which the reader is asked to share in the configuration of a new world whose rules and modes of being are not a mimesis of the reader's own world.

Up to this point in the analysis, we have been talking about diegetic and metadiegetic resources employed to foreground ontology in *Tamazunchale*. We will now move to linguistic and tropologic means of achieving the same end.[28] Among the former, we could cite the (limited, as compared to other Chicano/a texts) use of *caló*,[29] some instances of bilingualism, as well as what McHale calls "lexical exhibitionism," which would include the Borgesian lists of books towards the end of the novel;[30]

and the markedly elevated style that Fausto utilizes in his report to the viceroy, quoted in indirect free style in chapter 2.[31] In all cases, it seems, these resources are self-referential in that they succeed in drawing the reader's attention from the level of the plot to that of the linguistic means employed to tell the story (McHale 1987, 150).

Still more interesting is the treatment of metaphor and allegory. As noted by McHale, in postmodernist fiction metaphors and allegories have a dual ontological structure, inviting the reader to read allegorically but refusing to satisfy such an effort (142). Or, to quote Charles Jencks, "Post-Modern allegories are enigmatic because on the one hand you don't know exactly what the myth it is being compared to is. So instead of two things in focus, you've got two things that are out of focus" (1987, 47). Once again, we have a situation in which the text chooses not to choose between ontological (and literary) states of affairs, leaving the reader to decide which of the two possible routes (the metaphorical or the literal) to pursue; or rather, leaving the reader undecided and puzzled by the fact that she or he cannot just take one of the two routes and forget about the other. These metaphors and allegories play with the reader's expectations by proposing a figurative reading that they themselves question upon reverting to a literal meaning.[32]

A simple example of dual allegory in *Tamazunchale* will illustrate the point (after which we will move to a more complex and central case of allegory). Consider the story that Marcelino tells Fausto about his uncle Celso's remedy for old age (said to prolong life). The story, because it is told by Marcelino, acquires a certain magical and primitive tone that, as we shall see, the text refuses to confirm:

> If I remember . . . Celso started with a bag of stones all about the same size. You take the stones and make a little pile. You make is as high as you can, until you are sure no more stones can be put on top without falling. Then, and this is the hardest part . . . if you truly believe you can, you place one more stone on top. If it stays and does not fall, you will be strong as that last stone. Nothing can make you fall. (Arias 1975, 47–48)

Aside from the fact that the construction of the tower depends a lot on its builder's perception of when to put in the last stone, and aside from the fact that Marcelino may not recall it properly, the remedy's effectiveness is put into question even before the story is told, right after Marcelino assures Fausto "They say it puts new life back in the old skeleton" (47). Fausto, juggling the metaphorical and the literal, plays the part of the devil's (literality's) advocate as if to compensate for the allegorical turn that the narrative is about to take: "What about the rest of me?" (47). It is not that Fausto misses the figurative sense of Marcelino's fossilized metaphor, but his identity as a postmodern character forces him to live and think in the space between the allegorical and the literal. The same is true, by the way, of another utterance by Fausto in which the subject is, once again, delaying death, and the results are an unavoidable super-position of literal and figurative meanings. The solemn tone with which Fausto asserts, when he first feels Death is nearby, "It can't happen, it won't happen! As long as I breathe, it won't happen" (12), suggests the force of an illocutionary promise to himself (something like "I will not tolerate it"). Literally, however, it is the simplest of truisms, since it is evident that as long as one breathes one is alive. Of course a promise like Fausto's is impossible to fulfill, especially when one considers that humans have no control over death. But when one thinks not of humans but of characters, the fulfillment of his promise is not only possible but even plausible. To begin with, being a fictional character, Fausto does not really "breathe" at all. His mode of existence depends, as we saw, on narration, therefore, as long as he manages to keep the narration going he will live. Read with an eye for the literal, then, our allegory (the pile of stones) acquires an additional twist. Since the existence of a literary character depends not on breathing but on being part of the narrative, Fausto will undoubtedly live as long as he is able to keep piling up rocks one on another, as long as he keeps adding chapters/adventures one after the other—thus my previous analogy between Fausto and Scheherazade. Paradoxically, his dropping the last stone will be the end of his life, because his existence is process (narration), not stasis. The last stone/chapter will undoubtedly be the end—literally.

As for the second allegory I want to analyze, it will allow me to link this part of the analysis with my ensuing discussion of *Tamazunchale* as a self-reflective novel. It is perhaps one of the oldest literary allegories, that of the text as a road along which the characters (and the readers) journey. In this figurative sense, the allegory will actually propose to the reader a system of equivalences somewhat like this: road = life = text, as already noticed by Nieto (1986, 240, where she discusses previous uses of this allegory). This figurative meaning is supported in the novel by the "reading" that the inserted play (also entitled "The Road to Tamazunchale") offers us, and even by the scenographical treatment of the road in that play (an ascending ramp). As such, the allegory is fairly traditional and conventional. In a literal sense, however, the road happens to be just that: the textual space (page after paper page) traveled by

the characters (as well as by the reader's eyes) up to the last page, which
we turn as we would turn a last curve in a road to find our destination:
a sign in capital letters (in the postscript) that reads TAMAZUNCHALE,
much as a road sign would. This literal road is—as my title suggests—
full of detours and distractions, inasmuch as other texts/roads intersect
it, inviting the reader to wander off his/her path (convinced that all
roads inevitably lead to Tamazunchale). Thus we find interpolated stories (much as we did in *Don Quixote*) both from the oral tradition (the
legend of the volcano/lovers Popocateptl and Ixtacihuatl) and from several literary traditions (see, for instance, the first time that Fausto leaves
his house, on which occasion a mock symbolic knighting ceremony takes
place—reminding one once again of Don Quixote's procuring his im-
provised armor; see also the episode about David, and so on), not to
mention references to numerous other books, including the encyclopedias Fausto sold all his life. The interpolation of all these other narratives functions as a metaliterary warning for the reader (that this is a
story not a mimesis of "reality") and has "the effect of interrupting and
complicating the ontological 'horizon' of the fiction, multiplying its
worlds, and laying bare the process of world-construction" (McHale 1987,
112).

     In fact, *Tamazunchale* itself is presented to us as an interpolated text,
framed by two epigraphs in front of the text and an additional quote
from a tourist guidebook in the postscript. The opening frame is composed of a quote from the *Istoria de la Conquista de México* by Francisco
López de Gómara and an Aztec poem from the *Cantos de Huezozingo*.
This frame gives us as a point of departure for the story—the *roots* of
Chicano/a literature, as they were being identified at the time by the
critics: the Spanish colonial heritage on the one hand, and the pre-Hispanic indigenous component, on the other. The closing frame gives us,
rather ironically I would say, the Anglo-American contribution: a guide
for tourists. In between we have *Tamazunchale*, a text that is not only
concerned with exploration and conquest of an unknown land (the subject of López de Gómara's quote), nor with the leisurely exploration of a
"naturalist's and sportsmen's Eden" (postscript, n.p.), but with all that
and more. *Tamazunchale* is a text between texts (an intertext in the most
literal sense of the word) that purposely exploits its nature as a fictional
overlapping of worlds (including those worlds evoked in the frame).
Thus, we start our road from two quoted texts and arrive, at the end, at
another quoted text; and all we encounter in between are texts, and texts,
and more texts. In passing, and only because the frolicsome dimension
of postmodernist fiction so invites, I would like to mention an addi-

tional play on words that results from *Tamazunchale*'s frame. On our road to Tamazunchale we travel, as mentioned, from the opening frame (the *root*) to the closing frame, whose author is F. Toor. The inverted sequence *root/toor* is yet another of the in/transcendent games in this novel, one that alludes to a mode of being of the text as a mirror reflecting not reality but itself (and its associated literary worlds), a sort of Möbius strip or Brunelleschian optical box that stresses, once again, the text's undeniable self-referentiality and independence from outside norms.[33] As M. C. Africa Vidal has concisely put it, postmodernist fiction does not attempt to imitate or recreate reality as much as it tries to replace reality with signs of the real (1989, 55), the key element here being *signs*. In *Tamazunchale*'s case, the referent is not as much in the outside world as it is in other systems of signs (other texts) and in itself as a filter of linguistic/semic/visual realities.

A clear example of this change in referent is found (at the metadiegetic level) in the performance of the play "The Road to Tamazunchale." The coincidence in the titles of both the embedded play and the novel creates a confusion that makes the reader wonder about whether the novel is thus entitled because of the play or vice versa.[34] Furthermore, the fact that the actors in the drama play themselves (except for the character who plays Fausto) implies a duplication of their literariness. At the same time, the mere existence of the play produces a mirrorlike image of the author-text-audience relation in which all three elements are now fictional, or rather metafictional. In addition, the fact that Fausto is part of the audience and not a character in the play seems to suggest that, at this point in the story (a few pages away from the end), it does not matter which ontological or narrative level a particular character belongs to: as Tiburcio reminds the audience, we are all on the same road:

> Under his wife's coaching, he rambled to the end of his speech, explaining to his audience how they were all either coming from or going to Tamazunchale. "And we are too," he added. "We may not know it, but it's the same road. Everyone is on that road. *Sí compadres*, everyone! (83)

Including the readers, I might add. But *Tamazunchale* as a metaphor for the end is not (just) a euphemism for death. At this metaliterary (metaliteral?) level, as we saw, the word TAMAZUNCHALE (at the beginning of the closing frame, the postscript) is literally a sure sign of the end of the novel. In this sense, Tiburcio is right, since each and every character is literally on the road to TAMAZUNCHALE (or on *The Road to Tamazunchale*), on the road to the postscript, to the inevitable full stop where narration ceases.

IV

By way of conclusion, it is now time to go back to some of the questions left pending at the beginning of this chapter. I started by wondering about the continual crisscrossing of all kinds of borders that we have now had the opportunity to observe in more detail. Behind my question was the assumption that most other Chicano/a texts up to that point had framed the border-crossing issue in a political context—the United States–Mexican border—without venturing outside immediate social reality. As we saw, that geopolitical border also plays an important role in *Tamazunchale*, but it does not receive the almost epic treatment that it had previously been granted in novels such as Miguel Méndez's *Peregrinos de Aztlán*, or in countless poems and plays published or enacted throughout the U.S. Southwest. Crossing the U.S.-Mexican border is in *Tamazunchale* part of a larger picture in which all characters are crossers of one kind or another. When comparing the episode of Fausto smuggling the Mexican workers across the border with that of the wrestler jumping out of the TV set or that of Marcelino appearing all of a sudden in Los Angeles, we realize that they all have the same narrative status (that is, one is not more "real" than the others). The boundaries between "reality" and fiction have been erased, as I noticed, resulting in a novel that (for the first time in the context of Chicano/a letters) downplays epistemological issues while foregrounding ontology.

In fact, the continual crossing of boundaries in *Tamazunchale* could even be read as a commentary on the issue of ethnicity and identity as it was being dealt with in contemporary Chicano/a literature. While most other texts were operating with a fairly essentialist notion of identity and ethnicity (seeking to define it and then accepting that definition as an immutable given), the change of dominant (from epistemology to ontology) in *Tamazunchale* makes essentialist definitions impossible. Rather, characters are constantly being exposed to incidents that make them rethink themselves vis-à-vis the others. It happens to Fausto in the beginning of the novel, when he sees himself reflected in the mirror and thinks he is *"puro indio"* (13) just when he is planning his entrance into Cuzco as a conquistador. It happens to Evangelina when she is complaining about Mexicans being poor and dirty and Fausto forces her to remember how she married a Mexican street sweeper. It happens again in an episode in which Fausto talks to two young Chicanas at a bus stop and they discuss which one is prettier, the one with the hair dyed blonde or the one with natural hair (22–23). It happens to Marcelino, when he sees a black man for the first time and starts considering the issue of skin color in his own family (49). It happens to Jess, whom Fausto constantly call Jesús, even though he knows Jess doesn't like his name in Spanish (20). It happens to Tiburcio, when he is detained in a raid by the Immigration and Naturalization Service, in spite of his being a U.S. citizen (32). It happens, in sum, to most of the characters, whose identity and self-awareness seem to be constantly renegotiated in these cross-addressing episodes. On this subject (although his comments do not refer to *Tamazunchale*) Thomas Docherty has remarked something of interest to us while discussing McHale's idea of the change of dominant. What Docherty suggests is that in postmodernism "as a result of the priorisation of praxis over gnosis there is a corresponding attack upon the philosophy of identity ('Know thyself') and its replacement with a philosophy of alterity ('Acknowledge the unknowability of the Other')" (1993, 17). Inasmuch as *Tamazunchale* managed to propose such a philosophy of alterity (and I am suggesting that it did so by making ontological border crossing the decentered nucleus of its narrative world), it became a forerunner for later Chicano/a texts in which essentialist worldviews are replaced by explorations of difference (in gender, class, ethnicity, and other areas) and border identity.[35]

As a consequence of this radical difference that *Tamazunchale* showed with respect to other Chicano/a texts of the time, contemporary critics and readers were faced with a dilemma. Not able to dismiss the novel (which most people granted an undeniable literary value), they still had to deal with its problematic relation to the then-known corpus of Chicano/a letters.[36] The main question, at a time when Chicano/a literature was being defined (and overdefined) in almost every critical publication was thus: Is this a Chicano novel? Or, for the somewhat less aggressive, How is this a Chicano novel? On the one hand, the most militant of the critics (such as Mariana Marin) were quick to dismiss the novel as non-Chicano/a since it did not conform to the dialectical modes of presentation of social realities that Marxist critics saw as exemplary of the Chicano/a novel. On the other hand, those critics who wanted to incorporate *Tamazunchale* fully into the existing canon could not simply portray Arias's novel as part of any of the narrative trends then being identified as constitutive of Chicano/a literature (and thus recall Lomelí and Urioste's idea of *Tamazunchale* creating a new dimension). A defensive tone prevailed among those who first championed Arias's work, of which the following almost apologetic concluding remarks by Marvin Lewis (who also considers *Tamazunchale* to be a magical realist novel) could still be representative in 1977:

> Unlike most other Chicano novels, *The Road to Tamazunchale* is not basically concerned with social problems of the Chicano. At times allusions are made to these problems in the past in an effort to place the present in its proper perspective. They are handled on a symbolic rather than a literal level. . . . Through a fusion of Chicano themes and an archetypal quest Ron Arias has created an autonomous work of literature which has to be judged first as fiction and not as a mere reflection of social reality. (52)[37]

Given that context, I am proposing that the enthusiastic and quickly overwhelming assignment of the novel to an already prestigious literary movement from Latin America, magical realism, was a twofold strategy for Chicano/a criticism. On the one hand, it did make sense in terms of tracing literary resonances for *Tamazunchale*, so nobody could claim it was a far-fetched critical move; on the other, it was probably the only (or at least the most powerful) response that critics could come up with at the time to deal with *Tamazunchale*'s radical novelty. By creating a certain distance between *Tamazunchale* and other Chicano/a texts (ironically sending Arias's novel back across the border as the INS would have done to Tiburcio), the question of its Chicanism was somehow attenuated. First, by affiliating *Tamazunchale* with an already existing and distinguished movement, its quality was left out of the question. Then, by sending it to Latin America (albeit rhetorically), the critics felt less pressed to deal with the issue of Chicanism immediately.

The last of my questions that still needs to be addressed, then, is why *Tamazunchale* was not read in the more immediate context of postmodern fiction written in English in the United States (particularly striking if one considers the many similarities that I have pointed out in notes, as well as others that could easily be added). What is at stake, of course, is an element of literary history in writing that would have meant a drastic difference in *Tamazunchale*'s critical reception. Namely, had *Tamazunchale* been read as part of the U.S. (literature in English) context instead of being read in terms of the Latin American scene,[38] it probably would have been perceived as a formative text of a new literary movement (U.S. postmodernism), and not as a mere continuation of an existing one (magical realism), in the same way that writers like John

Barth are not referred to as *followers* of Latin American magical realism but rather as *creators* of U.S. postmodernism. The fact that cultural nationalism was quite strong among Chicano/a critics in the 1970s is probably at the root of the problem, since few of them at the time wanted to perceive Chicano/a literature as a part of the overall U.S. literary (or social) map, preferring an antagonistic relationship with the colonial power that the United States was perceived to be. For *Tamazunchale,* a text whose subject is border crossing, this was indeed an ironic fate: to be forced across the border in order to find a space in the literary map of its time.

Notes

1. The novel has been published four times (with several reprints). All quotes will be from the 1992 Doubleday edition.

2. For an account of criticism as well as other points, see my discussion below.

3. It should be noted at this point that *Tamazunchale* is one of the few urban novels that Chicano/a literature had produced at the time. This, combined with the fact that the city happens to be Los Angeles (where the largest Chicano/a-Mexican population in the U.S. resides) could be a reason for the mobility of Arias's characters. Yet, another 1975 novel set in Los Angeles (Alejandro Morales's *Caras viejas y vino nuevo*) had its protagonists confined to a Chicano/a segregated space for the most part. The only other possible precedents of *The Road to Tamazunchale* (in terms of the treatment of space) would possibly be Daniel Venegas's *Las aventuras de don Chipote o cuando los pericos mamen* (1928) and Oscar Zeta Acosta's *Revolt of the Cockroach People* (1973). For further comments on *Tamazunchale* as an urban novel, see Lewis (1977, 49).

4. This type of unexpected spatial juxtaposition could very well have a precedent in surrealism. However, as Achille Bonito Oliva has noticed (in a different context, that of the plastic arts), postmodernist (or trans-avant-garde, as he calls it) contiguity does not produce dissonance "but establish[es] the possibility of an unexpected outflow, crisscrossed and animated by a light sensibility" (1981, 42). Bonito Oliva discusses linguistic juxtaposition (of styles, for example, which also happens in *Tamazunchale*, where slang coexists with archaic colonial Spanish), but I believe that his reflections can be extended beyond the stylistic realm.

5. At this point, of course, David is also somewhat of a crossover from William Faulkner's "A Rose for Emily." For these as well as other intertextual presences in *Tamazunchale*, see Martínez and Nieto.

6. In this and other discussions about diegetic levels I am appropriating the terms as defined by Gérard Genette in his *Narrative Discourse.*

7. The reader should be warned that this is a synopsis of most of the episodes that I will be analyzing later on. Repeated references to these episodes therefore lie ahead. About embedded stories see Todorov (1992, 70–73).

8. I am deliberately using Chicano in the masculine to refer to this canon in formation since few women writers were included at the time. For a preliminary approach to issues of canonicity, see J. Bruce-Novoa's "Canonical and NonCanonical Texts."

9. Although I have used several critical sources in writing and documenting this chapter, I would like to acknowledge here McHale as the main source of theoretical inspiration, which explains the abundant references to his work through the course of my essay.

10. For an example of the influence of Latin American writers on U.S. postmodernists, see Barth's *Friday Book*, where he acknowledges the impact of the works of Borges and García Márquez on his own.

11. Although I have no space here to go into a detailed analysis of *Tamazunchale*'s first reviews, it is interesting that since the beginning, Chicano/a reviewers have been the ones to consistently compare Arias's novel with its Latin American counterparts. The two 1976 reviews by Chicanos/as (that of Lomelí and Urioste, and that of Judy Salinas) confirm the point (there are no 1975 reviews by Chicanos/as, with the exceptions of some comments by Juan Rodríguez in his rather sui generis newsletter *Carta Abierta*). By contrast, non-Chicano/a reviewers writing in 1975–76 already stressed the international and U.S. connections that *Tamazunchale* might evoke in a reader's mind, while refraining from commenting on magical realism. Thus, Alan Cheuse emphasizes the imaginary and the blurring of borders in the novel, and he suggests parallels with B. Malamud and I. B. Singer, limiting his comments on Latin America to possible "touches of Central American mythologies" (1975, 4). A year later (1976), Robert Bonazzi praises the mixture of fantastic and realistic modes and refrains from comparing Arias's text with others. Reviews become a little less meaningful after 1977, when major articles on *Tamazunchale* start to be published; the tendency, nonetheless, continues, although now the comparison with magical realism is pervasive.

12. An additional problem springs from Saldívar's use of the terms "North" and "South America." It is to be supposed that Saldívar refers to the U.S.A. and Latin America, respectively. But magical realism, as is well known, is a phenomenon manifested in both South America (Colombia, for instance) and North America (Mexico), not to mention Central America.

13. Both the diachronic sequence and the synchronic series are terms that I am taking from H. R. Jauss's *Toward an Aesthetic of Reception*.

14. Of course, when talking about such a change of dominant, one should keep in mind that it means a change in the relative importance of epistemology and ontology, and not a total substitution of one for the other (see McHale 1987, 11).

15.   Though I do not want to engage in literary typology, representative examples of those trends would include José Antonio Villarreal's *Pocho* (bildungsroman), Richard Vásquez's *Chicano* (realist presentation of episodes), Raymond Barrio's *Plum, Plum Pickers* (expressionism), Oscar Zeta Acosta's *Autobiography of a Brown Buffalo* (autobiographical novel), and Rolando Hinojosa's *Estampas del Valle* (description of customs). For an analysis of how Hinojosa's work both resembles and distances itself from traditional *costumbrismo*, see my *Rolando Hinojosa y su "cronicón" chicano*, chapter 2.

16.   Tzvetan Todorov has called this type of characters "Narrative-men" in an essay by that title. In discussing the *Arabian Nights*, Todorov asserts: "If all the characters incessantly tell stories, it is because this action has received a supreme consecration: narrating equals living. The most obvious example is that of Scheherazade herself, who lives exclusively to the degree that she can continue to tell stories" (1992, 73). Albeit Fausto does not face beheading, he is nonetheless aware that his existence depends on the narrative. Whether Fausto is the (detached) narrator of some of the episodes or not (an aspect that Arias's critics have neglected so far, but that should be crucial for those who insist that everything happens in Fausto's mind), his life only goes on as long as it is told to a readership. Classic precedents aside, other self-conscious characters are numerous in postmodernist novels. Muriel Spark's *Comforters* gives us a few examples (Caroline among them).

17.   A reference to the deathbed monologue as a genre (in relation to *Tamazunchale*) had been already made by Lomelí and Urioste, who compared Arias's text with Carlos Fuentes's *La muerte de Artemio Cruz* (1976, 41).

18.   A similar crossing occurs in Guy Davenport's *Da Vinci's Bicycle*, in the story "The Haile Selassie Funeral Train." In it the train traverses countries that are noncontiguous by our geographical standards. Note, incidentally, that Marcelino's crossing from Peru into Los Angeles is also related to a funeral procession, which his appearance disrupts.

19.   A comparable instance of characters entering the world of movie production occurs in William Burroughs's *Soft Machine*, where we also find anachronisms and many other strategies I am discussing here. My intention in pointing out these coincidences is to (at least minimally) contextualize *Tamazunchale* in the global and the U.S.A. literary arenas. In no way am I claiming extensive parallels between any particular novels and Arias's, nor am I trying to limit the parallels between them to any one characteristic. All I am trying to do is demonstrate that *Tamazunchale* shares most of its forming traits with other postmodernist novels. For further texts that would share some of these characteristics, the reader is urged to read McHale's analysis of the respective strategies.

20.   Anachronism is a frequent technique in Ishmael Reed's fiction. A parallel example to the one found in *Tamazunchale* can be observed in Reed's *Flight to Canada*, where twentieth-century aviation technology is said to exist in the nineteenth century.

21. Similar misattributions are found in other postmodernist texts. A fine example would be this from Donald Barthelme's "Paraguay": "[T]his Paraguay is not the Paraguay that exists in our maps. It is not to be found on the continent, South America; it is not a political subdivision of that continent, with a population of 2,161,000 and a capital named Asunción" (1968, 30).

22. Also in *The Comforters*, by Muriel Spark, Mrs. Hogg appears and disappears (much as Marcelino does in *Tamazunchale*), leaving doubts about whether she is alive or dead or what kind of existence she has.

23. For postmodernism, warns McHale, cinema and TV are no longer sources of inspiration; rather they provide internal (parallel) worlds that interact with those of the main diegetic level (1987, 128). For an example of other books where this occurs, see Burroughs's *Soft Machine*. The jumping of one character from one diegetic level to another is a technique very much in favor among postmodern writers. In John Barth's *Giles Goat-Boy*, on the other hand, the protagonist meets a character who is reading *Giles Goat-Boy*, precisely the scene in which their meeting takes place. For a reader familiar with the Latin American tradition, a similar overlapping of worlds occurs in Julio Cortázar's story "Continuidad de los parques." On a different level, it should also be recalled that Don Quixote (in the second volume) gets to read and enjoys the first volume of his adventures when he finds it at a press in Barcelona. Though the motif is old, its postmodernist uses make it more radical.

24. A poignant example of this type of borrowing is found in *Imaginative Qualities of Actual Things*, by Gilbert Sorrentino, where one of the characters marries Lolita, the main character in Nabokov's book by that title. In the Chicano/a literary sphere, an example from the 1980s is found in *The Brick People* by Alejandro Morales, where characters from Latin American novels get together to play cards (this is, by the way, Morales's way of recalling/borrowing a similar episode from Carlos Fuentes's *Terra Nostra*). For a typology of literary borrowing, see Rabinowitz 1980. For a detailed treatment of the concept of "transworld identity" in postmodernist fiction, see McHale (1987, 16–18).

25. The term "informed reader" is taken from Stanley Fish. For a further characterization of the informed reader see Fish 1980, 48.

26. Symbolically, as Judy Salinas and others have suggested, Fausto's action is also evocative of Xipe Topec's skin shedding, in itself a symbol of springtime renewal of life (Salinas 1976, 112). From a linguistic point of view, this relativism is a clear sign of polyphonic otherness, further emphasized in Arias's novel by bilingual puns (Tamazunchale/Thomas and Charley) as well as by the constant tension between Spanish and English.

27. See, for instance, the absolute lack of surprise with which students in New Tammany College welcome the goat-boy in Barth's *Giles Goat-Boy*. For an analysis of this attitude (which he calls "banality") in postmodernist fiction, see McHale (1987, 74–77).

28. In using the word "tropologic," I am mostly interested in the second meaning that the word "tropology" is given in *Webster's New Universal Unabridged*

Dictionary, second edition: "a method of considering or interpreting Scripture in a figurative as well as a literal sense."

29. The most detailed description of *caló* that I know of has been proposed by Rosaura Sánchez in her *Chicano Discourse*: "*Caló* as an urban code is a synthesis of the different varieties spoken by Chicanos in the Southwest, for it incorporates standard Spanish, popular Spanish varieties, loanwords from English and even code-switching. It is primarily characterized by its penchant for innovativeness in its expansion of the lexicon to produce an argot, the slang of young Chicanos, primarily male" (1985, 128). In *Tamazunchale,* the few examples that we find of *caló* serve mainly to characterize Mario as a *cholo.* See, for instance, his way of addressing Fausto in the following quote: "Hey, *ese!* . . . Forget the sheep" (Arias 1975, 29; emphasis added).

30. "Fausto purchased more books than they could carry. Diaries, journals, crates of paperbacks, encyclopedias in five languages, a Nahua grammar, a set of Chinese classics, a few novels by a promising Bulgarian author, a collection of Japanese prints, an illustrated Time-Life series on nature, an early cosmography of the known and unknown worlds, a treatise on the future of civilization in the Sea of Cortez, two coffee-table editions on native American foods, an anthology of uninvented myths and three boxes of unwritten books" (Arias 1975, 99).

31. "Before leaving Huancayo he composed an elegant, detailed report to the viceroy. Numerous violations of trade and customs regulations by well-organized native elements . . . bound to undermine authority" (ibid., 14). In chapter 12, a scroll is found by Jess (while he searches for a will), who is unable to read it. The following conversation with Carmela then takes place:

"What's it say?"
"I don't know, it's got a lot of big words . . . "
"Spanish?"
"I don't know, it looks foreign." (97)

32. An example of this type of allegory could be found in Barth's *Giles Goat-Boy,* where the relatively simple allegorical interpretation (university = world) is problematized in a series of revelations experienced by its protagonist.

33. As the reader may recall, there are other inversions in *Tamazunchale* that would help support my point about the novel being a sort of Möbius strip. Among them, one could cite the opposite paths taken by Fausto and Marcelino, the two-way movement of characters out of and into TV sets, the several crossings of the U.S.–Mexican border, David's "resuscitation" and his return to the world of the dead (with the help of Marcelino, who mummifies him), and so on. About Brunelleschi and his "optical box," see Louis Marin's analysis (1980, 307–8).

34. For a postmodernist discussion on titles (and subtitles) see Barth 1984, ix–xiv.

35. Among the best known of which one could cite Gloria Anzaldúa's *Borderlands,* Sandra Cisneros's *House on Mango Street,* and Arturo Islas's *Rain God.*

36. The issue has been summarized as follows by J. Bruce-Novoa: "Most critics tacitly agree to the existence of a category of important works which probably

should be read, but that once again are not considered entirely Chicano in that they do not address directly ethnic issues. Examples are *The Road to Tamazunchale* by Ron Arias and the aforementioned [John] Rechy novels" (1986, 130).

37. Up to a certain point, Tomás Rivera's foreword to *Tamazunchale* was the first apologetic defense of Arias's novel's Chicanismo (by claiming universality for both *Tamazunchale* and the Chicano/a novel of the future). Gingerich (in a 1977 review and later in his article) abounds in references to this same issue, and so does Bernice Zamora in a (rather late) 1978 review, from which the following quote is of interest: "What differentiates *The Road to Tamazunchale* from other Chicano novels is its lack of pretension in avoiding the `Escape into Aesthetics,' and its transcendence of a conspicuous eagerness to please by blatant social statements of reform" (1978, 227–28).

38. Although one should not lose sight of Nelly Richard's caveat on magical realism's prestige from a center/periphery perspective: "For almost the first time, Latin America finds itself in a privileged position, in the vanguard of what is seen as novel. *Even though it only finds itself in this position within a theoretical framework formulated elsewhere,* Latin American cultural practices are deemed to have prefigured the model now approved and legitimized by the term `postmodernism'" (1993, 467; my emphasis).

References

Acosta, Oscar Zeta. *The Autobiography of a Brown Buffalo.* San Francisco: Straight Arrow, 1972.

———. *The Revolt of the Cockroach People.* San Francisco: Straight Arrow, 1973.

Africa Vidal, M. Carmen. *¿Qué es el posmodernismo?* Alicante, Spain: Universidad, 1989.

Anzaldúa, Gloria. *Borderlands/La Frontera.* San Francisco: Spinster/Aunt Lute, 1987.

Arias, Ron. *The Road to Tamazunchale.* 1975. Garden City, N.Y.: Doubleday, 1992.

Barrio, Raymond. *The Plum, Plum Pickers.* Sunnyvale, Calif.: Ventura, 1969.

Barth, John. *Giles Goat-Boy.* Garden City, N.Y.: Doubleday, 1966.

———. *The Friday Book.* NY: G. P. Putnam's Sons, 1984.

Barthelme, Donald. *City Life.* NY: Farrar, Straus & Giroux, 1968.

Bonazzi, Robert. Review of *The Road to Tamazunchale. Library Journal* 101.3 (1 February 1976): 546.

Bonito-Oliva, Achille. "The International Trans-Avant-Garde." *Flash Art* 104 (1981): 36–43.

Bruce-Novoa, Juan. "Canonical and Non-Canonical Texts." *The Americas Review* 14.3–4 (Fall–Winter 1986): 119–35.

Burroughs, William S. *The Soft Machine.* New York: Grove, 1961.

Calvino, Italo. *Invisible Cities.* 1972. Translated by William Weaver. Reprint, Orlando, Fla.: Harcourt Brace Jovanovich, 1974.

Candelaria, Cordelia. "Ron Arias." In *Dictionary of Literary Biography: Chicano*

Writers, First Series. edited by Francisco A. Lomelí and C. Shirley, 82:37–44. Detroit: Bruccoli Clark Layman, 1989.

Cardenas de Dwyer, Carlota. 1977. "International Literary Metaphor and Ron Arias: An Analysis of *The Road to Tamazunchale,*" In *The Identification and Analysis of Chicano Literature,* edited by F. Jiménez, 358–64. Binghamton, N.Y.: Bilingual Press, 1979.

Castillo, Ana. *The Mixquiahuala Letters.* Binghamton, N.Y.: Bilingual, 1986.

———. *Sapogonia.* Tempe, Ariz.: Bilingual, 1990.

Cheuse, Alan. "Death of Chicano Everyman." (book review). *Los Angeles Times,* 7 December 1975, 4.

Cisneros, Sandra. *The House on Mango Street.* Houston, Tex.: Arte Público, 1984.

Davenport, Guy. *Da Vinci's Bicycle.* Baltimore: Johns Hopkins University Press, 1979.

Docherty, Thomas, ed. *Postmodernism: A Reader.* New York: Columbia University Press, 1993.

Eco, Umberto. *The Role of the Reader: Explorations in the Semiotics of Texts.* Bloomington: Indiana University Press, 1979.

Fish, Stanley. *Is There a Text in This Class? The Authority of Interpretive Communities.* Cambridge: Harvard University Press, 1980.

Fuentes, Carlos. *La muerte de Artemio Cruz.* Mexico: Fondo de Cultura Económica, 1962.

———. *Terra Nostra.* Mexico: Joaquín Mortiz, 1975.

García Márquez, Gabriel. "El ahogado más hermoso del mundo." 1968. In *La increíble y triste historia de la Cándida Erédira y de su abuela desalmada,* 47–56. Reprint, Buenos Aires: Sudamericana, 1990.

Genette, Gérard. *Narrative Discourse: An Essay in Method.* 1972. Translated by Jane E. Lewin. Reprint, Ithaca, N.Y.: Cornell University Press, 1980.

Gingerich, Willard. "Chicanismo: The Rebirth of a Spirit." *Southwest Review* 62.3 (Summer 1977): vi–vii, 302–4.

———. "Ronald Francis Arias." In *Chicano Literature: A Reference Guide,* edited by Julio A. Martínez and F. Lomelí, 51–64. Westport, Conn.: Greenwood Press, 1985

Hinojosa, Rolando. *Estampas del Valle.* Berkeley, Calif.: Quinto Sol, 1973.

Islas, Arturo. *The Rain God.* Palo Alto, Calif.: Alexandrian, 1984.

Jauss, Hans R. *Toward an Aesthetic of Reception.* Translated by Timothy Bahti. Minneapolis: University of Minnesota Press, 1982.

Jencks, Charles. Interview with Hugh Cumming. *Art & Design* 3.7–8 (1987): 45–47.

Lewis, Marvin. "On the Road to Tamazunchale." *Revista Chicano-Riqueña* 5.4 (Fall 1977): 49–52.

Lomelí, Francisco A., and Donaldo W. Urioste. *Chicano Perspectives in Literature: A Critical and Annotated Bibliography.* Albuquerque, N.M.: Pajarito, 1976.

Marin, Louis. "Toward a Theory of Reading in the Visual Arts: Poussin's *The Arcadian Shepherds.*" In *The Reader in the Text,* edited by S. R. Suleiman and I. Crosman, 293–324. Princeton: Princeton University Press, 1980.

Martín-Rodríguez, Manuel M. *Rolando Hinojosa y su "cronicón" chicano: Una novela del lector*. Sevilla, Spain: Universidad de Sevilla, 1993.

Martínez, Eliúd. "Ron Arias' *The Road to Tamazunchale*: A Chicano Novel of the New Reality." 1977. In *Contemporary Chicano Fiction*, edited by Vernon E. Lattin, 226–38. Reprint, Binghamton, N.Y.: Bilingual Press, 1986.

McHale, Brian. *Postmodernist Fiction*. N.Y.: Methuen, 1987.

Méndez, Miguel M. *Peregrinos de Aztlán*. Tucson, Ariz.: Peregrinos, 1974.

———. *El sueño de Santa María de las Piedras*. Guadalajara, Mexico: Universidad, 1986.

Morales, Alejandro. *Caras viejas y vino nuevo*. Mexico: Joaquín Mortiz, 1975.

———. *The Brick People*. Houston, Tex.: Arte Público, 1988.

———. *The Rag Doll Plagues*. Houston, Tex.: Arte Público, 1992.

Nieto, Eva Margarita. "The Dialectics of Textual Interpolation in Ron Arias' *The Road to Tamazunchale*." In *Contemporary Chicano Fiction*, edited by V. E. Lattin, 239–46. Binghamton, N.Y.: Bilingual Press, 1986.

Pereira, Teresinka. Review of *Modern Chicano Writers*, edited by J. Sommers and T. Ybarra-Frausto. *Revista Chicano-Riqueña* 7.3 (Summer 1979): 58–59.

Rabinowitz, Peter. "'What's Hecuba to Us?' The Audience's Experience of Literary Borrowing." In *The Reader in the Text*, edited by S. R. Suleiman and I. Crosman. Princeton: Princeton University Press, 1980.

Reed, Ishmael. *Mumbo Jumbo*. New York: Bantam, 1973.

Richard, Nelly. "Postmodernism and Periphery." In Docherty 1993, 463–70.

Rodríguez, Juan. "Comments on *The Road to Tamazunchale*." *Carta Abierta* 1 (October 1975): 1; and *Carta Abierta* 2 (November–December 1975): 1.

Saldívar, Ramón. *Chicano Narrative: The Dialectics of Difference*. Madison: University of Wisconsin Press, 1990.

Salinas, Judy. Review of *The Road to Tamazunchale*, by Ron Arias. *Latin American Literary Review* 4.8 (Spring–Summer 1976): 111–12.

Sánchez, Rosaura. *Chicano Discourse: Socio-Historic Perspectives*. Rowley, Mass.: Newbury House, 1983.

Sommers, Joseph, and Tomás Ybarra-Frausto. *Modern Chicano Writers*. New York: Prentice-Hall, 1979.

Sorrentino, Gilbert. *Imaginative Qualities of Actual Things*. New York: New Directions, 1971.

Spark, Muriel. *The Comforters*. London: Macmillan, 1957.

Todorov, Tzvetan. *The Poetics of Prose*. 1977. Translated by Richard Howard. Reprint, Ithaca, N.Y.: Cornell University Press, 1992.

Vásquez, Richard. *Chicano*. Garden City, N.Y.: Doubleday, 1970.

Venegas, Daniel. *Las aventuras de don Chipote o cuando los pericos mamen*. 1928. Reprint, Mexico: Secretaría de Educación Pública, 1984.

Villarreal, José Antonio. *Pocho*. Garden City, N.Y.: Doubleday, 1959.

Zamora, Bernice. Review of *The Road to Tamazunchale*, by Ron Arias. *Atisbos* 3 (1978): 226–68.

Feeding the "Hunger of Memory" and an Appetite for the Future

The Ethnic "Storied" Self and the American Authored Self in Ethnic Autobiography

BARBARA FREY WAXMAN

Theorists on autobiography, even those ordinarily using a Western European male model as the basis of their theorizing, acknowledge with respect the complexity of the genre in its representation of the "truth" or the "reality" of the "self"; in particular, postmodern approaches to autobiography claim the impossibility of a master narrative of the truth and relish the notion of the multiplicity of selves that an autobiographical text can never entirely capture. Paul John Eakin's queries suggest how difficult it is for the autobiographer to express referential truth about an integral self in a unified text: "What is the obligation of the writer to the personal integrity of his or her subject and story? How is it possible to honor the obligation to referential truth without determining first whose is the truth to be told?" (1989, xix). Philippe Lejeune confronts these problems by declaring: "If [autobiographers] make mistakes, distort, . . . in relation to what we can assume to be reality, this distortion is their very truth!" (1989, 134). Distortions develop in part because there are two systems operating within autobiography: a referential system linking the textual self to "reality" and committed to producing "the image of the real"; and a literary system, in which a self not formerly in existence is created through language and the author is committed to producing "the effect of the real" or verisimilitude (22, 126). While the autobiographer's aim of conveying *the* truth about the self as "complete subject" is an impossible dream, according to Lejeune, nevertheless,

207

autobiographers and their readers persist, fueled by their "desire for reality" (131–32). Bell and Yalom also subscribe to this idea that "the autobiographical 'I,' however fugitive, partial, and unreliable, is indeed the privileged textual double of a real person, as well as a self-evident textual construct" (1990, 2).

This problematizing of the genre of autobiography intensifies when we add to it considerations of gender and ethnicity. What feminist critics such as Sidonie Smith have recently theorized about gender in autobiographies can also help us to theorize about ethnicity in autobiographies. Smith makes three points in particular that are relevant here. First, she argues that the Western European patriarchal model of autobiographies privileges "the autonomous or metaphysical self as the agent of its own achievement" and opposes that self to the world, thereby endorsing a view of the human being that values individual integrity and devalues "personal and communal interdependency" (1987, 39). Women autobiographers frequently subvert this ideology of individualism and advocate interdependency and community, suggests Smith. I would add: many ethnic autobiographers also challenge the ideology of individualism, and consequently their stance toward the world, including their readers, is far from adversarial. Second, Smith writes that the woman autobiographer's "very voice in its enunciations remains haunted and haunting; for the language she appropriates has been the instrument of her repression" (42). I would add that American ethnic autobiographers similarly work with the tools of their oppressors—the American culture and the English language—and that they are painfully aware of this as they write. Finally, Smith explains the female autobiographer's challenge of having to deal with double discourses: she struggles "to negotiate a doubled identification with paternal and maternal narratives" (42). The ethnic autobiographer must similarly negotiate a double discourse: the ethnic narrative and the American mainstream narrative. With this double discourse, ethnic autobiographies commonly attempt to balance individualism and community; American English and their ethnic group's linguistic sensibilities; and American cultural values and pursuits and ethnic traditions and beliefs.

Using Smith's first two points as background to further discussion of her third point, I would like to examine in more detail these negotiations of double discourses in order to offer the following tentative theory of ethnic autobiography. The ethnic autobiographer, like all autobiographers, aims to carve out, in the act of writing, new versions of the self. For the ethnic writer, however, the new versions of the self are self-consciously shaped within the context of the American mainstream culture;

he or she aims to construct an American identity by authoring this auto-biography. This goal is attempted in four ways, representing respectively four salient characteristics of the ethnic autobiography: first, through writing a story about language, with an intellectual but also a richly sensuous attention to the qualities of English; second, through asserting the right to be an author, using this language to create the autobiography and exalting the political and cultural roles of the author; third, through self-conscious reflection on the genre of autobiography and on the act of writing an autobiography, acknowledging what an autobiography can do, publicly and privately, for identity formation; and fourth, by forging an intimate relationship with the American reader through a confessional stance (Lejeune argues that confession is "the center of the autobiographical domain" [1989, 125]) that enables the author to pull himself or herself into the center from the margins of American culture and to stake out a future there.

However, the aim and process of achieving an American identity as an American author are not in themselves what makes ethnic autobiographies unique. The uniqueness lies in the textual negotiations between these American-auctorial stirrings of individualistic identity and the pull of past ethnic identifications, what Richard Rodriguez calls the "hunger of memory," the desire to repossess the past ethnic communal life and familial contexts of identity formation. Ethnic autobiographers continually feed this hunger of memory and resist the hegemonic American culture by retelling and reinterpreting stories of their family life and their past selves. These ethnic family stories of lived reality interact with their stories of American authorship, of language, writing, and readership, together constructing the dynamic border identities of these autobiographical subjects. I would like to illustrate this theory of ethnic American autobiography by briefly turning to Rodriguez's *Hunger of Memory*, Maxine Hong Kingston's *Woman Warrior*, and Philip Roth's *Patrimony*.

In *Hunger of Memory*, Rodriguez establishes in his prologue, titled "Middle-Class Pastoral," his professional role as a middle-class, assimilated American writer; Raymond Paredes sees this assumption of his literary artist's role as the completion of a "conversion experience" guided by his education (1992, 281). The prologue also reveals Richard's ambivalence about this role: although he declares that this is a book about his early and persistent obsession with language and with how language "determined" his "public identity," he also describes his book as "essays impersonating an autobiography," as if to suggest not only that he is creatively revising the genre of autobiography but also that he is marginally an autobiographical writer and uncomfortable in his role. The prologue also introduces his ambivalence about his education and process of growing up: his is an American story of upward mobility, but it is also a story of loss, of an increasingly cool indifference toward his Mexican origins: "Aztec ruins hold no special interest for me. I do not search Mexican graveyards for ties to unnamable ancestors" (1982, 5). Nor does he wish in his autobiographical narrative to glorify his lower-class background; that would be hypocritical, because he has chosen and worked for his middle-class status. Paredes argues that Rodriguez smugly reasserts the privilege of the middle class and implies that there is cool alienation between the middle class and the working class (1992, 286–87). However, I hear regret in his tone as Rodriguez writes of the growing silence between himself and his parents, a chasm created by his education, which kept him still reading the Spanish of Lorca and Marquez but also claiming as his Montaigne, Shakespeare, and Lawrence—none of whom his parents had ever read. He calls himself "a comic victim of two cultures" (1982, 5). This prologue and the first chapter focus on language as an emblem of his struggle to negotiate the two cultures, to move between two discourses. Unlike Paredes, who posits that *Hunger of Memory* does not "manifest any tension between the forces of assimilation and the allegiances of ethnicity and class" (1992, 287), I read his textual negotiations as fraught with conflict and guilt, at least over ethnicity, if not over class.

Chapter 1 discusses further the relation between the public language of English and his private language of Spanish, celebrating with nostalgia the narrator's childhood memories of "the intimate speech my family once freely exchanged" (6). He recalls the sounds of Spanish versus English to his ears as a five-year-old. The English of *los gringos*, the language of power, was "never pleasing" with its "high nasal notes" (14), while the *español*, the language of their otherness, was the language of belonging and individualized specialness, the language of "joyful return" (16). Although Paredes claims that Rodriguez gives us no vivid picture of life within his Mexican-American culture, no sense of "children's games or rhymes, . . . of a grandmother's cure for *empacho* . . . no legends . . . , no stories of the Mexican Revolution" (1992, 285), his memories are there; they are just focussed symbolically on language. He feeds the hunger of memory by offering remembered stories of Spanish as a language in which he rejoiced at home; he lovingly describes "that military drum roll, the twirling roar of the Spanish r" (1982, 18), as opposed to descriptions of his parents' halting, "heartbreaking" English and its unsettling effect on him. There are also stories of his family's gatherings and interactions flavored by Spanish, and of his conversations with his grandmother, in which she told him stories about her life on a farm in Mexico and her work as a seamstress, conveying the timbre of intimacy in her voice and her caressing *español* (39). At the same time, he narrates tales of the clashes between public (American/English language) and private (Mexican/Spanish language), such as when the nuns from his school visited his parents at home and persuaded them to allow Richard to practice his English at home, spoiling the sanctuary of their "Spanish" home. His own ambivalence about Spanish is revealed in his confession that during his middle years, his tongue halted by guilt, he had great difficulty pronouncing his Spanish confidently; he had become a *pocho*, an assimilated Mexican American who had left his native society behind (28–29).

Perhaps to circumvent these clashes and conflicts, to redress this "original sin" against his family of exchanging English for Spanish (30), he argues a controversial position against bilingual education, asserting that Hispanic schoolchildren should learn English as a ticket into the mainstream culture; he will not undermine the school's distinct role of public, sociopolitical indoctrination (to train citizens for public life in American society), nor will he "trivialize the nature of intimate life—a family's 'language'" (12). Thus, in this chapter Rodriguez describes and feeds the hunger of his ethnic memory by reliving some of his childhood experiences, revisiting "the golden age of [his] youth" (26), especially while examining his two disparate linguistic lives. At the same time, he knows and names himself, at age seven, not as Ricardo Rodriguez but as *Rich-heard Road-ree-guess*, an American citizen (22, 27), who has a right to speak the public language of English and to develop his "public individuality" (26–27) in order to enter the public arena and reap its "social and political advantages" (27), first as a student and later as a writer.

In his final chapter Rodriguez reflects on his act of writing his intellectual autobiography as a middle-class American citizen, his view of the genre, and his readers. As Paredes rightly observes, *Hunger of Memory* is self-consciously academic and culturally sophisticated, "eager to establish its intellectual respectability" (1992, 287). This intellectual prowess demonstrated by his writing is a prominent part of his autobiographical persona. He also writes to make public his private life, to deconstruct the bipolarity that has split his life; I think he defuses some of the tensions between his public and private lives by writing this autobiography, even though Paredes argues that Rodriguez believes "no one can live dual roles—public and private identities . . . —comfortably" (289).

The autobiography represents a less-than-ambiguous break with his family: the very nature of the genre of autobiography is antithetical to the outlook of his parents, who would protect the privacy of the family. In writing his intellectual autobiography and confessing his alienation from his family, he embarrasses his mother, who has asked him not to "publish" the private life of his family. He also distorts his parents' words even when he quotes them, because, as he confesses, he has pulled their language out of its private context. Moreover, it embarrasses his mother that he writes these private thoughts for *los gringos*, the educated Americans whom he identifies as his audience. Yet he disagrees with his mother; he feels compelled to write to transcend his public/private conflict over language. He suggests that the deeply personal has a place in our American culture, and that strangers may be its best recipients: "There are things too personal to be shared with intimates" (1982, 185).

Rodriguez concludes, then, that authorship, his use of the English language, has helped him to understand himself; it has helped shape his identity as an American and completed his individuation from his parents. Paredes observes that his autobiography "intends to demonstrate Rodriguez's literary mastery of English as conclusive proof . . . of his assimilation" (1992, 293). Despite his assimilation, however, he must also continue to feed the hunger of memory, to revisit the borderland of his ethnicity in reminiscences, as he does in his concluding vignette about memories of his family's shared Christmas dinners. These dinners, conflated into one scene, are presented as not really warm and nurturing; they reveal the alienation of the younger generation from the parents, who for the most part are silent onlookers as their children converse and eat; there is unappeased hunger in Richard as he contemplates the silence of his father at the end of this gathering.

By writing this book, then, Rodriguez has not only carved out a public niche for himself but has also struggled, not entirely successfully, to negotiate the chasm between public and private, between Mexican and American, between Spanish and English. In claiming for himself a tensive public voice without entirely relinquishing the private one and declaring his entry into intellectual adulthood without relinquishing all the conflicts of this entry, he writes a "lyric of rhetorical angst" that is characteristic of many American ethnic autobiographies (Saldívar 1992, 307). Although recent critics such as José David Saldívar have denounced his language of rhetorical angst as marketable—hence insincere—and have seen Rodriguez as a conservative sellout to assimilation (307–8), I nevertheless read his text's voices as those of honest angst and regret-filled, though chosen, alienation, as well as of pride in making it into intellectual, cultured, middle-class America.

Similar negotiations of double discourses exist in Hong Kingston's autobiography. There is some controversy among Chinese American critics of Kingston, which Sau-ling Cynthia Wong has astutely surveyed and analyzed (Wong 1992, 252-60), about whether her text should be considered as autobiography; critics complain that it contains too much fiction and is too idiosyncratic, too unrepresentative of Chinese American experience, and thus misleading for white readers who might generalize about Chinese (and Chinese American) culture from reading it. However, these objections to the book's meanderings of the imagination in search of the spirit of a person's life and her storied selves do not exclude it from classification as autobiography, I would argue, because this genre has always blurred the distinctions between fiction and truth in the subjective rendering of peoples' identities. Moreover, as Wong contends, "autobiography cannot, by definition, be more than *one* person's life story; thus it cannot be fully trusted" to be representative of a collectivity (259). Nor does Hong Kingston ever claim to be a cultural exegete or purveyor of cultural authenticity; Wong rightly observes that Hong Kingston's "protagonist has eschewed the facile authority which self-appointment as guide and spokesperson could confer on her" (266). Hers is a uniquely personal story of the developing self and not intended to apply to "all" Chinese Americans. Wong thus characterizes the book as an autobiography and the book's "discursive space" as "between the two poles of the 'double consciousness'"—a space defined by W. E. B. Du Bois's concept of the "insider" who is aware of her cultural experience while writing, aware of the "outsider's" scrutiny of her "difference" (Wong 1992, 265). In other words, like Rodriguez, Hong Kingston in the act of writing the book attempts to negotiate double discourses in order to forge an ethnic identity.

These negotiations of double discourses are complicated further by the gender oppression existing for women among her Chinese kin. She strives in her book to adapt the Chinese mythology of the woman warrior to an American context, transforming herself into her own version of woman-warrior-as-American-writer to avenge the ethnic wrongs suffered by her people in the U.S. and to resist her Chinese culture's dismissal of women. In her act of writing *Woman Warrior*, she tries to exorcise the cadre of ghosts haunting her that have been conjured by her mother's Chinese cultural sensibility. Yet this haunting crew also galvanizes her imagination so that Hong Kingston is inspired to create stories out of her family's Chinese history and heritage. If her stories misrepresent Chinese folk materials, as some of her Chinese-American critics have claimed, these inaccuracies are, Wong has argued, "simply indications of how far removed from it the protagonist has become" (1976, 268) and indicative of how much she is therefore impelled to use her imagination to reconstruct the culture of her origin. She offers us, for example, the tale of No Name Woman, her father's sister, whose name has been expunged from her family's history for some unmentionable sin but whose life story Hong Kingston resurrects by imagining it for us. Telling of the education and adventures of Fa Mu Lan also energizes her to overcome the submissive and negative role that is more commonly expected of Chinese womanhood and to take on the alternative role of female fighter and defender of a cause. She, moreover, tells the story of her mother's experience as a medical student and her brave exorcism of a "sitting ghost," again as a way through language to talk herself into banishing her own metaphorical sitting ghosts, aspects of her Chinese heritage that paralyze and smother her in her American cultural milieu. She revels in the riches of her Chinese culture's mythology and folk tales and is subject to her own mother's hypnotic abilities as a storyteller.

In telling her tales in *Woman Warrior*, Hong Kingston models herself on her mother, Brave Orchid; she tells "talk stories," longing to learn more of her Chinese heritage and identity, while also at times trying on the linguistic outlook of her American existence. Like Rodriguez, she scrutinizes English; she praises its liberatory directness in contrast to the superstitious Chinese tendency to protect (hide) the truth through misleading or unreliable language: "The emigrants confused the gods by diverting their curses, misleading them with crooked streets and false names. They must try to confuse their offspring as well, who, I suppose, threaten them in similar ways—always trying to get things straight, always trying to name the unspeakable" (5). The American logical outlook, its simplicity and belief that "mysteries are for explanation," pleases her: "Shine floodlights into dark corners: no ghosts" (205); interestingly, however, she registers her appreciation of American directness here through the indirection of a metaphor, blending her two cultures linguistically. At one point the author rages at the "lies" her mother tells in all her stories and at her inability to distinguish between true accounts and made-up tales (202). As her mother puts it, "We like to say the opposite" (203). As an American writer, Hong Kingston often, but not always, prefers to write to readers/strangers what she feels most deeply about, especially her frustrating (non)communications with her mother and her mother's insulting assumptions about her and her femaleness.

While she names herself an American writer, Hong Kingston's text also expresses her (and her mother's) understanding, via the Chinese language, of the power of words ("Be careful what you say. It comes true. It comes true," 204), including her sense that her words have the power to resuscitate her aunt, No Name Woman, and also her fascination with all the Chinese versions of the word "I," the complex conceptualizing of identity in the Chinese culture. Her book's language conveys the notion that Hong Kingston and her narrator are several selves. Moreover, her love for the Chinese tradition of "talk story" is evident in the story in "A Song for a Barbarian Reed Pipe" that closes the book. It tells about her grandmother, a lover of theater, and the family's attendance at the theater in China. It also speculates on the performance they might have seen of the songs of Ts'ai Yen, the poetess. Hence it is a story of a story about language, the language of the play, and the language of the poetess in her life's history. This talk story, the beginning of which the narrator's mother had told her and the end of which she has created, is a perfect negotiation, in structure and symbolic content, of Hong Kingston's American auctorial identity and her Chinese aesthetic and political identifications. The poetess in the speculative performance that Hong Kingston fabricates had been snatched from her native Chinese tribe at age twenty and forced to dwell among a barbarian tribe. While there, Ts'ai Yen composed her own angry, sad, and yearning songs about China and her family, which she sang to the accompaniment of the barbarians' flutes.

The tale concludes with her decision to depart for the Han lands and to claim them as her home (Wong 1992, 270); the narrator remarks that one of the songs she had created while in exile is preserved in her own Chinese culture and played with their instruments. The song "translated well"; it made a successful discursive and aesthetic negotiation between the two cultures, just as Hong Kingston's text does. As Wong puts it, the final pages "celebrate not return from the remote peripheries to a waiting home but the creation of a new center through art" (270); they celebrate the author's own making of cultural meaning and identity. Her re-creation of the tale is an individuating act that separates herself, American-born, from her Chinese mother while at the same time acknowledging her cultural and emotional debts to Brave Orchid. It marks her entry into mature adulthood and emblematizes her creation of her literary or storied self, the enactment of her role as Chinese American writer—one who will "translate well" the complex truths of her mediations between her Chinese and American cultural contexts. Through the tale, Hong Kingston feeds the hunger of ancestral and familial memory while satisfying her appetite for her future as an American author.

Philip Roth undertakes similar negotiations in *Patrimony*, a text that is both a biography of his father Herman Roth and an autobiography of Philip Roth in relation to his father (just as Kingston's is an autobiography of herself and a biography of her mother and other female family members important to her identity). Roth recreates stories of Herman's past, his youth in the 1912 Jewish immigrant neighborhood of Newark, and offers details about his family's cultural heritage that help appease the hunger of memory, such as the tale of his deposit of his tefillin in a locker at the Y and the passing on of the shaving mug of his grandfather, Sender Roth. Some of these stories he puts in Herman's voice, his father recounting them in dialogues with Philip. Readers hear his reminiscences about the old neighborhood in Newark and anecdotes about life in the Jewish retirement communities of Florida. Herman's narrative is often a "meandering saga" of "the mundane existence of an ordinary immigrant family," in which he recalls neighborhood people's intricate family relationships—what Roth calls Herman's sacred text, his Deuteronomy, his Americanized version of the history of Israel (1991, 190). These stories Roth captures in a "Yiddishized" English similar to Kingston's mother's "Chinafied" English.

The narrator also joins himself to his father's secular Jewish culture by using some Yiddish. For example, as he retells his father's tale of the abandonment of the tefillin in the locker at the Y and figures out the reason for this act, he determines that the Y is the center of Jewish life for his father and his cohort. His explanation is peppered with Yiddish: "[T]he locker room of the Y, where they undressed, they schvitzed, they stank, where . . . they kibitzed and told their dirty jokes, and where, once upon a time, they'd made their deals—that was their temple and where they remained Jews" (96). Using the words "kibitzed" (to shoot the breeze or engage in small talk) and "schvitzed" (sweated) marks Philip as a member of his own ethnic world. Yet in this same episode the language of his interpretation of Herman's act as "inspired by a personalized symbolic mythology as eccentric as Beckett's or Gogol's" (94) also places him squarely within the intellectual, "artsy" mainstream of American culture. He is also the cultured American in a passage about his grandfather's shaving mug. After nostalgically describing the mug's connection with the Jewish Sabbath and summarizing his Jewish immigrant grandfather's history, he says, "His mug emitted the aura of an archaeological find . . . it had the impact on me of a Greek vase depicting the mythic origins of the race" (28). Both voices and discourses represent Philip Roth's narrator, the American Jewish writer's storied self.

In traversing these double discourses, Roth's narrator attempts to build a bridge across the "poignant abyss" of culture and education growing between himself and his father ever since high school, the kind of abyss Rodriguez writes about. Roth had tried to negotiate this chasm when in college through his fantasy that his father had merged with him; he had the sense that he was his father's "double or medium" as he pursued his studies (159–60). However, mature acts of language, such as the writing of this book, more firmly bridge the gaps between middle-aged adult son and elderly father. They also help Philip to make that transition into orphaned adulthood and full realization of his American and Jewish literary gifts, just as Hong Kingston's and Rodriguez's autobiographical acts marked and guided their transition into psychological and literary autonomy.

These stories of his father's recounted by Philip are sacred to Philip: in his affectionate retelling and reinterpreting of these tales from the perspective of the American-born son, Philip reveals his "holy" aim of preserving his family's history and capturing for the future his memories of his father. The book ends with these words: *"You must not forget anything"* (238), an echo of the earlier passage that articulates his aim in writing this autobiographical biography: "'I must remember accurately,' I told myself, 'remember everything accurately so that when he is gone I can re-create the father who created me.' You must not forget anything" (177). Self-consciously, Roth has attempted to capture "the lived reality" of his father's life and also to create a literary portrait of that reality (Lejeune's "effect of the real"), particularly during Herman's final years.

In recreating his father and his memories of Herman in the Yiddishized and American-cultured witty discourses of this text, Roth also recreates himself, Herman's American Jewish son, The Author. He conceives of this text as part of his *Patrimony*, his rich inheritance from his father, who had been in his own right a raconteur and humorist ("The jokes originate with [Herman]," he acknowledges to one of his fans [46]). His literary *Patrimony* is apparent in this passage: "[H]e taught me the vernacular. He *was* the vernacular, unpoetic and expressive and point-blank, with all the vernacular's glaring limitations and all its durable force" (181). In remembering Herman, Roth clearly wants to reaffirm his own status as an American *Jewish* writer. So he offers us these vignettes of Jewish life: he has memory-ties to Herman's old Jewish neighborhood; he has Sender Roth's shaving mug, which his grandfather had used in the local barber shop every Friday afternoon in preparation for the Jewish Sabbath; he recounts stories of anti-Semitism at Metropolitan Life Insurance during Herman's years there, challenging the gentile business world to deny the truth of the stories and asserting his status as fighter for a Jewish cause. Roth also shores himself up against Jewish critics across his career with his father's praise, explaining that his "fiercely loyal and devoted father . . . had never found a thing in my books to criticize—what enraged *him* were the Jews who attacked my books as anti-Semitic and self-hating" (188). Establishing his roots in Herman and Herman's cultural milieu in writing this book, Philip reinscribes his identity as *Jewish* American writer.

At the same time he reflects on his role as (American) autobiographer and biographer. In concluding self-consciously with a symbol-laden dream he had had about Herman's death, in which his father had been envisioned as a defunct American warship in the waters off Newark, with himself as "a small fatherless evacuee" on the pier waiting to be rescued (237), he notes that "every major theme of his life was encapsulated there, everything of significance to both of us." He then proceeds succinctly to list these themes, frankly and smoothly discharging the biographer's last important summing-up task. But as postmodern autobiographer, he recounts another dream, his father's return to chide him for dressing his corpse inappropriately, which he interprets as his father's judgment upon him for writing this biographical book exposing Herman's life while Herman was dying, "in keeping with the unseemliness of my profession" (237); in this respect Herman (or Philip's projection of him) resembles Mrs. Rodriguez. Herman's criticism, the narrator suggests, is a judgment by *the* father, to which sons, in most cultures, must submit, because of the very nature of the father/son dyad. Rodriguez eventually does so too in his recent autobiographical book, *Days of Obligation: An Argument with My Mexican Father*; David L. Kirp suggests that in this book Rodriguez, more than in his first book, "pays a kind of homage to his Hispanic and Indian selves—his surmise that Mexico had nothing to teach him turned out to be quite wrong" (1992, 42). Daughters like Hong Kingston similarly do obeisance to mothers in their life stories. To Herman Roth's judgment about his book, Philip willingly submits because in writing *Patrimony*, he has followed "the inscription on his [father's] coat of arms": he has remembered everything (1991, 124). His proud role of the American Jewish son as the biographer of a Jewish immigrant father is self-consciously analyzed, and he acknowledges that in this text he has created his father's storied selves; he has dressed his corpse in words, as a way of remembering. As an autobiographer, he has also created his own storied selves: the bereft Jewish son and the American Jewish writer.

Thus, like the texts of Rodriguez and Hong Kingston, *Patrimony* nourishes both the ethnic hunger of memory and the auctorial appetite for an American (literary) future, creating a border identity for the autobiographical subject in double discourses that display the characteristic tensions of ethnic autobiography. The source of the tensions in these texts is that ethnic yearnings for the past (a marginalized existence) usually compete with American ambitions for the future (a mainstream existence); for the ethnic autobiographer to feed one (and to familiarize readers with the textual experience of it) is temporarily to stint (and defamiliarize) the other. A neat hybridity is impossible—too fictive even for autobiographical writings that only promise "the effect of the real" self, not a referentially "real" textual self. Unappeased hunger and disease thus mark the ethnic autobiography even when its author has boldly staked out a place in the very center of American culture.

References

Bell, Susan Groag, and Marilyn Yalom, eds. *Revealing Lives: Autobiography, Biography, and Gender.* Albany: State University of New York Press, 1990.

Eakin, Paul John. Foreword to Lejeune 1989.

Kingston, Maxine Hong. *The Woman Warrior.* New York: Vintage, 1976.

Kirp, David L. "Beyond Assimilation." Review of *Days of Obligation: An Argument with my Mexican Father,* by Richard Rodriguez. *The New York Times Book Review,* 15 November 1992, 42.

Lejeune, Philippe. *On Autobiography.* Minneapolis: University of Minnesota Press, 1989.

Paredes, Raymond A. "Autobiography and Ethnic Politics: Richard Rodriguez's *Hunger of Memory.*" In Payne 1992, 280–96.

Payne, James Robert, ed. *Multicultural Autobiography: American Lives.* Knoxville: University of Tennessee Press, 1992.

Rodriguez, Richard. *Hunger of Memory: The Education of Richard Rodriguez.* New York: Bantam, 1982.

Roth, Philip. *Patrimony.* New York: Simon and Schuster, 1991.

Saldívar, José David. "The School of Caliban: Pan-American Autobiography." In Payne 1992, 297–325.

Smith, Sidonie. *A Poetics of Women's Autobiography.* Bloomington: Indiana University Press, 1987.

Wong, Sau-ling Cynthia. "Autobiography as Guided Chinatown Tour? Maxine Hong Kingston's *The Woman Warrior* and the Chinese-American Autobiographical Controversy." In Payne 1992, 248–79.

Chinese-U.S. Border Crossings
Ethnic, National, and Anthropological

MAYFAIR MEI-HUI YANG

In 1981, on my first trip to mainland China from the U.S. as an anthropologist, I crossed over a border vaster and deeper than the Pacific Ocean. It was a journey over multiple borders—ethnic, linguistic, cultural, national, discursive, and political-economic—each ramifying the other. At that time, China had just started to open up to the Western and capitalist world, and tourists, business people, and scholars were allowed inside the borders. While people outside China were learning about the new egalitarian and state-controlled society created by the Communist Revolution (1949), and the extent of the psychic, moral, and cultural damage of the Cultural Revolution (1966–76), those inside China were finding out about the decadence and alluring wealth of the capitalist societies. Perhaps the best way to describe this experience of border crossing is to provide a Chinese woman's account of crossing in the opposite direction. For Li Qian, Americans seem so carefree and fun-loving.

> Sometimes I envy this way of life. I think Americans are very lucky, but then, I also think that it is a very limited life. They do not have a very deep appreciation of life . . . when you spend your whole life floating in sugar water [*paozai tangshui li*], then you don't see a lot of things. It's like climbing Huangshan or Taishan [famous mountains in China]: those who live at the top have the world at their feet. It's a good view, but they've only

got a limited perspective from up there. It's only by starting at the bottom and climbing laboriously upward to the top that you can have the full perspective of life. You know, experience the world at all different levels. As a Chinese, I've had this experience. For more than 30 years China was closed off from the world, nobody inside knew anything about the outside. I've climbed from the 19th century right into the 20th, when I came to the U.S. I've experienced both . . . I'm satisfied that I've had a full life.

What I would like to discuss here is that elusive thing which we can call "perspective" or "point of departure" in anthropological discourse. The account just given is a Chinese woman's perspective on the advanced industrialized West. It is not a perspective that can be found in most English-language anthropological treatises, where the native point of view is bracketed and treated as part of the data and generally does not inform the theoretical discussion or telos of analysis. Most anthropological writing is undertaken by Westerners addressing Western issues and concerns and speaking to a Western audience. The issue I'd like to explore is whether it is possible to build into anthropological discourse and cultural critique a different point of view and a different array of contextualizations for ethnographic practice and writing. That is to say, anthropology must recognize its role as what Edward Said called "traveling theory" (1983) and all the dangers and promises this role can bring. The danger is to impose a Eurocentric vision in the description and analysis of other societies, which often has profound consequences when these societies come to adopt this vision. Such was the case in twentieth-century China when the adoption of Western social evolutionism, Marxism, or a discourse of modernity led to a wholesale rejection and self-inflicted destruction of Chinese culture (Yang 1996). At the same time, can anthropology also speak to and address issues of non-Western cultures by building into its discourse points of view that will enhance its reception in destinations other than the West?

China has the dubious distinction of being home to one-fifth of the human species. Yet very little is heard from within this national and cultural zone by those outside, and what is heard is not quite understood. In writing about China in the English language, now the most powerful language in the world, how can an anthropologist of Chinese descent and Western education position herself and select a point of departure? This is not just a question of epistemology, for what is at stake is to ensure that the specificity of China's situation does not get obscured in the act of translation across borders, and, at the same time, to make anthropological discourse more available and usable to Chinese social thinkers and writers on both sides of the border.

Since my own Chinese ancestry has played an important role in shaping both my fieldwork and my thoughts and writings on China, I would like here to examine myself as both subject and object of anthropological analysis. I was born in Taiwan but went abroad at the age of five. In the 1970s I arrived in the U.S. and attended high school. Like my parents, who had left the Mainland for Taiwan, I am also part of the Chinese diaspora, which since the nineteenth century has scattered Chinese first in Southeast Asia and then in other parts of the world. The topic of what forces made so many people leave their home country deserves an extended analysis. Suffice it to say for now that something was going wrong in China;[1] otherwise, why did the opium sold by Western imperialists find such a ready market in nineteenth-century China, and why did so many leave, in wave after wave of emigration—of which the latest was in the aftermath of 4 June 1989?

Before I came to the United States, my national and cultural identities as a Chinese were more or less intact. It was the encounter with the potent forces of assimilation in the U.S., an immigrant country par excellence, that started to erode my axis of orientation. At the same time, what was made available to me as a substitute identity, the category of "Chinese American," did not feel comfortable or adequate. Those who identified with "Chinese American" seemed to be second- and third-generation "ABCs" (American-born Chinese) who did not speak or read Chinese and did not keep track of current events in China, Taiwan, or Hong Kong. It seemed that, buried within much of the discourse of ethnic and minority difference in the U.S., were powerful forces of assimilation to an American and Western cultural situation, albeit now a reformed and self-declared "multicultural" one.

The study of China offered a way of addressing the state of dislocation and disorientation that comes from having national borders within, which was not possible with the American discourse of ethnic minorities. Anthropology thematized the cultural difference I struggled with, while at the same time, anthropology's dominant impulse, objectivism, allowed me to hover in a scholarly, detached space in between nationalities and cultures. This objectivism was quickly abandoned once I got to China, at about the same time that objectivism was also called into question from within Western anthropology.

As an on-the-ground anthropologist dealing with the mundane facts of everyday life in China, I was often able to pass as a Chinese. Speaking

Mandarin in north China, my accent could be attributed to my coming from the South. In the South, my accent was easily explained as being from the North. While I told everyone whom I got to know well in China that I was from the United States, I was careful for their sake not to dispense this information too easily in front of their neighbors, acquaintances, or colleagues. Instead, I tried to let them decide whether they wanted to make this knowledge public. Since China's relationship with Taiwan was still on a precarious footing in the early 1980s, I was also initially careful as to whom I revealed my Taiwan origins, but by the mid-1980s this was no longer a concern.[2]

There were both advantages and disadvantages in having a Chinese ancestry and being able to render my origins invisible. It enabled me to experience at first hand the ways that a Chinese treats and interacts with other Chinese and to compare these with my experiences in Taiwan. It also allowed me to see and hear things that might ordinarily be withheld from what are called "foreigners." At the same time, as I came to internalize or reinternalize the emotions of being a native Chinese, I often lost the detached perspective that is needed to recognize and examine some outstanding social features. One of the emotions that I internalized and that sometimes diminished my fieldwork effectiveness was fear. It was a dull fear, usually a constant presence in the background, censoring my every utterance and movement. And then at times it erupted into a major preoccupation that saturated my every thought and movement.

In the first half of the 1980s in China, the culture of fear was still a powerful force in constraining actions and enforcing reticence of speech in everyday life. To be sure, it was a milder form of the culture of terror that reigned during the Cultural Revolution, but for me coming from another world, the culture of fear was-palpable as one of the main sources of culture shock. The political atmosphere in Beijing at that time was probably comparable to that of Poland in the 1970s, where even the removal of Stalinist-type direct threats to one's personal security did not signal a dramatic change in the habits of wariness and self-protection (Nowak 1988). The atmosphere in Beijing became significantly more relaxed in the late 1980s until the trauma of 4 June 1989, after which it is said that things returned to the climate of the early 1980s. The economic prosperity of the early '90s brought another wave of political relaxation on the part of society, if not on the part of the state.

One of the reasons why I was so susceptible to the culture of fear may have been the split in my subjectivity between being an "overseas Chinese," a "Chinese American," and a native Chinese. The category "overseas Chinese" *(huaqiao)* belongs firmly within a Chinese discourse that constructs it as people of Chinese ancestry who have maintained their language, culture, and ties of kinship with the "Motherland," who live in Chinese communities abroad, and who do not regard their current host countries as their primary point of orientation. In common usage, *huaqiao* often refers to overseas Chinese in Asia, while *huayi* often designates those living in European or North American countries.

The category "Chinese American" designates an American of Chinese ancestry and is also part of a new American discourse that, since the 1960s, has come to replace an older discourse of the Euro-American "melting pot." This new discourse affirms ethnic diversity while resting on a common ground of assumptions and values that are shared with the dominant Euro-American culture. Besides these two subject positions, the fact that I was so often mistaken for a native and treated as one in China meant that with the passing of time and the acquisition of more of the native habitus of thought, feeling, and action, the moments when I came to adopt elements of native subjectivity gradually increased.

This triangular subject composition made it all the easier for me to lose sense of any subject grounding; thus free-floating and open-ended in subjectivity, I became highly attuned to the culture of fear. Had I subscribed to a firm American subjectivity, I would have paid more attention to the protection that a U.S. passport provided me, and perhaps I would not have felt as vulnerable. The fact that I could pass as a native meant that people were not put on their guard while conversing with me. While this made for a rich participant-observation experience, it also made me prone to feeling guilty and afraid of being discovered as an impostor and spy, thus more easily becoming a subject of the culture of fear. At the same time, I was also not a real native, and so did not possess a developed and sophisticated immune system to handle and contain fear, as well as the anger that arises when one is so often thwarted by the bureaucratic system. Nor was I schooled in the everyday tactics of subverting and neutralizing the encompassing power of this system. Thus I was triply vulnerable: first, as a semi-native, I came to share with other natives the subjective experience of living in a culture of fear. Second, being brought up elsewhere, I also felt the fear that comes from not being versed in the ways the society has of dealing with it. I would probably never attain the level of stoic dignity, equanimity, or bravado and defiance that I have known in some natives. Finally, as an outsider who sometimes posed as an insider, I became susceptible to the fear that the masquerade would be uncovered, and my true identity, whatever that was, would be revealed.

I have attempted a self-analysis in order to show that the pervasive model of anthropological and cultural studies epistemology, the dualistic theme of The West and The Other, is no longer adequate to deal with the postmodern world of knowledge. Even though most anthropologists experience sharp ruptures in their sense of self when in the field, most textual reconstructions still delimit the anthropologist as a firmly rooted Western subject.

Of course, in recent years reflexive anthropology has challenged the universal knowing subject or Archimedean point of view in anthropological discourse. This universal subject, which speaks as the omniscient narrator of traditional "objective" anthropology, has been revealed to be in the end, merely a localized Western point of view. However, reflexive anthropology has often replaced the universal knowing subject with a relativized *Western* subject—a self-critical subject, to be sure, but still one that takes as its point of departure the world of the West. This has the ironic effect of reinforcing and re-reifying the West and thus bolstering its strength.

The space opened up in recent years for self-reflexivity on anthropological representations of the Other has had a salutary effect of widening the possibilities and goals of anthropological inquiry. Interpretive anthropology has sought to contextualize and historically situate both the Other and the observing and writing Subject. Calls for "thick description," for understanding the "native's point of view" (Geertz 1973, 1984), and for dialogic and polyphonic representation (Clifford 1988) are all part of an awareness of the specificity and relativity of the subject positions of observer and observed. The notion and practice of "anthropology as cultural critique" (Marcus) are also historically informed. They represent the recognition that the cultural forms around the world today are not the products of an essential native culture but bear the effects of Western imperialism and capitalism, which must be subjected to critique both abroad and at home in the West. While thankful for the creation of this "experimental [and self-critical] moment" in Western anthropology, I submit that the project of interpretive anthropology must be pushed much farther and that the promise of a decentered, polyphonic, and critical anthropology has yet to be realized in more diverse ways.

Anthropology as Western self-critique has the problem of reducing the understanding of another culture into an exercise in finding solutions to problems and questions that issue from a Western milieu. The Other culture merely serves as a staging ground or experimental case for addressing and playing out issues that are of concern in the West.

That is, the anthropologist travels thousands of miles to live in another culture in order to bring back material that will help the West better criticize and improve itself. This renders anthropology insensitive to issues and concerns that arise out of native experience and native self-understanding, and can foreclose the possibility of understanding and joining in native self-critique.

At times, the elevation of Western self-critique is almost as Eurocentric as the old colonial attitudes of Western superiority, because it continues to assign such a central role to the West. Western self-critique, it is presumed, will also serve to improve conditions for the Other, since the Other's historical context is one of Western colonialism and therefore dependent on the West's self-critique. Even Edward Said, a major figure in the critique of the West, has expressed reservations about the basic assumption

> that the whole of history in colonial territories was a function of the imperial. . . . [There] has been a tendency in anthropology, history, and cultural studies to treat the whole of world history as viewable by a Western meta-subject, whose historicizing and disciplinary rigor either took away or, in the post-colonial period, restored history to people and cultures "without" history. (1986, 59)

Understanding the Other cannot be reduced to a cultural critique of the West. By merely reversing the terms of the old colonialist discourse so that now the Other is valorized while the West is criticized, certain strains of reflexive anthropology still overprivilege the role of the West as the one needing and producing critique. If anthropology is to be more relevant to contemporary contexts outside the West, it cannot restrict itself to a critique of Western colonialism. A way must be found to accommodate and engage with different cultural critiques from the "Natives' point of view," critiques of new forms of power that have emerged in the postcolonial period.

The ethnographic process, it seems to me, involves at least two dimensions of interpretation. In the first dimension, the anthropologist engages in the work of observing, listening, investigating, describing, transcribing, understanding, and explicating the expressions and practices of a particular Other. The second dimension is a metarealm of understanding that, on the one hand, includes native metainterpretive frameworks, natives' self-positioning and self-critiques of their own culture in a certain world-historical context, and, on the other hand, includes the metainterpretation of the anthropologist learning, debating, and engaging with native frameworks of understanding and critique. For the anthropologist, the work of this metainterpretive dimension involves not only talking to representative or average native practitioners and informants, but also engaging with the thoughts of native critical thinkers, reformers, or persons who have reflected deeply upon their own society and the experience of modernity. Only by engaging in the work of this metainterpretation can the anthropologist proceed to figure out how the cultural elements under study might fit into the natives' own larger historical context. While the first dimension of interpretation of the Other has received much attention and refinement in recent anthropological discourse, the second has seldom been thematized.

Having called for the incorporation of native critiques in anthropological endeavors, I am also aware of the difficulties and hazards of this enterprise. In addressing some problem areas in a social milieu not one's own, not only is there the old danger of imposing Western values but there is also the problem of uncritically adopting wholesale the self-critique of the natives. In the case of Chinese intellectuals in the current reform period in China, there is a general sentiment of rejection and condemnation of what is taken as Chinese culture, Confucian tradition, and "feudal thought," things that allegedly hold China back and prevent it from catching up with the West. Two books, *The Ugly Chinese (Chou-e de zhongguoren)* written by Taiwan author Yang Bai, and *The Deep Structure of Chinese Culture (Zhongguo wenhua de shengcen jiegou)*, by Sun Longji, an American-trained Hong Kong writer, were extremely popular in the 1980s in urban and intellectual circles in China. Both excoriated the Chinese people for a whole panoply of bad character traits. In the Chinese intellectuals' critique of an essentialized Chinese culture, the West is generally held up, implicitly or explicitly, as a paragon of progress, enlightenment, and virtue. The most vivid expression of this sentiment is in the 1988 TV serial "River Elegy" (*He Shang*), in which the most sacred symbols of Chinese culture—the Yellow River, the dragon, and the Great Wall—are reinterpreted and denounced for representing violence against a helpless people, autocratic despotism, and conservative isolationism (Wakeman 1989). In the last scene, there is an airborne view of a muddy and sluggish Yellow River, which flows out of the land mass of China to join and blend itself with the openness, dynamism, and liberation of the blue ocean, standing for the modern West. Whether condemning Chinese culture or praising the West, these views share a common assumption, that culture is an essence that endures through time.

Faced with this native self-critique, the anthropologist from the West must resist the urge to label Chinese intellectuals "Orientalist" or exemplars of colonized, *comprador* mentality. In these labels lies the insistence that the Other plays a role for a West nostalgic for premodern times, a role of native "authenticity" and purity, a role no longer possible nor desirable, it seems, for much of the contemporary non-Western world.[3] This Western, self-critical perspective also implies that China's problems can all be attributed to the experience of colonialism and capitalism, to external imperialist forces. It does not account for the degree to which the forces of modernity introduced from without have, over the course of the twentieth century, not only destroyed certain aspects of tradition but have also strengthened selective elements of Chinese tradition so that the arrangement of power in China today, however novel, still has a very familiar Chinese flavor.

On the other hand, in confronting the essentialist self-critique of Chinese intellectuals, my own inclination is to point out that while it can serve as a galvanizing discourse for cultural renewal and innovation, it also suffers from its ahistorical perspective. To ascribe to Chinese culture an intrinsic timeless nature, and to blame this nature for various inadequacies in the modern world, overlooks what a perspective that is sensitive to historical context would recognize: much of what can be critiqued in China today are modern forms of power and control found elsewhere in the world in other experiences of modernity. In examining the nature of power in contemporary China, one would have to concur with Michel Foucault that the power of "administration over the ways people live" and the oppositional struggles it has engendered are "transversal" processes in the modern world. "That is, they are not limited to one country. Of course they develop more easily and to a greater extent in certain countries, but they are not confined to a particular political or economic form of government" (Foucault 1983, 211).

In constructing a historical framework for understanding state socialist China, both Western self-critique and Chinese self-critique seem to be inappropriate. It seems to me that the weakness of both self-critiques is that they still subscribe to a clear-cut and isomorphic set of binary oppositions: the West and the Other, the East vs. the West, tradition vs. modernity. In the postmodern world, the sheer number and variety of transnational, cross-cultural and discursive border crossings accompanying human movements, communications media and the circulation of commodities (Rosaldo 1989; Appadurai 1990; Anzaldúa 1987) have together begun to affect the self-understanding and practice of anthropology. There is a recognition that the discipline can no longer remain wedded to a discourse of fixed borders between a Western knowing subject and a pure and culturally integral object of the Other (Clifford 1988). There are also suggestions that the outmoded organic holistic model of culture might be replaced by a Foucaultian vision of modern transnational and translinguistic discursive formations (274). Given these modern border crossings, it no longer seems adequate to mount a critique either of the West or of Chinese tradition.

The Western anthropological subject has already started to be broken up from within by the three-pronged corrosive force of class, race/ ethnicity, and gender. At the same time, anthropology has also experienced an influx of non-Western practitioners, both in the form of students from other lands coming to study in the West and as members of anthropology departments and programs set up in countries outside of Europe and North America. Yet we have seen few of these developments translated into real changes in the knowing subject of anthropological discourse. It is perhaps time to fragment this integrated Western knowing subject and show how not only "cultures" but also the knowing subject are being increasingly traversed by lines of transcultural and transnational border crossings.

In other words, a further pluralization of anthropological and ethnographic subject positionings is in order. And this pluralization must be broader than that stemming from the three-pronged corrosive force (gender, race/ethnicity, and class distinctions) at work now in reflexive anthropology and cultural studies. The bulk of this multi*ethnic* discourse, it seems to me, is limited to the construction of an "American" multiculturalism and is a project that does not engage adequately with the realities of trans*national* border crossings. The kind of pluralization I am calling for will address issues stemming from transnational border crossings of anthropological subjectivity. The liminal subject position in which I have situated myself, as neither insider nor outsider, both subject and object of knowledge, may be taken as an instance of a decentered anthropological knowing subject.

In an insightful article on the writings of Edward Said, the literary critic Abdul JanMohamed outlined four types of modern border crossings between the Third World and the West: those of the exile, immigrant, colonialist,[4] and scholar/anthropologist. The subjectivity of the exile is marked by a sense of absence and loss of the home culture. This "structural nostalgia" is accompanied by a general indifference "to the values and characteristics of the host culture" (JanMohamed 1993, 101). At the same time, the enforced distance between the exile and his or her homeland can produce a renewed and profound linkage between the exile and the formative culture of birth. In contrast, the immigrant is propelled by a "desire to become a full-fledged subject of the new culture" (101) and by a tendency to shed the habits and foci of the old subjectivity.

Both exile and immigrant are in turn differentiated from the colonialist and anthropologist who "apprehend the new culture, not as a field of subjectivity, but rather as an object of/for their gaze" (102). Whereas the exile and immigrant must confront the issue of "a rupture between and a re-suturing of individual and collective subjectivities" (101), the colonialist and anthropologist are not troubled with a profound realignment or threat to subjectivity. However, while the colonialist actively represses or lacks any desire to become a subject of the native culture, the anthropologist's approach to the problem of "going native" is much more complex. In order to understand the Other, the anthropologist must learn the native language and culture, which can often open up the borders of his or her subjectivity. However, the professional and epistemological strictures of anthropology have usually ensured that the anthropologist reasserted the detached stance of "objectivism" and maintained a clear borderline between the West and the Other.

The traditional strengths of anthropology (long-term fieldwork, immersion in another culture, openness to cultural difference, and understanding the natives' point of view) notwithstanding, when it comes to anthropological subjectivity, the border between the West and the Other has been clearly demarcated and maintained. The native point of view can be described and appreciated, so long as everyone remembers that it is on the other side of the border and the roles of knower and the known are not to be confused. JanMohamed's pairing of exile and immigrant as border crossers who approach a host culture as a "field of subjectivity" and who experience a profound rupture and repositioning of their subjectivities suggests another course for the anthropological knowing subject. What it suggests is that in both fieldwork and ethnographic writing, elements of native subjectivity must be allowed to mingle with and reshape Western anthropological subjectivity. The anthropologist must seek to become not only like the exile who gains a certain perspective on his or her own culture while residing in another culture (Marcus and Fischer 1986), but especially like an immigrant who starts to absorb a new subjectivity, interprets the world from its standpoints, and acts upon its historical concerns as if she were a new member of that culture. Understanding and engaging with native self-interpretations of historical context and native self-critiques are a step toward dissolving the monolithic Western subject of knowledge, whether this subject is one engaged in self-promotion or self-critique. In this way, anthropology will become more available and relevant as a discourse with which a wide variety of cultural and discursive subjectivities in the modern world can engage.

Much of reflexive anthropology is compatible with the advocacy of "multiculturalism" in the U.S. I want to argue that the decentering of a Western anthropological knowing subject cannot be restricted to the issues of multiculturalism as they are presently formulated. American multicultural discourse not only conflates the three terms of exile, ethnicity, and immigrant but also privileges the latter two terms. It would certainly be salutary for anthropology to incorporate the new subject positions of various ethnic and immigrant minorities, but it is still the critique and improvement of the West. The figure of the immigrant or ethnic is oriented towards the Western center even while criticizing it, while the exile is oriented in a different direction towards another center. Whereas the immigrant or ethnic tries to escape an imposed marginalization by struggling to be included in the center, the exile is engaged in a willed state of self-displacement and self-imposed marginalization. The immigrant or ethnic minority demands the right to join and be recognized by the host or dominant culture, while the exile insists on maintaining an identity with the home culture and resists merging in with the new environment and easing into a new home. For anthropologists residing in the West, it is the figure of the exile who wills her own homelessness, it would seem, who provides a subject position that will truly decenter anthropology from the West. However, this position is often maintained at a high personal cost. The other way to a multiplex and truly transnational anthropology is of course the development of anthropological thought in non-Western countries or locales, but in many areas there are certain barriers to this.

The question of a decentered anthropological subject position from which to formulate diagnoses of China's modern afflictions challenges not only Eurocentrism but also the "center" of contemporary Chinese culture. At a time when the center of Chinese culture in the world (whether the political capital of Beijing or the heartland of China) is often unable to articulate the concerns of a significant portion of people who call themselves Chinese, it is on the peripheries of Chinese culture where dynamic cultural innovations and self-questioning will have to take place (Tu 1991; Lee 1991). This periphery is the product of the waves of Chinese diaspora in the nineteenth and twentieth centuries—people fleeing warfare, impoverishment, and political persecution in the troubled Mainland. It includes the Chinese societies of Taiwan, Hong

Kong, and Singapore, as well as Chinese communities scattered in what Western anthropologists call the "core," that is to say, the societies of the West. The two latest waves of this diaspora are the 1980s and '90s migration of ethnic Chinese to North America, Europe and Australia (Tu 1991, 21–22). Therefore, it should be remembered that one society's core is another's periphery.

The notion of periphery implies the importance of distance, geographical or subjective, for diagnosis and cultural critique of the center. Just as the anthropologist of Western subjectivity gains an insight into the modern West by studying primitive and peasant societies on its periphery (Marcus and Fisher 1986), overseas Chinese immigrants and exiles can come to a new understanding of Chinese culture while being away from the Mainland. Geographical distance produces subjective distance. For the immigrant and exile, long separation from the homeland means that part of the self disengages itself from identification with the homeland, so that the home culture becomes "objectified" to a certain extent. No longer is the home culture part of the new everyday reality in which the subject is situated; now the subject discovers within herself a habitus that does not fit in with the new surroundings. The contrast that the subject notices between the features of the host culture and those of the home culture relativizes the habitus of old as only one among many ways of dealing with the world. For the immigrant eager to embrace a new subjectivity of the host culture, the objectified self becomes the target of criticism, repression, and efforts at self-transformation. For the exile, however, this objectified self becomes a focus for self-reflection and self-renewal as the subject reaffirms the ties that hold the self to the home culture.

Although geographical distance produces subjective distance, it is not the sole determinant for subjective distance. Even without spatial distance, the subject can come to feel that one part of herself does not fit in with her cultural environment. The portion of herself that does not fit triggers an internal distanciation mechanism that renders the subject a marginal person without the experience of migration. The Czech notion of an "internal exile" where the subject maintains a private space or sanctuary from the depredations of state-infused culture is an example of the importance of marginality in state socialism (Lee 1991, 220–21). Internal exile can also describe the subjectivity of any cultural critic who engages in self-critique within his or her homeland. Without geographical distance, cultural self-critique is facilitated when a division emerges within the self, establishing a distance between the critical self and the self who is identified as part of the object of critique. In fact, it can be argued that self-critique in its very nature implies an internal division and a distanciation mechanism.[6] If cultural critique is indeed predicated on subjective internal divisions, then it is not surprising that one frequently encounters critique either among marginal people or on the peripheries of a culture. In the case of China, cultural diagnosis and critique from the periphery takes on added significance, because the present political situation makes it impossible to speak at the center.

This anthropological subject is a product of the Chinese diaspora who came to the U.S. in the 1970s, fashioned herself as an immigrant, only to find the label "Chinese American" unsatisfactory because it sought to make her into an American minority subject. Through the study of China she inadvertently recuperated the persona of "overseas Chinese," thus switching from the subjectivity of immigrant to exile. When she went to China as an anthropologist, one part of the experience was that of a culture-shocked Western subject of knowledge trying to understand an alien culture. The other part was that of an exile returning home after a long absence, sadly and unpleasantly reminded of all the familiar reasons why she left. Fieldwork was a mixture of the Western subject becoming an immigrant to China and the overseas Chinese subject who, on the one hand, empathized with all the joys and sufferings of the mother culture and, on the other hand, objectified it as an afflicted part of herself that needed to be diagnosed and healed. By recognizing the "overseas Chinese" and the "Chinese American" components of this ethnographic subject, and by accepting rather than rejecting the process and the possibilities of "going native," she becomes part of a larger movement of decentering the Western knowing subject while attempting to create a new form of discourse that is useful and relevant to ongoing projects in native self-understanding, self-critique, and reform.

Notes

1. I believe that the economic problems were only the most visible signs of a much larger cultural malaise, which has yet to be understood.

2. In 1988, the Taiwan government formally allowed its citizens to visit the Mainland.

3. Trinh T. Minh-ha has written about a Western insistence on native authenticity: "I am also encouraged to express my difference. My audience expects and demands it; otherwise people would feel as if they have been cheated: . . . We came to listen to that voice of difference likely to bring us *what we can't have* and to divert us from the monotony of sameness. They, like their anthro-

pologists whose specialty is to detect all the layers of my falseness and truthfulness, are in a position to decide what/who is 'authentic' and what/who is not" (1989, 88).

4. The category of colonialist can be stretched to include the modern Western businessman and woman of the postcolonial era.

5. Hong Kong Chinese, especially from the professional, middle, and upper classes, are leaving in order to escape the uncertainties of life after the Communist mainland takes over the territories in 1997.

6. I thank Abdul JanMohamed for sharing his insights on this topic with me.

References

Anzaldúa, Gloria. *Borderlands/La Frontera: The New Mestiza*. San Francisco: Spinster/Aunt Lute Books, 1987.

Appadurai, Arjun. "Disjuncture and Difference in the Global Cultural Economy," *Public Culture* 2.2 (1990): 1–24.

Bai, Yang. *Chou-e de zhongguoren* (The ugly Chinese). Taibei: Lin Bäc Chubanshe, 1985.

Clifford, James. *The Predicament of Culture: Twentieth Century Ethnography, Literature, and Art*. Cambridge: Harvard University Press, 1988.

Clifford, James, and George E. Marcus, eds. *Writing Culture: The Poetics and Politics of Ethnography*. Berkeley: University of California Press, 1986.

Foucault, Michel. "The Subject and Power." In *Michel Foucault: Beyond Structuralism and Hermeneutics*, edited by H. Dreyfus and R. Rabinow. 2d ed. Chicago: University of Chicago Press, 1983.

Geertz, Clifford. *The Interpretation of Cultures*. New York: Basic Books, 1973.

JanMohamed, Abdul R. "Worldliness-without-World, Homelessness-as-Home: Toward a Definition of the Specular Border Intellectual." In *Edward Said: A Critical Reader*, edited by Michael Sprinker. London: Basil Blackwell, 1993.

Lee, Leo Ou-fan. "On the Margins of the Chinese Discourse: Some Personal Thoughts on the Cultural Meaning of the Periphery." *Daedalus* 120.2 (1991).

Marcus, George E., and Michael M. J. Fischer. *Anthropology as Cultural Critique: An Experimental Moment in the Human Sciences*. Chicago: University of Chicago Press, 1986.

Nowak, Krzysztof. "Covert Repressiveness and the Stability of a Political System: Poland at the End of the Seventies." *Social Research* 55.1 (1988) and 55.2 (1988).

Rosaldo, Renato. *Culture and Truth: The Remaking of Social Analysis*. Boston: Beacon, 1989.

Said, Edward. *The World, the Text, and the Critic*. Cambridge: Harvard University Press, 1983.

———. "Intellectuals in the Post-Colonial World." *Salmagundi* 70–71 (1986).

Shweder, Richard, and Robert Levine, eds. *Culture Theory: Essays on Mind, Self and Emotion*. Cambridge: Cambridge University Press, 1984.

Sun, Lonji. *Zhongguo Wenhua de "Shenceng Jiegou"* (The "deep structure" of Chinese culture). Hong Kong: Taishan, 1983.

Trinh T. Minh-ha. *Woman, Native, Other: Writing ,Postcoloniality, and Feminism*. Bloomington: University of Indiana Press, 1989.

Tu, Wei-ming. "Cultural China: The Periphery as the Center." *Daedalus* 120.2 (1991).

Wakeman, Frederic. "All the Rage in China." *The New York Review of Books*, 2 March 1989: 19–21.

Yang, Mayfair. "Traveling Theory, Anthropology, and the Discourse of Modernity in China." Paper presented at the Fourth Decennial Association of Social Anthropologies Conference, Oxford University, England, July 1993.

———. "Tradition, Traveling Anthropology, and the Discourse of Modernity in China." In *The Changing Nature of Anthropological Knowledge*, edited by Henrietta Moore. London: Routledge, 1996.

The Collective Self
A Narrative Paradigm in Sky Lee's
Disappearing Moon Cafe

LIEN CHAO

It is about 140 years since the Chinese settled in Canada. As a group of immigrants, they have made indispensable contributions to the development of the west coast of Canada and to the construction of the Canadian Pacific Railway (the CPR) British Columbia section, which for the first time unified Canada geographically and strengthened the nation politically. Nevertheless, as a visible minority group, the Chinese Canadians were historically depicted by the dominant groups as nonassimilable, and thus racially undesirable in Canadian society.[1] In Canadian history, Chinese immigrants were the only people forced to pay increasing head taxes upon landing; they were also the only group excluded from immigration to Canada because of their race.[2] The Chinese were disenfranchised, deprived of citizenship rights and excluded from most professional jobs up to the 1950s. The Chinese Canadian community also suffered a historical sex ratio imbalance because early Chinese immigrants were almost exclusively male laborers.[3] In addition to the sex ratio imbalance, the general anti-Chinese racism in society made it impossible for Chinese men to meet women of other races. Chinese bachelor-laborers were a historical phenomenon without parallel elsewhere except in North American Chinatowns. Sociologist Peter Li summarizes the Chinese Canadian experience:

Aside from the indigenous people, no other racial or ethnic group had experienced such harsh treatment in Canada as the Chinese. . . .

By the turn of the century they had been virtually reduced to second-class citizens in Canada. Subjected to social, economic, and residential segregation in Canadian society, they responded by retreating into their own ethnic enclaves to avoid competition and hostility from white Canadians. Ironically, these unfavorable external conditions enabled ethnic businesses and associations to thrive in the Chinese community. (1988, 1–2)

In mainstream cultural areas, such as Canadian literature, Chinese Canadian writers writing in either official language were so few in number that a racial minority voice was virtually nonexistent. This collective silence has made the community consistently vulnerable to both misrepresentation and underrepresentation in Canadian society. Furthermore, the nonexistence of the Chinese as speaking subjects in Canadian culture deprives contemporary Chinese Canadians of a history and of a significant cultural identity. The context of Canadian social history, in which Chinese immigrants and their descendants were silenced by the groups in power and their contributions to Canada were denied recognition, is a colonial condition. To break through the historical silence, contemporary Chinese Canadian writers have engaged in a dialogue with the existing versions of Canadian history. This paper illustrates the narrative strategy of dialogue used effectively by Chinese Canadian writers to decolonize the historically silenced community, to reclaim the denied collective history, and to redefine personal identities. For a better-focused illustration, Vancouver writer Sky Lee's novel *Disappearing Moon Cafe* (1990),[4] which embodies the narrative paradigm of the collective self, will be examined. The collective self epitomizes a process of transforming the historical silence and marginality of the community to a narrative voice of resistance.

The social-historical context in which contemporary Chinese Canadian writers grew up in the 1950s, the 1960s and even in the 1970s was a systematic denial of what they were. Published in 1979 in the first joint anthology by Chinese and Japanese Canadians, the following statement locates the connection between the dominant cultural representations and the denial of Asian Canadian history:

What has characterized our experiences growing up Asian Canadian has been a sense of separation from all things Asian

Canadian. We learned little about our ancestors, the pioneers who had made this land grow, "caught silver from the sea", laid the rails that had bound British Columbia to Canada. Our school books didn't deal with the Vancouver racial riots of 1887 and 1907, or the World War Two expulsion, incarceration and later dispersal of the Japanese Canadians, or the disenfranchisement of both peoples until the late 1940s. (Chu viii)

The denial of Asian Canadian experiences in Canadian history and in school curricula precipitates the deprivation of Asian Canadian identity. Thirteen years after the publication of the first joint anthology, a 1992 community publication, *Jin Guo: Voices of Chinese Canadian Women,* cries out in a similar way. The editorial committee points out:

[W]hen you're growing up here, there are no books that speak about your own experience. All the books are about white Canadians. It's a feeling that you have no place here. You're not even represented in Canadian literature. . . .

There's a real need now, more than ever, to make our voices heard—to get together and reclaim our histories. (Chinese Canadian National Council, 1992, 227, 234)

However, this double marginality—their experiences as a Canadian racial minority group being marginalized, and consequently their Canadian identity being denied—ironically gave the first generation of Chinese Canadian writers a desire to break the community's hundred-year silence and to do so in English. The development of Chinese Canadian literature foregrounds a discursive resistance to mainstream Canadian discourse that historically discriminated against nonwhite and non-European Canadians and marginalized their experience as the Other. M. M. Bakhtin observes: "Responsive understanding is a fundamental force, one that participates in the formulation of discourse, and it is moreover an *active* understanding, one that discourse senses as resistance or support enriching the discourse" (1981, 280–81). Bakhtin's theory of discursive dialogism, which emphasizes the "responsive" activities in all rhetorical forms, necessitates a form of dialogue and a responsive discursive paradigm, such as the collective self, in contemporary racial minority literatures.

In Chinese Canadian literature, the narrative forms of dialogue are widely used to connect a young narrator with an elder, and sometimes even with the dead ancestors. As a metonymic device, dialogues connect the speaking subject with the silent ancestors, signifying a process of rereading the colonial past and redefining the self as a part of the community. The Vancouver poet Jim Wong Chu's poem "old chinese cemetery: kamloops July 1977" captures the connection between the poet's identity and the community's unrecognized history:

> like a child lost
> wandering about
> touching feeling
> tattered grounds
> touching seeing
> wooden boards
>
> etched in ink
> etched in weather
> etched in fading memories
> etched
> faded
> forgotten
>
> I walk
> on earth
> above the bones
> of a multitude
> of golden mountain men
> searching for scraps
> of memory
>
> like a child unloved
> his face pressed hard
> against the wet window
>
> Peering in
> for a desperate moment
> I touch my past.

(Wang-Chu 1986, 21)

The search for an individual identity and for a poetic voice leads the poet to the deserted Chinese railway laborers' burial ground. Those who in history were silenced collectively by a discriminatory nickname "Chinamen" provoke the poet to break their silence. Suddenly the poet seems to have located his lost self in the scattered bones of the unknown "golden mountain men," whose contributions to Canada were denied recognition in recorded Canadian history. The moment connects the poet with the community's hundred years' silence; its impact on individuals today is emphasized in the final line "I touch my past." The connection between the searching poet and the silent bones underlines the narrative paradigm in Chinese Canadian literature—the collective self, a process of rewriting the community's history and redefining the individuals' identities.

Sky Lee's novel *Disappearing Moon Cafe* embodies the narrative paradigm of the collective self at the thematic, narrative, structural, and linguistic levels. The metonymic device of dialogue connects the character-bound narrator Kae Ying Woo, a fourth-generation Canadian-born Chinese woman, with the memories of her maternal great-grandfather Wong Gwei Chang, who was a community leader for several decades before his death in 1939. The novel is set in Vancouver's Chinatown, where thousands of Chinese bachelor-laborers initially landed to build the Canadian Pacific Railway in the 1860s. Lee depicts four generations of the Wong family, whose lives are witnesses of one hundred years of Chinese Canadian history from the 1880s to the 1980s. Furthermore, dialogue joins the narrator with the four generations of women involved in the Wongs, who appear as wife, paper-bride, mother, daughter, wet nurse, surrogate mother, waitress, businesswoman, victim of incest and suicide, and so forth. Lee also delineates a collective "her-story" as a part of community history in which Chinese women have to fight a double survival battle in a misogynist culture and a racist society.

To represent the hundred years, Lee employs two narrative frameworks: one is a classical prologue/epilogue structure set in character Wong Gwei Chang's mind before 1939, which enables him to review the experience of the bachelor-laborers in the nineteenth and early twentieth centuries. The other narrative framework is centered around the character-bound narrator Kae Ying Woo, who tells the stories of the four generations of the Wongs in the body of the novel in contemporary time. What is framed in Wong Gwei Chang's memories in the prologue and epilogue is metonymically an equivalent to the condition of silence, like the Chinese railway workers' burial ground in Jim Wang-Chu's poem, since Wong Gwei Chang died in 1939, eight years before the Chinese Exclusion Act was revoked in 1947 (see note 2). The prologue/epilogue contains accumulated historical data of the Chinese laborer generation, but as this generation was never given an opportunity to express its solitude and mistreatment in racist Canadian society, the historical data were not mentioned in existing Canadian history. The attempt to articulate their experiences in English necessitates a dialogue between contemporary Chinese Canadians and the dead Golden Mountain men. Kae Ying Woo, a member of the fourth generation, reinterprets the experiences of her great-grandfather, his generation, and even the generation before him. The textual and structural relationship between the prologue/epilogue and the body of the novel embodies the dialogue between the contemporary Chinese Canadians and the past generations. The following paragraph captures the dialogue between the searching narrator and the Chinese Canadian collective in order to break through the silence and invisibility of the community:

> I wonder. Maybe this is a chinese-in-Canada trait, a part of the great wall of silence and invisibility we have built around us. I have a misgiving that the telling of our history is forbidden. I have violated a secret code. There is power in silence, as this is the way we have always maintained strict control against the more disturbing aspects in our human nature. But what about speaking out for a change, despite its unpredictable impact! The power of language is that it can be manipulated beyond our control, towards misunderstanding. But then again, the power of language is also in its simple honesty. (180)

The impact of the historical silence and invisibility of the community extends to the narrator's generation. In order for the latter to gain a voice in Canadian society, her generation has to reclaim the unrecognized community history by breaking through the secret code of silence.

As a form of narrative strategy, dialogue transforms the silent historical data frozen in Wong Gwei Chang's memories into a postcolonial voice in English. One of the historical events that Lee chooses to highlight in Wong Gwei Chang's memories is the bone hunting organized by the Chinese Benevolent Association in British Columbia in the 1890s. In the novel Wong Gwei Chang is the one asked to take on the task in 1892 of collecting the widely scattered bones of the deceased Chinese railway laborers along the completed CPR in order to have them sent back home for a proper burial. Lee's descriptions of Wong Gwei Chang's bone-hunting journeys pose a protest against the existing CPR history, in which little is mentioned, if at all, about the seventeen thousand Chinese railway laborers recruited directly from China and Hong Kong to build its British Columbian section (Yee 17), nor did the CPR history record the six hundred Chinese who died in the construction, even though the number was a conservative estimate given by Andrew Onderdonk, the railway contractor of this section (Wickberg 1982, 24).

Another historical event highlighted in Wong Gwei Chang's memories is the boycott organized by the Chinese community in Vancouver against the "Janet Smith" bill in 1924. The depiction of this event recalls an anti-Chinese prosecution in Canada. As a community leader, Wong Gwei Chang can see that racism is behind the accusation of a Chinese houseboy as the suspect in a white maid's murder: "A no-good chinaboy sniffing after white women's asses" (76); so it is for his race rather than his crime that the Chinese houseboy is judged and sentenced by the public and by Canadian law. The Chinese community organized a successful boycott against a further legislative attempt to pass a bill that would prohibit white women from working in close proximity to the Chinese (227). Had the bill been passed, it would have sentenced the whole race of the Chinese to be seen as criminals by legitimizing the existing racial discrimination and segregation. These historical events highlighted in Wong Gwei Chang's memories provide a counterweight to the denial of Chinese Canadian experience in existing Canadian history and a rewriting of the dominant history from the viewpoint of the Chinese Canadian community.

Wong Gwei Chang's memories are presented by an interplay of first-person and a third-person narrative voices. Lee chose to have Wang Gwei Chang's memories retrieved and reconstructed in a third-person narrative, while Kae Ying Woo's own experience as a contemporary Chinese Canadian woman is narrated in the first-person. The interplay of the double narrative voices in the body of the novel effectively constitutes the dialogue between the narrator and the community's past—the self and the collective. This interplay further indicates that the collective, although being silenced, is always grounded as an overall social-historical context in which the self exists and is defined. The reinterpretation of Wong Gwei Chang's memories by the first-person narrator Kae Ying Woo constructs a historical perspective of the Chinese immigrants in the nineteenth-century while acknowledging that this perspective is a contemporary rereading and a rewriting of that historical period.

Lee's narrative strategy of dialogue with double voices, in which Wong Gwei Chang is not the first-person speaking subject of his generation but like a silent historical document for his great-granddaughter to decipher, illustrates the relationship between silence and discourse coherently. Derrida notes that silence cannot be said in *logos* but can be indirectly and metaphorically made present by its *pathos* (Derrida 1978, 37, 38, 72). This *pathos* merges textually from a combined reading of the beginning of the prologue, "he remembered . . ." (Lee 1984, 1), and the ending of the epilogue: "He closed his eyes, the heavy chant of the story-teller turning to mist in his head" (237). The reliance of Wong Gwei Chang's generation on Kae Ying Woo for a voice arouses *pathos* in the reader. By giving voice to their experience, the narrative appropriates the silenced Chinese laborers in history. The inevitable displacement of the silenced with a narrative and the inadequacy of words, which can only partially recall the silence through the writer's attempt but can never revive what has been silenced in history, further arouse *pathos* in the reader. The classical narrative structure of the prologue/epilogue that encloses Wong Gwei Chang's memories sustains the "resistance" of that silence metonymically and politically. The limited power of words that can only partially reconstruct the silenced in a fictional world fur-ther challenges the narrator and the reader with *pathos* by having what had been the silenced printed in a language that initially ordered such a silencing procedure. The double narrative voices, which connect the com-munity with the individuals, are best embedded in a family setting.

Disappearing Moon Cafe is a family saga adopted and adapted to en-able the writer to use the Wong family and its business site, a Chinese restaurant named Disappearing Moon Cafe, as a microcosm to repre-sent the Chinese Canadian collective, especially the Chinese Canadian women's collective in the last hundred years. Lee's employment of this traditional narrative form embraces an immediate structural irony: since Chinatown has suffered a historical sex ratio imbalance, the majority of the Chinese laborers have never had families. Traditionally a family saga is centered on characters with the same family name; it depicts the birth and death, rising and falling, growth and decline of the lineal male dy-nasty. This narrative form is deconstructed in Lee's novel to represent an unusual kinship among the Chinese bachelor-men. Wang Gwei Chang realizes that this unusual kinship and companionship among the Chi-nese laborers has kept the community together like a family through many years' hardships: "year after year, right or wrong, they had al-ways been loyal to each other. How many lonely, softhearted nights, respectfully attentive to the would-be heroics of laundrymen and gar-deners, they had all played surrogate wives to each other" (226). In ad-dition to the history of the bachelors, Lee also writes the "her-story" of the Chinese women as part of the community history to be recovered.

Lee appropriates the male orientation in the traditional family saga by telling stories about the four generations of the Wong women in a continuous battle for equality. Kae Ying Woo's psychological need to search for her identity becomes acute after she has given birth to her son. She is troubled by her unwilling acceptance of the physical change in her body and the possible loss of her researcher's job at the Howe Institute (121), and she questions the overwhelming expectation of a young professional female to fit her life into the institution of marriage and traditional motherhood. Kae Ying Woo's personal crisis leads her to seek an explanation in the Chinese women's collective. Nevertheless, since the collective is denied in the recorded history, the narrator decides to reclaim it by telling the stories of her mother's side, saying, "My mother's side is more vibrant, to my way of thinking" (20).

Kae Ying Woo's search leads her to the "Temple of Wonged Women" as the narrator puns later (209), in which she learns the personal battles of the four generations of the Wong women are interrelated. Kae's great-grandmother Lee Mui Lan came to Canada in 1924 at age forty-four as the wife of the richest Chinese businessman in Vancouver Chinatown. She has no other personal identity, however, except what her marriage provides her with: "She was simply the mother of Gwei Chang's only son. Stamped on her entry papers: 'A merchant's wife.' A wife in name only, she relied heavily on him for her identity in this land, even though the hard distance remained on her husband's face. And this she could only bear in silence" (28).

Kae Ying Woo also finds out her grandmother Chen Fong Mei is a paper-bride. Her entry in Canada costs her in-laws head tax at immigration and money to bribe the investigating government officers to secure her landing status. As a paper-bride, Fong Mei is expected to be a reproductive machine by her mother-in-law Mui Lan, who

> wanted a grandson to fulfil the most fundamental purpose to her life. A baby with a brow as clear and as promising as his future. A little boy who came from her son, who came from her husband, who also came lineally from that golden chain of male to male. The daughters-in-law who bore them were unidentified receptacles. (31)

When her daughter-in-law shows no signs of fertility five years after her marriage, Mui Lan steps in to interfere as a mother-in-law, attempting to dismiss Fong Mei from the Wongs: "If the first wife cannot bear a son, then she stands aside for another" (60). She then hires a poor waitress, Song An, from the restaurant to sleep with her son in order to produce a grandson for the Wongs. To fight for her survival, Fong Mei mates with Wong Ting An, who is probably Wong Gwei Chang's son from a liaison before his marriage to Mui Lan. Fong Mei gives birth to two daughters and a son in eight years, while learning to handle business accounts and real estate. The waitress gets pregnant by someone other than Mui Lan's son, just as Fong Mei had done, but later the waitress refuses to give her son to the Wongs.

From her mother's old housekeeper, her nanny Seto Chi, Kae Ying Woo finds out that in the "Temple of Wonged Women," her aunt Suzi is the most deeply wronged one of all. Suzi is a scapegoat sacrificed by various social institutions including her mother's parental authority. The writer locates a historical cause in Suzi's tragedy as well: "Since 1923 the Chinese Exclusion Act had taken its heavy toll. The rapidly diminishing chinese-canadian community had withdrawn into itself, ripe for incest" (147). Suzi, who mates with her half-brother Morgan without knowing that they both descended from Wong Ting An, is mistreated by her mother. In order to conceal her own past, Fong Mei accuses and punishes her daughter for committing an unforbidden crime: "You'll never marry him. You are going into Greenwood, a prison for cheap sluts like you. I've already made all the arrangements. And that thing in you is a deformed monster, so I'm giving it over to the government to raise" (203). Suzi commits suicide after the hospital purposely deforms her baby son at birth because her mother Fong Mei had indicated to the doctor that the baby was an unwanted illegitimate.

Kae Ying Woo realizes in the "Temple of Wonged Women" that each Wong woman's struggle is connected with the collective cause of women's rights. Kae Ying Woo's grandmother Fong Mei single-handedly wins her own identity as a mother and as a successful businesswoman. The poor waitress Song An, hired to be the surrogate mother by Mui Lan, brings up her son Keeman to triumph. Kae Ying Woo's mother Beatrice is married to Keeman despite Fong Mei's objection. Suzi's suicide is the strongest protest against the institutional control and legitimation of women's reproduction for maintaining patriarchal order in society. Although Fong Mei later becomes a matriarch like her mother-in-law Mui Lan, sharing the power of the patriarchy and practicing its control over her daughter Suzi's pregnancy and labor, Lee allows the ghost of Fong Mei to make a recantation to her granddaughter Kae Ying Woo:

> (The ghost signals for silence. She wants to go on.) Fong Mei: "what if I had refused to have children for men and their namesake? Then my daughters would have been free to have children for their own pleasure as well, and then how free we all would have been! . . . What is this Wong male lineage that had

to be upheld at such a human toll? I once thought it was funny
that I could take my revenge on the old bitch and her turtle son.
Another man's children to inherit the precious Wong name, all
their money and power. I forgot that they were my children! I
forgot that I didn't need to align them with male authority, as if
they would be lesser human beings without it. (189)

Fong Mei's recantation calls for a collective awakening to repudiate the
overall cultural representations of the masculine experiences or male
lineage as the dominant social force. The collective awakening also calls
on women to free themselves from a historical bondage that is partly
prolonged by a self-imposed slavery. At her mother's recantation, Suzi's
ghost cries out for justice: "All this bondage we volunteer on ourselves!
Untie them! Untie me!" (189). The collective awakening needs more than
a requital to Suzi's ghost; what is needed to untie the "Temple of the
Wonged Women" is a female saga that does not follow the father's name
or one ethnic origin.

Lee explores the unrecorded female collective from the beginning
of the Chinese settlement in Canada. She composes the her-story by
devaluating the flawed male dynasty. Wong Gwei Chang's memories in
the prologue record his survival experience with a native woman, which
is unknown to the Wongs. He was rescued by Kelora Chen in a bone-
hunting journey in 1892. Kelora was born of a native woman and a white
man, but raised by a Chinese bushman, Chen Gwok Fai. Chen Gwok
Fai assimilated into the native tribe that Kelora and her mother belonged
to, and at the same time he taught Kelora to speak Chinese. In the prologue, Wong Gwei Chang and Kelora have performed the native ritual
of nuptials accordingly: "'It's the custom,' Chen [Gwok Fai] said, 'to
give a gift when you take a wife'" (15). But it is in the epilogue that the
reader finds out Wong Gwei Chang's later being called by his mother in
China to do family duty is actually a family-arranged marriage with
Lee Mui Lan. After Wong Gwei Chang comes back from China, he finds
a boy named Ting An at their old hut, but Kelora is dead. This underde-
veloped episode, which is locked in Wong Gwei Chang's memories in
the prologue/epilogue, not only suggests an unrecorded mixed kinship
between the Chinese Canadians and the native people, but the exploitation of the latter's generosity by immigrants of all races.

Lee's careful development of the character Ting An presents a
political statement. Ting An starts in the bushes as a lost child who is
half Chinese, a quarter native, and a quarter Caucasian. He then becomes a devoted friend of the Wongs, a capable business manager for

the restaurant, a spokesperson for Chinatown against the imposition of the "Janet Smith" bill, and a long-time lover and companion for the lonely Wong daughter-in-law Fong Mei. Despite all he has done for the Wongs, he is never treated or loved as he deserves by the rest of the Wongs. His final break away from Wong Gwei Chang climactically relocates his lost self in the collective of the Eurasians, which voices a strong political protest. Wong Gwei Chang recalls before his death that Ting An decided to change his last name back to Chen, his mother's maiden name (232) and decided to marry, after years of secret mating and waiting in disappointment for Fong Mei to leave her husband, Wong Gwei Chang's legitimate son. Ting An refuses to be further patronized by the Wong last name or by the father/son relationship, which is never clarified by Wong Gwei Chang until Ting An's rebellion:

> "I am your father," Gwei Chang had to answer. "I gave you my name because you're my son." Ting An smirked at him.
> "Don't you know that you are my son?" Gwei Chang asked.
> "A Chang, you have always treated me like family," Ting An said hesitantly at first, then continued with too much deliberation. "All these years, I wanted to thank you for the protection of the Wong name, sir. I will always be very grateful to you for all that you have done for me." (233)

Ting An's lifetime identity as a hired worker in Wong Gwei Chang's business rather than a son in his family furthers the issue of the exploitation of the native people. The final outcry of his anger and his thorough rebellion against Wong Gwei Chang's offer of the family name demonstrate the power of the silenced upon its transformation into words. The power of the silenced exists also in its resistance to being appropriated by a discursive regularity or a social legitimacy; in this case the expectation of legitimacy is a traditional Chinese cultural value deriving directly from the institution of marriage and male linearity. The following conversation captures Ting An's irreconcilable resistance to internal discrimination inside the Chinese community:

> After a while, Gwei Chang said, "Keep the Wong name. It is yours. Eventually, I'll find you a real wife from China. Marrying this female is absolutely out of the question for you."
> "A real wife from China," Ting An repeated in disbelief. He shook his head from side to side, as though something rattled in his head. A suspicion perhaps, but he kept interrupting him-

self. His eyes narrowed at Gwei Chang, only to dart away a couple of times. Then a bewildered expression, as though he realized something for the first time in his life. . . . Finally, he turned to Gwei Chang, his eyes wicked with hate.

"Like your real wife from China?' he asked. "Not a dirty halfbreed, buried somewhere in the bush?" (233)

Together with Kelora Chen, who exists in Wong Gwei Chang's memories only, the two characters—Kelora and Ting An, mother and son—stand out as political statements. The experience of the two characters challenges all non-native groups in North America who have made their settlement and prosperity in this land at the expense of the native people. The presence of the two characters reminds the reader of the worst discrimination and marginalization experienced by the native peoples, the Métis and the Eurasians. The expression of their experience in words challenges the narrowly defined racial divisions and the institutionally determined legitimacy that separates people through discrimination. The characterization of Ting An and Kelora Chen speaks referentially of a self-awareness among the contemporary Chinese Canadians of their own racial phobia.

In rewriting the community history, Kae Ying Woo relocates her lost identity in ambiguous and entangled human relationships, which never follow the fathers' last names. Kae Ying Woo is perhaps the great-grand-daughter of Wong Gwei Chang and Kelora Chen rather than of her official great-grandmother Mui Lan. She is possibly the granddaughter of Fong Mei and Wong Ting An, rather than of her official grandfather Wong Choy Fok. On her father's side she is probably the granddaughter of the poor Chinese waitress Song An and an unknown gambler grandfather. The revelation of the unrecorded, illegitimate kinship that has actually kept the community together repudiates the superiority of patriarchy. Kae Ying Woo's realization that the unrecorded mixed kinship is the human resource challenges the male lineage. Further, her acceptance of the old nanny Seto Chi as her "other mother" and her "(trans)parent" rewrites patriarchal social order with female social connections. It is critical that the narrator concludes that "family sagas" in the traditional sense cannot convey her characters' experience: "No wonder no one writes family sagas any more!" (127, 128). The narrator's exploration proves that traditional definition of legitimacy attached to father's last name and the efforts society makes to sustain male superiority are not only highly problematic but also prohibitive to understanding women's experience and defective in composing a female saga.

In addition to Lee's narrative framework of prologue/epilogue, double narrative voices, and her rewriting of the family saga with a female her-story, her overall employment of an episodic narrative mode of short passages helps to bring past, present and future onto one platform, individual and collective into ongoing dialogues. Instead of following a traditional chronicle, Lee tells her stories in a great number of episodes; their length varies from half a page to ten pages. These episodic entries appear to be assembled almost freely within the period of one hundred years, achieving a narrative effect of equal interaction. With these episodic entries, the writer juxtaposes community events with personal experience, and especially with Chinese Canadian women's experience, in a mutual interaction. Without imposing dominance or submission to the events, the episodic narrative mode undercuts the traditional male orientation and male dominance in a family saga by assigning women's experience a parallel position. The writer juxtaposes the outcomes of the historical events with the reinterpretations of these events from a contemporary point of view. Without telling the complete story chronologically in one entry, the episodic narrative mode breaks up the traditional narrative order, especially chronology. The climaxes of the stories and the outcomes of the historical events are deferred until several chapters later, or even until the epilogue, to avoid any realistic illusions. On the whole, the episodic narrative mode helps to facilitate the dialogues between the past and present, self and collective, male and female, without ordering the participants. The interactions gradually and effectively define the contemporary Chinese Canadians; their personal identities are related to the collective history and her-story of the community.

The metonymic device of dialogue is also demonstrated linguistically in the novel. Lee inserts phonetic and morphemic translations of Chinese words as intrusive elements into the predominantly English syntax. The insertions of the Chinese elements not only create a dramatic uncertainty or a nonmeaning to decenter the imperialist language but also implants a hypothesis of linguistic hybridization resulting from the dialogues between the two languages and two cultures. However, the insertions of Chinese phonetic and morphemic translations are limited to the parts about Kae Ying Woo's great-grandmother, grandmother, and their generations. For example, when Mui Lan defends her arrangement to hire the waitress to be a surrogate mother, she says to her daughter-in-law Fong Mei, "[N]o one can accuse the Wong family of having 'wolf's heart and a dog's lung'" (61). The Chinese metaphor *langzin-*

goufei,[5] or having a wolf's heart and a dog's lung, suggests a person who is less than humane. The metaphor might not be appreciated by an average English reader, since the wolf and the dog are not necessarily considered cruel animals, especially not more cruel than some human beings. However, the word-to-word translation of the idiomatic Chinese saying, and its insertion into the English syntax, provides the reader with the flavor of the Chinese language. Contrastingly, Lee chooses contemporary English for Kae Ying Woo's generation, indicating the bilingual language skills and the linguistic assimilation of the fourth generation into mainstream culture. The possibility of mutual appropriation between the two cultures and two languages also helps to reveal the discursive paradigm of the collective self as a new definition for the Chinese Canadians.

Lee names the prologue "Search for Bones," which foregrounds the predominant Chinese Canadian literary trope. The metonymic trope of following the nineteenth-century railway laborers' footprints in search of their bones along the CPR, thus in search of the community history, is widely employed in Chinese Canadian writings, such as in Jim Wang Chu's poem quoted above. Repeated adoption of the trope bespeaks the political and psychological need of contemporary Chinese Canadians to have a recognized collective history. The choice of this trope proclaims a transformation from a Chinese Canadian historical trope of silence and invisibility to a postcolonial trope of speech. Lee's choice of a female narrator/researcher in her first-person narrative empowers the doubly marginalized Chinese Canadian women. By naming the epilogue "New Moon," Kae Ying Woo realizes the freedom she gains from rewriting the Chinese Canadian collective and especially from composing the her-story of "Temple of Wonged Women." Her exclamation that "[a]fter three generations of struggle, the daughters are free!" indicates such a new era in the 1990s (209). Regarding the subtitles of the prologue and the epilogue together with the body of the novel in between, the reader can see that the embedded narrative paradigm of the collective self working as a unifying force throughout the novel. Kae Ying Woo's friend Hermia Chow sees the unity of this narrative paradigm in the production of *Disappearing Moon Cafe*:

> Do you mean that individuals must gather their identity from all the generations that touch them—past and future, no matter how slightly? Do you mean that an individual is not an individual at all, but a series of individuals—some of whom come

before her, some after her? Do you mean that this story isn't a
story of several generations, but of one individual thinking
collectively? (189)

Obviously the writer expects the reader to come to this realization as
much as Hermia Chow does. "The collective self" cannot be separated
in reading Chinese Canadian literature or in discussing the community
history, because the collective is created by the individual(s), hence the
identity of the individual(s) emerges from the collective and from creating the collective.

In this chapter, I have briefly summarized the social-historical context in which Chinese Canadians were silenced for about a hundred years:
their contributions to Canada were denied recognition, and consequently
their Canadian identity as a member of this racial minority group was
denied. The historical silence of the community, ironically, engenders
contemporary Chinese Canadian writers with a resistance to being further silenced or remaining invisible. Chinese Canadian writers are engaged in a collective literary endeavor to reclaim the denied community
history in order to redefine its individuals today. Dialogue between the
contemporary speaking subjects and the community elders or the dead
Golden Mountain men becomes the predominant literary trope widely
adopted by the first generation of Chinese Canadian writers writing in
English.

Sky Lee's novel *Disappearing Moon Cafe* contains the geographical
setting for depicting the collective history. The relationship between the
narrator Kae Ying Woo, who speaks in the first person, and characters of
older generations whose experiences are depicted in the third-person
narrative, constitutes dialogues between the speaking subject and the
community's denied history. The relationship between the prologue/
epilogue in which Wong Gwei Chang's memories are enclosed and the
body of the novel in which the enclosed historical data are deciphered
structurally enhance the dialogue between the narrator and the community. Overall it is the narrator Kae Ying Woo and the contemporary
generation who need to speak for the historically silenced generations.
It is in her narrative that the community's denied past is given a voice,
and, at the same time, in the process of speaking for the collective values
Kae Ying Woo relocates her own identity.

Lee's narrative demonstrates an awareness of the economy of writing in English. Her adoption of the episodic narrative mode completely
breaks up the traditional chronological narrative order and disrupts the
neutralizing power of syntax in writing. The episodic entries bring past

and present, the individual and the collective, men and women, into equal parallel positions for paradigmatic interactions. The result is an overwhelming metonymical effect of an inseparable relationship between the collective and the self, the impact of the community's past on its individual members today. In the inseparable collective self, the self, although acting as the speaking subject, is always comprised and contextualized by the collective, while at the same time it composes the collective from the contemporary point of view. Thus the self and the collective become mutually constitutive in this narrative paradigm.

Disappearing Moon Cafe also appropriates the traditional form of the family saga in order to delineate the community history and especially the unrecorded Chinese Canadian women's her-story. In the collective her-story, the reader learns of Chinese Canadian women's historical experience of being treated as reproductive machines for producing male heirs to carry on the fathers' names. The characters' struggle to empower themselves leads to a collective awakening—a recognition of their own equal participation in marriage, family, and other social affairs—and to challenge the traditional superiority of the male sex. The adaptation of the family saga for a female saga itself indicates a postcolonial dialogue between a racial minority woman writer and the English literary tradition. Along with Lee's other narrative strategies, her novel is a political and linguistic dialogue with existing Canadian history and with the English language in which Chinese Canadian experiences were historically marginalized. Derrida observes "language can only indefinitely tend toward justice by acknowledging and practising the violence within it" (Derrida 1978, 117). Coming from a suppressed racial and cultural minority, Chinese Canadian writers have attempted to decentralize the imperialist language and its signifying system. They have developed a discourse of resistance that is exemplified in Sky Lee's novel *Disappearing Moon Cafe*. It is this discourse of resistance that connects the collective with the individual and starts to bring justice to the community and the individuals who were historically treated with injustice.

Notes

1. Canada, House of Commons, *Debates* (Macdonald), 12 May 1882, 1287 and 1477. Canadian politicians in the nineteenth and part of the twentieth centuries used anti-Chinese, anti-Oriental racism to promote their careers. The above parliamentary document records the first Canadian prime minister Sir John A. Macdonald's denunciation of the Chinese race as "an alien race in every sense

that would not and could not be expected to assimilate with our Aryan population."

2. British Columbia made Chinese immigrants pay $10 head tax in 1884; immediately after the Canadian Pacific Railway was completed, Bill 156 was passed, imposing a $50 head tax on every Chinese upon landing; this head tax increased to $100 in 1900 and to $500 in 1903. On 1 July 1923, the Chinese Exclusion Act came into effect; during the next twenty-four years, only forty-four Chinese entered Canada. The 1923 Chinese Exclusion Act was revoked in 1947. In British Columbia Chinese were finally given the right to vote only in the spring of 1949.

3. In the 1880s, the sex ratio imbalance among the Chinese in Canada was 1.2 percent female to 98.8 percent male (one female to eighty-two males]. In 1924, the ratio was 6 percent female out of a total Chinese population of forty thousand in Canada (about one female to sixteen males]. Only in 1981 did the sex ratio among the Chinese in Canada finally reach an equilibrium. See Harry Con, Ronald J. Con, Graham Johnson, Edgar Wickberg, and William E. Willmott, in Wickberg 1982, 26; Lee 1984, 162.

4. Sky Lee, *Disappearing Moon Cafe* (Vancouver and Toronto: Douglas & McIntyre, 1990). The novel won the 1990 City of Vancouver Book Prize and was shortlisted for the Governor General's Award in the same year. Page references will be noted in the text.

5. According to the *Chinese-English Dictionary*, *langxin-goufei* means: (1) rapacious as a wolf and savage as a cur; cruel and unscrupulous; brutal and cold-blooded; (2) ungrateful.

References

Bakhtin, M. M. *The Dialogic Imagination*, Edited by M. Holquist. Austin: University of Texas Press, 1981.

Canada, House of Commons. *Debates* (Macdonald). 12 May 1882, 1287 & 1477.

Chinese Canadian National Council, Women's Book Committee. *Jin Guo—Voices of Chinese Canadian Women*. Toronto: Women's Press,1992.

Chu, Garrick, et al. *Inalienable Rice: A Chinese and Japanese Canadian Anthology*. Vancouver, B.C.: Powell Street Revue and The Chinese Canadian Writers Workshop, 1979.

Derrida, Jacques. *Writing and Difference*. Translated by Alan Bass. Chicago: University of Chicago Press, 1978.

Lee, Sky. *Disappearing Moon Cafe*. Vancouver and Toronto: Douglas & McIntyre, 1990.

Lee, Wai-man. *Portraits of a Challenge: An Illustrated History of the Chinese Canadians*. Toronto: Council of Chinese Canadians in Ontario, 1984.

Li, Peter S. *The Chinese in Canada*. Toronto: Oxford University Press, 1988.

Wang-Chu, Jim. *Chinatown Ghosts*. Vancouver, B.C.: Pulp, 1986.

Wickberg, Edgar, et al., eds. *From China to Canada: A History of the Chinese Communities in Canada*. Toronto: McClelland and Stewart, in association with the Multiculturalism Directorate, and Department of State, 1982.

Wu, Jinrun, et al. *A Chinese-English Dictionary*. Beijing: Commerce Press, 1982.

Yee, Paul. *Saltwater City: An Illustrated History of the Chinese in Vancouver*. Vancouver and Toronto: Douglas & McIntyre; Seattle: University of Washington Press, 1988.

"This is my own, my native land"
Constructions of Identity and Landscape in Joy Kogawa's Obasan

KARIN QUIMBY

Where do any of us come from in this cold country? Oh Canada, whether it is admitted or not, we come from you we come from you. From the same soil, the slugs and slime and bogs and twigs and roots.

—Joy Kogawa

The importance of the landscape to the formation of a national identity has been a significant concern in much North American literature. However, the literature that grew from the European expansion on the North American continent has dominated conceptions of how the land has helped to shape a national and continental identity. Nina Baym and Annette Kolodny have investigated the ways in which the European conquest and westward expansion have read the American land as female, and how this reading has served to support mythic configurations in which male agency is gained through the objectification of the female. Baym finds that in order to support the myth of the Euro-American westward-moving male individual, the land has often been conceptualized in "unmistakably feminine terms" (1989, 1153). She further asserts that the mythic configuration of the land-as-woman limits the possibilities of female auctorial and subject agency by the fact that the human female is displaced by the land. She articulates the two specific femaled roles that the land represents within the Euro-American male paradigm: "The role of the beckoning wilderness, the attractive landscape, is given a deeply feminine quality. . . . It has the attributes simultaneously of a

257

virginal bride and a nonthreatening mother; its female qualities are articulated with respect to a male angle of vision" (1155). Working with
the same gender and historical focus, Annette Kolodny also uncovers
prominent Anglo-mythic constructions of the North American landscape,
finding similar gendered readings of the American land.[1]

While Baym and Kolodny's studies remain important feminist critiques of male definitions of the North American landscape, they fail to
address histories or figurations of the land other than European American ones. Joy Kogawa's *Obasan*, which tells a Japanese Canadian story
situated significantly in response to a specific history and landscape,
presents an opportunity to investigate a historical and mythic trajectory
of the land that is neither Eurocentric nor male. The landscape functions, in *Obasan*, to signify the problems of national and personal identity when the Japanese Canadians are forced into internal exile during
World War II. Naomi, the young female protagonist and narrator,
struggles, as an adult looking back on this experience, to arrive at a place
of understanding what is perhaps an irreconcilable paradox—how she
and her people could have been exiled upon their own native land. This
specific dilemma represents the broader problem faced by immigrant
and native people who share a dual or multiple national or racial identity. By investigating the way the landscape works to shore up dominant histories and identities, and hence to marginalize others, I hope to
emphasize, as Gloria Anzaldúa does so powerfully in *Borderlands/La
Frontera: The New Mestiza*, the ways in which physical terrain defines the
vast categories of identity, politics, nationality, and history. Exposing
the dominant perceptions of the land will serve to clear a space, then, to
acknowledge the rich variety of experience that informs a single geographical site.

Although a geopolitical border separates Canada and the United
States, and there are also national and ethnic differences between Baym
and Kolodny's studies and Joy Kogawa's narrative, all of these texts are
informed by the same continental expanse of land and contest a similar
mythic paradigm of European westward expansion and gendered constructions of the land. Therefore, it is useful to investigate the ways in
which these texts play upon each other and construct new meanings of
identity fostered upon this terrain. Understanding the land as intertextual
is crucial in allowing for the complexity of identities that appear to be
formed on some sense of a common ground. As Trevor Barnes and James
Duncan remark: "[P]laces are intertextual sites because various texts and
discursive practices based on previous texts are deeply inscribed in their
landscapes and institutions. We construct both the world and our actions

towards it from texts that speak of who we are or wish to be" (1992, 7–8). Reading Baym and Kolodny's feminist studies along with Kogawa's novel provides another way to intertextually examine the ongoing shaping of North American identities that refuses the narratives and meanings usually arrived at from the male Eurocentric point of view.

It is Kogawa's very foregrounding of the landscape that offers the most compelling challenge to the Eurocentric inscription of identity that has served to colonize the imaginations of the people on the North American continent. Indeed, one might consider Kogawa's emphasis on the landscape in her novel as a strategic response of resistance to the dominant history of Canada. By having Naomi investigate and imagine her identity through landscape imagery, Kogawa issues both a poetic and political challenge to a vast history of colonization that reached its most terrible expression for the Japanese Canadians in the exile they were forced to endure. I shall investigate how Naomi shapes her identity, and through implication a collective experience, through her interaction with and readings of the landscape in its natural, political, and mythic forms.

Annette Kolodny's most recent writing on the landscape, "Letting Go Our Grand Obsessions: Notes Toward a New Literary History of the American Frontiers" (1992), forays into new territory in which she proposes a reopening of the frontier of literary history by "thematizing frontier as a multiplicity of ongoing first encounters over time and land, rather than as a linear chronology of successive discoveries and discrete settlements" (13). Joy Kogawa's semiautobiographical novel, *Obasan*, constructs a thematics of the land that historicizes the Japanese Canadian eastward expulsion and exile during World War II, and as such opens a provocative new frontier. Kogawa writes explicitly of the Canadian landscape, showing how the Japanese Canadian history of forced exile from the British Columbia coast to the detention site of the Slocan ghost town and finally to the Alberta prairies significantly affects the identity of the young female protagonist, Naomi. Naomi's identity forms as she locates and relocates herself and her family in the shifting figurations of the landscape across which she is forced to move. The very idea of a homeland is radically destabilized through this history, and thus assertions of national identity are problematized as well. The paradox of the riddle "We are both the enemy and not the enemy" (Kogawa 1981, 70) acts as a central theme throughout the text and is figured repeatedly as the Japanese Canadians experience the paradox of being exiled upon their own native land. The representations of the landscapes across which Naomi and her family are forced to move serve to show how unstable national and gender identities are and how identities are shaped by the intersection of historical circumstances and the physical landscape.

A significant concern in *Obasan* is how Naomi makes sense out of this forced exile. There is little in Kogawa's text that suggests that "the role of the beckoning wilderness, the attractive landscape, is given a deeply feminine quality" (Baym 1989, 1154). The wildernesses of Slocan and the Alberta prairie, as the sites of exile and dispersal, are hardly inviting and are figured, rather, as "the middle of the earth" (Kogawa 1981, 111), and "the edge of the world" (191). Kogawa's very construction of the Canadian landscape and the female identities that are formed and reformed on this land thus contests the privileged literary history that emerged from the European expansion on the North American continent, which, as Nina Baym and Annette Kolodny have shown, situates a male Adamic hero inscribing himself upon a femaled wilderness. Kogawa clearly moves beyond this Euro-American male paradigm that disallows female agency and instead writes a compelling personal and collective history of the Japanese Canadian experience that does not retreat into an oppositionally gendered reading of the land but crosses and confronts the privileged histories of this land while formulating an idea of what it means to be a Japanese Canadian woman. Naomi's search for national and personal identity reflects what Paul Lauter has suggested appears in much marginalized literature, in which "the problematic of self consists more often of its emergence within conflicting definitions of community and continuity" (1990, 16). Certainly Naomi's experience of exile, in which the Japanese Canadian community is dislocated and her immediate family fractured, addresses just these problematics of self.

The poetic epigraph to the novel poses a riddle, the working out of which continues through the narrative. This epigraph also constructs a semiotic system drawn from the landscape, introducing specific signs that will recur with shifting significations:

There is a silence that cannot speak.
    There is a silence that will not speak.
Beneath the grass the speaking dreams and beneath the dreams is the sensate sea. The speech that frees comes forth from that amniotic deep. To attend its voice, I can hear it say, is to embrace its absence. But I fail the task. The word is stone.

This poetic riddle suggests the movement of a person burrowing under the earth to an underground sea in search of the "freeing word." A psychological move into the unconscious is revealed through the consecutive motions of descent into the earth and sea; the speaking dreams are located "Beneath the grass" and beneath these dreams/grass is a sea, an "amniotic deep." In this underground sea, with its implication of the womb, "the speech that frees" is located. Figuratively, a return to the mother is called for, but as later learned, the mother is absent, thus Naomi cannot yet hear this voice or speak the words that would free her from the silence. The landscape acts as a maze through which Naomi must travel in the search for the mother and for herself. Erika Gottlieb suggests: "[T]he task imposed upon the reader [is] to puzzle out nuances in the natural landscape as they become key elements in *the* human drama" (1986, 51). Although Gottlieb attempts to work toward resolutions to the riddles of identity posed in *Obasan,* showing that it is "less through the people than through the landscape that she approaches the troubled questions of her Canadian identity" (42), she does not address the problematics in these landscape representations which often reveal the paradoxes of being exiled on one's native land, and thereby resist resolution.

Chapter 1 takes up the same figures of grass, sea, and underground stream, moving the imagery from a poetic epigraph to a prose narrative that is bound to a specific location and history. The movement from the grass to the underground sea in the epigraph is refigured in the narrative by the grass on the Alberta coulee becoming an image of the sea: "'Umi no yo,' Uncle says, pointing to the grass. 'It's like the sea'"(1). Naomi and her grandfather travel each year to this coulee near his home in Alberta in a ritual, as later learned, in which the grandfather intends to tell Naomi of her mother's fate in Nagasaki. He has been unable to tell her for eighteen years. Faced again this year with her uncle's silence, Naomi's thoughts significantly turn to the earth upon which she is sitting. The narrative shifts discourses at this point, from the interpersonal to an interior discourse in which the land is central: "My fingers tunnel through a tangle of roots till the grass stands up from my knuckles, making it seem that my fingers are the roots. I am part of this small forest. Like the grass, I search the earth and the sky with a thin but persistent thirst" (3). Rooting herself to the land in this manner, while indicating a yearning for something else, is a recurring gesture, often occurring in response to the many silences Naomi confronts when she thinks of her absent mother. In rooting herself to the land Naomi not only indicates her need to ground the self but also claims an identity literally and significantly positioned on Canadian land.

Naomi positions herself historically upon the Canadian land as well.

Looking out over the coulee she imagines: "Everything in front of us is virgin land. From the beginning of time, the grass along this stretch of prairie has not been cut" (2). This implied gendering of the land recalls Nina Baym's suggestion that a woman writer must sometimes figure the land in gendered terms because of the "archetypal resonance of the image" (1989, 1155). But Naomi suggests neither the possibility of agency nor a violence against a femaled land as Baym also posits might be characteristic. Instead, the image of a "virgin" land is followed by a recounting of a historical use of the land by the native Canadians as a buffalo jump. Together with the image in which she burrows her fingers into the grass, figuratively becoming part of the land, Naomi claims a position on a landscape to which she belongs as much as the native peoples before her. Naomi's figurative integration into the grassy land, along with her historical conjurings, which connect her present physical position with the precolonial images of the land, makes a powerful and insistent claim of identity that evolves from the landscape.

Naomi further conflates the images of the Native Canadians and the Japanese Canadians by imagining her uncle, as he sits next to her, likewise belonging to the land: "Uncle could be Chief Sitting Bull squatting here. He has the same prairie-baked skin, the deep brown furrows like dry river beds creasing his cheeks. All he needs is a feather headdress, and he would be perfect for a picture postcard—'Indian Chief from Canadian Prairie'—souvenir of Alberta, made in Japan" (2). Combining the native and immigrant identities destabilizes the idea of an oppositional and monolithic national and ethnic identity, offering another possibility of identity. This image also subverts the Euro-American proprietary tradition represented in Robert Frost's poem, "The Gift Outright": "The land was ours before we were the land's. / She was our land more than a hundred years / before we were her people" (31).

Locating the Japanese Canadian identity upon a landscape in which they are both native and other, Kogawa constructs a history of Canada and Japanese Canadians in which she examines the paradox of belonging and not belonging, of displacement and home. Naomi's brother Stephen later expands upon this paradox with a riddle: "It is a riddle, Stephen tells me. We are both the enemy and not the enemy" (70). Disrupting the possibility of a homogeneous identity or idea of home creates a destabilized space from which Naomi begins to reconstruct her history and identity.

Naomi's own position on the land and the identity that forms from her complex relationship with the landscape is first reflected in the sexual abuse that is perpetrated upon her by Old Man Gower. Naomi figures herself into the landscape in multiple positions when remembering this abuse. The landscape itself continually shifts significations, creating a multilayered narrative. Referencing Hélène Cixous and Luce Irigaray's theories, in which they posit a "female" language as one that is nonlinear and plural, opposing the logocentrism in "male" language, Shirley Geok-lin Lim suggests that many "Asian American women's texts [are] characterized ... by multiple presences, ambivalent stories, and circular and fluid narratives" (1990, 290–91). Although this claim of female discourse cannot be limited to women writers, it is useful in suggesting and constructing the possibilities of plural identities, and indeed, in Naomi's construction of her identity through landscape images, there are multiple presences and nonlinear shifts of significations.

Throughout Naomi's telling of the sexual abuse, she situates herself within a changing landscape. The wilderness first denotes safety: "To be whole and safe I must hide in the foliage, odourless as a newborn fawn" (Kogawa 1981, 63). The forest growth is protection from the invading, splintering male abuse. Similarly, while she is half-dressed in Gower's bathroom she worries: "If Stephen comes he will see my shame. He will know what I feel and the knowing will flood the landscape. There will be nowhere to hide" (64). If the landscape signifies safety, then the male gaze represents danger and the predator.

The forest as a sign of safety is immediately subverted, however, when Naomi imagines herself as "Snow White in the forest, unable to run. He [Gower] is the forest full of eyes and arms. He is the tree root that trips Snow White. He is the lightening flashing through the sky" (64). Gendering both forest and sky as male reverses the mythic construction posited in Baym and Kolodny's studies, in which the wilderness is femaled and awaiting the mark of the male hero. Despite this reversal, the result is the same; the male forest engulfs and entraps the female, thus reinscribing a terrorizing patriarchal paradigm within which female agency is impossible. Juxtaposing the figurations of wilderness as both safety and imperilment suggests, again, the paradoxes contained within the formation of Naomi's identity and implies again the thematic of Stephen's riddle, "We are both the enemy and not the enemy."

The tree recurs as a central sign in the text, and the resulting split from the mother because of the male abuse is signified through this sign. Naomi first remembers her mother as a tree and herself a part of this tree: "I am clinging to my mother's leg, a flesh shaft that grows from the ground, a tree trunk of which I am an offshoot" (64). The forest now contains both danger (male) and security (female). The merged mother and daughter are torn apart by male intrusion, and, manifested in secrecy, the result is a splitting and silencing of the daughter: "But here in Mr. Gower's hands I become the other—a parasite on her body, no longer of her mind. my arms are vines that strangle the limb to which I cling" (64). The silenced daughter strangles the mother, the other female self. By presenting the multiple positions within which Naomi imagines herself responding to and figured in the landscape, Kogawa represents the necessary complexity of an identity that forms through subjugation and abuse. That is, Kogawa implies that for Naomi a linear or single sense of identity is impossible, which contrasts with the dominant mythic confrontations with the landscape represented later in the text by the Anglo hero, the "Giant Woodsman."

The actual exile into the Canadian interior utilizes the same discursive sign system that began the narrative. The expulsion into the wilderness is figured using metaphors of the land, sea, and stone. Naomi's exile develops and reflects the condition of her identity using the language and imagery of the landscape: "There is no beginning and no end to the forest, or the dust storm, no edge from which to know where the clearing begins. Here, in this familiar density, beneath this cloak, within this carapace, is the longing within the darkness" (111). Her identity takes on what becomes in the novel a familiar boundaryless shape, a wilderness encloses her and she figures herself as an animal covered by a "carapace," a shield against the unknowing, the darkness. The "longing" she feels is strikingly similar to the "thin but persistent thirst" (3) she imagines in the first chapter, when she takes on the form of grass. In both instances Naomi transforms into another shape when a desire for the absent mother is implied. The wilderness invokes not only the experience of forced exile but signals the displacement Naomi feels because of her absent mother. Naomi languishes within this rootless state, unable to find an edge from which to create meaning. Meaning is made, however, when, juxtaposed against this personal account of her lost and fluid state, there comes a very public pronouncement: a date, 1942. This transforms Naomi's personal state into a political and historical statement.

Naomi's personal identity is contingent upon the questions of identity raised by the Japanese Canadian community's exile. The expulsion into the Canadian wilderness represents the near erasure of an entire race of people. Lim suggests: "Kogawa's novel deliberately rewrites a body of communal stories (the infamous history of Japanese Canadian wartime detention and nuclear holocaust in Nagasaki), reweaving these old fibers into new cloths" (1990, 291-92). Naomi figures the community expulsion in terms similar to her personal experience: "We are going down to the middle of the earth with pick-axe eyes, tunnelling by train to the Interior, carried along by the momentum of the expulsion into the waiting wilderness" (Kogawa 1981, 111). The forest's engulfment of the entire community is figured as a descent into the earth and suggests the erasure against which Naomi and her family struggle. Again, the forest is hardly the beckoning femaled frontier that informs so much of the European American histories of the North American continent.

Kogawa emphasizes instead a Japanese Canadian experience by referencing the beginnings of their history on the North American continent: "We are those pioneers who cleared the brush and the forest with our hands, the gardeners tending and attending the soil with our tenderness, the fishermen who are flung from the sea to flounder in the dust of the prairies" (112). Re-presenting the Japanese Canadians as pioneers, gardeners, and fishermen of the Canadian land and sea at the moment of their expulsion powerfully undercuts their perceived status as enemy and alien, and calls forth the paradox in Aunt Emily's statement "After all we're Canadians" (104).

The Nakane family's exile to Slocan, a former ghost town in the Canadian Interior, implies the recurring theme of erasure not only by the idea of inhabiting a ghost town but by the erasure Naomi discovers when she returns to Slocan twenty years later and finds that "Not a mark was left. All our huts had been removed long before and the forest had returned to take over the clearings" (117). The absence or erasure of site and sign inform Naomi's construction of history and identity and the actual return to Slocan prefaces Naomi's reconstruction of her experiences there as a child.

Naomi remembers the house in Slocan into which her family moved and recalls it being significantly earthlike. The house is a dilapidated structure that appears to grow from the forest floor: "a small grey hut with a broken porch camouflaged by shrubbery and trees. The color of the house is that of sand and earth. It seems more like a giant toadstool than a building . . . from the road the house is invisible" (121). The house not only grows from the forest floor but occupies a figurative space beneath the earth as well, recalling again the movement underground in the epigraph. Naomi thinks: "Although it is not dark or cool, it feels underground" (121). By figuring the house as submerged into the earth, the boundaries of home are ruptured. Biddy Martin and Chandra Mohanty examine, in their article "Feminist Politics: What's Home Got To Do With It?," the "configuration of home, identity, and community . . . as a concept and desire" (1986, 191). They define their idea of home to contain at least two specific modalities: being home and not being home. "Being home" refers to the place where one lives within familiar, safe, protected boundaries; "not being home" is a matter of realizing that home was an illusion of coherence and safety based on the exclusion of specific histories of oppression and resistance, the repression of differences even within oneself. Because these locations acquire meaning and function as sites of personal and historical struggles, they work against the notion of an unproblematic geographic location of home. (169)

The absence of familiar, safe, and protected boundaries of the house in Slocan obtains through the blurred boundaries between house and land. If the figurative walls of home transform into a toadstool, then the idea of home must extend, in this instance, to include the landscape. Both the house and forest become, then, the site of "personal and historical struggle." This melding of home and identity into the landscape, a construction that recurs throughout the text, always also contains within it the paradox of being a Canadian exiled upon one's own land. Even as a child, Naomi is imbued with a sense of being home and not being home at the same time.

The modality of "not being home," as constructed by Martin and Mohanty, is informed by a female subject who grows up with the "notion of a coherent, historically continuous, stable identity" (195), a position from which she breaks out by choosing to live in homes and neighborhoods unfamiliar to her. *Obasan* is written from a much different subject position. The history of forced exile informs the notion of home, and Naomi's complex working out of "not being home" transforms this modality into an even more radical site of resistance; as a Japanese Canadian, Naomi cannot ignore or repress the "differences" within herself as she is continually viewed by the dominant, racist government as "other." Because home is not only the metaphorical four walls but the land as well, increasing the possibility of radical displacement, Naomi must constantly resist submersion and reassert her rightful position on her native Canadian land. Thus, the Canadian landscape becomes both the concrete and metaphorical notion of home with which Naomi struggles.

As a young girl exiled to the forest without knowing explicitly why, Naomi also struggles with her identity using images appropriate to her age and place.[2] She recounts the story of Goldilocks in a way that both signals her desire for a stable sense of home and exposes the story's traditional ethnocentric reading:

> In one of Stephen's books, there is a story of a child with long
> golden ringlets called Goldilocks who one day comes to a quaint
> house in the woods lived in by a family of bears. Clearly, we are
> that bear family in this strange house in the middle of the woods.
> I am Baby Bear, whose chair Goldilocks breaks, whose porridge
> Goldilocks eats, whose bed Goldilocks sleeps in. Or perhaps this
> is not true and I am really Goldilocks after all. In the morning,
> will I not find my way out of the forest and back to my room
> where the picture bird sings above my bed and the real bird
> sings in the real peach tree by my open bedroom window in
> Marpole? (Kogawa 1981, 126)

Naomi imagines herself as two identities in the story. From living in a
forest, Naomi reads the story from an object position linked to place; she
and her family become the family of bears. Yet, she also imagines herself
as Goldilocks, which signals a desire to return to a subjectivity that allows agency; it is Goldilocks who acts, who breaks things, who eats and
sleeps. From her physical experience of place, Naomi identifies herself
as Baby Bear living in a forest home, but through imagination and desire, she also identifies with Goldilocks's subject agency; thus, she is
simultaneously object and subject, agent and captive. The obvious fact
that Goldilocks is Anglo further problematizes Naomi's desire for subject agency; implied in the fairy tale is the assumption that one must be
Anglo in order to act, a position certainly supported by Naomi's experience of exile. By exposing the traditional ethnocentric reading of this
fairy tale, Naomi also deconstructs a monolithic subject position, she is
neither victim nor agent, but both.

After three years of living in Slocan, the Japanese Canadians are
again dispersed. Naomi figures the leaving using forest imagery and
reading the tale of the Giant Woodsman into the situation:

> The day we leave, the train station is a forest of legs and bodies
> waiting. . . . We are all standing still, as thick and full of rushing
> as trees in a forest storm, waiting for the giant woodsman with
> his mighty axe. He is in my grade-two reader, the giant wood-
> cutter, standing leaning on his giant axe after felling the giant
> tree (179).

Just as in the Goldilocks tale, in which Naomi imagines herself and her
family as the bears, identifying with the object position, so too does she

imagine herself, and others on the train with her, in the object position of trees, waiting to be felled by the giant woodsman. Annette Kolodny and Nina Baym both suggest that a figure such as the woodsman is a representation of the mythic Adamic hero who acts with individual agency against a femaled wilderness. Here, the Japanese Canadians become this wilderness, a gendered position within the Anglo-mythic paradigm that Naomi invokes with this tale. Thus, rather than forging into the wilderness in the agent position, they are object to be acted upon and destroyed by the Anglo-mythic hero. Yet, read another way, this victim status is also subverted in that as trees, they are part of the land and belong integrally to the Canadian soil. The felling of these trees signifies a destruction of the Canadian land, suggesting perhaps that the assault on the Japanese Canadians is also a simultaneous assault on Canadian national identity. Read as such, Naomi's identity takes on a complexity that dismantles a status as pure victim, again foregrounding a central problem in the text: that of occupying simultaneously multiple identities and positions.

Naomi's experience with the landscape, too, is complex. For instance, the mountain landscape surrounding Slocan is sharply contrasted with her later experience of the Alberta prairie, the location of their second exile. Beauty and life surround her in Slocan: "The rain, the warmth bring to bloom the wildflowers that hide beneath the foliage. Everywhere is the mountain's presence. our bones are made porous" (139). Thus, despite the exile, Naomi has moments of joy and wonder, and is kept alive by the landscape. But when she and her family are forced even further inland, to the prairie, the imagery is quite different, reflecting the death and destruction of her family and other Japanese Canadian families.

The second exile relocates Naomi's family on the Alberta prairie. In response to the new landscape, Naomi imagines herself on an edge: "We have come to the moon. We have come to the edge of the world, to a place of angry air. Was it just a breath ago that we felt the green watery fingers of the mountain air? Here, the air is a fist" (191). Their position on the edge is further signified by Naomi's awareness of the arrangement of homes on the farm to which they move. Not only is the house into which they move smaller than the one in Slocan, but, she states: "Our hut is at the edge of a field that stretches as far as I can see . . . " (192). Furthermore, Naomi notices that "We are at the far end of a large yard that has a white house in the middle" (191). The farmer's residence, as compared to their hut, is a "real house" (192). Such literal placement on the margin signifies not only Naomi's family's position but the situation of the other Japanese Canadians who were not allowed to return to their coastal homes after the war was over.

Living on and farming this desolate land is figured as debilitating and nearly deadly: "All the oil in my joints has drained out and I have been invaded by dust and grit from the fields and mud is in my bone marrow. I can't move anymore . . . there is no escape" (194). Naomi is captive in this landscape, choked not only by the oppressive conditions, the extreme heat and cold, but by the Orders-in-Counsel that forbid the Japanese Canadians to return to their homes. The land invades and dulls Naomi, figuratively perpetrating the displaced violence of the racist government orders. The land is now the enemy, just as the government is the enemy.

Another important process in Naomi's subject construction is her deconstruction of official history. As an adult woman, Naomi rereads newspaper clippings Aunt Emily had collected during the war. Naomi counters the "official" facts with her memory of living and working in the Alberta beet fields in a way that reasserts her experience on the land and constructs a specific history from this position. A newspaper clipping she finds in Aunt Emily's folder is one entitled "Facts about evacuees in Alberta" and shows a smiling Japanese Canadian family with a caption reading: "Grinning and Happy" (193). Naomi powerfully counters this "official" history by telling her own facts: "The fact is I never got used to it and I cannot, I cannot bear the memory. There are some nightmares from which there is no waking, only deeper and deeper sleep" (194). By challenging this official history, Naomi does wake from sleep: "'Grinning and happy' and all smiles standing around a pile of beets? That one is telling. *It's not how it was*" (197; emphasis mine). The process of reconstructing her history requires Naomi to remember and tell of the painful years on the Barker farm.

Naomi's reconstruction of her life in Alberta significantly depicts her position on and as part of the landscape. The trope of submersion in the earth reoccurs. For relief from the heat, Naomi spends time either in a root cellar, a "damp tomb," situated significantly underground, or in a swamp in which "The water is always muddy, so brown that we cannot see the submerged parts of our bodies at all" (200). In both cases relief from life on this land implies death, and Naomi figures herself as a submerged, dying self. The tree, which has appeared throughout the text with various meanings, reappears in the swamp, this time explicitly representing death: "The only tree here is dead" (204). Further, Naomi is "sitting motionless as the dead tree" (205), again implying her identification with this figure. During this time on the Barker farm she is informed

of her father's death and news of her mother's fate in Nagasaki reaches
Obasan and Uncle. Again, the landscape signifies these shifts in consciousness and identity.

Naomi does not learn of her mother's death until many years later.
The family minister is the one who finally reads the letter to Naomi and
her brother. After the reading, Sensei begins a prayer, but Naomi refuses
to listen and instead significantly turns her attention to the earth and
sky:

> I am not thinking of forgiveness. The sound of Sensei's voice
> grows as indistinct as the hum of distant traffic. Gradually the
> room grows still and it is as if I am back with Uncle again, lis-
> tening and listening to the silent earth and the silent sky as I
> have done all my life . . . I close my eyes . . . Mother. I am listen-
> ing. Assist me to hear. (240)

Rejecting the Christian discourse and shifting to a discourse that
significantly links the earth and sky to the mother, Naomi suggests now
that a reclamation of the land also means reclaiming the mother. The
possibility of collapsing into a "mother earth" archetype, by which is
typically implied a safe and nurturing site remains, however, impossible for Naomi to envision. When she remembers, or recreates her
mother from memory, Naomi figures her in problematic and paradoxical terms. She imagines the mother as a fluid force that never allows her
the stability she desires: "You are the tide rushing moonward pulling
back from the shore . . . I sit on the raft begging for a tide to land me
safely on the sand but you draw me to the white distance, skyward and
away from this blood-drugged earth" (241). Naomi imagines her mother
as the ocean underneath her, a destabilizing force, moving her away
from the paradoxical earth that is at once a "safety of sand" and a "blood-
drugged earth." The drawing away of self to the "white distance" radically depositions and destabilizes Naomi. This poetic, dreamlike passage
represents not only fluid identity boundaries but, through its blending
of narrative and poetic forms, destabilizes boundaries in writing as well.[3]

The imagery shifts again and the tree now signifies the mother: "A
Canadian maple tree grows there where your name stands. The tree utters its scarlet voice in the air. Prayers bleeding. Its rustling leaves are
fingers scratching an empty sky" (241). The image of Canada's national
tree planted in Japan, signifying the mother, is again a powerful yet problematic claim of identity. That the tree stands in place of the dead mother

who met her fate partially because Canada denied her the right to return again invokes the paradox of Stephen's riddle: "We are both the
enemy and not the enemy" (70). The tree also recalls the photograph
that shows Naomi as a young girl, hanging onto her mother's leg: "Your
leg is a tree trunk and I am branch, vine, butterfly. I am joined to your
limbs by right of birth, child of your flesh, leaf of your bough" (242–43).
But Naomi counterposes this image of life with: "The tree is a dead tree
in the middle of the prairies" (243). The multiple significations of the
tree suggest the necessary vicissitudes, the crossings of identity one encounters when coming to terms with paradoxes such as being exiled
upon one's own native land and in embracing the absent mother. Naomi's
struggle to recreate the mother thus also represents her rereading of her
position on Canadian land and within Canadian history.

Historicizing herself as a Canadian, Naomi turns again to locate her
identity within the landscape in a passage that is both an appeal to and
an indictment of the nation of Canada:

> Where do any of us come from in this cold country? oh Canada,
> whether it is admitted or not, we come from you we come from
> you. From the same soil, the slugs and slime and bogs and twigs
> and roots. We come from the country that plucks its people out
> like weeds and flings them into the roadside. We grow in ditches
> and sloughs, untended and spindly. We erupt in the valleys and
> mountainsides, in small towns and back alleys, sprouting up-
> side-down on the prairies, our hair wild as spiders' legs, our
> feet rooted nowhere. We grow where we are not seen, we flourish
> where we are not heard, the thick undergrowth of an unlikely
> planting. . . . We come from Canada, this land that is like every
> land, filled with the wise, the fearful, the compassionate, the
> corrupt. (226)

Naomi's entreaty challenges the people of Canada, and indeed of all
lands, to recognize injustice and to acknowledge histories of people who
are not of the dominant group. Her claim of Canadian national identity
is here in its most potent form wherein she demands recognition and
valorization of her lived history.

Naomi returns, finally, alone to the coulee. Grieving over the mother,
she wonders what is left after the body rots: "Up through the earth come
tiny cries of betrayal. There are so many betrayals—departures, deaths,
absences—there are all the many absences within which we who live

are left" (245). Included in these betrayals is the white Canadian betrayal of the Japanese Canadian citizens, a betrayal from which Naomi too must heal.

Naomi's final prayer returns the imagery to the forest, signaling the eventual and perpetual organic return to the earth and implying perhaps that it is not until death that those of all colors belong equally to the land:

> Father, Mother, my relatives, my ancestors, we have come to the forest tonight, to the place where the colors all meet—red and yellow and blue. We have turned and returned to your arms as you turn to earth and form the forest floor. Tonight we read the forest braille. See how our stained fingers have read the seasons, and how our serving hands serve you still. (246)

It is in this position, finally, on the earth, that Naomi both reads and inscribes her history and thus claims her place on the Canadian soil.

Joy Kogawa's *Obasan* constructs a history of the Japanese Canadian experience of exile during World War II, raising questions of national identity problematized by the paradox of being exiled upon one's own native land. This destabilized idea of a homeland is figured through Naomi's responses to the different sites to which she and her family are forced to move. The Canadian landscape is the actual and figurative space upon which Naomi constructs her identity, and by doing so inscribes a Canadian history through claiming a place on Canadian land.

Notes

1. See Kolodny 1984 and Kolodny 1975, in which she emphasizes the psychological motivations in constructing the land as female, suggesting that the European male figurations of the North American continent are informed by the desire for total gratification on both a filial and sexual metaphorical level. In contrast, the imaginative play of white pioneer women focuses "on the spaces that were truly and unequivocally theirs: the home and the small cultivated gardens of their own making" (1975, 6). These private spaces, she suggests, "implied home and community, not privatized erotic mastery" (xiii).

2. King-Kok Cheung suggests that Kogawa's use of fairy tales provides a way to critique the outrageous official government history of the Japanese Canadian internment without directly confronting it. Cheung's project is to show the power of silence in *Obasan*; thus she posits that Kogawa confronts dominant Canadian history "without raising her voice. Instead, she resorts to elliptical

devices such as juvenile perspective, fragmented memories, and reveries, Western fairy tales and Japanese fables—devices that at once accentuate fictionality and proffer a 'truth' that runs deeper than the official records of the war years spliced into the novel" (1993, 129).

3. Lim suggests that *Obasan* "shows an interest in prose experimentalism; mixing genres; crossing boundaries of prose and poetry; combining the work of memory and history, fact and reverie, and fiction; the discourse of myth and legend. . . . and the discourse of bureaucracy and law" (Lim 1990, 291).

References

Barnes, Trevor J., and James S. Duncan. "Introduction: Writing Worlds." In *Writing Worlds: Discourse, Text and Metaphor in the Representation of Landscape,* edited by Trevor J. Barnes and James S. Duncan, 1–17. New York: Routledge, 1992.

Baym, Nina. "Melodramas of Beset Manhood: How Theories of American Fiction Exclude Women Authors." In *The Critical Tradition: Classic Texts and Contemporary Trends,* edited by David H. Richter. New York: St. Martin's Press, 1989.

Cheung, King-Kok. *Articulate Silences: Hisaye Yamamoto, Maxine Hong Kingston, Joy Kogawa.* Ithaca: Cornell University Press, 1993.

Frost, Robert. *In The Clearing.* New York: Holt, Rinehart, and Winston, 1942.

Gottlieb, Erika. "The Riddle of Concentric Worlds in *Obasan.*" *Canadian Literature* 109 (Summer 1986): 34–53.

Kogawa, Joy. *Obasan.* Boston: David R. Godine, 1981.

Kolodny, Annette. *The Land Before Her: Fantasy and Experience of the American Frontiers, 1630–1860.* Chapel Hill: University of North Carolina Press, 1984.

———. *The Lay of the Land: Metaphor as Experience and History in American Life and Letters.* Chapel Hill: University of North Carolina Press, 1975.

———. "Letting Go Our Grand Obsessions: Notes Toward a New Literary History of the American Frontiers." *American Literature* 64.1 (1992): 1–18.

Lauter, Paul. "The Literatures of America: A Comparative Discipline." In *Redefining American Literary History,* edited by A. LaVonne Brown Ruoff and Jerry W. Ward Jr., 9–34. New York: The Modern Language Association of America, 1990.

Lim, Shirley Geok-lin. "Japanese American Woman's Life Stories: Maternality in Monica Sone's *Nisei Daughter* and Joy Kogawa's *Obasan.*" *Feminist Studies* 16.2 (1990): 289–312.

Martin, Biddy, and Chandra Mohanty. "Feminist Politics: What's Home Got to Do With It?" In *Feminist Studies/Critical Studies,* edited by Teresa de Lauretis, 191–212. Bloomington: Indiana University Press, 1986.

A Concluding Essay
Narratives for a New Belonging—
Writing in the Borderlands

ROGER BROMLEY

Given the provenance of this book it is not surprising that each chapter addresses a similar theme, but it is quite remarkable how almost every author, without any prior consultation, has drawn upon a common pool of concepts, terms, problems, and secondary references, all of which might be broadly grouped under the rubric "postcolonial." This is, of course, not an unproblematic term, as it gives priority to a Western perspective and privileges, even while seeking to deconstruct, imperial histories. In this concluding chapter I want to draw together some of the mutual concerns of the writers of this book, highlight a number of issues and problems and, with specific reference to a representative sample of multiple texts that transgress generic borders, try to situate the main themes of this volume by means of a particular conjunctural historical and cultural analysis.

One of the principal issues that recurs throughout is that of binarism, with the corresponding oversimplifications that result from the insistent polarities of either/or, self/other, black/white, and so forth. This binarism has been instrumental in establishing those essentializing norms of identity which, whether in terms of sexuality, class, gender, or "race," have marginalized and oppressed increasing numbers of people. This volume speaks of, from, and across many of these margins and argues for plurality, fluidity, and always emergent becoming. It also seeks to renew those severed links between self and the collective, to shape a critically imagined solidarity, a healing, out of discursive rupture.

Several of the chapters use Bakhtin's concept of the *dialogical* as one means of challenging the oppositional presumptions of border, division, exclusionary thought, and absolute difference. The dialogical is an inclusive, never finalized interactivity, an opening up and a breaking down; it is also a resource in a communal, many-voiced storying. Combined with this use is also an awareness of the ways in which, although almost all the texts referred to are written in a colonizer's language, this language has been dislocated and acted upon, violated even, so that, in Marlene Nourbese Philip's terms, "the historical realities are not erased or obliterated" (Philip 1989, 85). Transformation and textual negotiation are key features of the uses of language in border writing; this is also true of its narrative practice.

Speaking of the colonizer's language reminds me of the dangers of homogenization and of collapsing a number of discourses into one. Similarly, Jolly in her essay on Gordimer and Head makes a crucial point about the tendency to construct a single, new other—the colonized or the marginalized—to replace now-discredited versions of the other. As I remarked earlier about the problems in using the concept "postcolonial," we need to avoid the, by now, conditioned reflex of using "colonization" as a catchall metaphor for a range of distinctively different oppressions. Western cultural critics, in particular, and/or those working within Western institutions, could, unwittingly, run the risk of adding yet another "distinct cultural invariant" to what Samir Amin calls "Eurocentrism" (Amin 1988).

This volume is subtitled "Resistance Literature and Cultural Borders," and while its principal concerns are with memory and history, and transnational, cross-cultural, and discursive border crossings, many of the writers are also sensitive to the fact that borders are within persons and communities, as well as within discourses. Each *textual* journey over multiple ethnic, linguistic, cultural, national, and political-economic borders has to be articulated with the historical and contemporary journey of the exile, immigrant, and refugee. They are journeys of displacement, alienation, pain, loss, and, perhaps even in the end for some, of opportunity. The subject of address, the object of representation, unvoiced and invisible, the border crosser met and meets that hostility reserved for the stranger who comes today *and* the discriminatory and exclusionary legislation shaped for the stranger who stays, or might stay, tomorrow. In the words of bell hooks, quoted in the introduction: "We could enter that world but we could not live there."

Sliding Against the Masks of Newer Selves

Since 1989, with the collapse of bureaucratic socialism in Eastern Europe, the end of a bipolar power system, and Bush's announcement of a "new world order," there has been an increasing sense of a fundamental political, social, economic, and cultural *impasse*, a breakdown in ways of thinking the future. The focus in this chapter is on particular narratives as "goods to think with and as good to think with," but before examining these narratives as cultural resources for new possibilities, of new belongings, I want to briefly look at two recent works of political analysis as a way of framing my argument. One, Francis Fukuyama's *End of History and the Last Man* (1992), is already an international best-seller and an immensely influential, if deeply controversial, book; the other, Samir Amin's *Eurocentrism* (1988), is not widely known beyond academic and political activist circles. Both propose a historical and philosophical setting for the twenty-first century from radically differing perspectives.

Fukuyama argues that a consensus concerning the legitimacy of liberal democracy as a system of government has emerged over the past few years and that this liberal democracy may constitute the "end point of mankind's ideological evolution," "the final form of human government," and, as such, constitute "the end of history"(xi). He is using history in the Hegelian sense as a "single, coherent, evolutionary process, when taking into account the experience of all peoples in all times" (1992, xii). It is this evolutionary process that has ended, according to Fukuyama, leaving liberal democracy as the only coherent political aspiration that spans different regions and cultures around the globe. He constructs a universal, directional history that guarantees an increasing homogenization of all human societies, regardless of their historical origins or cultural inheritances. All countries undergoing modernization, he asserts, "must *increasingly resemble each other* "(xiv; my emphasis), i.e., follow the pattern of a unitary nation-state, economically rational (liberal capitalist) and predicated upon the existence of global markets and the spread of a universal consumer culture.

The driving force of this directional history is what Hegel analyzed as "the struggle for recognition," or Plato's third part of the soul, *thymos*, or "spiritedness" (xvi). I shall be examining narratives that are very much concerned with value, recognition, and self-esteem, and it is interesting to note that Fukuyama argues that "the propensity to feel self-esteem arises out of the part of the soul called *thymos*" (xvii), and that Hegel had asserted, with the coming of the American and French revolutions, that history comes to an end because the longing that had driven the historical process—the struggle for recognition—has now been satisfied in a society characterized by universal and reciprocal recognition. No other arrangement of human social institutions is better able to satisfy this longing, and hence no further progressive historical change is possible.

The homogenizing and universalizing process that Fukuyama describes as necessary for the establishment of "a world made up of liberal democracies" involves an imperialism that is economic, political, social and, above all, *cultural*. I say "above all" cultural, because capitalism's need for surplus and unequal accumulation means that standardization can only ever be achieved through cultural imitation at a consumerist level; economically, politically, and socially the peripheral nations will remain fundamentally unequal.

The idea of central and peripheral nations is developed in Samir Amin's *Eurocentrism*, in which, he argues, Eurocentrism "is a culturalist phenomenon in the sense that it assumes the existence of irreducibly distinct cultural invariants that shape the historical paths of different peoples."(1989, vii). It is this notion of "distinct cultural invariants" that the narratives examined in this chapter challenge at the level of structure, trope, and word, as well as in the terms of gender, ethnicity, and sexuality.

Without referring to Fukuyama, Amin shows how Eurocentrism is anti-universalist yet presents itself as "universalist" through its claims that imitation of the Western model by all peoples is the only solution to the challenges of our time. Amin does not oppose this Eurocentrist paradigm—the primary ideological construct of capitalism—with a universalist Marxist alternative, because this, he argues, also understood Europe as "the model for everything." Both liberal capitalism and its Marxist alternative inhabit the same cultural impasse confronted by what Amin considers to be fundamentalist, provincial, and "inverted Eurocentrisms."

Any critique of the core of the Eurocentric dimensions of capitalist culture has to be produced at the level of the fundamental transformation of economic, political, and social practice, but if, as Lyotard says, "narration is the quintessential form of customary knowledge" (1984, 28), narratives that transgress, violate, and subvert ideas of essentialism, invariance, and transhistorical constants may be goods/good to think with in the search for a new theory of culture—fluid, dialogical, and transnational. A mode of analysis is needed that locates specificity, difference, and historical particularity but does not remain located within, or enclosed by, either *provincial* cultural models or cross-cultural generalizations; instead, it recognizes aspirations for universalism in the diasporic and the nomadic. Against *mimicry*, these narratives offer, in unresolved, arbitrary, and contradictory ways, decentering, deterritorialization and, in Amin's phrase, "delinking"—the unharnessing of cultural narratives from the Eurocentrist paradigm and its culturalist distortions. Liberation struggles, whatever forms they take, will challenge the "end of history" and the "eternal west," but narratives enable us to hypothesize, speculate, and write against the grain of prevailing empires of truth and value.

It is not surprising, perhaps, given that America, and its adjacent "Americas," is the principal source of the current form of the cultural phenomenon of Eurocentrism, that the transgressive, boundary narratives I will consider have been written within its immediate domain. In each text, to a greater or lesser extent, assimilation to a Europeanized or a Euro-Americanized version of cultural identity is an ever-present option or challenge—to be fully "human" is to be westernized (a Eurocentrist term of approval). To propose an "otherness" that is not simply marginalized, minoritized, or celebrated for its right to irreducible difference—culturally evasive and relativist—is to work towards a concept of transnational value that marks "a rupture with everything that submission to the law of international value implies; in other words, it implies delinking" (Amin 1989, 123).

The word "rupture" is an appropriate way of describing the narrative condition of the texts under scrutiny: Maxine Hong Kingston, *The Woman Warrior* (1977); Bharati Mukherjee, *Jasmine* (1989); and Gloria Anzaldúa, *Borderlands/La Frontera* (1987). Each text concentrates upon a figure on the boundary, at the crossroads (a "chiasmic" figure), on the frontier. In a sense (in a literal sense), the crossing never takes place, because the "other side" is precisely that—the site of the minoritized/marginalized figure's "othering." What does happen is, with all their ambivalences and unresolvedness, the narratives open up conditions for, the possibilities of, in Anzaldúa's words, "the new *mestiza*." A *mestiza* is a person of mixed ancestry; but what I shall try to argue is that these narratives work both with "ancestry" and with "progeny"—a proleptic condition of a new belonging: mixed, ambivalent, ambiguous, postessentialist. The narratives work along what Rosaldo calls "cultural border zones [that] are always in motion, not frozen for inspection" (1989, 217). "Othering" is a method of preservation, a homogenizing, a freezing for inspection. *Rupture* is the key trope for the kind of narrative that confounds/confronts "othering."

Gloria Anzaldúa says, in *Borderlands,*

> The new *mestiza* copes by developing a tolerance for contradic-
> tions, a tolerance for ambiguity. She learns to juggle cultures.
> She has a plural personality, she operates in a pluralistic mode—
> nothing is thrust out, the good, the bad and the ugly, nothing
> rejected, nothing abandoned. Not only does she sustain contra-
> dictions, she turns the ambivalence into something else. (1987,
> 79)

In a sense, each of the narratives operates by turning *ambivalence* into
something else while, at the level of form, remaining ambivalent and
contradictory—*on the boundary*. It is this characteristic which marks the
texts as postcolonial, postimperial, and postnationalist while each one's
condition of emergence, its *emergency*, is marked by the indelible traces
of empire, colonization, and cultural nationalism. Despite this, or perhaps because of it, they are narratives that help us to "think" a twenty-
first century "marked by borrowing and lending across porous national
and cultural boundaries that are saturated with inequality, power, and
domination" (Rosaldo 1989, 217).

Another "dislocated" writer, Marlene Nourbese Philip—born and
educated in Trinidad and Tobago, now living in Canada—provides us
with another valuable means of imagining/imaging a "new belonging."
In her poem, "She Tries Her Tongue; Her Silence Softly" (1989), she in-
stalls an extract from *The Practical Guide to Gardening*:

> It is important, when transplanting plants, that their roots not
> be exposed to the air longer than is necessary. Failure to observe
> this caution will result in the plant dying eventually, if not im-
> mediately. When transplanting, you may notice a gently rip-
> ping sound as the roots are torn away from the soil. This is to be
> expected: for the plant, transplanting is always a painful pro-
> cess. (59)

Each of the narratives in question *is* a transplantation, as well as being
about transplantation; and roots, old soil, and new soil are all changed
by the process—the "plant" is not simply assimilated to the new soil,
rerooted. The rerooting is also a rerouting, hence the proliferation of
journey metaphors throughout the texts. Above all, each narrative constructs "a painful process" of arrival and departure, flight and return
(mentally, if not literally), rupture and explosion, decentering and
delinking, rape and disfigurement, the losing of tongues and the loos-
ening of tongues, reterritorialization and deterritorialization. The trans-

planting is never final but always in process; the gently (and not so gently) ripping sound is continuous; and the tearing away of roots never finally completed. Above all, each narrative is marked by tropes of excess. For each writer, this is not simply a matter of theme but an urgent formal challenge—how to construct such a transgressive narrative, the journey from periphery to center, from Third World to First World: across codes, across references, and across heavily "policed" zones of identity. It is a journey against "origin," against supposed authenticity, and, above all, against irreducible cultural absolutes. Another imperative is, in Marlene Philip's terms, for the writer to use language in such a way "that the historical realities are not erased or obliterated," given the pressure of imperial cultures to erase and obliterate the "realities" of the "other" in all ways except those in which they are constituted in their colonized "otherness." As Philip says, "[T]he language as we know it has to be dislocated and acted upon—even destroyed -so that it begins to serve our purposes" (85). *Dislocation* is a significant trope in each text.

Each of the narratives uses a memoir/autobiographical form and is written in English (although for Gloria Anzaldúa this is not an adequate description, as she punctures/interrupts/traverses her primary use of English with Castilian Spanish, North Mexican dialect Spanish, Tex-Mex, and Nahualt—a way of revealing that the actual physical borderland, the U.S./Mexican border is also a junction of languages, a juncture of cultures, and an intersection of psychological, sexual, and spiritual borderlands that has no specific territorial signified). This interference/interreference enables her to write about identity, as D. Emily Hicks points out in *Border Writing: The Multidimensional Text* (1991), in ways that come close to Deleuze and Guattari's notion of deterritorialization.

Each narrative is both an individual story and, *explicitly*, a cultural narrative—bicultural or varicultural, in each instance. The biculturalism is rehearsed throughout as the primary site of narrativity, with discontinuous frames to mark the contrapuntal codes/references as a way of unsettling ideas of origin, center, authenticity, and the representational—all features of the culturalism discussed earlier. I mention these issues, especially the explicitness of the cultural narrative, because, as Raymund A. Paredes says (Payne 1992, xxvii), "the quintessentially modern literary figure [is] the solitary observer, immune to involvement in anything he surveys."

For reasons of gender, ethnicity, or sexuality (or a combination of any, or all, of these) the primary figure in each narrative is excluded, initially, from the fullness and wholeness of identity and language, except in so far as these are imposed partially and prescriptively. Each text

is a de-scripting/de-scription, an unwriting laterally placed alongside
the ostensible "telling." Many marginalized people find/found themselves—in an echo of patriarchal and slave culture—denied the power
to name, and are renamed (as was their landscape) by the European
stranger or through religious hegemony. In *Jasmine* (1989), the epony-
mous figure is variously Jyoti, Jasmine, Jazzy, Jase, and Jane—all the
namings of others/males. The woman, doubly colonized in this text, as
so many black females are, is screened from her own body (throughout
the *narrated time* she is pregnant), as it becomes a site of exploitation and
profoundly antihuman use; she is abducted, brutalized, and raped by
the sailor upon whom she depends for passage from the Third World to
the First World. The enclosed nature of that passage, the confinement
and violation in the impoverished/dirtied hotel room, the blood of the
murdered sailor (a sacrificial exchange for the woman's blood), and, later,
the circumscription of her body by pregnancy—all trace out the dangers and impurities confronting the boundary crosser, the "othered" traveling to the construction site of her/his othering. The narrative makes
space for her body and her voice, but not without extensive violence.

Bharati Mukherjee says in "A Four Hundred-Year-Old Woman,"

> I was born into a class that did not live in its native language. I
> was born into a city that feared its future, and trained me for
> emigration. I attended a school run by Irish nuns, who regarded
> our walled-off school compound in Calcutta as a corner (for-
> ever green and tropical) of England. My country—called in
> Bengali *desh*, and suggesting a homeland rather than a nation of
> which one is a citizen—I have never seen. It is the ancestral home
> of my father and is now in Bangladesh. Nevertheless, I speak
> his dialect of Bengali, and think of myself as "belonging" to
> Faridpur, the tiny green-gold village that was his birthplace."
> (1991, 24)

Desh has become for her a merger of Faridpur and Manhattan, but
she resists the hyphenated ascription "Indo-American" or any other form
of cultural ghettoization. She regards herself as an immigrant whose
investment is in the American reality—as an American writer. On the
surface this sounds like a simple matter of assimilation, of yielding to
the dominant culture. It is, actually, a refusal of nostalgia and exoticism,
a claim to be "as American as any steerage passenger from Ireland, Italy,
or the Russian Pale" (25). As a writer her literary agenda "begins by
acknowledging that America has transformed *me*. It does not end until I

show how I (and the hundreds of thousands like me) have transformed America" (25). This agenda, continuous and presumably never-ending, is a challenge to the culturalist phenomenon—with its assumption of the existence of irreducibly distinct cultural invariants—of Eurocentrism for which the United States is now the prime medium. This phenomenon—the culture of capitalism—is a five hundred-year-old "man"!

Mukherjee acknowledges that there are parts of herself that remain Indian (a contestable category from a critical perspective) and, in a memorable and, for my analysis, definitive phrase, there are "parts that slide against the masks of newer selves" (26). The fluidity of sliding and the variability of masks mark so much of these new kinds of narrative of displacement—narratives of process and becoming, of renewing and reclaiming. She says that it is her duty to "give voice to continents" but also to redefine the nature of American and what makes an American. For Fukuyama, Eurocentrist America gives voice to continents by homogenization and universalization, but, for him, the nature of American is an unproblematic given, a natural category. Mukherjee's "material" is transformation, not preservation; her stories are "about the hurly-burly of the unsettled magma between two worlds" (27). The "hurly-burly" is a collocation, a figure of commotion and confusion—a matter of structure, not just theme. "Unsettled" describes the larger project that I am trying to locate, as does "magma" with its suggestion of varying strata, amorphousness, and liquidity. Given America's current global hegemony, her theme "the making of new Americans" has a bearing on the issues raised earlier in connection with Amin's *Eurocentrism*. The crucial point is whether these "new Americans" melt into the prevailing ideological constructs of liberal capitalism or actively engage in "delinking." I speak metaphorically, but, arguably, narratives can have a function in making a space for that critical distance necessary to the breaking of the post-1989 ideological gridlock.

Bharati Mukherjee speaks of being "aware of [herself] as a four-hundred-year-old woman, born in the captivity of colonial, pre-industrial, oral culture and living now as a contemporary New Yorker"(27), but she does not place that colonial, pre-industrial, oral culture in *the context* of contemporary New York—a center/periphery polarization based upon unequal development in which the history of one is dependent upon the history of the other.

The epigraph to *Jasmine* is a quotation from James Gleick's *Chaos:* "The new geometry mirrors a universe that is rough, not rounded, scabrous, not smooth. It is a geometry of the pitted, pocked, and broken up, the twisted, tangled and intertwined"—a timely reminder in a period of

renewed provincialism (nationalism) and "ethnic cleansing" that, sys-
temically, the world is interdependent and that round and smooth categories like self, ethnicity, and nation have become pitted, pocked, and
broken up, and that narratives are needed that articulate the twisted,
the tangled, and intertwined.

Jasmine begins in an astrological framework (and with a sentence
that links the medieval with the postmodern), a moment of cultural fa-
talism that the narrator describes as "lifetimes ago"—seventeen years
from the point of narrating, but "ideological" lifetimes in her sliding
selves and fluid masks. The chapter ends with the narrator's refusal: "I
know what I don't want to become" (5). The negative actually contains
a positive, but it rejects the specificity and detail of the astrologer who
proposes an absolute closure, an ending at the very beginning.

The opening chapter locates a fundamental *ambivalence* that operates throughout the narrative. The astrologer foretells her widowhood
and exile, a prophecy designed to contain her and determine her: "what
is to happen will happen." The prediction removes all possibility of
agency; in foretelling it forecloses: "Bad times were on their way. I was
helpless, doomed. The star bled" (4). It is a system of gendered pattern-
ing : "Go join your sisters," the man with the capacious ears commanded.
"A girl shouldn't be wandering here by herself" (4). The "wandering"
enables Jasmine to defy not the "facts" of the prophecy but its design
and intention to render her less than human.

In the last section of the chapter the narrator is swimming and makes
a discovery:

> Suddenly my fingers scraped the soft waterlogged carcass of a
> small dog. The body was rotten, the eyes had been eaten. The
> moment I touched it, the body broke in two, as though the water
> had been its glue. A stench leaked out of the broken body, and
> then both pieces quickly sank. That stench stays with me. (5)

The chapter is constructed around two "memory" events: the astrologer's
prediction and the dead dog in the water. The girl is encircled. She chooses
to remember the dismembered body that her touch had broken in two—
a touch that "announces" the leaking and broken body of the narrative
that follows and predicts the dangers to her own body as its ownership
and use are contested throughout the text—named by men—shuttling
between identities. The "glue" that holds together her body is the water
that enables her to travel from Amsterdam to Florida, her identity dis-

torted by illegal documents, her body dismembered by the grotesque Half-Face, the trawler captain. The stench of the dog is overlaid by the new memory of the stench of the captain's blood after she has murdered him.

The death of the narrator's father, gored by a bull; her husband, by a bomb meant for her; and her killing of the sea captain are all "fragmentations" of the patriarchal body, necessary regressions and sacrifices. Like the dismembered dog, each death focuses on a violation of the Body; it explodes/breaks up the completed, finished product. The narrative is, hence, opened up in a way that allows the woman's *body* (in her "original" culture designed/destined to be isolated, alone, fenced off from all other bodies as female—negated) to be translated from her repressed "beginning" to a point where signs of its unfinished character, of its growth and proliferation, are foregrounded; its protuberances, offshoots, and convexities are made apparent. The ever unfinished nature of the body is made visible: conception, pregnancy, death throes are all shown.

Analogically, the narrative itself has a similar "body," and unfinished nature, of growth and random proliferation, an amorphousness that refuses the shapings of others. Jasmine grows and changes but her child is, narratively speaking, never born: the deferment, the retardation, the unfinalizability is critical. Her banker partner is shot and is wheelchair bound, a neighboring farmer hangs himself, Iowa, the Middle West, a landscape of fertile pastures, becomes a place of decay and death, of endless repetition, a terminus. Bud, her partner, and the neighbor—Darrel—have become immobilized; their belonging has been too long.

The narrative shifts, slides, moves synchronously and laterally, overlaps and intertwines; it braids "feudal" reference with electronic discourse; it splits, dissolves, scars, and pries open the sealed and discrete—leaks India into Iowa, and Iowa into India. Her assumed surname—Ripplemeyer—neatly sounds out her ambivalence, both ripple and mire. The narrative is mobilized by an image of revisiting—the woman traveling in time and space is more than Jasmine, and other than Jasmine, the Third World woman: "[W]hich of us was raped and raped and raped in boats and cars and motel rooms? (127). She meets "monstrous" America, "liberal" America, and "middle" America—each one locked into its own limits. In Clearwater, Florida, the narrator has an experience whose *ambivalence* helps to situate her for the next phase of her journey from rape, through brief stay in a "Third World" compound, to East Coast America:

In one of the department stores I saw my first revolving door.
How could something be always open and at the same time
always closed? She had me try out my first escalator. How could
something be always moving and always still? (133)

These questions staple the remainder of the narrative together and
are their staple form. Their undecidability becomes her medium : the
undocumented living in the fluidity of American character (in Florida she
mimics an American voice and an American walk as a strategy of
"documentation") and the American landscape. She jumps "tracks," dis-
tancing herself—her widowhood disguised in T-shirts and cords—from
Indians living in America but retired behind ghetto walls. The text, with
its fractures, spirals, and syncretisms, avoids the cultural and linguistic
ghetto of closure and coherence, of teleology/astrology: "[N]othing was
rooted anymore. Everything was in motion" (152).

I have concentrated almost exclusively on the transformations of
the narrator, limited though they are by the need for "assisted" passage:
"I have had a husband for each of the women I have been. Prakash for
Jasmine. Taylor for Jase. Bud for Jane. Half-Face for Kali" (197). However, there is another "other" figure in the text, Du Thien, the Vietnamese refugee boy adopted by Jane and Bud. He is "the brightest boy in the
camps. The boy who survived" (155). His survival, like Jasmine's, is
based upon adaptation. His electronic "obsession" becomes him: he *is*
the circuits he reshuffles, combining new functions. His genius is for
scavenging, adaptation, appropriate technology. Finding himself in
America, he founds himself through "recombinant electronics," by al-
tering "the gene pool of the common American appliance." The "American" could not survive in Vietnam; the Vietnamese American lives out
his "hyphenization" by constantly changing shape; his name, Du, *sounds
out* many possibilities—due, jew, do, dual, a personal pronoun in German,
zoo (the phonetic Vietnamese reminding us of the less than human
"gooks"):

At school they say Du's doing so well, isn't he, considering.
Considering what? I want to say. Considering that he has lived
through five or six languages, five or six countries, two or three
centuries of history; has seen his country, city, and family butch-
ered, eaten filth in order to stay alive; that he has survived every
degradation known to this century, *consider all those liabilities,*
isn't it amazing that he can read a Condensed and Simplified
for Modern Students edition of *A Tale of Two Cities?* . . . Du's

doing well because he has always trained with live ammo, without a net, with no multiple choice. . . . Once upon a time, like
me, he was someone else. We've survived hideous times. I envy
Bud the straight lines and smooth planes of his history.
Until Harlan. Always, until Harlan. (214)

The litany of excess in the first half of the quotation, the hyperreality,
has become the condition of numberless people in the "periphery"—a
condition of fissure and rupture and unending violence. This has superseded the "realism" (narrative and political) of "straight lines" and
"smooth planes," which are now the fairy tale of "once upon a time."
The "real" is grotesque, another order of fairy tale: "[W]e've hurtled
through time tunnels. We've seen the worst and survived. Like crea-
tures in fairy tales, we've shrunk and we've swollen and we've swal-
lowed the cosmos whole" (240).

Du and Jasmine share this provisionality; they are figures of continuing metamorphosis, sojourning awhile in various spaces, not living
in one place. The episodic and the interstitial *is* their condition. Not living in the world, but the world that they make up, invent, as a condition
of survival living in them. Both are explosive, volcanic—tornadoes and
rubble-makers. Bud, the banker, "enters" their world, fascinated by the
exotic/erotic and, simultaneously, guilt-ridden, as it is a world generated by capitalism's need for surplus in imperial markets; he is shot by
Harlan, a local victim, bankrupted by the same economic process.

Both Jasmine and Du have only partial affiliations, disinterested
identities, tactical belongings. The narrator says, at one point, "How
many more shapes are in me, how many more selves, how many more
husbands?" (215). The gendered and ethnicized "others" write back,
script their own "otherness" in flight and fluidity, temporariness and
the transitional. Both leave Iowa for California, separately. Traveling west
to another boundary, beyond which is "their" East, they arise from nowhere and disappear into a cloud. Jasmine leaves Bud and goes away
with Taylor, in love but also seeking another form of "glue" to prevent
her body from breaking in two, another means of transformation: "greedy
with wants and reckless from hope" (241).

Hope has motivated the narrative, recklessness shaped its condition:

Adventure, risk, transformation: the frontier is pushing indoors
through uncaulked windows. Watch me re-position the stars, I
whisper to the astrologer who floats cross-legged above *my*
stove? (240)

The ambivalence of the opening chapter returns, staging the "known" of astrology with the unknown risks and illusions, perhaps, of agency: "[W]atch me re-position the stars". The frontier is, remember, *pushing*, not being pushed *by* the subject. Du and, to a certain extent, Jasmine overcome what Deleuze and Guattari call the paranoic impulse to reterritorialize (they have no territory, or belonging as such—their "belongings" are always carried with them, decentered and deracinated) and intensify the schizophrenic tendency of capitalism, *partially* forming deterritorialized flows that are no longer subject to the constraints of commodity exchange. *Partially* . . . but then narratives are only good to think with, goods to think with—cultural modelings, not programs of social action. At the end of the narrative, Jasmine still only knows what she does not want to become.

One of the pioneering examples of the kind of formative narrative that I am describing was Maxine Hong Kingston's controversial *The Woman Warrior*, first published in 1976. Ostensibly a work of autobiography, its narrative method worked against, and broke down, some of the prevailing currencies and conventions of such writings. It is not my purpose here to rehearse the controversies that the book has aroused, as these have been dealt with most effectively by Sau-ling Cynthia Wong (1992).

The major objection has been to its generic status. Is it an autobiography or a work of fiction seeking to validate itself, or be validated by Euro-American publishers, as "ethnic" autobiography? Much of the debate has been stimulated by the book's formal and stylistic characteristics—its formative nature, its unfinalizability, and its speculative (playful, even) fictionalization. To some critics, an autobiography has to be referential, a document shaped by a bildungsroman model. This is what has been called "epireading" by Krause—"a reading which proceeds under the privileging of 'action' and 'speech', transposing the written words on the page into a somehow corresponding human situation of human persons, voices, characters, conflicts, conciliations" (Krause 1984, 226). *The Woman Warrior* treats the irreducible and the irreconcilable; it refuses anything other than an arbitrary closure. The writing itself is constitutive and makes possible a "graphireading" that "deals with writing as such and does not think of it as transcribing an event properly construed as vocal and audible" (Krause 1984, 226). This is, essentially, what I mean by *formative* writing and it is a condition that is shared by all of the texts I am referring to. These are discourses with manifold and complex horizons, and with forms that remind us we are in the world of narrative, not the phenomenologically constituted "real" world.

In this sense, *The Woman Warrior* can be read as an extended series of cultural reflections/speculations on the specifics of the gendered experience of an Asian American woman.

In the opening chapter, "No Name Woman," we can see how the writer is excavating the sites of old, silent narratives to make new, articulate ones. Memory, timing, and the writing itself have been manipulated to produce metaphor out of loss, absence, and the suicide of her aunt, the no-name woman. The aunt had belonged to her village in China by virtue of birth, family, and residence; but her death, and that of her newborn child, at the bottom of the family well mark the depth (in all senses of the word) of her "not belonging." The writing images/imagines the life, the birth, and the death, and names them through the evolving narrative, but does not literally name the aunt whose presence/absence is mourned by her American-born, ethnically Chinese niece: "The Chinese are always very frightened of the drowned one, whose weeping ghost, wet hair hanging and skin bloated, waits silently by the water to pull down a substitute" (22). The "substitute" is metaphor—that distance or separation from referential identity, a figure of usurpation and transgression. The writing itself is the reparation, the "substitute," pulled down, so to speak, so that the aunt can belong.

The book is subtitled "Memoirs of a Girlhood Among Ghosts," and the opening chapter begins in this way: "In China your father had a sister who killed herself. She jumped into the family well. We say that your father has all brothers because it is as if she had never been born" (11). She can only be manifested (ghostlike) through the process of writing—itself a form of birthing ("she had never been born") that erases the "as if" of the mother's statement. It is through a tropological structure, a figure of writing and reading, of *substitution*, that the complex mutuality of aunt/niece belonging can be achieved: a consuming of biases that produces a fluid identity that is neither Chinese nor European, but a shifting and sliding Chinese American compound. The compound itself denotes the bicultural focality and the double tracking of the perspective and the writing itself: a discourse of agency, possibility, and self-creation in the face of death/ghosts/loss and negative belonging. (Non-Chinese are referred to as "ghosts.")

This opening chapter, "No Name Woman," uses the figure of prosopopeia, a term from rhetoric in which an imaginary or absent person (the aunt is both, in a sense) is represented as speaking or acting (de Man, 1984). The chapter takes the form of an address or apostrophe to an absent, deceased, passive, and voiceless entity. The writing speculates upon and invents the aunt's reply, and confers upon her the power of speech and action ("'you must not tell anyone,' my mother said, 'what I am about to tell you'")—it creates a mask or face. Autobiography is a means by which one's name is made as intelligible and memorable as a face, and the opening chapter generates this naming/facing process for both the "no-name woman" and the belonging/not belonging Chinese/ American, American/Chinese writer, Maxine Hong Kingston. It is a chapter about nomination and transition, the giving and taking away of faces, figuration coming through disfiguration—"wet hair hanging and skin bloated." It is also an epitaph. When the aunt became pregnant by an unknown man, not her husband, the villagers destroyed her family house, ritually wearing masks. The writing becomes the inscription of the "never said," a phrase which is also used in the chapter as a reference to desire.

The literal figure of the dead aunt may be an image gathered from suppressed family memory, from traces of the real person herself, the "drowned-in-the-well-sister" (the text reproduces it as an indissoluble compound word), but she is also a "Spirit," nothing less than infinity, hence the metaphorical use of her as a continuous being. The figure is given a new belonging: homelessness-as-home, in Abdul JanMohamed's phrase (1992). The literal aunt and the figural aunt become one: the fiction of the voice-beyond-the-grave, in de Man's formulation; she is a chiasmic figure, empowered to cross the conditions of death and life with the attributes of speech and of silence: transitional and transitory.

The survivor (the woman warrior) speaks in the person of the dead and in her own person contrapuntally, because identity is cultural, never simply individual: "Unless I see her life branching into mine, she gives me no ancestral help" (Kingston 1981, 16). The writing is the branching: a meditation upon transgression and rupture, a mourning that gives rise to the discovery of writing. Belonging is a figuration that conflates the experience of disappearance, loss, and bereavement (by focussing upon the death of another, as substitute for oneself) with the experience of finding a space through writing/speaking: a coming to speech in, and through, narrative. The adversarial figure—a rival almost—of family experience is turned into a threshold of creativity/ of belonging.

De Man refers to a section of Wordsworth's essays upon epitaphs in which he speaks against metaphor:

If words be not . . . an incarnation of the thought but only a clothing for it, then surely they will prove an ill gift; such a one as those poisoned vestments, read of in the stories of supersti-

tious times, which had power to consume and alienate from his
right mind the victim who put them on. (1984, 79)

By analogy, the writing of autobiography may not, after all, be simply
the expression of a life but a disfiguring (and refiguring), and a consuming and alienating process in which the reading/writing constructs a
varifocal effect: a displacement/defacement through metaphor, *against*
absolute and essentialist belongings, and for a complex, multilayered,
and dynamic pattern of syncretism—out of the past, out of death, out of
the adversarial. Each narrative studied here is a "poisoned vestment"
(investment) with the power to consume and alienate—the power of
the chiasm and the borderland.

The use in autobiography of prosopopoeia to posit the voice or the
face of the other means that what is lost is not "life" but that belonging
which can only be accessible in the privative way of understanding, characterized by the taking away or removal of something, and the loss or
absence of some quality normally (literally) presumed to be present: self-
identity as a given or fixed identity. The restoration of mortality, through
the dialogue with the dead in "No Name Woman," deprives and disfig-
ures to the precise extent that it restores and *creates* (or it restores *by*
creating) the other, the absolute stranger: the dead aunt. The writing is a
way of creating a relationship with severance and separation; a discourse
of mutuality in which both remembering self and other are dislocated,
unhinged. A narrative has emerged, out of emergency (what does it mean
to be a Chinese-American female ?) and out of denial and erasure. As
always, the writing is not a transcription but a rewriting, a de-scripting
of prescriptions. The aunt is commemorated and given birth to. It is "a
story to grow up on" (13), a way of thinking the future, of survival and
possibility, by trying to name the unspeakable past. The writing engenders—in all senses of that word—"a prodigal aunt," a figure of excess in
the sense that the speculative vestment-narrative enables her to exceed,
go beyond, the subject identities in which she is invested. This includes
the investments and appropriations of the niece's doubly articulated
narrative. In one version, she is engendered as the obedient and passive
raped woman—"Women in the old China did not choose" (14). In another, the "aunt crossed boundaries not delineated in space" (15) and
she is given the power of agency and choice, figuring (and figuring in)
her own desire—"the enormities of the forbidden"(15). "She" becomes,
for a hypothetical moment, the active subject of her own verbs/actions—
"she looked"; "she liked." In another narrative incarnation she is imaged

as "a wild woman" free with sex, but this is rapidly erased as a possibility (then and now—for aunt or her) by the narrator.

In the spaces of not knowing, in the interstices of distance, forgetting, and desire, the writing combs "individuality" and "eccentricity" into the narrative, delinking and deterritorializing both "Chinese woman" and "Chinese American" woman from any transhistorical subjectivities or irreducible absolutes of identity. The narrator's mother had told her "once and for all, the useful parts" (13) of the aunt's story, the instrumental and moralizing parts. The narrative has to recover the discarded and the suppressed. The recovery can never be archival, since those traces have been erased, but must be imaginary—the entry, the breath, and the mutual spaces : the secret voice and separate attentiveness of the aunt:

> And one day he [the grandfather] brought home a baby girl, wrapped up inside his brown western-style greatcoat. He had traded one of his sons, probably my father, the youngest for her. My grand-mother made him trade back. When he finally got a daughter of his own, he doted on her. They must all have loved her, except perhaps my father, the only brother who never went back to China having once been traded for a girl. (17)

There are a number of complex substitutions in this extract, and out of the "probably" and the "perhaps" the writing process produces its own echo through its vagrant and extravagant forms; analogically rehearsing the break the aunt had made in the "roundness" of the village, its homogeneous space. The narrative is linked with, but constructed *against*, the "personal, physical representation of the break she had made in the roundness" (19) by bringing the aunt into the future (the time of writing, the niece's recall) and disengaging her from her overdetermined present/presence: "homelessness-as-home." The writing re-presents the extreme pain of the aunt's labor in a style that is "unhinged," obliterative, spatial: out of time. She gives birth in a pigsty, a place of dirt, glad to have a fence enclosing her because the language has become a form of splitting and opening—she is "a tribal person alone." The writing is seeking to find analogues for the experience of the woman being taken out of her body as, finally, the child is expelled out of *her* body. The child, like the mother, has no marker, no name; she is joined to the mother only in separation: ghostlike. The narrative *speaks* both mother and child; names, marks, and memorializes as the text labors and gives birth in an act of substitution and propitiation. The aunt and child are rescued from the "ghosts massed at crossroads," that site of transgression, magic and female power: the space of dangerous memories.

The writing is similar to shamanistic practice as defined by Taussig in *Shamanism, Colonialism and the Wild Man* : "[T]he power of shamanism lies not with the shaman but with the differences created by the coming together of shaman and patient . . . the joint construction of the healer and the sick in the semantically generative space of annulment that is the colonial death space" (1987, 460). "No-name Woman" is a joint exploration of the semantically generative space in which the aunt is treated as if she had never been born; both niece and aunt are healed by the mutuality of the writing process. In the words of Joy Harjo's poem "Anchorage":

> Everyone laughed at the impossibility of it, but also the truth. Because who would believe the fantastic and terrible story of all of our Survival those who were never meant to survive? (1983, 15)

Gloria Anzaldúa is a Chicana *tejana* lesbian-feminist poet and fiction writer who has also been active in the migrant farmworkers movement. Her poem "To live in the Borderlands means you" ends in the following way: "To survive the Borderlands you must live *sin fronteras*, be a crossroads" (1987, 195), which links with the crossroads and survival themes *and* forms of the writings discussed so far. Anzaldúa's book *Borderlands/La Frontera* (1987) is a complex, multilayered text that refigures questions of language, class, ethnicity, gender and sexuality in ways which demonstrate how each is, in Stuart Hall's words, something "constructed, told, spoken, not simply found" (1988, 45), a product of social and historical contingency. The work is a major contribution to the revisions of notions of identity politics currently being explored in those "marginal locations as spaces where we can best become whatever we want to be while remaining committed to liberatory black liberation struggle" (hooks 1989, 54).

Borderlands can be places that defy the closure of frontier/ border/ boundary and spaces similar to what Trinh T. Minh-ha calls "the interval," " a space in which meaning remains fascinated by what escapes and exceeds it. . . . displacing and emptying out the establishment of totality" (1990, 96). They are also points of confluence, analogous to what Paula Gunn Allen, another writer of complex ethnicities, describes:

My life is the pause. The space between. The not this, not that,
not the other. The place that the others go around. Or around
about. It's more a Mobius strip than a line. (1987, 151)

The geographical borderland of Gloria Anzaldúa's book is the U.S./
Mexican border, but this is simply the site for the "local" narrative that
extends into psychological, sexual and spiritual borderlands and the
unique positionings consciousness takes at these confluent streams. She
also crosses the borders and opens up the margins of other discourses—
historical, mythological, political, linguistic, and literary- traditionally
enclosed by disciplines, subjects, and genres. The writer becomes the
"officiating priestess at the crossroads" (1987, 80), a figure of continual
creative motion engaging in the shamanistic practice described above.
The new *mestiza*, like the writing process itself, is a "morphogenesis," a
term that Anzaldúa takes from Ilya Prigogine's theory of "dissipative
structures" and relates to a kind of birth that created unpredictable innovations (1987, 97). The text generates endless examples of rupture,
transgression, and nepantilism—of people torn between ways in the language of the Borderlands, the space of *los atravesados* : "the squint-eyed,
the perverse, the queer, the troublesome, the mongrel, the mulatto, the
half-breed, the half dead; in short, those who cross over, or go through
the confines of the 'normal'" (3).

Borderlands interrogates and unsettles notions of the homeland, cultural constructions of women, gender, the "other," power, and normative
sexuality. Anzaldúa sees in her chosen sexuality "a strange doubling,"
conventionally deviant and inverted but, potentially, with a magic aspect: "having an entry into both worlds," an evolving, unfolding, and
"sliding" signifier of agency and new *possibility*. From her background
as a lesbian, as a woman of color, and as, originally, a poor *tejana*,
Anzaldúa in her writing articulates the semantically generative spaces
between the different worlds she inhabits in a multiple discourse of category breaking, genre crossing, and constitutive forms—a new *mestiza*
at the level of style and structure: *una cultura mestiza*.

The work is poem, polemic, history and post-Christian spiritual
thesis—episodic, ex-centric, unfinalizable, transgressive, code/mode
switching, and excessive; she writes against white rationality by acknowledging the "forbiddens" of body and soul, so often consigned to the
margins as "dangerous memories." Anzaldúa sees a generative/germi-
native source in what she calls the Coatlicue state—"a rupture in our
everyday world" figuring in contradictions, as a *travesia*, a crossing that

she is best able to represent in passages of prose which focus on a third person "she," lost in textual spaces which open and contract:

> She has this fear that if she digs into herself she won't find any-
> one that   when she gets "there"   she won't find her
> notches on the trees   birds will have eaten all
> the crumbs   She has this fear that she won't find the way
> back. (43)

The "she" is distanced, severed from the writing "I," eye, and "they slit her from head to belly. *Rajada*" (43). As so often, the dialect usage does not act as a supplement or a repetition, but, in its phonetic emphasis and precision, has an explosive presence, the force of an irruption. It is this figure of the "slit" that Anzaldúa uses to construct her *caracter multiplice*—split between "the tongueless magical eye and the loqua-cious rational eye," *la rajadura*, the abyss, that only this new kind of mul-tiple writing can bridge and span.

I have referred throughout this chapter to the ways in which narra-tives work with birth imagery, and sections of *Borderlands* break up the temporal shapes of conventional syntax and generate a fractured, diz-zying, spatial language as, again and again, the writing tries to make "sense," and approaches reconciliation (of magical eye and rational eye), only to

> "cross over," kicking a hole out of the old boundaries of the self
> and slipping under or over, dragging the old skin along, stum-
> bling over it. It hampers her movement in the new territory,
> dragging the ghost of the past with her. It is a dry birth, a breech
> birth, a screaming birth, one that fights her every inch of the
> way. (49)

Borderlands is divided into two main sections—"Atravesando Fronteras/ Crossing Borders" (pages 1 to 91) and "Un Agitado Viento/Ehecatl, the Wind" (pages 102 to 203). The first section is arranged in seven parts, principally written in prose but constantly switching codes, references, and registers as a way of signalling, structurally, the unsettled and unset-tling nature of anxiety, unrest, boundaried and boundless—which en-ables the creative process, the shamanistic, shape-changing performance to take place. The cultural shifts that are recorded throughout the text, which are the text, constitute the new *mestiza* who/which will "survive

the crossroads." Surviving the crossroads is the dream, the energy, the
new belonging of all of the narratives in this chapter: "the green shoot
that cracks the rock" (82), the progeny of a struggle of borders:

> Because I, a *mestiza*,
> continually walk out of one culture
> and into another,
> because I am in all cultures at the same time,
> *alma entre dos mundos, tres, cuatro,*
> *me zumba a cabeza con lo contradictorio.*
> Estoy norteado por todas las voces me hablan
> simultaneamente.
>
> (77)

Each of the narratives analyzed has been concerned with undocumented
women and women without documents. The gaps in documentation,
the "illegal" status of women, have been extended beyond the literal
sense to produce a work of breaks, passages, and bridges at a metaphorical level. Written against homogeneity, each text in its irregular
and interstitial form is an irruption, a threshold crossing, a renewal of
valorization. There is a certain regression to amorphousness, prior to
creativity and empowerment.

In a cultural landscape overfreighted with negative signs and flat
horizons, each writer has produced a virtual structure, striving to find
an analogical vocabulary, an analogical form of discourse that is appropriate for the opening up of a potentially different order. Nature, mythology,
religion and history are all raided/quarried for borrowings to express
the new *mestiza* in an irreducible language, sacral but not mystifying.
The writings become modalities of orientation, means of founding possibility: constructions of space for thinking a new belonging, a settlement for new creativity, new symbols and rituals: a reclaiming.

In a contribution to a debate with Alex Callinicos published in *Socialist Review* in April 1992, Fukuyama writes:

> If we are unwilling to become the contemptible last man, sim-
> ply filling our lives with consumerism, then in a certain sense
> we will long to live for ideals or to struggle against the society
> which created such a flat horizon. In a way, we start history by
> becoming first men who are engaged in bloody besieged battles
> to simply prove we are human beings and can involve ourselves.
> (20)

He *means* "men" and I think he has in mind the Trumps and the Max-
wells, those Nietzschean "supermen" who know that the "desire for
unequal recognition constitute[s] the basis of a livable life" (1992a, xxiii),
and who strive contemptuously against what they conceive as the slav-
ish morality of liberal democracy. In *The End of History and the Last Man*,
Fukuyama cites Nietzsche as founding the philosophy which acts as a
criticism of his thesis of universal recognition (derived from Hegel) that
led him to argue that liberal capitalist democracy marks the end of history as it offers the only viable model for the future: "a world made up
of liberal democracies" (1992, xx). The *Socialist Review* contribution is a
slightly amended version of the introduction to the book, but the final
section (quoted above) uses "we" in a sense that seems to align the writer
quite unequivocally with the critique from the Right that demonstrates
the irreducible contradiction of liberal democracy.

The gendered, martial language suggests that, in the first instance,
the response to "supermen" is necessarily a feminist one. I say "in the first
instance" because the response also needs to include class, race, and sexuality. The narratives in this chapter, and throughout this volume, address
lives filled with, or emptied by, consumerism; they seek to establish vocabularies, codes, and "improbable" discourses that *embody* new ideals and
struggle against flat, and flattened, horizons. In a way, *they* start history
by becoming first peoples (original and originating people) who are
engaged in their own bloody, besieged battles for meaning, space, and
recognition as human beings of a new belonging founded in sacrifice
and struggle. Cultural politics are no substitute for other levels of social
and political action, but new narratives *(storia)* can have a crucial role:

> Stories are important. They keep us alive. In the ships, in the
> camps, in the quarters, field, prisons, on the road, on the run,
> underground, under siege, in the throes, on the verge—the sto-
> ryteller snatches us back from the edge to hear the next chapter.
> In which we are the subjects. We, the hero of the tales. Our lives
> preserved. How it was, how it be. Passing it along in the relay.
> That is what I work to do: to produce stories that save our lives.
> (Bambara 1985, 41)

Throughout this volume we have been speaking of transgressions,
excesses, and extremes as ways of searching for new communions/com-
munities and new subjectivities, means of linking the self with the collective, and I should like to conclude with a brief extract from a poem by
Tom Paulin:

After extremity
art turns social
and it's more than fashion
to write the word "we."

(Paulin 1992)

References

Allen, Paula Gunn. "The Autobiography of a Confluence." In *I Tell You Now*, edited by Brian Swann and Arnold Krupat. Lincoln: University of Nebraska Press,1987.

Amin, Samir. *Eurocentrism*. Translated by Russell Moore. London: Zed Books, 1989.

Anzaldúa, Gloria. *Borderlands/La Frontera: The New Mestiza*. San Francisco: Aunt Lute Books, 1987.

Bambara, Toni Cade. "Salvation is the Issue." In *Black Women Writers*, edited by Mari Evans. London: Pluto Press, 1985.

de Man, Paul. *The Rhetoric of Romanticism*. New York: Columbia University Press, 1984.

Fukuyama, Francis. "The End of History?" *Socialist Review* 152 (April 1992): 18–20.

———. *The End of History and The Last Man*. London: Penguin, 1992.

Giroux, Henry. *Border Crossings: Cultural Workers and the Politics of Education*. London: Routledge, 1992.

Hall, Stuart. "Minimal Selves." In *ICA Documents 6: Postmodernism and the Question of Identity*. London: ICA, 1987.

Harjo, Joy. "Anchorage." In *She Had Some Horses*. New York: Thunder's Mouth Press, 1983.

Hicks, D. Emily. *Border Writing: The Multidimensional Text*. Minneapolis: University of Minnesota Press, 1991.

hooks, bell. "The Politics of Radical Black Subjectivity." In *Talking Back*. Boston: South End Press, 1989.

JanMohamed, Abdul R. "Some Implications of Paulo Freire's Border Pedagogy." *Cultural Studies*, Winter 1992, 107–17.

Kingston, Maxine Hong. *The Woman Warrior: Memoirs of a Girlhood Among Ghosts*. London: Picador,1981. First published in the USA, 1977.

Krause, David. "Reading Bon's Letter and Faulkner's *Absalom, Absalom!*," *PMLA* 99.2 (March 1984): 225–41.

Lyotard, Jean-François. *The Postmodern Condition*. Minneapolis: University of Minnesota Press, 1984.

Mukherjee, Bharati. "A Four Hundred-Year-Old Woman." In *Critical Fictions*, edited by Philomena Mariani. Seattle: Bay Press, 1991.

———. *Jasmine*. London: Virago Press, 1991. First published in the USA, 1989.

Paulin, Tom. "To the Linen Hall." In *Selected Poems, 1972–1990*. London: Faber, 1992.

Payne, James Robert, ed. *Multicultural Autobiography: American Lives*. Knoxville: University of Tennessee Press, 1992.

Philip, M. Nourbese. *she tries her tongue, her silence softly breaks*. London: The Women's Press, 1993. Originally published in Canada, 1989.

Rosaldo, Renato. *Culture and Truth*. Boston: Beacon Press, 1989.

Taussig, Michael. *Shamanism, Colonialism, and the Wild Man*. Chicago: University of Chicago Press, 1986.

Trinh T. Minh-ha, "Documentary is/Not a Name." *October* 52 (Spring 1990).

Wong, Sau-ling Cynthia. "Autobiography as Guided Chinatown Tour? Maxine Hong Kingston's *The Woman Warrior* and the Chinese-American Autobiographical Controversy." In Payne 1992.

CONTRIBUTORS

ARTURO J. ALDAMA completed his doctorate in Ethnic Studies at the University of California at Berkeley, where he wrote on mestizo and mixed-blood writers in literature. He served as editorial assistant for *An Other Tongue* (Duke University Press, 1994), and has been designated a national scholar by the Teachers of Chicano Literary Arts (TECLA).

ROGER BROMLEY was educated at the University of Wales, the University of Illinois at Urbana-Champaign, and the University of Sussex. For twenty-one years he lectured in literary and cultural studies at the University of Portsmouth. Currently, he teaches in the Department of English and Media Studies at Nottingham Trent University. He has published numerous articles and contributed chapters to more than a dozen books. His book *Lost Narratives* was published in 1988 and, at present, he is completing a study of popular culture and politics in late-nineteenth-century England.

LIEN CHAO, born in Hangchow, China, came to Canada in 1984 to do her M.A. and completed her Ph.D. in English at York University. Her dissertation is "Beyond Silence: Chinese Canadian Literature in English." She is also working on a novel entitled "My Mother and Her Daughters."

JOHN HAWLEY (editor) is Associate Professor of English at Santa Clara University. He has edited *Writing the Nation: Self and Country in the Post-Colonial Imagination* (Rodopi, 1996).

SUZETTE HENKE is Morton Professor of Literary Studies at the University of Louisville. She is author of *Joyce's Moraculous Sindbook: A Study of "Ulysses"* (1978) and coeditor of *Women in Joyce* (1982). Her publications in the field of modern literature include essays on Virginia Woolf, Anaïs Nin, Dorothy Richardson, Doris Lessing, Linda Brent, Janet Frame, Samuel Beckett, W. B. Yeats, and E. M. Forster. Her recent book *James Joyce and the Politics of Desire* was brought out by Routledge in 1990. She is presently working on a study of "women's life-writing" in the twentieth century.

TREVOR JAMES is Dean of the Auckland Consortium for Theological Education, affiliated to the University of Auckland. He has published extensively on the literature of New Zealand.

ROSEMARY JOLLY is Assistant Professor of English at Queen's University, Canada. She is author of *Colonialization, Violence and Narration in White South African Writing* (1996). She has published on postcolonial theory, South African literature, and the work of Wilson Harris. She is presently coediting a collection of essays on writing in the new South Africa.

MANUEL M. MARTÍN-RODRÍGUEZ is Assistant Professor of Spanish and Portuguese at Yale University. He has published on Rolando Hinojosa, Sandra Cisneros, Xavier Villaurrutia, Alejandro Morales, and Ivan Silen and the poetics of alterity.

LYN MCCREDDEN is a lecturer in the Department of English Language and Literature, Deakin University, Australia. She teaches contemporary literary theory, Victorian literature, and feminist poetics, and has published on James McAuley and Australian romanticism.

MARY O'CONNOR teaches at the State University of South Dakota. The essay published here is part of a larger study entitled *Through the Cracked Looking-Glass: The Irish Woman Poet Imagines Subjecthood*. The study examines the development of Irish women poets, with specific attention to the work of Medbh McGuckian, Eavan Boland, and Nuala Ní Dhomhnaill.

KARIN QUIMBY is a doctoral candidate in the Department of English at the University of Southern California. She has published on Asian American literature and lesbian film and culture.

GAYLE WALD is currently Assistant Professor of English at George Washington University. Her chapter is work-in-progress from *Crossing the Line: Racial Passing in Twentieth-Century American Literature and Culture,* forthcoming from Duke University Press.

BARBARA FREY WAXMAN is Professor of English at the University of North Carolina at Wilmington. Her first book is *From the Hearth to the Open Road: A Feminist Study of Aging in Contemporary Literature* (Greenwood Press, 1990), and she has also edited a collection of essays, *Multicultural Literatures Through Feminist/Poststructuralist Lenses* (University of Tennessee Press, 1993).

MAYFAIR YANG, born in Taiwan, is Associate Professor of Anthropology at the University of California, Santa Barbara. Her book *Gifts, Favors, and Banquets: The Art of Social Relationships in China* (Cornell University Press, 1994) addresses the problem of state power and personal relations.

NEJD YAZIJI received her doctorate in Comparative Literature at the University of Texas at Austin. The title of her dissertation is "Questioning the Nationalist Paradigm: Toward a Post-Colonial Narrative Critique."

BERNICE ZAMORA is Assistant Professor of English at Santa Clara University, where she teaches Native American and Chicano literatures.

INDEX